MANAGEMENT OF LAKES AND PONDS

MANAGEMENT OF LAKES AND PONDS
Second Edition

GEORGE W. BENNETT

Head, Aquatic Biology Section
Illinois Natural History Survey
and Professor of Zoology
University of Illinois
Urbana, Illinois

VNR VAN NOSTRAND REINHOLD COMPANY
NEW YORK   CINCINNATI   TORONTO   LONDON   MELBOURNE

Van Nostrand Reinhold Company Regional Offices:
New York   Cincinnati   Chicago   Millbrae   Dallas

Van Nostrand Reinhold Company International Offices:
London   Toronto   Melbourne

Manufactured in the United States of America

Published by Van Nostrand Reinhold Company
135 West 50th Street, New York, N.Y. 10020

Published simultaneously in Canada by
Van Nostrand Reinhold Ltd.

15   14   13   12   11   10   9   8   7

FOREWORD

In the struggle for existence that occupies the time of all living things, there is a constant effort on the part of an organism to increase its numbers in the face of a rigid, demanding, and peripherally hostile environment which tends to reduce these numbers. This struggle goes on unconsciously, as far as we know, among all organisms but man. Man, though, is so peculiarly endowed with reason, and the ability to think of the future and to plan for it, that he takes an active hand in this game of numbers with the intention of enhancing his own well-being.

Much of man's activity, either directly or indirectly, is aimed at manipulating populations. He increases the number of wheat plants, and then finds that he must reduce the numbers of Hessian flies. He increases the numbers of sheep, and then must do something about their parasites. He increases the numbers of grouse or rabbits, and then must occupy himself with controlling the diseases of these game species. He wishes to harvest lake trout in the Great Lakes, and runs head-on into a much more efficient harvester in the sea lamprey, with which he must compete or which he must eradicate.

From the beginning of man's emergence as a factor in the environment he has used other organisms as stepping stones toward his own ascendency to the wavering pinnacle upon which he has now placed himself. The earliest evidences of man are artifacts related to his food requirements. Among these we find such things as spears and hooks for the capture of fishes.

The art of fish and game management had its roots in man's attempts to manipulate populations. But a new phenomenon appeared within the present century, and much of it after the first two decades had passed. This has been the changing of the *art* of management to the *science* of management. As we learn more and more about fish and game, we learn that these organisms often react to a situation in an empirical, predictable way, and that the old wive's tales and rules of thumb which governed the art just a little while ago have been found to be erroneous unless they happen to be based on what we now know to be scientific fact.

The great amount of knowledge which exists for a field such as fish management becomes so hidden in the literature, and sometimes so abstruse to the nonspecialist, that it must be brought together and interpreted by one who is conversant with the field. This is what Dr. Bennett has done in this book.

There is certainly a need for organized information on fish management. According to a survey published by the Fish and Wildlife Service, more then twenty-five and one-quarter million Americans fished for sport in 1960. They spent 2.7 billion dollars doing it. That the need is growing is evidenced by a similar survey made five years earlier which showed that at that time there were about twenty-one million fishermen who spent more than 1.9 billion dollars. During that half-decade the number of sport fishermen in the United States increased by an average of about a million a year.

I believe that there is a real chance that soon human interest in fish will, throughout the world, make the complete circle. So far as we know, man's initial interest in fish was as a dietary item. In many nations with poorly fed populations this is still the case. With the distressing increase in the number of human beings, we all may soon have to harvest every source of food, which could make the stream through a pasture or an artificial impoundment an important asset for people whose protein resources need to be increased. This represents another and possibly more important reason for people to manage fish populations.

Furthermore, as this need for food grows throughout the world, we find that man is making it more difficult to get his nourishment. He doesn't know what to do with the wastes of his economy, wastes which easily get into our waters and which are often injurious to aquatic life. In his frantic attempt to get all possible food from each arable acre, he finds that he must protect his growing foodstuffs from competing organisms, and his methods of destroying these competitors may demand the use of materials which again may be detrimental to aquatic organisms. This poses a dilemma of great magnitude and significance.

For these reasons, this book should have a great audience, and the information it contains should be of importance and value to a large segment of our population.

People who take up sport fishing may vary from those handy with a shovel to those skilled in manipulating an electron microscope. These individuals start to fish when they are so young that they can hardly hold a pole, and stop when they are so old that the same difficulty faces them. And all, whether they enjoy fishing or not, must eat. To these people this book will, in part or in the whole, be a useful reference.

Urbana, Illinois
October, 1970

Harlow B. Mills

PREFACE TO SECOND EDITION

Time passes swiftly and even more rapid are the changes that go with it. The second edition, called *Management of Lakes and Ponds,* is an expansion of the first edition and again is directed toward pond owners, fishermen, and fishery biologists; also, the same chapter arrangement has been retained.

A tremendous amount of water-oriented research has been published since 1962 and the author has experienced great difficulty in deciding what papers were the more significant, which of these should be included, and how far to go in describing the development of new lines of research. Much has been accomplished in the exploration of water pollution and the effects of various types of pollutants on the aquatic environment and its inhabitants. It seems important that those having a professional or layman's interest in water and fish are made aware of the several types of pollutants and their effects. For this reason a summary discussion of aquatic pollutants has been added to Chapter 3.

Other chapters have been enlarged where necessary to include recent management-oriented research in various aspects of fishery biology.

Dr. Harlow B. Mills, now retired as Chief of the Illinois Natural History Survey, accepted the task of critic for the second edition. Fortunately for the author he has given of himself in a far greater capacity as a consultant, an editor, and as a primary source of encouragement when the "going" became difficult. As in the first edition, I am indebted to the members of the Aquatic Biology Section of the Illinois Natural History Survey, particularly Drs. D. Homer Buck, William F. Childers, Donald F. Hansen, Robert C. Hiltibran, R. Weldon Larimore, and William C.

Starrett for consultations, figures, and some of their unpublished research information. Also I wish to thank Dr. Philip W. Smith for information on the taxonomy of some Asian and African species of fish mentioned in this book and Mr. H. Wickliffe Adkins for editorial reading.

Dr. George Sprugel, Jr., Chief of the Natural History Survey and himself a former fishery researcher, recognized the problem of integrating the vast amount of recent data and gave special consideration in reducing the author's other assignments during the period of writing.

Miss Mary Frances Martin, Technical Assistant and Secretary for the Section of Aquatic Biology, supervised and prepared the manuscript with the able assistance of Mrs. Sheryl Ammirati and Mrs. Sherry Thacker.

I wish to express my appreciation for the counselling and editorial work of Mr. George Narita, Editor of the Professional and Reference Book Division of Van Nostrand Reinhold Company.

October, 1970   George W. Bennett

PREFACE TO FIRST EDITION

Any book that is written and published probably stems from the belief of the author that there is a need for such a book. Therefore it seems only fair that the preface should let the reader know for whom the book is intended. This one was planned as a general reference for the professional fishery biologist, and for the recreation expert assigned to the task of producing hook-and-line fishing in the artificial impoundments of parks and forest preserves. It will interest fishermen who wish to be informed on lake-management matters, and should serve as a baseline from which research biologists in warm-water fisheries launch further investigations. Students of aquatic biology and fishery management will find both theory and practice here, as well as references for further reading on many subjects.

A sincere effort has been made to recognize and acknowledge those researchers whose activities have contributed to a well-balanced theory of management and to avoid the pitfalls of oversimplification in management. Out of respect for biological variability, I usually have avoided specific directions, such as, for example, how to stock a lake. Rather, I have tried to show the range of *reasonable* stocking and its relationship to the range of potential results. Our purposes will have been satisfied if the reader gains enough insight into what might happen, and why, to appreciate the danger of fish management by cookbook methods, and hence seeks to make use of the general principles of management, as well as the sources of information available, in the realistic solution of management matters that may come his way as a professional biologist and citizen.

The organization of the present book was devised to achieve these purposes. First a brief, concise view of fish culture is presented to place the modern approach to the management of artificial lakes and ponds in a proper perspective. Next, artificial aquatic habitats are distinguished from natural bodies of water, and described, and, as much as is feasible, categorized. Then, the ecological interrelationships of fishes and lake habitats are investigated and the implications for the professional manager are discussed. After a reasonably thorough treatment of such large concepts as carrying capacity, productivity, growth, reproduction, competition, and predation, the book comes to grips with the theory and techniques of management per se. Now, the complex problems of fishing mortality and natural mortality are handled before concluding with chapters on sensory perception and behavior in sport fishing and the commercial aspects of this most popular of all outdoor sports.

No attempt has been made to avoid technical matter, although technical terminology has been reduced to a minimum and the mathematical approach to population dynamics has been relegated to a list of papers, many of which will be available in the nearest university library. For the convenience of the student and individual pond owner who will be using the book, important terms and concepts are defined when they are first presented. No scientific names of fishes appear in the nine chapters of this book; however, the scientific names as well as the common names of all fishes mentioned may be found in the Appendix. A few scientific names other than those of fishes appear in the text, most of which are the names of aquatic plants as given by Fassett.*

Any author who completes a book is indebted to many people. In this respect, I have been very fortunate in receiving the counsel of all of the members of the Aquatic Biology Section of the Illinois Natural History Survey. I am particulary indebted to Drs. William C. Starrett, R. Weldon Larimore, and Donald F. Hansen of our Section editorial committee for giving of their own time to read and criticize this manuscript.

Dr. Harlow B. Mills, Chief of the Illinois Natural History Survey, has contributed greatly through his encouragement, his suggestions for improving certain areas in each of the nine chapters, and through his special ability to recognize and point out the author's bias regarding several controversial subjects.

---

*Fassett, N. C., 1957, A Manual of Aquatic Plants, with revised Appendix by A. C. Ogden, University of Wisconsin Press, Madison. Wisconsin.

Mr. Royal B. McClelland, Executive Secretary of the Illinois Federation of Sportsmen's Clubs and Editor of *Illinois Wildlife* magazine, has read the manuscript through the eyes of a fisherman and lake owner, and has suggested changes to make the book more understandable and readable.

Much of the original planning for subject matter included in Chapter 6 came from discussions with Mr. Sam A. Parr, Executive Assistant for the Illinois Department of Conservation, and Mr. W. W. Fleming, Director of Fish and Game, Indiana Department of Conservation. This chapter on theories and techniques of management was later presented to Mr. William J. Harth, Superintendent of Fisheries, Mr. Al Lopinot, Chief Fishery Biologist of the Illinois Department of Conservation, and to other professional fishery biologists with the Department for general discussion at the 1961 meeting of Illinois aquatic and fishery biologists. I am grateful for the suggestions offered at this meeting.

Many people furnished invaluable cooperation as lake and pond owners willing to allow the collection of fish and fishing in their waters. These cooperators would number more than a hundred. Of these, I have space to mention a few: Mr. William Utterback and Mr. David Malcomson, each of whom owns a number of gravel-pit ponds and who not only allowed us to use these ponds for research but gave of their own time to assist in research activities; Mr. Faye H. Root, Assistant Professor of Camp and Park Management at the University of Illinois Robert Allerton Estate near Monticello, who has arranged for our use of 4-H Club ponds and has given cooperation in many ways; and Mr. Max McGraw, owner of the Fin'n Feather Club, who has built special ponds for research and has furnished creel and management data from ponds and lakes on the club property for our use.

I especially wish to acknowledge the valuable assistance of Miss Mary Frances Martin, Technical Assistant and Secretary for the Section of Aquatic Biology, who was always willing to help in various phases of this work, and of others who have typed material, a page at a time. My wife, Mary Ellyn, read the manuscript at each stage of progress for spelling, punctuation, and meaning.

I do want to express my appreciation to Dr. Peter Gray and Messrs. Ross, Chastain, and Hart of the Reinhold editorial staff for their constant encouragement and assistance in improving my manuscript.

Urbana, Illinois
April 1962   George W. Bennett

CONTENTS

MANAGEMENT OF LAKES AND PONDS

1

HISTORY OF FISH MANAGEMENT

Fishery management can be defined as the art and science of producing sustained annual crops of wild fish for recrecational and commercial uses.[34] It is not synonymous with fish farming, or the production either of hatchery fish for put-and-take fishing or fish fry and fingerlings for stocking. Nor does it consist merely of regulations which control the take of kinds, numbers, and sizes of fish (as when limits are placed upon fishing seasons) any more than that it is restricted to "habitat improvement" per se.

Nonetheless, fishery management makes use of knowledge gleaned from fish farming, the products of the hatchery, legal assistance to regulate fishing, and methods of habitat modification. These facets of fishery husbandry and knowledge can be employed only when integrated into a master plan that eliminates physical and physiological barriers to the well-being of the fishes selected for management. Thus, as stated above, fishery management is defined as the art and science of producing sustained annual crops of wild fish for recreational and commercial uses. The reasons that we have stressed the words "art" and "science" should soon be apparent.

Studies of fish production in Lake Erie[32,61] have illustrated the complexity of factors influencing the fish in an aquatic habitat by showing that turbidity and plankton abundance control the size of surviving year classes of important commercial fishes. Here the crop of fish available for capture in any given year was not related to fishing intensity in past seasons but to the amount of topsoil carried into the lake during some preceding year when the fish being studied were hatching. Although

1

naturally no amount of legal regulation of the fishery can be expected to change such a cause-and-effect relationship, the fishery would be changed by intensive soil-conservation practices on the land in the watersheds tributary to Lake Erie. This points up the importance and complexity of fishery management; however, its history is bound up with the broader term "fish culture."

We might somewhat arbitrarily divide fish culture and management into three overlapping time periods—a division that has its greatest relevance to the student of fish management. The first, which stretches from its earliest development in the pre-Christian era to about 1900 A.D., is characterized by classical fish culture. The second, which roughly covers the period from 1900 to the 1930's, represents the first gropings (often blind and erroneous ones) toward the manipulation of wild populations. The third, which began in the 1930s and extends to the present time, is identified with the development of modern ideas and methods related to managing "wild" fish in natural and artificial waters.

Thus, fishery management as an integrated science is rather recent, and it may be said to have had its beginnings when fishery biologists began to study fish populations as complete units. Nevertheless, to recognize the importance of what went before, one must consider the historical records of pond-fish culture that began with the earliest historical writtings.

EARLY POND-FISH CULTURE

In almost all written history there are references to fish ponds or fish culture. A study of these records reveals that the Chinese were well versed in raising fish many years before the time of Christ.[16] Also, it can be seen that the Romans copied the techniques of this art at a very early time, although they probably added nothing to the knowledge of fish culture beyond that which existed in the ancient Chinese civilization.

Pond-fish culture spread through Europe during the Middle Ages. The first carp ponds were built in Wittingau (Czechoslovakia) in 1358, and for the next 400 years in Europe this was the center for raising pond fish.[40] During this period, fish culture became quite complex. For example, carp culture very early demanded specialized holding areas, such as spawning and hatching ponds (where fry were allowed to grow during the first summer) and growing and fattening ponds. Further, in the fall, carp had to be moved to deep wintering ponds. Special strains of carp were developed, much as various strains of domestic animals have been produced. Thus, from the 15th to the 18th centuries, with this growth in complexity, men, such as   North,[41] Boccius,[8] and others, presented detailed techniques for raising pedigreed carp and other common fish useful for food. These investigations have been continued up to the present, and much progress has been made in understanding the many facets composing the pond habitat for fish.

Since pond-fish culture in Europe represented food production, it supplied a cash crop that was harvested much as any other farm crop. However, this type of "farming" has not been profitable in North America until very recently[30] because of an early and extensive development of commercial fishing for wild unmanaged fresh water and marine populations which provided a more than adequate amount to supply domestic demands. For example, the commercial yield of freshwater fishes from the Illinois River (Illinois) alone was 24 million pounds in 1908;[57] the catch was composed mostly of carp, buffalo fish, and catfish and was largely shipped by rail to eastern markets. In fact, it is interesting to note that special strains of carp imported to this country from Europe in the 1880s and liberated into unmanaged waters soon reverted to the original wild type. However, in the period since 1908, the fisheries of the Great Lakes and coastal marine waters have largely supplanted those of inland rivers and smaller lakes, so that now the commercial operations in inland rivers are much reduced, except those for catfish, which always have a ready market.

THE DEVELOPMENT OF HATCHERIES

A normal outgrowth of European fish-culture practices brought to this country by immigrants was the development in the United States of hatcheries to supplant the natural production of young wild fish. The earliest hatcheries were privately operated, usually for the production of trout. Dr. Theodatus Garlick, the Rev. Dr. John Bachman, and Seth Green were all operating private hatcheries prior to 1865.[64] In 1872, at the urging of the American Fish-Culturists' Association, the Congress of the United States enlarged the duties of the newly formed Fish Commission to include the propagation if fish.* In 1875 both federal and state governments were operating hatcheries for the artificial production of fish. The late 19th and the early 20th centuries were marked by attempts at hatchery production and stocking of the kinds of fish useful for sport and food in the more important waters. Many of these attempted introductions resulted in failure for the following reasons: a lack of understanding of physical and biological limitations, the release of the fishes into habitats unsuitable for them, and the inability of fishes to survive predation and/or to compete with other organisms already present in the waters.[11] These failures were primarily due to the fact that at that time

*U.S. Comm. of Fish. Rept. 1872-73 (1874).

the science of fish ecology was practically unknown, whereas the art and science of fish culture were well advanced.

This was the heyday of the men engaged in the artificial propagation of fish. States vied with one another in the race to put out larger and larger numbers. "Paper fish" flourished in the reports of hatchery superintendents; numbers were important; little else mattered.

Moreover, in the late 19th century only a few trained professional biologists were employed by state conservation departments; most of the limnologists and ichthyologists were attached to universities and were given little or nothing to say in formulating the programs of conservation departments. The scientists and fish culturists came together at the annual meetings of the American Fisheries Society. The latter probably thought that the only practical contribution the scientists could make was to identify some strange fish or aquatic insect, and during this period the university biologists were primarily engaged in taxonomic and distributional studies. Undoubtedly, some of the statements of the "practical men" at the American Fisheries Society meetings mildly irritated the biologists, but not sufficiently to cause them to become crusaders. After all, at that time, they had little real information on the ecology of fishes, except in a broad, general way.

This divergence of beliefs was clearly illustrated in Illinois in the 1880s and 1890s when Professor Stephen A. Forbes and his group of scientists were studying the biology of the Illinois River. Concurrently, the Illinois Fish Commission was working in this area, but with the primary objective of rescuing the fish stranded by the receding waters of early summer along the Illinois and Mississippi Rivers.

Forbes's emphasis is clear; he recognized the loss of fish as a natural phenomenon![22] "As the waters retire, the lakes (of the Illinois River bottoms) are again defined; the teeming life which they contain is restricted within daily narrower bounds, and a fearful slaughter follows; the lower and more defenseless animals are penned up more and more closely with their predaceous enemies, and these thrive for a time to an extraordinary degree." Fish stranded in landlocked pools were either preyed upon by other, larger fish or by amphibians, reptiles, fish-eating birds, or mammals; or if the pools dried completely, the fish died and decayed where they lay exposed. Since these victimized fish were mostly small ones, the products of the current reproductive season, Forbes and his colleagues recognized them as being in excess of the small number required to maintain the population at a constant level. They realized that this apparent waste was normal and had been occurring on the overflow lands of large rivers for many thousands of years.

The Illinois State Fish Commission, on the other hand, engaged crews of men with seines and wagons to rescue these fish for stocking in other lakes or for release in open water. These crews usually operated each year from the time the fish became stranded in the spring, until the waters had receded to their usual summer low-water levels.[3]

Professor Forbes must have recognized that this program was entirely useless, not only because the fish were "expendable" but also because their survival was in doubt when they were seined up and transported during hot weather. Yet, judging from the publications of that time, there was no animosity between Professor Forbes and the State Fish Commissioners. Perhaps the former realized that the Commission was responding to the desires of the public.

It is against this background that we can visualize the important place hatcheries held in the minds of fish culturists at that time. The products of inland hatcheries were trout, salmon, whitefish, walleye, largemouth bass, smallmouth bass, northern pike, muskellunge, and several other species propagated for stocking in special locations. Since hatchery operators were thoroughly convinced of the worth of their effort, they scarcely gave any thought to the way in which fish managed to survive before the hatchery was developed.

Hatchery superintendents and fish-and-game department officials on both state and federal levels expended considerable effort to convince the public that hatchery fish were needed to maintain populations in the face of advancing civilization—a drive which gave great impetus to the hatchery movement. However, almost no effort was made to determine the final disposition of hatchery fish or to estimate the importance of the hatchery product on the basis of fish stocked per acre of water. Since such questions were dangerous to the hatchery movement they were simply avoided. It is interesting to note that the hatchery movement was so successful that even today the otherwise uninformed layman inquires about recent stocking of the waters in which he plans to fish. In later sections of this book, we will see some of the important ways the hatching of fish is useful in fishery management.

EARLY ATTEMPTS AT MANAGEMENT

In spite of the emphasis on artificial propagation of fish in hatcheries, some of the early investigations were not directly related to artificial fish propagation. These studies helped to pave the way for the modern concept of fishery management which is the subject of this book.

Before 1759, Hederstrom[24] recognized rings of growth on the vertebrae of fishes as representing annuli; later other biologists discovered the growth rings on the scales of fish, but Borodin[9] and Barney[1] were responsible for bringing a method of aging fish from scales to the attention of fisheries workers. Wiebe[64] and Juday et al.,[31] were among the first to do comprehensive experiments with fertilizer materials in water and to measure the increase in plankton resulting therefrom. Surber[53] tested sodium arsenite as a chemical for the control of aquatic vegetation. The first electric fish shocker for research purposes was developed by Burr.[10] Markus[37] investigated the relationship between water temperatures and the rate of food digestion in largemouth bass. Thompson[56] tagged fish and studied their migration in rivers.

Several potentially useful studies were undertaken earlier. Dyche[17] observed that interspecific predation between largemouth bass and bluegills might favor bluegills rather than bass. Barney and Canfield[2] studied the fish production of an 0.22-acre pond over a period of five years and gathered some evidence that production and total standing crop were related to the lengths of the food chains of the fishes introduced. The first record of the use of the bass-bluegill combination was published in 1902.[44] Barney and Canfield[2] used largemouth bass, crappies, and bluegills, or bluegills alone prior to 1922.

A comprehensive inventory of theories on fishery management in 1938 was given by Hubbs and Eschmeyer[25] in *The Improvement of Lakes for Fishing*. Dr. Hubbs, then head of the Michigan Institute for Fishery Research, and Dr. Eschmeyer, one of his students recognized for his independent thinking, pooled their experiences and hypotheses and built, with a strong assist from Leopold's concepts of game management, a thesis that populations of fish in lakes could be managed as well as terrestrial vertebrates. Actually, they had very little to go on, but they based their thesis on the assumption that if game habitat could be improved by the addition of cover on land, fish habitat must be deficient of cover under water and could be improved in the same manner. So the book begins with a section on improving cover, based on the theory that such cover is one of the larger needs.

Other subjects discussed were managing plant growths, bettering spawning conditions, regulating the fluctuations of water levels, preventing erosion and silting, and many more. In discussing the handling of populations with stunted growth, the authors advocate the following: *(1)* increase food (however, without suggestions as to how to go about it), *(2)* avoid overstocking, and *(3)* reduce the population by liberalizing size limits, season limits, and bag limits, as well as by destroying nests, by planting fish-eating game fishes and, as a last resort, by killing the entire population as Dr. Eschmeyer had already done at the time the book was published. In all, there are twenty types of fish-management practices described, none of which had yet been carefully tested.

Evidence that the authors were still affected by the earlier beliefs and operations is to be found under the subject, Place of Lake Improvement in Fish Management:

"At least for the near future, lake improvement cannot be foreseen as a substitute for the long-recognized practices in fish management (restrictive and protective legislation, law enforcement, and the introduction of fish and the stocking of artificially propagated and reared fish.[35]) Methods of lake improvement would need to be enormously perfected, before this new practice, if ever, could be expected to replace the older means of maintaining the fish supply." (Bracketed matter mine.)

Hence, the book, *The Improvement of Lakes for Fishing* is important in that it initiates a rather bold break with the past, points toward the future and presents a precise picture of 1938 views; the actual lake-management data which it contains is of less significance.

IMPORTANCE OF STUDYING TOTAL POPULATIONS

An important step in the understanding of fish-management problems was the census taken of populations of fish by the poisoning or draining of lakes so that a population could be observed as a unit.[4,19] Such a census was particularly enlightening when conducted on a lake population with past stocking and fishing records available, because, under such circumstances, the effects of stocking could be evaluated as could the quality of fishing associated with a specific population. Almost immediately it became evident that there was never a shortage of fish; in fact, usually there appeared to be an overabundance of individuals, particularly of the fish of smaller sizes.

When many complete fish censuses became available, some of the causes for poor fishing were obvious: *(1)* an excess of undesirable fish, that is, the domination of these populations by species of no interest to anglers, with the number of acceptable fish so reduced that the chances of catching one was remote; *(2)* an excess of desirable fish where the populations of hook-and-line species were so large the over-population led to stunting and few individuals were large enough to interest fishermen. This type of information gave direction to attempts at fish management, something that had been lacking before.

At this time, several studies of entire populations helped to give us an understanding of certain aspects of population dynamics. Thompson,[57] who took periodic samples of the fish populations of Lake Senachwine (Illinois) with wing nets and used the mark-and-recovery method* of population estimation, came to the conclusion that the "fine" fish component of this population (consisting of largemouth bass crappies, bluegills, and other centrarchids) totaled between 50 and 55 lb/acre,

---

*Thompson's method was improved upon by Z. E. Schnabel (*Am. Math. Monthly* 45 (6), 348-352 (1938)) and others. (See references for Chap. 7).

regardless of whether the lake level was high and the area was 6000 acres in extent or whether it was reduced by drought to 3000 acres or less. Moreover, the poundage was constant from year to year, in spite of a cycle of size and numbers. In certain years there were ten times as many fish as in other years, but the average weight of an individual was only one-tenth as great. This was a crappie-dominated cycle, wherein a dominant brood of crappies curtailed the survival of its own young and those of other species until this brood was decimated by natural mortality. Then another dominant brood was produced and the cycle was repeated. The cycle shifted between high numbers and black crappies with low numbers of white crappies and bluegills, and moderate numbers of white crappies and bluegills with low numbers of black crappies. Hence this investigation demonstrated that, in spite of constancy of poundage, continual changes might be taking place among the fishes of certain populations.

One of the most significant studies, in that it helped to show the true position of hatcheries in fish management, was that of Carbine,[13] who followed the spawning and hatching of nest-building centrarchids in Deep Lake (Michigan). Fry were sucked through glass tubing from nests guarded by males (to give identification of kind) and counted. Carbine estimated that the hatch of fish per acre in Deep Lake exceeded one-half million during a single spawning season. Thus, he was able to demonstrate that the hatching success of fishes in natural lakes was as high or higher than that observed in fish hatcheries.

THE SIGNIFICANCE OF POND STUDIES

Several investigators working with fish in ponds demonstrated the capacity of fish populations to expand and contract in relation to the capacity of the habitat to support them[54] and the relationships between length of the food chains and poundages of fish supported.[58]

Probably the most extensive pond research unit in North America was developed between 1934 and 1944 by H. S. Swingle and E. V. Smith at the Alabama Polytechnic Institute (now known as Auburn University), Auburn, Alabama. This excellent unit consisted of more than 100 ponds which could be drained and refilled and which ranged in size from one-tenth of an acre to more than one acre. These ponds were used for developing simple pond-management techniques which could be used by laymen for increasing the fish yield of farm ponds. Recommendations that worked well in the region of Auburn, Alabama, caught the interest of sportswriters throughout the country, and many magazines of national circulation published articles on the Alabama methods of pond management. The Soil Conservation Service, the foremost pond-sponsoring agency in the United States, and many state conservation departments, put to use the recommendations of this research unit.

The national publicity on pond management stimulated such widespread interest that many states developed programs of pond research on their own. It soon became evident that the same kind of fishes that produced satisfactory hook-and-line yields in Alabama ponds, when stocked in the recommended numbers in ponds in other parts of the country, did not behave as they did in Alabama. This was not only because the habitats and fish food complexes were different, but also because the behavior and physiology of the fishes varied within the limits of their natural range. It followed that the program of stocking fingerling bass and bluegills in certain ratios in one part of the country might not produce satisfactory populations for fishing in other regions in spite of the fact that the fish were considered the same.

Fishery biologists began to study life histories of many common warmwater fishes in small controllable waters and to test other combinations of fishes as well as that of largemouth bass and bluegills, with the objective of finding new combinations that would work as well or better than the bass-bluegill combination. Soon many states developed their own stocking recommendations for largemouth bass and bluegills, and some recommended the stocking of bass or some other piscivorous species with one or with several omnivorous species, often excluding the bluegill.[33,38]

The importance of pond studies was not in the development of combinations of kinds and numbers of fishes to be stocked;—or in the demonstration that fertilization with inorganic and organic fertilizers would increase production and the standing crops of fishes;—or was the proof that relatively small waters could furnish excellent fishing of primary significance. More important were the basic concepts that were developed from studying small populations in habitats of limited extent where an investigator could exert more or less control over a good many facets of his semiartificial ecosystem, or modify the ecosystem in some manner and in varying severity, and measure the impact upon the fishes through exposing the entire population.

These studies demonstrated that fish populations in ponds were restricted by limitations imposed by the pond habitat, so that the addition of more fish, per se, would not increase the poundage of fish beyond certain levels. They exposed unsuspected competition between species of fishes for food and space, particularly among the young, and demonstrated that growth rates were density-dependent, and not controlled by set growth patterns. They also exposed some rather exact relationships between certain species of fishes and their environments, information that could be used to advantage in management.

Most of these discoveries could not have been made in larger waters because of the physical inability to control any significant part of the fish population or the related ecosystem, and it would be preposterous to attempt to "see" the whole fish population of a large lake in relation to its habitat at any season.

If we assume that the behavior of populations of fishes in ponds and in larger lakes is governed by the same ecological principles, the information supplied by pond studies could be judiciously applied to larger waters. For example Van Oosten,[60] who studied the commercial fish production of the Great Lakes for many years, was unable to find proof of changes in the relative abundance of fishes due to competition between species. Yet the rapid sequence of species that has followed the spread of the sea lamprey[43] has left little doubt that interspecific competition is as severe in the Great Lakes as in any waters. Once we are aware of the potential of this factor in small waters, we can find an explanation for changes that we see taking place elsewhere.

LAKES AND RESERVOIRS

Natural Lakes

The glacial lakes of the world have been studied by limnologists for almost 100 years and much information is available on their physical, chemical, and biological properties. All of the glacial lakes predated modern man and were probably involved in the evolution of higher fishes. Some of the predator-prey relationships that are so highly developed between the fishes and other vertebrates and invertebrates no doubt originated during the more recent glacial periods.

Natural lakes probably contain a greater variety of animals than do artificial man-made waters because the long period of their existence makes possible immigration and evolutionary diversification as well as development of predator-prey reproduction potential relationships. These relationships were often a guarantee that the fish involved would survive and be able to fill their ecological niches in spite of great ecological pressures.

Although many of these relationships in natural lakes have been upset by man's removal of certain components of the system, those which are left may function with enough efficiency to maintain a situation of continuous well being for the fishes; this balance is less likely to be maintained in man-made and man-stocked reservoirs, where the animal populations consist of easily migrating species, accidental introductions, and those organisms selected and released in these waters by man.

Natural lakes not only require less management than do artificial ones, but they often do not lend themselves as well to management. The reasons will be made obvious in later sections of this book. Because management techniques are often less useful and less applicable to natural than to artificial waters, more emphasis will be placed on the management of man-made ponds and reservoirs than on natural lakes.

Artificial Reservoirs

The progress of fish management in large reservoirs has been detailed by Jenkins.[27] In the early 1920s many large reservoirs were constructed for flood control and hydroelectric power and among the first studied was Lake Keokuk, which is a low-dam impoundment on the Mississippi River near Keokuk, Iowa.[14,23]

As construction gained momentum in the 1930s, studies of new reservoirs consisted primarily of inventories of plankton, bottom fauna, and fish,[39,62] but provided, in addition to these inventories, opinions on how to improve the fish-producing capacities of the reservoirs.[63] In the latter part of the 1930s, a number of reservoirs, previously furnishing excellent fishing, became poor. Consequently, some biologists concluded that, after an initial high productivity brought about by the decay and utilization of the organic matter present at impoundment,[12,18] we could expect these large impoundments to become aquatic deserts. A team of fishery biologists, employed by the Tennessee Valley Authority to investigate the fish populations of its reservoirs,[21,55] concluded that there was insufficient evidence to substantiate this belief.

Fish Cycles in Reservoirs. The work of the TVA in this direction was strengthened by the studies of others and, in time, biologists, who had seen fishing in a number of new water-supply reservoirs change from excellent to very poor in a matter of a few years, were ready to predict a reservoir fishing cycle:[5]

"At the first spawning season (May—June) after the reservoir is filled and stocked with fish, the young of largemouth bass will be very abundant. These will grow rapidly to legal size and produce excellent bass fishing for about three years. Moderate numbers of young crappies, bluegills, and other sunfish and bullheads may be produced during the first spawning period. These will grow rapidly to large average sizes and add to the excellence of fishing.

"Carp, buffalo, and suckers, as well as some other fish present in the stream flowing into the impoundment will move into the lake in small numbers and produce some young the first season.

"During the first few years the reservoir will be clear except immediately following heavy rains, and the recreational attractions other than fishing, such as swimming and boating, will be at their maximum.

"Reduced recreational values will be apparent in about the length of time that the original spawn of bass survives (usually four to six years). By this time the bass fishing will be largely gone. Crappies and bluegills will be present in such large populations that they will have become small, stunted, and unattractive to fishermen; carp and other rough fish will have multiplied so successfully that their bottom-feeding activities will continually stir up the bottom mud. The lake will remain turbid throughout the year, regardless of periods of dry weather, and will have lost much of its attractiveness to fishermen and bathers. Many of the aesthetic values of boating will be gone. The conditions will be entirely the result of changes in the relative abundance of certain fishes, and as the primary function of the reservoir is to supply water, and not recreation, almost nothing can be done to bring back conditions that were obtained in the early years of impoundment."

As a result of investigations of small impoundments not used for water supply, many examples were available by 1946 to show that the chemical treatment or the draining of such small impoundments to remove undesirable populations similar to those that developed in water-supply reservoirs entirely eliminated "aquatic desert" conditions, and that once these impoundments were restocked with desirable fish they again became very productive. Thus, the theory of Ellis[18] that high fish production in the early years of impoundment resulted from organic decay in the new lake basin was largely disproved, since this cycle of production could be repeated as often as the reservoir was completely drained (or poisoned) and restocked with small numbers of fish.[6] In addition, the hypothesis of progressive loss of fertility that had been advanced could be attacked in some situations since the amount of flooded vegetation in a lake basin was too meager, in relation to the huge volume of water impounded, to produce a "hay infusion" that would result in an initial high fish production.

Recent Advances in Management. In 1945 the Federal Office of River Basin Studies was formed. Within the framework of this organization, biologists could appraise the fishery resources of a river before a federal impoundment was built and thereby estimate the effect of the impound-

ment on the resource. Although these benefits or losses were incorporated in the cost-benefit ratios prepared by the U.S. Corps of Engineers, the predicted gains or losses of a fishery seldom influenced the
decision to build a reservoir.

In 1944, Norris Reservoir (Tennessee) was opened to year-round fishing: the results were so encouraging that Tennessee dispensed with a
closed season on all of its remaining reservoirs in 1945, as did Ohio that
year and some additional states shortly thereafter.

After World War II there was a marked expansion of studies of fish
populations in reservoirs, particularly in the states of Tennessee, Kentucky, Missouri, Oklahoma, Texas, and California. In many instances
there seemed little to be done that would have any effect upon the fish
population of a large reservoir, and the fishermen and biologists were
forced to go along with fish-population changes resulting from natural
biological sequences.[45]

A more dynamic approach to reservoir problems was activated when
plans for a National Reservoir Research Program were developed prior
to 1960 and money was provided in the Federal Bureau of Sport Fisheries
budget to begin work in 1961.[50,51] Reservoirs on the upper Missouri
River, i. e., Lewis and Clark, Fort Randall, Big Bend, and Oahe, were
included, and headquarters for these North Central Reservoir Investigations were located in Yankton and Pierre, South Dakota. These reservoirs
range in size from 30,000 to 324,000 acres and stretch along some 800
miles of the Missouri River.

In 1963 the Reservoir Research Program began a comparison between
Bull Shoals and Beaver Reservoirs on the White River in Arkansas. At
this time Bull Shoals was fifteen years old and Beaver Reservoir was new.
Headquarters for the White River Reservoir investigations were located
in Fayetteville, Arkansas.

As with any new approach to a resource study, it is considered appropriate to inventory the resource in order to learn its extent. In 1966 the
National Reservoir Research Program counted 1065 reservoirs exceeding 500 acres which at average annual pool levels totaled 8,953,000 acres.
Greatest total areas of impounded waters were in the Missouri River
basin in Arkansas, in the White and Red River basins, in the Gulf and
South Atlantic regions, and in the Columbia River basin. Natural
lakes that had their surface areas expanded through damming the outlets
were excluded from this count unless such damming doubled or more
than doubled the original area, or *storage capacity*. According to Dr. Robert
M. Jenkins, Director of the federal reservoir program, an annual increase
in acres of impounded water amounted to about 3 1/2 percent per year

from 1960 to 1967, and it has become evident that, exclusive of Alaskan waters and the Great Lakes, there are more acres of large man-made lakes than there are of natural lakes.

On the basis of records from about 150 reservoirs, the fishing pressure on reservoirs is around 11 fisherman-days per acre per year with an average harvest of approximately 1 1/2 pounds of fish per fisherman-day. "Using these averages, it was estimated that about 97 million fisherman-days were expended on the reservoirs in 1966 with a catch of 170 million pounds of sport fish and angler expenditures of about 485 million dollars."[50]

In the 1950s, reservoir management had been reduced to about five phases of operation: *(1)* The manipulation of water levels to favor certain species and depress others.[7,20,26,29,42,65] *(2)* The addition to reservoirs of certain species not originally present, in order to contribute directly to the creel or to "fill in" indirectly the trophic levels in the food chain of some important fish already present. Good examples of the first type of addition are to be found in the introduction of the white bass and striped bass (the striped bass was isolated in the Santee-Cooper Reservoir and then added to Kentucky Lake). The introduction of the threadfin shad is an example of a fill-in fish to improve food conditions for game fish.[28] *(3)* The control of over-abundant rough fish and/or forage fish to reduce their competition with game fish for food and space. There was a need for more efficient methods of controlling these undesirable fish, of which the rough fish species were buffalo fishes, carpsuckers, carp, drum, etc., and the forage fish, which were usually gizzard shad. *(4)* An increase in the harvest of hook-and-line fish. This was done through year-around open seasons, enclosed fishing docks, heated for the fisherman's comfort, the creation of temperature gradients, installation of brush piles, and by other means of attracting and holding fish in concentrations where fishermen could harvest them in the most efficient manner possible. *(5)* Publicity so that the public would know "where to go and when" to catch fish. Newspaper stories of catches stimulated interest and induced fishermen to go fishing, and also furnished information on where fishes were being caught.

Reducing Undesirable Populations. In the management of large reservoirs there has always been a need for the development of more efficient methods for the reduction of undesirable populations.

Fishery management in water-supply reservoirs received a great stimulus through the granting, by the Public Health Departments of some states, of permission to use rotenone for the control of undesirable fish in these reservoirs. The Public Health Department of the State of Oklahoma prior to 1954 permitted the use of rotenone to kill gizzard shad in a water-supply reservoir. Other states soon followed this lead (Illinois in 1956) until many states now sanction the use of rotenone for the removal of excessive populations of gizzard shad by partial poisoning, or for the poisoning of all fish in a reservoir with subsequent restocking of new populations of selected species.

In no case has the use of rotenone or the presence of dead fish for the short period before they are picked up and hauled away from the lake had any noticeable effect upon the water supply after it has gone through the usual filtration and chlorination. In many water-supply reservoirs where the rooting of rough fish had kept the water continuously muddy, the complete poisoning of these fish stopped mud-stirring activity and greatly reduced the task of water treatment because of the much-reduced problem of filtering out suspended silt. Water-supply reservoirs, renovated and restocked with desirable fish, regained all their former recreational values—fishing, swimming, boating, and aesthetics.

CHANGES IN FEDERAL AGENCIES DEALING WITH FISHING, HUNTING, AND OTHER OUTDOOR RECREATION

Historically, the addition of new bureaus and the reorganization of old fish and game departments of the federal government have significance. The Fish and Wildlife Act of 1956 passed by Congress called for reorganizing the Fish and Wildlife Service into two bureaus, namely, a Bureau of Commercial Fisheries and a Bureau of Sport Fisheries and Wildlife.[46,47] The Bureau of Sport Fisheries and Wildlife was further divided into Sport Fisheries, Technical Services, and Wildlife Divisions, with an overall administrative Office of Budget and Finance. The Technical Services Division was to assist the Sport Fisheries and Wildlife Division with problems of Engineering, Federal Aid, Lands, and Statistics.

The Division of Sport Fisheries is composed of three operating branches: Extension and Training, Fishery Biology, and Fish Hatcheries.

The Bonner Boating Bill passed by the 85th Congress and known as the Federal Boating Act of 1959 was designed to promote greater boating safety. The Act provided that all boats powered by motors of more than 10 horsepower must be registered. State governments had until April 1, 1960·to set up their numbering and registration systems or the task was to be taken over by the U.S. Coast Guard. Most states organized their own boat-control systems by the deadline.[48]

On April 2, 1962, the Bureau of Outdoor Recreation was created in the U.S. Department of the Interior under reorganization authority given by the 82nd Congress in 1950. The purpose of the new bureau was "to serve as the focal point within the Federal Government for the many activities related to outdoor recreation."[52]

An improvement in the water quality of lakes, rivers, and coastal waters has resulted from the passage of a series of antipollution laws beginning with the Water Pollution Control Act of 1956 (Public Law 660). This law authorized grants for construction of municipal waste-treatment works and for state and interstate programs of pollution abatement. The Water Pollution Control Act was amended in 1961 (PL 87-88), supporting an increase in funds for construction grants incorporated in the original Act, plus monies for research, training and demonstrations by public and private agencies, institutions, and individuals. The Water Quality Control Act of 1965 (PL 89-234) stimulated the various states to develop standards of water quality for their waters: it increased money for construction grants, and supported research and development to demonstrate new ways of controlling pollution.

It was amended in 1966 by the Clean Water Restoration Act (PL 89-753), which introduced the concept of pollution control within units consisting of watersheds or drainage basins, and supplied grants to help pay for basin planning. Under this amendment a part of the functions formerly handled by the Department of Health, Education, and Welfare was transferred to the Department of the Interior. Congress is now (1969) moving in the direction of greater controls on oil pollution, pollution from vessels, acid mine wastes, and pollution affecting the Great Lakes.*

FUTURE OUTLOOK

Much has been spoken and written about the effects of a bad environment on the individual, yet no one has yet defined the components of an optimum human environment. The champions of "progress" want to express values only in terms of dollars, whereby a game fish is worth $4.00 to 8.00 per pound, one mallard is supposedly equivalent to $2.00, a goose to $6.00, and the value of a park is equal to the dollars spent by park visitors".[36] I have indulged in such economic evaluations myself. If we continue to follow such practices, those resources having aesthetic and ethical values alone will continue to disappear at a rapid rate. It seems that we are much more able to measure the *costs* of changes contributing to a higher-quality environment than to measure the *benefits* derived from it.

---

*The Conservation Foundation for Aug. 29, 1969, 1250 Connecticut Ave., N.W., Washington, D.C.

Nearly a dozen years ago DeVoto,[15] a man of letters, wrote: "But though my tastes are metropolitan and I have no urge to be active in the wilds, I agree with the outdoorsmen; life would be intolerable if I could not visit woods and mountains at short intervals. I have got to have the sight of clean water and the sound of running water. I have got to get to places where the sky-shine of cities does not dim the stars, where you can smell land and foliage, grasses and marshes, forest duff and aromatic plants and hot underbrush turning cool. Most of all, I have to learn again what quiet is.

"Nothing in this is sentimental or poetic. It is necessity."

Many of us are impressed by the ground swell of public opinion concerning depredations on the American environment: the flooding of stream valleys or public parks of high aesthetic value and beauty to furnish water supplies for sewage dilution; the elimination of forested areas for lumber or superhighway construction; the fouling of bodies of water or the loss of open spaces because they are available and "don't really belong to anybody." There is a rapidly growing segment of the American public that is becoming more and more determined and articulate against those who would further debase our environment with "progressive improvements." These people may recognize "that the same measures that make life itself possible in the distant future also make for a more interesting and pleasing environment in the immediate future."

The preservation of at least a part of the natural landscape may be hoped for, and these areas can be augmented through the creation of more "artificial" recreational areas not excessively manicured with mowers and trimmers, nor made unnatural with too many exotic trees and shrubs. Eventually such artificial areas, if left alone, will revert to a natural look.

Water adds to aesthetic values and recreation potential, and the farm pond, originally built chiefly for livestock, has demonstrated its potential for fishing, boating, and swimming and is recognized as an attractor of wildlife. Such small impoundments usually do not demand areas for which there are greater and competing uses. Land owners build ponds, either for their own use, for rental to outdoor groups or sportsmen's clubs, or to increase the value of poorer, nonagricultural segments of their property. Thus the pond-building movement continues to boom with recreational uses often exceeding those of water supply.

The development of larger impoundments for community water supplies will continue until a large part of the more desirable sites will be in use. In most instances water-supply reservoirs will be available for public water-oriented recreation.

The U.S. Corps of Army Engineers has already created reservoirs or has developed plans for impoundments on nearly every stream in the United States with any record of primary or secondary flood damage. The U.S. Army Engineers, once strictly dam builders and navigation channel maintainers for flood control and river barge traffic, have raised their sights to include recreation, water supply, and sewage dilution. There are suggestions that they are broadening their viewpoint to consider methods of accomplishing water manipulation goals other than through big dam building, particularly where there are strong objections to dams because they would cause losses of nonmeasurable aesthetic values already present and recognized.

As gun-control laws and trespass become more restrictive to sportsmen who wish to hunt, opportunities for fishing will become more widely distributed and more readily available. Research on reservoirs will find new methods of fish management for such waters, increasing the opportunities for success in sport fishing.

In the following chapters I have described the known characteristics and dynamic processes of warmwater fish populations. These must be thoroughly understood and appreciated before one can apply management. Although the principles governing such populations are broad, any application to a selected population is specific and hence requires understanding, not only of these general principles, but also of all the ramifications of a current situation.

REFERENCES

1. Barney, R.L., 1924, "A confirmation of Borodin's scale method of age determination of Connecticut River shad," *Am. Fish. Soc. Trans.* 54, 168-177.
2. Barney, R. L., and Canfield, H. L., 1922, "The farm pond and its productivity," *Fins, Feathers and Fur,* 30, 3-7.
3. Bartlett, S.P., 1893, *Report of Board of Illinois State Fish Commissioners to the Governor of Illinois, Oct. 1, 1890 to Sept. 30, 1892,* pp. 1-22.
4. Bennett, G.W., 1943, "Management of small artificial lakes," *Illinois Nat. Hist. Surv. Bull.* 23(3), 357-376.
5. Bennett, G.W.,1946, "Pond talk - II," *Illinois Wildlife,* 1(2), 8-10.
6. Bennett, G. W., 1947, "Fish management — a substitute for natural predation," *North Am. Wildlife Conf. Trans.* 12, 276-285.
7. Bennett, G.W., 1954, "The effects of a late-summer drawdown on the fish population of Ridge Lake, Coles County, Illinois," *North Am. Wildlife Conf. Trans.* 19, 259-270.
8. Boccius, G., 1841, *A Treatise on the Management of Freshwater Fish,* J. Van Voorst.
9. Borodin, N., 1924, "Age of shad (*Alosa sapidissima* Wilson) as determined by the scales," *Am. Fish. Soc. Trans.* 54, 178-184.
10. Burr, J.G., 1931, "Electricity as a means of garfish and carp control," *Am. Fish. Soc. Trans.* 61. 174-182.

11. Buss, K., 1967, "The evolution of fish stocking in the United States," *Penn. Angler* 36(10), 16-18.

12. Cahn, A. R., 1937, "The fisheries program in the Tennessee Valley," *Am. Fish. Soc. Trans.* 66(1936), 398-405.

13. Carbine, W.F., 1939, "Observations on the spawning habits of centrachid fishes in Deep Lake, Oakland County, Michigan," *4th North Am. Wildlife Conf. Trans.* 275-287.

14. Coker, R.E., 1930, "Studies of the common fishes of the Mississippi River at Keokuk," *Bull. U.S. Bur. Fish.* 45(1929), 141-225.

15. DeVoto, B., 1955, "Hell's half acre, Mass.," *Harpers,* (Sept.), 10-19.

16. Duhaldi, J.B., 1735, *History of the Chinese Empire,* Vol. 1, p. 35.

17. Dyche, L.L., 1914, "Ponds, pond fish, and pond fish culture," *Kansas State Dept. Fish. and Game Bull.* 1, 1-208.

18. Ellis, M.M., 1937, "Some fishery problems in impounded waters," *Am. Fish. Soc. Trans.* 66(1936), 63-75.

19. Eschmeyer, R.W., 1938, "The significance of fish population studies in Lake management,"*3rd North Am. Wildlife Conf. Trans.,* 458-468.

20. Eschmeyer, R.W., and Jones, A.M., 1941, "The growth of game fishes in Norris Reservoir during the first 5 years of impoundment," *North Am. Wildlife Conf. Trans.* 6, 222-239.

21. Eschmeyer, R.W., and Tarzwell, C.M., 1941, "An analysis of fishing on the T.V.A. impoundments during 1939," *J. Wildlife Management,* 5(1), 15-41.

22. Forbes, S.A., 1925, "The lake as a microcosm," *St. Lab. Nat. Hist. Bull.* 15(9),537-550.

23. Galtsoff, P.S., 1924, "Limnological observations in the upper Mississippi, 1921," *Bull. U. S. Bur. Fish.* 39, 347-438.

24. Hederstrom, H. 1759, *Ron Fiskars Alder Handl. Kunal. Vetenskapsakademin (Stockholm)* 20, 222-229, in. *Inst. Freshwater Res. (Drottingholm)* 40(1959), 161-164.

25. Hubbs, C.L., and Eschmeyer, R. W., 1938, *The Improvement of Lakes for Fishing,* Inst. for Fish. Res. Bull. No. 2, pp. 1-233.

26. Hulsey, A. H., 1957, "Effects of a fall and winter drawdown on a flood control lake," *Proc. 10th Ann. Conf. S.E. Assoc. Game and Fish Comm.* pp. 285-289.

27. Jenkins, R.M., 1961, *Reservoir Fish Management—Progress and Challenge,* Sport. Fishing Inst., Washington, D.C., pp. 1-22.

28. Jenkins, R.M., and Elkin, R.E., 1957, "*Growth of the White Bass in Oklahoma,"* Oklahoma Fish Res. Lab. Rept. No. 60 pp. 1-21.

29. Jeppson, P., 1957, "The control of squawfish by use of dynamite, spot treatment, and reduction of lake levels," *Progressive Fish Culturist* 19(4), 168-171.

30. Johnson, M. C., 1959, "Food-fish farming in the Mississippi delta," *Progressive Fish Culturist* 21(4), 154-160.

31. Juday, C., Schloemer, C.L., and Livingston, C., 1938, "Effect of fertilizers on plankton production and on fish growth in a Wisconsin lake,"*Progressive Fish Culturist,* 40, 24-27.

32. Langlois, T.H., 1948, "North American attempts at fish management," *Bingham Ocean, Collect.* 9(4), 33-54.

33. Larimore, R.W., 1957, "Ecological life history of the warmouth (Centrarchidae)," *Illinois Nat. Hist. Surv. Bull.* 27(1), 1-83.

34. Leopold, A., 1933, *Game Management,* Chas. Scribner's & Sons, New York, pp. 1-481.

35. Lucas, C.R., 1939, "Game fish management," *Am. Fish Soc. Trans.* 68(1938), 67-75.

36. Macinko, G., 1968, "Conservation trends and the future American environment," The Biologist, 1(1-2), 1-19.

37. Markus, H. C., 1932, "The extent to which temperature changes influence food consumption in largemouth bass," *Am. Fish. Soc. Trans.* 62, 202-210.

38. Meehean, O.L., 1952, "Symposium on farm fish ponds and management," *J. Wildlife Management* 16(3), 233-288.

39. Moore, E., 1931, "A follow-up program on the impounded waters of the Sacondaga Reservoir," *Am. Fish. Soc. Trans.* 61, 139-142.
40. Neess, J., 1949, "Development and status of pond fertilization in central Europe," *Am. Fish Soc. Trans.* 76(1946), 335-358.
41. North, R., 1713, *Discourse of Fish and Fish Ponds,* E. Curll, London.
42. Shelds, J.T., 1958, "Fish management problems of large impoundments on the Missouri River," *Am. Fish. Soc. Trans.* 87(1957) 356-364.
43. Smith, S.H., 1968, "Species succession and fishery exploitation in the Great Lakes," *J. Fisheries Res. Board Can.* 25(4), 667-693.
44. Stranahan, J.J., 1902, "Fish culture on the farm," *Am. Fish. Soc. Trans.* 31, 130-137.
45. Stroud, R. H., 1948, "Growth of the basses and black crappies in Norris Reservoir, Tennessee," *J. Tenn. Acad. Sci.,* 23(1), 31-99.
46. Stroud, R. H., 1956, *Broad Public Interest to Prevail,* S.F.I. Bull. No. 56, p. 1.
47. Stroud, R. H., 1956, *Federal Reorganization and the Sport Fisheries,* S.F.I. Bull. No. 60, pp.. 1-2.
48. Stroud, R. H., 1958, *Small Boat Legislation,* S.F.I. Bull, No. 83, p. 5.
49. Stroud, R. H., 1966, "American experience in recreational use of artificial waters," in *Man-Made Lakes,* Inst. Biol., New York, pp. 189-200.
50. Stroud, R. H., 1967, *Reservoir Research Progress Report,* S.F.I. Bull. No. 183, pp. 1-3.
51. Stroud, R. H., 1967, *Reservoir fishery Resources Symposium,* S.F.I. Bull. No. 184. pp. 1-5.
52. Stroud, R. H., and Jenkins, R.M., 1962, *Bureau of Outdoor Recreation Established,* S.F.I. Bull. No. 126, pp. 1-2.
53. Surber, E.W., 1931, "Sodium arsenite for controlling submerged vegetation in ponds," *Am. Fish. Soc. Trans.* 61, 143-148.
54. Swingle, H.S., and Smith, E.V., 1939, "Increasing fish production in ponds," *4th North Am. Wildlife Conf. Trans.,* pp. 332-338.
55. Tarzwell, C.M., 1942, "Fish populations in the backwaters of Wheeler Reservoir and suggestions for their management," *Am. Fish. Soc. Trans.* 71(1941), 201-214.
56. Thompson, D.H., 1933, "The migration of Illinois fishes," *Illinois Nat. Hist. Surv. Biol. Notes,* 1, 1-25.
57. Thompson, D. H., 1941, "The fish production of inland streams and lakes," *A Symp. on Hydrobio.,* Univ. of Wisconsin Press. Madison, Wisc., pp. 206-217.
58. Thompson, D. H., and Bennett, G.W., 1939, "Fish management in small artificial lakes," *4th North Am. Wildlife Conf. Trans.,* pp. 311-317.
59. Thompson, G. H., 1913, "Protection of the undersized fish," *Am. Fish. Soc. Trans.*
60. Van Oosten, J., 1939, "The present status of the United States commercial fisheries of the Great Lakes," *4th North Am. Wildlife Conf. Trans.* pp. 319-330.
61. Van Oosten, J., and Hile, R., 1947, "Age and Growth of the lake whitefish, *Coregonus elupeaformis* (Mitchill) in Lake Erie," *Am. Fish. Soc. Trans.* 77, 178-249.
62. Wickliff, E.L., 1933, "Are newly impounded waters in Ohio suitable for fish life?" *Am. Fish. Soc. Trans.* 62(1932), 275-277.
63. Wickliff, E.L., and Roach, L.S., 1937, "Some studies of impounded waters in Ohio," *Am. Fish. Soc. Trans.* 66(1936), 78-86.
64. Wiebe, A.H., 1929, "The effect of various fertilizers on plankton production," *Am. Fish. Soc. Trans.* 59, 94-106.
65. Wood, R., 1951, "The significance of managed water levels in developing the fisheries of large impoundments," *J. Tenn. Acad. Sci.* 26(3), 214-235.

2

AQUATIC HABITATS

There are many kinds of aquatic habitats showing a great variety of physical, chemical, and biological characteristics. Many of these are inhabited by fishes, which are, of necessity, as diverse in body form and physiology as are the habitats in which they live.

The relationships of fishes to their aquatic environments are the subject of Chapter 3. In this chapter we will describe some static (nonflowing) water habitats that are important in sport fishing, and which, to some degree, lend themselves to fish management. Man-made waters, e.g., ponds, artificial lakes, and reservoirs, will receive more consideration than natural lakes. Much information on the latter is already available in treatises on limnology. Flowing-water habitats, e.g., brooks, streams, and rivers, have been omitted entirely and, for the most part, trout and other coldwater species are mentioned only where they bear a relationship to warmwater habitats or fishes. The literature on trout and trout management probably exceeds that for all warmwater fishes and its integration here would go beyond the objectives of this book.

NATURAL LAKES

Glacial Lakes

Limnologists have a complex technical classification of standing waters based primarily on their physical and chemical characteristics and secondarily on biological characteristics which are dependent on the physical-chemical properties of the environments. The limnologist's terminology for the types of lakes in which our interest lies are *oligotrophic* (oligo, little;

trophic, food) and *eutrophic* (eu, good; trophic, food). A general term for *oligotrophic lakes* might be *trout lakes* because they are suitable for trout, land-locked salmon, whitefish, various coldwater herrings, and sometimes grayling. *Eutrophic lakes* have physical-chemical characteristics such that coldwater fishes cannot live in them during summer months. They are satisfactory for largemouth bass and this species is nearly always present. Therefore, we may justify giving *eutrophic lakes* the common name of *bass lakes.*

Very briefly, the characteristics of these two types of lake are as follows:

Oligotrophic (trout) lakes: deep lakes, often large in size, located in regions where the substratum is usually rocky and the soils limited in amount and relatively sterile (Fig. 2.1). These lakes are thermally stratified in summer but with a large volume of water in the profundal zone that contains abundant oxygen all through the period of summer stratification. Fishes are characteristically salmons, trouts, chars, ciscoes, and graylings, all supported in relatively small populations because of the sterile environment. Oligotrophic lakes usually support less than 20 lb. of fishes per surface acre.

Eutrophic (bass) lakes: depths intermediate to shallow, variable in surface area, located in regions with a higher range of soil fertility than that of oligotrophic lakes. Such a lake is thermally stratified in summer but with reduced or zero oxygen in the profundal zone, making it an unsuitable habitat for fish during this period. Fishes are characteristically largemouth bass, white bass, white and black crappies, bluegills and other sunfish, buffalo, channel catfish, bullheads, carp, and suckers. Populations of 100−150 lb. of fish per acre are not uncommon.

Both *oligotrophic* and *eutrophic* lakes become thermally stratified in the warm seasons when layers of water at various depths will not mix with one another due to differences in water density (weight) associated with temperature differences. In both, the warmer layer of water at the surface circulates from the action of wind, and the volume of water below the surface becomes sealed off from direct contact with the air. For a more detailed explanation of the ramifications of thermal stratification, see Welch, Ruttner, or Hutchison.[23,37,50] A brief discussion of thermal stratification and loss of oxygen in several types of standing waters has been included on page 44 of this chapter.

Distribution of Glacial and Other Kinds of Natural Lakes

Various regions of the United States show a predominance or absence of the several kinds of natural lakes. In the northeastern region lakes are largely glacial in origin and are both deep (trout lakes) and shallow (bass

Fig. 2.1 Glacial lakes pass through several recognized stages in the process of aging; oligotrophic (infertile trout lakes) to eutrophic (fertile bass lakes) to distrophic (bog lakes filled with aquatic vegetation, and usually unsuitable for fishes). This is an oligotrophic or trout lake in the Boundary Waters Canoe Area, Superior National Forest, Minnesota. *Courtesy U. S. Forest Service.*

lakes). The growing season is relatively short and both coldwater and warmwater fish are found abundantly.[7]

In the Southeast, natural lakes are shallow and were formed by receding oceans, changing river systems, earthquakes, and dissolution of limestone deposits. Of an estimated 955,000 acres of lakes in the Southeast more than 78% of this water is in Florida and about 11.5% in Louisiana.

In the north central region there are more than 40,000 natural lakes of over 10 acres: 17,000 in Minnesota, 11,000 in Michigan, and 8,700 in

Wisconsin. Only a few glacial lakes are south of the northernmost states. Sterile oligotrophic lakes are found in the northern counties of these states and eutrophic lakes in the more southern parts.

Most of the lakes in the Rocky Mountain region are above the 4000-foot level. Waters are cold and suitable for trout. These lakes originated from glacial or volcanic action and originally contained native species of trout. Native rainbow and brook trout, the exotic brown trout, and some other species have been widely stocked in these waters.

Natural lakes in the Southwest are rare. Most of the natural lakes of North America are glacial in origin although there are a small number of lakes formed by other natural phenomena, such as dissolution of mineral deposits, earthquakes followed by land sinkings, sand "blowouts" that become lakes when water tables rise, flood-plain lakes created by changing river channels (oxbow lakes), and others.

Marshes

Marshes are included here because some glacial lakes are bordered by them and rivers may find their sources in them. They are important as spawning grounds for several species of fishes, including the northern pike, and are used as nesting areas for ducks and other water birds.[46]

Marshes have great capacity for taking up water during wet periods, filtering out silt, and gradually releasing clear water during periods of drought; for these reasons, rivers that originate in marshes or pass through them show less turbidity and have a more constant flow throughout the seasons than those which are dependent on surface runoff of cultivated lands.

MAN-MADE LAKES AND PONDS

Artificial lakes are of two kinds: *(1)* water impoundments for some definite purpose, such as flood control, water supply, or recreation, and *(2)* water-filled depressions from which surface materials or mineral deposits have been removed. It is interesting to note that these bodies of water show a considerable diversity of aquatic habitat. Thus, artificial lakes (such as lateral-levee lakes along large rivers, navigation pools created by low dams across river channels, or deep mainstream storage reservoirs) may be biologically quite similar to natural lakes, whereas, impoundments across small or temporary drainage channels may contain a limited biota, i.e., few species. In fact, when these latter lakes are in densely populated regions, the aquatic animals (primarily birds and mammals) that customarily inhabit remote regions and shun close association with man are almost entirely absent. The heavy use of a lake by recreation seekers may even drive away animals that are only moderately man-shy.

Neither coots nor migrating ducks (where protected) are wary of man, but they may leave a lake if boat traffic becomes heavy.

When some of the animals that ideally constitute the natural complex of undisturbed standing waters are absent from artificial lakes, interrelationships of the living organisms that are present will differ from those found in the more primitive environment. Thus when man is critical of the kinds and sizes of fish that an artificial lake produces in contrast to a natural one in some remote region, he is not making a proper comparison. The differences in animal populations inhabiting natural and artificial lakes will be considered further in Chapter 5.

There is a natural movement of plants and animals in an area of little direct human interference. Since most artificial lakes have not been in existence as long as natural ones, certain organisms have not yet had the time or the opportunity to populate or adjust to these newly created waters.

Some organisms move about much more readily than others, many of the smaller forms being carried by the wind as spores, seeds, eggs, or resting stages that are protected from desiccation by waterproof coverings. Aquatic animals and plants might be arranged in a scale of decreasing ability to traverse the gap between one body of water and another, with some moving in almost as soon as a new lake has been created, and others arriving less rapidly. In fact, opportunities for the movement of some aquatic organisms may be so infrequent as to require many years for their arrival by natural means, and others may never breach the gap. Certain organisms may gain entry as a result of accident or stocking by man. Because of these variations in migration time and the relatively short age of artificial lakes, populations of their organisms are usually simpler than those of natural ones, with fewer species.

Motivation for the construction of artificial lakes varies with our need for water. Today in the United States we inhabit all of our arable lands, and must devise ways to supply water for diverse uses. Although sometimes water problems are related to too much water, usually the amount is inadequate or availability is not synchronized with need.

At the turn of the century, engineers envisioned multiple uses for impoundments. Reservoirs were built by community, state, and federal efforts to supply water for cities and industries, to irrigate dry lands, and to generate power. More recently, impoundments have been constructed to supply water for navigation during dry seasons, to control floods during abnormally wet ones, and even to dilute sewage during periods of low water flow. However, it was not until the 1930s that many reservoirs were built solely for recreational purposes, because aquatic recreation had little or no recognized monetary value prior to this time.

After the drought and depression years of the 1930s, considerable interest centered on farm ponds, largely as a result of the United States Soil Conservation Service, which became active during that period. Not only were ponds promoted as sources of water for stock but also for their usefulness as a general farm-water supply for orchard spraying, fire protection, limited irrigation in dry years, and for recreation in the form of fishing, swimming, and boating. Furthermore, the damming of eroded gullies stopped the movement of soil downhill so that impoundments created by these dams could be combined with contour plowing and strip cropping as an integral part of the soil and water-conservation plans.

Other types of artificial bodies of water resulted from man's activities in digging at the earth's surface for clay, sand and gravel, limestone and other rocks, and coal and other minerals. The empty holes incidentally became filled with water and formed ponds and lakes.

These, then, are the artificial waters available for fish management. They are often more manageable than natural lakes because they are man-created, their ecologies are more simple, and they are so engineered that they can be better manipulated. In some, construction was originally planned to give maximum recreational values; in others, recreational uses followed an original but transitory resource such as the removal of gravel.

THE FARM POND

The most common type of artificial impoundment and the least expensive to create is probably the woods or pasture pond made by building an earthen dam across a small intermittent watercourse (Fig. 2.2). Superficially, these ponds seem to be the simplest type of aquatic habitat, and perhaps they are; however, intensive investigation of the physical, chemical, and biological characteristics of ponds indicates that even this type of habitat is so far from simple that an exact duplication of any pond is nearly impossible.

No one knows the exact number of farm ponds in the United States, but in a 1960 report of the U.S. Bureau of Sport Fisheries and Wildlife,[27] Dr. Willis King estimated that since World War II the Bureau has stocked from 30,000 to 40,000 farm ponds annually, which would approximate a total of 450,000 to 600,000 in this fifteen year period. Because many ponds had been built prior to World War II, it is quite possible that a total number exceeds a million.

A rough estimate of the farm ponds in Canada in 1961 would be in the neighborhood of 10,000.[38] Most of these ponds have been developed by individual land owners or as a business enterprise for raising trout.

Fig. 2.2 Pasture pond formed by damming a small intermittent watercourse.

Purposes of Farm Ponds

When farmers who had built ponds were asked to list their reasons for
doing so, 80% gave water for livestock as a reason; 70% wanted to provide fishing; 13% to provide irrigation water; 9% for swimming; 5%
for wildlife; and 4% for all other uses.[27] Many farm families are interested
in various forms of outdoor recreation, and the farm pond may be the
center of these activities: fishing, swimming, picnicking, hunting, boating, and, in the north, ice skating.

Engineering Considerations for Farm Ponds

Engineering specifications for ponds vary for parts of the country in
accordance with differences in rainfall, runoff, tightness of soils, and
types of vegetative cover. Ponds must be deeper in the north than in the
south in order that the cold winters and thick ice do not result in loss of
fish (Fig. 2.3). Increased depth is also a boon to regions characterized by
long periods of dry weather. In planning the shoreline of the pond, any
extensive water areas less than two or three feet in depth should be
eliminated, because shallow waters may become choked with aquatic
vegetation such as cattail and bulrush, which may form a continuous
band around a pond edge.

Fig. 2.3 A partially drained pond. The deep area near the center of the picture was specially constructed to permit fish to congregate there in winter.

A satisfactory pond must have an adequate water supply that carries a low silt load. This water supply may be runoff from lands managed under a soil-conservation program, or from springs, flowing wells, or very small streams.[12] The pond should be impounded behind a well-built dam with a spillway adequate to carry off flood waters. Trees and brush should not be allowed to grow on the dam, or continuously around the shore of the pond. The pond should be supplied with a drainpipe and valve large enough to allow fish to pass through the pipe out of the pond with the outflowing water.

Much attention has been given to the regional engineering aspects of pond construction by the United States Soil Conservation Service and the agricultural colleges of many state universities. Information for most localities of the United States is available for those wishing to construct ponds, and no attempt will be made here to consider more than a few of the simpler aspects of farm-pond construction.

Engineering methods for ponds in the southeastern U.S. are much different from those of northeastern, central, southwestern, or northwestern regions.

In the West, certain ponds (for example, in Colorado and Arizona) are used as sources of water for irrigation.[29] These ponds are pumped full and then are partly drained to irrigate crops during a 24-hr period. These irrigation ponds fluctuate as much as 10 ft. and the water is usually cold. Such ponds do not provide satisfactory fish habitats.

However, most ponds are built for uses other than irrigation and are more suitable for fish production, even though their primary function may be supplying water for stock or fire protection. Even if all ponds were built primarily for sport fishing, the engineering considerations for each section of the country would be highly variable.

United States Geological Survey quadrangle maps are very helpful for locating sites suitable for ponds. These maps show 5- or 10-ft contour lines on relatively small areas of land, so that it is possible to select on these maps locations for dams on intermittent water courses, to outline the pond shoreline above each selected dam site, and to estimate the approximate acreage of land sloping toward the pond site from which surface water will drain into the pond. Once the prospective builder has located all possible sites for his dam, then a local engineer experienced in pond construction can look over the actual sites, select the best ones, make test borings to determine soil strata under the dam sites, and plan the dams and spillway structures necessary to handle the estimated run-off.

Many ponds have been built without engineering assistance, and some of them have been successful. However, do-it-yourself pond building is not recommended beyond the preliminary steps described above because of the close tolerances between the runoff water handled and the type and size of spillway structure required for it. Thus, if the spillway is of the wrong type or is too small, the first flood may wash away the dam. On the other hand, if the watershed is not large enough in relation to the storage capacity of the pond, the pond may be full or nearly full only in wet weather. In dry years such a pond could become useless both for water supply and recreation.

Farm ponds usually range in size from 1/4 acre to several acres. Those smaller than about 1 acre are unsatisfactory for fishing.[41] Often when a pond or lake is planned to exceed 10 acres, the builder has in mind some commercial use, rather than farm water supply and recreation.

WHEN IS A POND A LAKE?

The question of when a body of water ceases to be a lake and becomes a pond has never been settled to everyone's satisfaction, and actually becomes a matter of semantics. According to some limnologists,[18] "a lake is thermally stratified, through most of the year, into an epi-, meta-, and hypolimnion.* Only a body of water conforming to this specification will

*Epilimnion (upper lake); metalimnion (middle lake or thermocline); hypolimnion (lower lake).

be considered when using the term lake." To many this definition is unsatisfactory because most small ponds built by damming steep-sided ravines are thermally stratified "through most of the year," although the stratification may be such that the upper edge of the hypolimnion is indefinite. In contrast, it seems illogical to call a large, shallow body of water a pond; for example, Chautauqua Lake, a natural basin in the floodplain of the Illinois River valley near Havana, Illinois, almost never shows thermal stratification. By definition this lake should be considered a pond, although it has a surface area of nearly 3500 acres.

In Oklahoma, 10 acres represents the arbitrary point of separation between lakes and ponds; thus bodies of water with smaller surface area are ponds and those with greater surface area are lakes.[26] However, Dr. W.C. Starrett suggests that the point of separation be set at 4 acres, and Veatch and Humphrys[22] consider Michigan waters of less than 5 acres as "lakelets and ponds." In any case, if we are not to use the terms interchangeably, the separation would have to be based on some arbitrary upper size limit for ponds, and any body of standing water above this limit should automatically be considered a lake, regardless of its limnological characteristics.

ARTIFICIAL LAKES FOR DOMESTIC USES

A great many artificial lakes have been constructed throughout the United States for urban and/or industrial water supplies. These artificial impoundments may vary in size from a few hundred acres to many thousands of acres. On these lakes, recreation is of secondary importance to water-supply uses, although an effort often is made to influence public opinion in favor of a proposed reservoir on the basis of its potential recreational attractions.

Water-Supply Reservoirs

Water-supply needs for towns and small cities frequently are met through the construction of artificial impoundments of intermediate sizes. In the East, an early attempt was made to restrict trespass on these water-supply reservoirs and thus to prevent their use for public recreation. Only recently has this policy been reversed. In the Midwest and West, almost no attempt has been made to restrict the recreational uses of water-supply reservoirs, and fishing, swimming, and boating are common. Where recreation is not restricted, a great deal of use may be made of water-supply reservoirs; however, water consumption holds priority, and when other uses conflict with the primary use, they must be sacrificed. As previously mentioned in Chapter 1, the health departments of some states have allowed the use of rotenone in water-supply reservoirs to control the overabundance of small stunted fishes, or dominant populations of bottom-feeding fishes responsible for stirring up the bottom mud. Rotenone in dosages great enough to kill fishes is nontoxic to warm-blooded vertebrates. A detailed discussion of the use of rotenone will be given later.

Reservoirs built for city and town water supplies are often created by damming permanent streams or small rivers. The smallest stream capable of filling the reservoir basin and also of supplying the annual needs of the community is the most practical choice. This is true because the silt load carried by a stream is roughly proportional to the size of its watershed, and the useful life of a reservoir depends upon the rate of silt deposition in its basin.

All permanent streams of any purity contain fishes. Some species cannot maintain their populations in impounded waters, others multiply excessively in reservoirs and create a constant turbidity through bottom-rooting activities. These latter species interfere with fishing by reducing the visibility for those that feed by sight, and also reduce aesthetic values for swimmers and boaters.

New water-supply reservoirs stocked with bass and pan fish usually go through a regular fishing cycle which requires about six or seven years from the time water is first impounded.[5] At the end of that time active measures must be taken if recreational and aesthetic values are to be maintained. These techniques will be discussed in Chapter 6.

Most water-supply reservoirs for cities in agricultural regions are relatively shallow because of the moderate slope of the land. These reservoirs are almost always thermally stratified in summer and lose their supply of oxygen in the deeper water.

Usually in rough or mountainous regions, water-supply reservoirs are comparatively deep and infertile.

NAVIGATION POOLS

In some of our larger rivers, locks and dams have been installed to maintain water depths for navigation. Examples of such rivers are the Mississippi, Ohio, and Illinois. Although these relatively shallow impoundments retain some current, the river rapids (important in the successful spawning of some fishes such as the blue sucker) have been largely eliminated. Navigation locks and dams are under the jurisdiction of the United States Corps of Army Engineers, which builds new dams, maintaining the present installations and also a river channel of a specified depth for the movement of towboats and barges.

Studies of the fishes living in the navigation pools of the upper Mississippi indicate that these pools support both an extensive sport and commercial fishery.[2,40]

Low dams across a large river will result in the permanent flooding of backwater areas adjacent to the river, except when the level of an upstream pool may be lowered to furnish water for navigation downstream. When this occurs, backwater lakes may be drained quite rapidly, sometimes to the detriment of their fish, particularly in winter when these backwaters are covered by thick ice.

LATERAL-LEVEE RESERVOIRS

Lowlands in the flood plains of rivers are sometimes protected from the river by levees; these lowlands are pumped dry for agricultural uses. When these areas are abandoned or reconverted into lakes with the levees still intact, they become lateral-levee reservoirs. These shallow reservoirs are very productive.

Some of them are supplied with stone and concrete spillways to allow the entrance of water from the adjacent river when it rises above the spillway crest. Then, as the river level recedes, water flows out of the lake until the spillway crest level is again reached. The water in such a lateral-levee reservoir may fluctuate moderately with changing levels in the river, e.g., when the level of the reservoir is below the spillway crest, due to slow seepage through the levee.

These lakes are quite turbid, due primarily to the action of wind.[25] They are productive of hook-and-line fish,[17,39] and at the same time may support a large commercial fishery for such river species as carp, buffalo, freshwater drum, and channel catfish.

MULTIPURPOSE RESERVOIRS

Large impoundments constructed by the federal government in many parts of the United States have been justified on the basis of a combination of uses, such as flood control, navigation, the generation of electric power, irrigation, and recreation. Not all of these values are assigned to one reservoir; usually irrigation is assigned in the arid west, navigation may be a localized or general assignment, and the generation of power requires a reservoir which will produce a dependable and constant source of water.

Some of these uses appear to conflict with one another. For example, flood control demands an empty reservoir much of the time to give maximum flood storage, whereas navigation and the generation of power require a full basin, since they may depend upon a continuous release of water from the reservoir. Furthermore, although recreation values may accompany a changing water level, they are gone when the reservoir basin is dry (as in some flood-control projects). Generally speaking, all needs do not occur simultaneously so there may not be intensive competition for water at any one time.

Apparent conflicts of purpose are resolved by assigning a range of levels to specific uses. First, the basic purpose is taken care of by setting a conservation-pool level or elevation near the bottom of the reservoir. Until this "absolute minimum" water level has been exceeded, no large amount of water will be released. In a reservoir of 24,000 to 30,000 acres, water at the conservation-pool level might create a lake of 3000 to 6000 acres. Then, other fractions of the reservoir's storage capacity may be assigned to power generation, navigation, or irrigation. Usually, the flood-control function belongs to the upper layer of reservoir capacity, which is drained off after each flood as rapidly as the river channel below the dam will permit (bank full), so that the upper lake in the reservoir will be available for storing water once again should another flood occur (Fig. 2.4).

In the operation of a multipurpose reservoir, water in the river channel below the dam is never allowed to exceed the top of the river banks (as long as any storage capacity exists in the reservoir), or to fall below a certain minimum flow in drought periods, even if this means using some

Fig. 2.4 Lake Wappapello (Missouri) outlet. This is a reservoir constructed for flood control and recreation. The boom above the gates is used for the removal of logs that may float into the outlet.

water assigned to the conservation pool. This minimum flow is so small in relation to the capacity of the conservation pool that there is little danger of ever draining the latter. The controlled release of water into the river channel below the dam insures a constant supply for agrarian users and towns situated on the river and maintains the fish population that inhabits the river below the dam. There are valid arguments against the construction of multipurpose dams, particularly on relatively flat terrain where the ratio of water stored to the land flooded by the reservoir is low.[28]

PONDS AND LAKES WITH EXCAVATED BASINS

Although lake and pond basins can be completely excavated with earth-moving equipment, this is infrequently done because of the high cost. However, sometimes the clay needed for a pond dam may be removed from the sides of the pond basin, so that the basin can be enlarged and deepened in the process of building the dam. Also, ponds are sometimes dug or enlarged and deepened in real estate developments or in other special locations where cost is of secondary importance.

There are many kinds of excavations made by man that become filled with groundwater and are eventually stocked with fish. These "holes" are excavations for the removal of gravel, limestone, stone, coal, or other near-surface mineral deposits. Some of these waterfilled pits are among the most attractive waters to be found south of the lake states, because they are comparatively clear. Recent construction of superhighways has resulted in many ponds where soil has been removed and used as fill to raise road grades.

Gravel-Pit Lakes

Gravel deposits have been transported and deposited by rivers which came from melting glaciers. Most of these deposits, although covered with soils, are readily located by test borings in regions where excavations (such as well drillings) or other evidence have shown the presence of gravel. Since considerable gravel is needed for road beds and as a component in hard surfacing, this product is in constant local demand. The sale of gravel, while not so remunerative as that of most other minerals, furnishes more than enough to pay for the cost of pond excavation. With a little planning, the excavations remaining when operations have been completed can become attractive recreational waters (Fig. 2.5).

When digging is done primarily to develop recreational ponds (often the case when gravel deposits are located under high-priced farm lands), plans may be made for the arrangement of ponds, the leveling of the spoil

Fig. 2.5 Gravel-pit ponds planned for recreational uses after gravel removal. Bodies of water were kept separated and stocked with various combinations of fishes, so that each pond could be easily renovated if fishing became poor. The square pond in the upper left is about 4 acres; a bathing beach and diving pier were built at its lower left corner.

banks, and the respreading of the top soil over leveled areas in order to greatly improve the pit area (Fig. 2.3). In regions where lakes and ponds are scarce, a well-planned recreational area superimposed on an abandoned gravel works may bring a better price than the original farm land, or, if strategically located and properly managed, produce annual income equal to, or exceeding, the income from farm crops.

A flooded gravel works may consist of a number of small ponds separated by levees of sand or clay. Often, when the pit owner decides to develop the area for recreation, his first thought is to connect all of these ponds. Experience shows that several isolated ponds are more easily managed for fishing than a single large one, and separated ponds allow a greater variety of fishing because species can be stocked in some that would not survive if placed in one large pond containing other more competitive fishes. However, no pond should have an area of much less than one acre, or it will be too small for satisfactory fishing.

The standing crop of fish supported by gravel pits may be lower than that of artificial ponds receiving direct surface runoff from farm lands; the fish-population size (weight) is related to the fertility of the surrounding land, in spite of the fact that there may be no direct surface runoff into the gravel-pit ponds.

The water level in a gravel-pit pond is that of the water-table level because the sand-bottomed basin will not hold water. This may be demonstrated by transferring water from one pond into another by a large pump. The pond from which water is being pumped may drop several feet and the other pond rise in proportion, but if the pump is stopped, water will seep out of the high pond and into the low one, so that within a very short time both will again be at groundwater level.

Since levels in gravel pits fluctuate from one to three feet during most years, this annual fluctuation should be taken into consideration when bottom contours are being planned. The exposure of large areas of the bottom, as a result of normal annual fluctuation, is unsightly and may be avoided if the more shallow areas are deepened.

Where gravel beds are extensive, gravel digging operations can be planned to create areas of open water up to four or five acres, or to create relatively narrow meandering channels. Once the spoil banks have become vegetated with trees, shrubs, and herbaceous plants, the latter arrangement is more attractive to anglers than is a large area of open water.

Gravel-pit ponds are usually thermally stratified in summer because they are surrounded by highlands that reduce the wind action of the water.

Strip-Mine Lakes

Strip-mine lakes result from the flooding of surface excavations after the removal of coal deposits. Layers of coal may vary in depth below the surface, and strip-mining equipment can operate at a profit on deposits as deep as 50-90 ft. Before the coal can be stripped, the topsoil and clay overburden must be removed. This operation is done with giant cranes supplied with digging buckets which pile the waste material in long ridges running parallel to the cuts they are making. As the coal in each cut is exhausted, the crane moves over to dig a new cut parallel to the other one, and the material from the new strip is piled into or along the previously exhausted excavation. Thus, strip mining actually turns land upside down (because the topsoil is buried under the clay overburden) and results in a series of long parallel ridges many feet high. In some stripped areas, water collects in the valleys between these ridges and forms long narrow lakes usually connected to similar lakes between other ridges by channels (Fig. 2.6). The last "cut" or strip that the crane makes before abandoning an area is not filled in and may form a lake several hundred

Fig. 2.6 Strip-mine area in winter with the tops of the spoil banks covered with snow. Frozen pond areas are visible in the lower left and center left. This area was about twenty-five years old and some trees had grown from a natural seeding of the spoil banks.

feet wide, as deep as 60 ft, and a mile or more long, depending upon the size of the stripped area, the depth of the coal, and the lengths of the booms of the stripping cranes.

Coal deposits are associated with deposits of sulfur, iron, and other minerals. When the abandoned mines are flooded, these minerals often dissolve and make the mine ponds too acid to provide a habitat for aquatic organisms.[31,8,9] However, ponds become less acid with age; the sulfuric acid may be buffered with calcium from limestone deposits and other carbonates, or the runoff water from higher lands may flush out the acid water. Occasionally, stripped lands adjacent to small rivers are flooded by the latter, resulting in a great change in the sulfate composition of the strip-mine water after the flood recedes. These ponds may range in pH from 2.0 to 8.0 or 9.0 depending on their stage of succession. Once the pH rises above 6.5 or 7.0 (neutrality) they will support fishes.

Strip-mine waters usually contain several hundred parts per million of sulfate; in one pond having a pH range of 7.2 to 8.0, fish were found living and reproducing although the water contained 1500 ppm of sulfate.

Strip-mine ponds vary considerably from one another in the weight of fish supported because of the great variation in their water chemistry. It is reasonable that fish production might be low in certain strip-mine waters, since many invertebrate animals and algae in the food chain are more sensitive than fishes to abnormal mineral content. But aging, weathering, flooding, and the annual accumulation of dust and leaves gradually build up the basic fertility and reduce the chemical imbalance of these waters until they become very fertile. The waters of the South Pollywog Association, an 80-yr-old strip-mine area in Vermilion County, Illinois, support populations of miscellaneous fishes as high as 750 lb/acre.

Quarry Lakes

A great deal of limestone is used in agriculture as limestone dust to neutralize acid soils and as crushed rock in road building and other construction. Other deposits of rock of value in building may be quarried from near-surface deposits. Quarrying and strip-mining operations are somewhat similar in that often the top soils and overburden are first removed, leaving the strata of limestone or other rock exposed. Since deposits of limestone are often below the level of the water table, quarrying operations depend upon pumps to remove the water as it seeps into the quarry pits.

After the valuable rock has been extracted, the pumps are stopped and the pits fill up to the level of groundwater (Fig. 2.7), forming one or several bodies of water. New limestone-quarry waters are usually quite infertile because they contain almost no phosphates, nitrates, or organic material. However, minerals causing hard water are present in abundance and organic nutrient materials may be carried into quarries through surface runoff from surrounding lands, so that the potential for fish production may increase quite rapidly as the water in the abandoned quarry ages.

Quarry ponds are similar to gravel-pit ponds and strip-mine ponds in that they are usually dependent on subsurface waters rather than superficial drainage. Also, they are thermally stratified in summer, due to their relatively great depths and to the limited action of winds on the surfaces of these ponds. In depth, quarry ponds may exceed gravel pits and strip mines.

Phosphate Pits

The mining of phosphate in Florida has created a number of water-filled pits in a region fairly close to Tampa.[11] The pits vary in size from 1/2 to 17 acres and in depth from 6 to 30 ft. These water-filled pits are very fertile and support dense blooms of phytoplankton as well as some types

Fig. 2.7 Ponds resulting from the quarrying of limestone are quite sterile and their waters are usually very clear. They make a satisfactory habitat for smallmouth bass.

of emergent higher aquatic vegetation. This is to be expected as the phosphate content of the water averages 0.5 ppm. These pits were used to increase water areas for public fishing after first being poisoned with rotenone and restocked with largemouth bass, bluegills, red-ear sunfish, channel catfish, white catfish, and Nile tilapia, *Tilapia nilotica*.

The main problem in using these water-filled pits as fish ponds was in the control of various algae, duckweeds, and other aquatic vegetation. Crittenden[11] recommended that the phosphate mining companies dig out unit areas of at least 150 x 1000 ft so that wind action might help in blowing floating surface vegetation to the downwind shore.

Borrow Pits

The construction of multiple-lane highways with their overpasses, clover-leaf entrances and exits, and other structures has required a great deal of soil for building fills and approaches. This material must be obtained from locations close by. The usual practice is to purchase small plots of land adjacent to the highway right-of-way and as near as possible to the construction sites. The depth of the resulting pits depends upon the area of land purchased, the amount of material needed at the highway site, and the quality of the material obtained. Excavations vary in area from one-half to several acres and may be as deep as 30 ft. These pits become filled up to the level of the groundwater.

Land plots purchased for road materials are usually in the form of rectangles and are excavated to form rectangular ponds (Fig. 2.8). These are much less attractive than are ponds with irregular curving shorelines, and some states have arranged with road contractors to modify their digging operations to produce more attractive waters. These pits are sold or leased for recreation areas after road construction has been completed.

Several states have purchased or leased borrow pits along superhighways for public fishing waters. Some are leased or purchased by private individuals or clubs for private fishing, or for pay-fishing lakes (Chapter 9).

LAKES BUILT FOR RECREATION

Within the past decade, many artificial lakes have been built *entirely* for the purpose of furnishing aquatic recreation (Fig. 2.9). There is scarcely any way in which recreation funds can be spent to produce such a large return over so long a period. At first, artificial lakes for recreation appear

Fig. 2.8 Borrow-pit ponds are common along new four-lane highways where clay fill material was needed for approaches to overpasses. These holes in the ground which rapidly fill with water to form ponds are frequently rectangular in shape and vary in depth with the need for fill material and the capability of the equipment used to dig them. Borrow pits are leased or purchased from road contractors and stocked with fish.

Fig. 2.9 Many lakes are built wholly for recreation. This is one of a number of state lakes in Alabama managed for public fishing. A slight daily charge for fishing helps defray the management costs.

to be expensive. However, costs of such public lakes can be amortized over the life of the impoundment[6] providing a long period of usefulness and consequently, an intangible return great enough to make them highly practical. Furthermore, where lakes are not built primarily for recreation, they still should be planned and constructed to allow easy management of their fish populations, and should have an outlet large enough for quick drainage and a sloping basin that will empty completely. From the standpoint of ease in management, it is more practical to build five 100-acre lakes than one lake of 500 acres.

A satisfactory site for a recreational lake requires a basin with a minimum area of shallow water (less than 4 ft deep). Shallows become problem areas because they frequently become choked with aquatic vegetation. When filled with dense, rooted aquatic plants, these areas are useless for fishing, boating, and swimming, and may become a breeding location for mosquitoes because the fish are unable to reach the mosquito "wrigglers." Extensive shallow areas are unnecessary for the successful reproduction of nest-building fishes as may be demonstrated in strip-mine and quarry ponds where shallows are very limited. In planning the height of a dam it is sometimes possible to raise or lower the proposed water level a few feet to give a minimum of shallow water.

Lakes built for recreation may be developed to any degree, that is, the grounds may be left in a relatively natural state with only access roads, or, on the other hand, there may be surfaced roads, boat docks (and boats for rent), bathing beaches, bath-house facilities, picnic areas, pavilions, and cabins.

The main problem in the day-to-day operation of public lakes built for recreation lies in conflicts between fishermen, swimmers, water skiers, and, in some cases, skin divers. The prevention of littering is always a problem.

Water skiing should be restricted to certain parts of lakes of more than 500 acres because a minimum of 50 acres is needed for each water skier and motor boat.[45] It may seem advisable to restrict water skiing to certain periods of the day as well.

PLANNING AN ARTIFICIAL LAKE OR POND

As was mentioned in connection with the planning of farm ponds, a layman may handle certain preliminary details of impoundment provided he can read a contour map and estimate land areas (see procedures for locating pond sites, p. 27).

Watershed, Runoff, Water Manipulation, and Silting

Rainfall, slope of land, and vegetative cover vary within certain limits, but a definite relationship exists between the volume capacity of a pond basin and the area of the watershed needed to keep that basin filled. Although usually it is impossible for the layman to calculate the volume capacity of a selected pond basin, he may, by the use of a quadrangle map, arrive at the approximate surface area of the basin and then consider this in relation to the area of the watershed. Where soils are relatively tight (for example, in parts of Illinois, Iowa, and Missouri) and the average annual rainfall is known, the approximate limits of range for the watershed are a minimum of 10 acres and a maximum of 50 acres to 1 acre of pond surface assuming a basin of average depth and contour. If the drainage area is less than 10 acres, insufficient runoff water will be available during dry periods. On the other hand, if the watershed is 50 or more acres, so much water in excess of pond capacity must be passed through the basin that a large and expensive spillway is necessary and excessive silting may occur. Probably the optimum ratio between watershed and pond surface area is in the neighborhood of 20 or 25 to 1 under the conditions listed above. Optimum relationships between the drainage area and the pond size and volume vary greatly among parts of the country with differences in rainfall, slope, soil types, vegetative cover, and evaporation rates.

Small ponds in the north central states having ratios of watershed to pond surface of less than 15 to 1 may be safely constructed with grass waterways to carry off excess water. However, where the watersheds and ponds are larger, spillways are usually constructed of concrete or stone.

It is unnecessary to screen spillways to prevent the departure of fish from a pond or lake, as only a small fraction of the fish population will leave. Screens across spillways have a way of becoming clogged during floods and sometimes are responsible for washouts of dams. It is more important to prevent fish from moving up over a dam from below, and spillways should be planned to provide insurmountable barriers to fish moving upstream.

There are many problems involved in handling water flowing in and out of a pond basin. Some of these are associated with differences in rainfall and evaporation rates. Others involve local situations such as variations in land scope and cover, quality of the water, control of water from a constant source (such as a spring or a flowing well), or the by-passing of excess water where the only suitable site for a pond is adjacent to a water course too large to be impounded. Solutions to most of these special problems will require the services of a competent hydraulic engineer.

Siltation of Reservoirs.   No impoundment of water is permanent, for moveable solid materials will be carried by inflowing waters and dropped in the basin as the current disappears. An understanding of reservoir sedimentation involves a consideration of erosion, transportation, and deposition of soil material. Ackermann and Corinth[1] have developed an empirical equation for the prediction of an annual rate of reservoir sediment deposition, based on studies made in the south and central parts of Illinois.

Sedimentation is an important consideration in reservoir planning because the life of a reservoir is measured by the number of years before the annual deposition of silt makes the reservoir useless.

The biological effects of silting over and above the mechanical reduction in volume, are variable because of differences in the sources of the material washed into the reservoir. Bottom soils have several important functions in the production cycle of fishes. Thus, if the silt contains organic matter, phosphates, and carbonates, the productive capacity will be increased; if the material is clay or sand and poor in nutrients, the production capacity may be reduced. Sometimes silt deposits in the upstream ends of reservoirs show successive layers of sediments, some of which are capable of increasing production and others which are not. These deposits originate from different sources within the reservoir watershed.

As a general "rule of thumb," the rate of silting in proposed reservoirs should not exceed 1% per year of the capacity of the original reservoir basin,* and a lower siltation rate is desirable.

THERMAL STRATIFICATION AND LOSS OF OXYGEN

Most ponds and lakes in the United States are thermally stratified during the warmer months. This stratification may develop in early March and extend well into November in the South. In the extreme north, summer thermal stratification may begin in late May or early June and end in late August or early September. Most artificial impoundments, with the exception of the deeper power and water-supply reservoirs contain no oxygen in the colder, deeper waters during the greater part of the period of summer stratification, although there may be oxygen in the lower waters early in the summer season, even after the lake has become thermally stratified. Gradually, however, the oxygen demand from decay and from respiration of bacteria, plankton, and other invertebrates, and fishes, uses up all of the available oxygen in the lower lake level (hypolimnion) so that this water may be completely devoid of dissolved oxygen.

Sometimes, dewatering structures (spillways) have their lake-side openings near the bottom of the lake, in order to expel oxygen-deficient water from far below the surface. For example, at Ridge Lake, Coles County, Illinois,[5] a tower spillway on the inner face of the dam was designed to release water from the bottom of the full lake each time runoff from rainfall raised its level. Studies of dissolved gases and bottom fauna in this lake indicated that the beneficial effect of this disposal of oxygen-deficient water was, at best, temporary. Even though oxygen was added to the deeper waters of the lake each time a substantial rain fell on the watershed, this new oxygen was so rapidly used up that no aerobic bottom organisms had an opportunity to develop.

Seasonal Thermal Stratification

Thermal stratification of lakes and ponds has its basis in the fact that water shows maximum density (weight) at 4°C. (39.2°F), becoming *less dense* (lighter in weight) both *above* and *below* this temperature. Let us consider the fact that soon after the ice melts in the spring, the temperature of the water in a lake rises to 4°C, bringing the entire lake to a uniform density. Then, winds blowing across the lake surface pile the water up on the downwind side, and in order to compensate for this,

*Personal communication with J.B. Stall, Hydraulic Engineer and Reservoir Sedimentation Specialist, Illinois Water Survey, 242 Water Resources Bldg., Urbana, Illinois 61801.

water passes downward across the bottom of the lake to the upwind side. The entire lake begins to circulate from top to bottom. As spring advances, however, there are days when the wind blows lightly or not at all, and the sun beating down on the lake begins warming the water on the surface, causing it to become less dense (lighter) than the colder water below. After the surface water has warmed a few degrees above the water in the lake depths, thermal stratification has begun and no ordinary wind will cause the light surface waters to invade the heavier deeper layers.

The surface water will mix with itself for a variable distance down, the depth depending upon the wind velocity and the area of lake surface exposed to it. The warm surface layer (epilimnion) tends to be thicker on large lakes than on small ones. The temperature of the epilimnion is about the same from top to bottom, but it may vary a few degrees during days when the surface is warming rapidly and winds are light.

Below the epilimnion is a layer of water (the thermocline or metalimnion) where the temperature of the stratum decreases rapidly as one progresses downward, that is, one degree centigrade per meter (about 1.7°F per yard) or more. The thermocline may vary in thickness in different lakes and at different times during the period of stratification. Although in large lakes the thermocline usually is a thinner layer than the epilimnion, in small ponds it may continue from the lower edge of the epilimnion to the pond bottom, eliminating a hypolimnion entirely.

In large deep lakes the volume of water below the thermocline (hypolimnion) tends to show a fairly uniform temperature. Where there is a significant temperature decrease as one moves downward, that change is less than 1°C per meter. As mentioned previously, lack of dissolved oxygen makes the hypolimnions of some lakes uninhabitable for all but anaerobic organisms. The rapidity and extent of dissolved oxygen loss is dependent upon the volume of oxygenated water and the respiratory demands made on this volume.

Variations in Thermal Stratification

Bardach[4] describes the progress of summer stratification in Lake West Okoboji, Iowa. In this lake, thermal stratification normally begins between May 15 and June 1 after the water below 30 m has already reached 10°C (50°F). Then, during the summer the hypolimnion warms up further, to 12° or 13°C (53.6° or 55.4°F).

However, in 1925, 1926, and 1950, when unusually heavy winds were recorded in late spring, West Okoboji did not form a thermocline until very late in the season or not at all; if it did form one it was situated at a greater depth than usual. In some years this abnormal stratification consisted of an upper warm layer, below which the temperature gradually dropped, as one progressed toward the lake bottom, until at 22m (72.2 ft) the temperature was 6°C lower than in the epilimnion [epilimnion, 20.6°C (69.1°F), and bottom 14.3°C (57.7°F)]. The vertical change in temperature was less than 1°C per meter so that by definition no thermostratification was ever completely broken up during the summer months. As mentioned previously, a similar type of stratification seems to be characteristic of many small artificial impoundments.

Fall Overturn

Summer thermal stratification is broken up in the fall by wind action after the epilimnion cools to approximately the same temperature as the hypolimnion and water densities are equalized. Gradually the entire lake begins to circulate as the winds create water currents across the surface and compensating currents develop across the lake bottom. Water that has remained trapped in the lake depths all summer again comes in contact with the surface layers where free and dissolved carbon dioxide has an opportunity to escape and the dissolved oxygen supply is replenished.

As fall progresses into winter, the lake water cools to 4°C (39.2°F) and below, and the colder upper layer becomes less dense. In the north a layer of ice seals the surface and the lake is again thermally stratified, with the ice and colder water above the mass of water at 4°C. As long as ice covers the lake very little circulation takes place. Some convection currents may be set up through the mild warming of water in contact with the bottom, but these warming forces are counteracted by colder water immediately under the ice. Once the lake is sealed from the air, the oxygen supply under the ice is dependent upon the photosynthetic activity of algae which in turn is supported by light transmission through the ice.

Attempts to Upset Thermal Stratification

Some attempts have been made to upset the thermal stratification of small lakes.[13,16,21,24,42,43] For example, 180 hours of pumping of warm surface water into the bottom of a small German lake increased the temperature of the bottom water by 5°C.[16] Also, this pumping initiated movements of water within the hypolimnion, causing an increase in its thickness, as well as a shorter temperature gradient within the thermocline.

In an experiment in a 3.6-acre Michigan lake, water was pumped from near the bottom (hypolimnion) to the surface. This caused a progressive increase in the depth of the upper warm layer of uniform temperature, a sinking of the thermocline (transition zone) at a nearly constant rate, and a decrease in the thickness of the hypolimnion as the bottom water was displaced. The upper limit of the thermocline was lowered from 13 to 25 ft, and the volume of the epilimnion was increased by 50%. An attempt was made to follow the movement of the cold bottom water after its release at the surface. Apparently the cool water became mixed rather thoroughly with surface water within the upper 4 to 5 ft.

Compressed air, released from perforated tubes on the lake bottom, has been used widely in winter to carry water currents from deep water to the surface and melt thick or snow-covered ice for the prevention of winterkill (Chapter 3, p. 77). This technique has been applied with some success in breaking up thermal stratification in summer. The thin streams of air bubbles escaping from holes in the plastic tubes create upward movements of water, some of which eventually reaches the surface.[13,24] This method is more efficient than the pumping of water either from the top to the bottom of the lake or from the bottom to the top.

Probably the most efficient method yet devised for carrying large amounts of water from the depths to the surface is through the use of an invention called a hydraulic air gun consisting of a tube 12 in. in diameter and 12 ft long supported vertically above the lake bottom. At the bottom of the tube is a chamber arrangement into which compressed air collects until the chamber is full; then a "bubble" of air large enough to fill the diameter of the 12-in. tube is suddenly released to pass up the 12-ft tube pushing water ahead of it and drawing water in behind it through holes near the bottom of the "gun." These "bubbles" are released intermittently, providing a good continuous flow of water through the gun. The water leaving the upper end of the 12-ft tube acts as a free turbulent jet which carries additional water along in its upward movement. Air comes in contact with water throughout the tube and after the escape from the upper end of the tube. Compressed air is supplied to the guns through tubes leading from a compressor on the lake bank.

Using a compressor that delivered 72 ft³ of air per minute, Wirth and Dunst[53] supplied six guns with air and estimated that they moved a total of 16.8 ft³ of water per second through the tubes. This water escaping from the ends of the tubes activated other water to increase the total upward movement to an estimated 84 ft³/sec, or 166 acre-ft/day. Tests run with the six air guns in Cox Hollow Lake (96 acres, maximum depth 29 ft), demonstrated that temperature stratification could be completely broken up in less than five weeks beginning with surface temperatures of 85°F and bottom temperatures of about 50°F. This destratification process may have significance in increasing fish production and controlling algal blooms.

THERMAL STRATIFICATION AND RESERVOIR OUTLETS

Reservoir outlets may be located near the top of the dam to release surface water, at intermediate depths to release subsurface water, or near the bottom to release water from the hypolimnion. The thermal stratification characteristics of the reservoir and the location of the outlet gates have much to do with the temperature and the oxygen content of the water released. From the standpoint of angling, experience has shown that fish congregate in the tailwaters of large reservoirs through upstream migration, and extensive sport fisheries have developed in these tailwaters[3,14,33,47,48] (see Chapter 7, p. 268).

The type of fishery which results is dependent upon (1) the temperature of the water released during the summer,[15] (2) what fish are available in the stream below, and (3) which ones may be stocked successfully in it. The temperature of the water, in turn, depends upon the vertical location of the outlet gates on the face of the dam.

Many large reservoirs are equipped with outlet gates at or near the bottom of the impounding dams (Fig. 2.10). Temperatures of water released through these gates range from 4 to 18.3°C (39.2 to 65°F), and may or may not contain sufficient oxygen for fishes; however, the water usually becomes aerated a short distance below the outlet of the dam, and in this location, trout are able to survive, and often grow very well, extending their range downstream until the water becomes too warm.[33] Where such a trout fishery has been developed, it usually has been necessary to modify the original water-release program designed by the engineers, since restriction of flow to only a few months per year is impractical from the standpoint of maintaining an artificial trout fishery. In addition, it is worth noting that the release of cold water alters the bottom faunal pattern from large warmwater species to small coldwater species, such as the insect families Tendipedidae, Simulidae, and Hydropsychidae, as well as snails and the scud, *Gammarus.*[33]

The tailwater discharge below Dale Hollow Reservoir is an example of a man-made trout stream.[32] This tailwater flows for 7.3 miles before it enters the Cumberland River in Clay County, Tennessee. When water is operating the three turbines the combined minimum flow is 5900 ft³/sec. When the turbines are not in operation there is a natural cold water discharge of 19 ft³/sec. Discharge schedules vary from year to year; shutdown periods of several days are common in the summer and fall, and levels of the tailwaters fluctuate within a 10-ft range.

The water discharge below the Dale Hollow Dam is always clear (turbidity less than 5 ppm and the water temperature of the discharge ranges between 7.2 and 13.3°C (45 and 56°F). The minimum discharge of 19 ft³/sec. has maintained a water temperature cool enough for trout in the upper three miles of the tailwater during extended shut-off periods. The best periods for trout fishing are on weekends when the turbines are shut down and water levels are low.

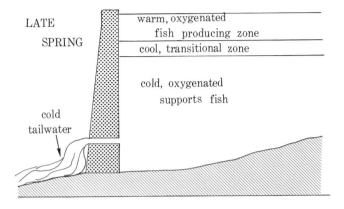

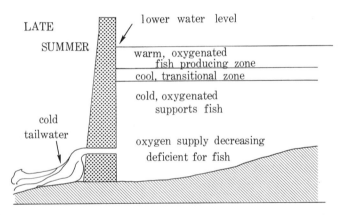

Fig. 2.10 Storage reservoirs with deep water outlets. A water-release program that will furnish an adequate quantity of water that is cold enough for a year-round trout stream often
supplies very fine fishing. However, trout must be stocked from hatcheries, as tailwater streams
usually are not suitable for natural spawnings. (Redrawn from Stroud, R. H., and Jenkins,
R. M., 1960, *Sport Fishing Inst. Bull. 98).*

Dale Hollow Reservoir dam is 178 ft high, and the water depth at
elevation 651 (spillway level) is 151 ft. The annual water level fluctuation
in this 30,000-acre lake is usually less than 25 ft.

Stroud and Jenkins[45] favor reservoir outlets located to release cold
water (often deficient in oxygen) from reservoir depths because there is
"a continuous discharge of oxygen-consuming decomposition materials
with the colder, deep waters." This prevents stagnation and makes "maximum reservoir volume available for use by fish life." At the same time,
the warm upper water is retained to promote fish production.

An interesting change in the temperature regime and in the fish population of Lake Taneycomo on the White River in southern Missouri took place after a second reservoir impounded by the Table Rock Dam was constructed in 1954, only 2 1/2 miles above the upper end of Lake Taneycomo.[15] Water released from the Table Rock Dam at a low level ranged in temperature between 4.4 and 15.5°C (40 and 50°F) and remained cold during the 2 1/2 mile flow into Lake Taneycomo. The effect of this cold water was to change a reservoir from a warmwater fish habitat to a cold one. Of the common warmwater fishes in Lake Taneycomo, only the bluegills survived in significant numbers after the change over to cold water. Growth rates of all warmwater species became much slower.

Rainbow trout were stocked in the upper end of Lake Taneycomo to sustain the fishery, and by 1962 and 1963, 99% of the fish caught in this area were rainbow trout; in the lower part of the lake these trout comprised about half of the catch. Cold water entering Lake Taneycomo from the Table Rock Reservoir either formed an advancing wedge below the surface or moved evenly along the bottom.

Excellent tailwater fishing for warmwater fishes may occur where water is released from a reservoir at surface or near surface levels (Fig. 2.11). These tailwater fisheries sometimes equal the fishing operations in the reservoir above the dam and sometimes they do not.[45] (see Chapter 7).

OTHER FACTORS AFFECTING THERMAL STRATIFICATION

Sometimes waters that enter lakes from feeder streams influence thermal stratification because such waters seek their appropriate density (weight) level. In south central Nebraska, a small reservoir built across Rock Creek (a stream originating from a large spring) always contained oxygen in the deeper water because the cold water entering from the stream moved along the lake bottom carrying dissolved oxygen with it.

In winter, water from tributary streams may be colder than the lakes into which they flow, forcing lake water from deeper layers upward toward the surface.[34] Cold, turbid waters entering Norris Reservoir (Tennessee) often formed a wedge of water between surface and bottom.[52,53] Water above and below this wedge was relatively clear, so that the vertical extent of the wedge could be defined on the basis of turbidity alone.

In small ponds thermal stratification may be affected by blooms of plankton algae which form a blanket near the surface, insulating the lower waters from light and the warmth of the sun's rays. For example, a farm pond adjacent to a barn lot near Illiopolis, Illinois, sampled in July 1939 showed an epilimnion 10 in. in thickness, containing a very dense

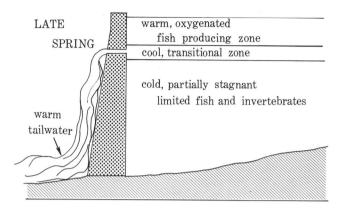

LATE
  SPRING

warm, oxygenated
  fish producing zone
cool, transitional zone

cold, partially stagnant
  limited fish and invertebrates

warm
tailwater

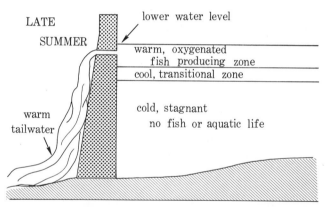

LATE
  SUMMER

lower water level

warm, oxygenated
  fish producing zone
cool, transitional zone

cold, stagnant
  no fish or aquatic life

warm
tailwater

Fig. 2.11 Storage reservoirs with shallow water outlets. Warmwater fishes congregate in these tailwaters, having migrated upstream from below. Tailwater fishing is very popular, and in a warm tailwater, fishermen may catch a variety of fishes. (Redrawn from Stroud, R. H., and Jenkins, R. M., 1960, *Sport Fishing Inst. Bull. 98.)*

"bloom" of plankton algae. The temperature throughout the epilimnion was 27.2°C (81°F), but at 13 in. below the surface the temperature was 21.6°C (71°F); a drop of 5.6°C (10°F) within 3 in. Also, the dissolved oxygen was entirely gone at 13 in. below the surface. In spite of these extreme conditions, this pond contained bluegills, some of which were caught in traps set at the surface level.

BIOLOGICAL PRODUCTIVITY OF WATER

The biological productivity of water is a function of the nutrient materials (organic and inorganic salts) dissolved in it and available from other sources.

The experiments designed to test the value of inorganic and organic fertilizers in pond fish production will be reviewed in Chapter 6; for the present it is sufficient to stress that the addition of organic or inorganic plant nutrients to a body of water facilitates an increase in the production of phytoplankton, which, in turn, causes an increase in the production of zooplankton and insect larvae and, somewhat later, of fish. Furthermore, increase in fish production is more pronounced among species that make direct use of the available phyto- and zooplankton organisms and insects than among those species of fishes that are piscivorous or have more specific food requirements. Changes brought about by the inadvertent addition of plant nutrients to lakes from any of several possible sources are defined as *eutrophication* and are considered undesirable because they reduce aesthetic values, change fish populations from more desirable to less desirable species, and create aquatic vegetation control problems.[19]

It can be demonstrated that in unpolluted natural waters the chemistry of soils in the lake basin and its watershed are related to the water of the lake in question.

The amounts of certain chemical compounds dissolved in natural waters are indicators of relative productivity. Several investigators have shown a positive relationship between alkalinity and fish production in lakes grouped as *soft water* (less than 50 ppm Methyl Orange alkalinity), *medium* (50-150 ppm), and *hard* (above 150 ppm). However, the greatest interruption of this relationship appears at about 40 ppm[30] and at levels greater than 40 ppm there seems to be no concise relationship between carbonate content and fish yield. No relationship could be found between fish yields and varying amounts of ionized hydrogen, carbon dioxide, or chlorides; there was no relationship between sulfates and production until the sulfates exceeded 300 ppm.[30] Table 2.1 shows a productivity classification of natural lakes (Minnesota) on the basis of total alkalinity and sulfate ions.[30]

Minnesota ponds containing amounts of phosphorus below 0.05 ppm had low fish yields.[30] Above a concentration of total phosphorus of 0.05 ppm, there was little difference in either average or maximum yield. Moyle concluded that the optimum concentration of total phosphorus might lie between 0.1 and 0.2 ppm; however, these phosphorus concentrations were usually associated with heavy algal blooms which were generally undesirable and created a danger through their ability to cause sudden oxygen depletion. Experiments with labelled phosphorus indicated that phosphorus in the epilimnion was very mobile and the littoral region was the most important contributor to the turnover of phosphorus in the epilimnion.[35]

Table 2.1   A Classification of Natural Lakes in Minnesota on the Basis of Total Alkalinity and Sulfate Ions [a]

Total Alkalinity (ppm)	Sulfate Ion (ppm)	Classification	Productivity	
			Fish	Plants
0.0-20.0	0.0-5.0	very soft	low	low
21.0-40.0	0.0-10.0	soft	low to medium	low to medium
41.0-90.0	0.0-10.0	medium hard	medium to high	medium to high
91.0 or more	0.0-50.0	hard	high	high
100.0 or more	50.0-125.0	medium alkali	high	high
100.0 or more	126.0-300.0	alkali	high	high

[a] From Moyle.[20]

LAKE SIZE AND PRODUCTIVITY

Prior to 1946, there seemed to be evidence of a straight-line negative logarithmic relationship between size of a lake and fish production, when all data then available were used.[36] These data included complete fish censuses of a number of small ponds, creel censuses as measurements of production on medium-sized waters, and commercial catches of fish on the larger lakes. No consideration was given to the possible effect of the geographical location of these waters or of regional soil fertility on production.

Later, when these data were reworked and consideration was given to location and soil fertility, the apparent relationship between size and productivity disappeared.[10,20] Information on yields from additional lakes (Minnesota)[30] in the form of average gill net ratios demonstrated that lakes of over 5000 acres in area were more productive than those of smaller sizes, whereas data from creel censuses indicated that lakes ranging in size between 500 and 1000 acres were more productive than those larger or smaller. One is forced to conclude that lake size alone has little significance as an index of productivity and that the water quality, the conformation of the lake basin, and the length of shoreline are much more important. Shallow lakes are more productive than deeper ones because the most productive zone is that influenced by the sun's rays.[20,22] Where this layer is in contact with the lake bottom, one may expect to reach a high level of production. Other factors, such as the length of the growing season,[50] also influence productivity.

REFERENCES

1. Ackermann, W. C., and Corinth, R. L., 1962, "An empirical equation for reservoir sedimentation," Ext. of Publ. 59 of I.A.S.H. Comm. of Land Erosion, p. 359—366.

2. Anon., 1944-1961., *Annual reports of the Upper Mississippi River Conservation Committee,* Bur. of Sport Fisheries and Wildlife, Minneapolis, Minnesota.

3. Baker, R. R., 1960, *Historical review of the Bull Shoals Dam and Norfork Dam Tailwater Trout Fishery,* Ark. Game and Fish Comm., pp. 229-236.

4. Bardach, J. E., 1955, "Certain biological effects of thermocline shifts," *Hydrobiologia.* 7(4), 309-324.

5. Bennett, G. W., 1954, "Largemouth bass in Ridge Lake, Coles County, Illinois," *Illinois Nat. Hist. Surv. Bull.* 26(2), 217-276.

6. Bennett, G. W., and Durham, L., 1951, "Cost of bass fishing at Ridge Lake, Coles County, Illinois," *Illinois Nat. Surv. Biol. Notes* 23,1-16.

7. Benson, N. G., Greeley, J. R., Huish, M. I., and Kuehn, J. H., 1961, "Status of management of natural lakes," *Am. Fish. Soc. Trans.* 90 (2), 218-224.

8. Campbell, R. S., Lind, O. T., Geiling, W. T., and Harp, G. P., 1965, "Recovery from acid pollution in shallow strip-mine lakes in Missouri," *Proc. 19th Indust. Waste Conf. (1964).* Eng. Ext. Ser. No. 117, Prudue Univ. Eng. Ext. Serv., Eng. Bull. 49 (1a), 17-26.

9. Campbell, R. S., Lind, O. T., Harp, G. L., Geiling, W. T., and Letter, J. E., Jr., 1965, "Water pollution studies in acid strip-mine lakes: changes in water quality and community structure associated with aging," Symp. on Acid Mine Drainage, Mellon Inst., Pittsburgh, pp. 188-198.

10. Carlander, K. D., 1955, "The standing crop of fish in lakes," *J. Fisheries Res. Board Can.* 12(4), 543-570.

11. Crittenden, E., 1965, "Florida phosphate pits for managed public fishing areas," *Proc. 17th Conf. S.E. Assoc. Game and Fish Comm.* pp. 237-242.

12. Davidson, V. E., and Johnson, J. A., 1943, "Fish for food from farm ponds," *U.S. Dept. Agr. Farmers' Bull.* 1938, 1-22.

13. Ford, M. E., 1963, "Air injection for control of reservoir limnology," *J. Am. Water Works Assoc.* 55, 267-274.

14. Frey, J. E., and Pierce, P. C., 1967, "The effects of cold water discharge on a downstream reservoir's temperature and oxygen levels," *Proc. 20th Ann. Conf. S.E. Assoc. Game and Fish Comm. (1966)* pp. 357-363.

15. Fry, J. P., and Hanson, W. D., 1968, "Lake Taneycomo: a coldwater reservoir in Missouri," *Am. Fish. Soc. Trans.* 97(2), 138-145.

16. Grim, J., 1952, "Ein See wird umgepflugt," *Allgem. Fischwirtschaftsztgo. Jahrg.* 77(14), 281-283.

17. Hansen, D. F., 1942, "The anglers' catch at Lake Chautauqua near Havana Illinois with comparative data on hoopnet samples," *Illinois State Acad. Sci. Trans.* 35, 197-204.

18. Hasler, A. D., and Einsele, W. G., 1948, "Fertilization for increasing productivity of natural inland waters," *13th North Am. Wildlife Conf. Trans. (1948),* pp. 527-555.

19. Hasler, A. D., and Swenson, M. E., 1967, "Eutrophication," *Science* 158(3798), 278-282.

20. Hayes, F. R., 1957, "On the variation in bottom fauna and fish yield in relation to trophic level and lake dimensions," *J. Fisheries Res. Board Can.* 14(1), 1-32.

21. Hooper, F. F., Ball, R. C., and Tanner, H. A., 1953, "An experiment in the artificial circulation of a small Michigan lake," *Am. Fish. Soc. Trans.* 82(1952), 222-241.

22. Humphrys, C. R., and Veatch, J. O., 1964, "Lake terminology," *Mich. State Univ. Agr. Expt. Sta. Water Bull.* 8(1961), 1-18.

23. Hutchison, G. E., 1957, *A Treatise on Limnology,* Vol. I. *Geography, Physics and Chemistry,* John Wiley & Sons, Inc., New York, 1015 pp.

24. Irwin, W. H., Symons, J. M., and Robeck, G. G., 1966, "Impoundment destratification by mechanical pumping," *J. Saint. Eng. Div. Am. Soc. Civil Engrs.* 92-SA6(5032), 21-40.

25. Jackson, H. O., and Starrett, W. C., 1059, "Turbidity and sedimentation at Lake Chautauqua, Illinois," *J. Wildlife Management* 23(2), 157-168.

26. Jenkins, R. M., 1958, "The standing crop of fish in Oklahoma ponds," *Proc. Okla. Acad. Sci.* 38, 157-172.

27. King, W., 1960, "A survey of fishing in 1959 in 1,000 ponds stocked by the Bureau of Sport Fisheries and Wildlife," *U.S. Fish. and Wildlife Circ.* 86, 1-20.

28. Leopold, L. B., and Maddock, T., Jr., 1954, *The Flood Control Controversy. Big Dams, Little Dams and Land Management,* The Ronald Press, New York, 278 pp.

29. Meehean, O. L., 1952, "Problems of farm fish pond management," *J. Wildlife Management* 16(3), 234-237.

30. Moyle, J. B., 1949, "Some indices of lake productivity," *Am. Fish. Soc. Trans.* 76(1946), 322-334.

31. Parson, J. D., 1958, "Literature pertaining to formation of acid-mine wastes and their effects on the chemistry and fauna of streams," *Illinois Acad. Sci. Trans.* 50(1957), 49-59.

32. Parsons, J. W., 1957, "The trout fishing of the tailwater below Dale Hollow Reservoir," *Am. Fish. Soc. Trans.* 85(1955), 75-92.

33. Pfitzer, D. W., 1954, "Investigations of waters below storage reservoirs in Tennessee," *19th North Am. Wildlife Conf. Trans.* pp. 271-282.

34. Powers, E. B., Shields, A. R., and Hickman, M. A., 1939, "The mortality of fishes in Norris Lake," *Tenn. Acad. Sci. J.* 14(2), 239-260.

35. Rigler, F. H., 1964, "The contribution of zooplankton to the turnover of phosphorus in the epilimnion of lakes," *Can. Fish. Culturist* 32, 3-9.

36. Rounsefell, G. A., 1946, "Fish production in lakes as a guide for estimating production in proposed reservoirs." Copeia, (1), 29-40.

37. Ruttner, F., 1953, *Fundamentals of Limnology,* Trans. by D. G. Frey and F. E. J. Fry, Univ. of Toronto Press, Toronto, Canada, 242 pp.

38. Smith, M. W., 1961, "Fish ponds in Canada--a preliminary account," *Can. Fish Culturist* 29, 3-12.

39. Starrett, W. C., and McNeil, P. L., Jr., 1952, "Sport fishing at Lake Chautauqua near Havana, Illinois, in 1950 and 1951-52," *Illinois Nat. Hist. Surv. Biol. Notes* 30, 1-31.

40. Starrett, W. C., and Parr, S. A., 1951, "Commercial fisheries of Illinois rivers: a statistical report for 1950," *Illinois Nat. Hist. Surv. Biol. Notes* 25, 1-35.

41. Stroud, R. H., 1956, *Farm Ponds,* S.F.I. Bull. No. 54, p. 7.

42. Stroud, R. H., 1959, *Artificial Circulation of Lakes,* S.F.I. Bull No. 86, p. 1.

43. Stroud, R. H., 1965, *Thermocline Artillery,* S.F.I. Bull. No. 165, p. 6.

44. Stroud, R. H., and Jenkins, R. M., 1960, *Warmwater River Fisheries at Dams,* S.F.I. Bull. No. 98, pp. 3-6.

45. Stroud, R. H., and Jenkins, R. M., 1960, *The Problem of Recreational Water Conflicts,* S.F.I. Bull. No. 105, pp. 1-2.

46. Stroud, R. H., and Jenkins, R. M., 1960, *Marsh Values,* S F.I. Bull. No. 106, p.7.

47. Stroud, R. H., and Jenkins, R. M., 1960, *White River Trout,* S.F.I. Bull. No.109, pp. 4-5.

48. Stroud, R. H., and Jenkins, R. M., 1961, *Availability of Tailwater Fishing,* S.F.I. Bull. No. 115, p. 2.

49. Thompson, D. H., 1941, "The fish production of inland streams and lakes," *A Symposium on Hydrobiology* Univ. of Wisconsin Press, Madison, Wisc., pp. 206-217.

50. Welch, P. S., 1935, *Limnology,* McGraw-Hill Book Co., In., New York, 471 pp.

51. Wiebe, A. H., 1939, "Density currents in Norris Reservoir," *Ecology* 20(3), 446-450.

52. Wiebe, A. H., 1941, "Density currents in impounded waters-their significance from the standpoint of fisheries management," *6th North Am. Wildlife Conf. Trans.* pp. 256-264.

53. Wirth, T. L., and Dunst, R. C., 1967, "Limnological changes resulting from artificial destratification and aeration of an impoundment," *Wisconsin Cons. Dept. Res. Rept.* 22, 1-15.

3

INTERRELATIONSHIPS OF FISH AND LAKE HABITATS

Several types of aquatic habitats were described in the preceding chapter. Now we will consider some of the components that make up an aquatic habitat, and the relationships of these components with fishes.

Water in a habitat for fish must carry dissolved useful gases, minerals, and other substances of kinds and amounts nontoxic to fish. However, the habitat also consists of physical features, basically the contours of the lake basin, with depths, high ridges, rocks, gravel beds, silt areas, marl deposits, stumps, and fallen trees. Growths of submerged aquatic plants, filamentous algae, and shoreline vegetation are a part of the physical habitat as well as of the biological environment. Other parts of the biological environment include the bacteria, plankton algae, fungi, aquatic invertebrate fauna, and a few kinds of vertebrates other than fish. Some of these organisms provide food, some are enemies, and others change with time, being enemies of small fishes first, and later, as these same fishes grow, becoming their food supply.

As indicated in Chapter 2, artificial impoundments, being proximate to man and recent in origin, harbor many abnormal and temporary ecosystems, since plant and animal lake inhabitants may be either slow or rapid invaders or may appear in unnatural or unusual combinations, and the stocking of fish by man is limited to the species he wants. In fact, man usually leaves it to other fish to find their own way into the lake he has created. Moreover, some aquatic forms that shun association with man seldom appear, and others that he dislikes are not permitted to enter (or at least to remain).

The status of a fish species in a lake may be directly related to its ability to compensate for the point of greatest maladjustment with its environment. The population density of fish of its own kind or of other kinds may be a factor in maladjustment to a given environment, since there is for all animals, a progressive decrease in the favorability of the environment associated with a progressive increase in population density, until growth and reproduction are inhibited. Hey[42] noted that when the two indigenous species of alga-eating tilapias *(T. mossambica and T. sparrmanii)* were released in equal numbers in South African sewer ponds, *T. sparrmanii* eventually disappeared. If a few *T. mossambica* were placed in a population of *T. sparrmanii*, the former disappeared. Neither of these species can be considered as basically predatory, but both will eat small fishes when they are available. Even nonpredatory species compete for food and space.

The biological domination man exerts over most lakes not only upsets interrelationships of aquatic organisms, but enters the picture in other ways, most commonly, perhaps, in water pollution from organic waste, commercial fertilizers, chemical waste, pesticides, thermal pollution, and silt. These pollutants are damaging to fishes in relation to the capacity of the recipient environment to absorb their effects without itself becoming detrimental to the fish populations. Of the various types of pollutants, waste chemicals and pesticides are almost uniformly undesirable, whereas sewage pollution from organic waste may represent a mixed benefit: organic sewage increases production after certain demands that it makes upon water are met.

THE PROBLEM OF POLLUTION IN AQUATIC HABITATS

A comprehensive discussion of aquatic pollution problems and their possible solutions would require more pages than are available here. However, it is important that those interested in fishery management have an appreciation for the range and seriousness of aquatic pollutants and possible ways to alleviate some of them.

If not seriously overloaded with irreversible pollutants, an aquatic ecosystem has the capacity to restore the quality of water. Thus, the level of introduction of most pollutants is closely related to, and is as important as, the kinds of pollutants that may be introduced. An obvious first step is in setting water-quality standards.[15] According to Surber,[89] good productivity of fish and aquatic life is dependent upon clear, clean water at favorable temperatures and with sufficient concentrations of needed dissolved gasses and solids. Siltation is one of the more damaging and widespread pollutants. For short periods fish can tolerate very high turbidities, but for longer periods turbidities of 100-200 ppm can be harmful. Temperatures of 93-96°F (or higher) are critical for most warmwater fishes. Oxygen levels should be about 5 ppm for warmwater fishes and

6 ppm for trout. The acid death point for pond fishes is around pH 4, and the alkaline death point is about pH 11. Chemical pollutants may kill fishes quickly, or in sublethal dosages may cause mortalities after long periods of exposure.

Some aquatic insects are more sensitive to pollution than are the fishes and may be used as indicators of reasonably unpolluted water. For example, an abundance of mayflies of the genus *Hexagenia,* that emerge during the summer months from most sections of the upper Mississippi River, indicate that the upper Mississippi in those sections is more riverlike than it is sewerlike.[33]

In contrast, the hordes of mayflies that used to be characteristic of Lake Erie are practically gone, and their nymphs (which formerly averaged 400 per square meter now average about 40 per square meter) have been replaced by pollution-tolerant worms. These worms have increased from 12 to 551 per square meter. These changes in the invertebrate faunal abundance have been paralleled by changes in the fishes from clean-water species such as ciscos, whitefish, and blue pike to more pollution-tolerant species such as white bass, sheepshead, smelt, and carp.[84]

Krumholz and Minckley[51] recorded a marked improvement in the water quality and fish population of the upper Ohio River eleven days after the closure of the steel industries, July 15 to November 7, 1959. Apparently as rapidly as the Ohio River water became improved, "clean water fishes" invaded the previously polluted areas, presumably moving in from nearby unpolluted waters.

Organic Pollution

Organic pollution originates from incompletely digested sewage which usually has some remaining biological oxygen demand when it is released. If the volume of incompletely digested sewage is small in relation to the volume of water into which it is released, the oxygen demand may be easily satisfied. In contrast, where the volume of sewage is as great or greater than the dilution water, as may be the case in periods of drought, the oxygen demand may remain unsatisfied for a long period of time and create an oxygen-deficient situation untenable for fish and aquatic invertebrates.

Completely oxidized sewage effluent often creates problems because of its heavy load of phosphorus. Phosphorus stimulates the growth of algae, which, in turn, create pollution problems when they die and decay. Nitrates are of lesser importance because, like the terrestrial legumes, some of the algae are capable of fixing atmospheric nitrogen.[61] The key to the prevention of over-fertile water lies in the removal of phosphorus.

This process has been accomplished in several ways. For example, to prevent sewage pollution in Norway's narrow fjords, organic sewage is mixed with 10—15% seawater and subjected to electrolysis. Phosphorus compounds in the sewage are precipitated as magnesium and calcium salts. These, together with sludge and suspended particles, adhere to magnesium hydroxide at the negative pole. Phosphates and sludge are in turn floated to the surface as a scum by means of hydrogen gas liberated during electrolysis, and scraped off. Chlorine developed at the positive pole is used for disinfection at the outlet.[83] Several other methods for removing phosphates from sewage effluent seem to be practical from the standpoint of cost. According to the *New York Times* for May 17, 1965, the U.S. Public Health Service has constructed a pilot plant to demonstrate the removal of phosphate from sewage.[80] Located at Lebanon, Ohio, the process used will make the water purer than it was originally at a cost of under one dollar per thousand gallons.

The costs of conventional primary and secondary treatment have posed problems which have been met easily. The treatment of the stubborn 10% remaining after secondary treatment is the real difficulty. Projected costs of treatment in the new Lebanon processing plant are 7¢ for secondary treatment, 8¢ for filtration, 10¢ for carbon absorption, 15¢ for electrodialysis, 10¢ for concentrate disposal, and 1¢ for chlorination, with a total estimated cost of 51¢ per thousand gallons (the 1965 cost of converting seawater to fresh water). The average national cost of conventionally supplied water is 30¢ per thousand gallons.[80]

Sources of phosphorus in streams and lakes are from human and animal waste, detergents, some manufacturing processes, and commercial fertilizers. Although much of the readily available phosphorus in agricultural fertilizer[5] is quickly fixed by the reactive iron and aluminum in the soil, it may be carried on silt particles in runoff water until it becomes deposited in a stream or lake bottom.[86]

In farming regions the main sources of nitrogen pollution are runoff from feed lots and manure piles, liquids from ground silos and septic tank fields, and liquid fertilizers that are accidentally or purposely released in waters. All of these are very toxic to fish and aquatic invertebrates. In some farming regions there are so many sources of nitrate available, including liquid nitrogen fertilizer, that these nitrates have percolated downward into the groundwater and into shallow wells to the extent that the latter have become useless.

According to a technical letter dated June, 1966, from the office of William C. Ackermann, Chief of the Illinois State Water Survey, about 25% of all water samples from Illinois wells of 50-ft depth or less have been found to contain an excessive concentration of nitrate. Nitrate poisoning is not uncommon and the U.S. Public Health Service has assigned a maximum limit of 45 mg/liter for drinking water. At present, the level at which nitrate becomes injurious to farm animals has not been established, because there are many factors that may influence action of the nitrate.

Chemical Pollution

1. Organic and Inorganic Chemical Waste. Manufacturing processes have produced a very wide variety of chemical waste products. Those that are not valuable enough to collect and reuse, or for which uses cannot be found must be discarded. Until recently many of these nonusable chemicals have been dumped in water courses as a means of getting rid of them. The toxicity of these waste chemicals to fishes is variable, but all of them contaminate the aquatic environment to a greater or lesser extent and some accumulate on the bottoms of water courses and smother or poison the bottom organisms without being toxic to fishes. In this way they may reduce the foods for some kinds of fishes.

For a listing of many of the chemical pollutants and their short-term toxicity to fishes one should refer to the California State Water Quality Control Board's publication, *Water Quality Criteria.*[56] Little is yet known of the long-term effects of many chemical pollutants that are being released in dosages not immediately toxic to fish and other aquatic animals.

2. Oil Refinery Pollution. Dorris, Copeland, and Patterson[22] have tested the value of holding ponds in the reduction or elimination of toxic substances associated with crude oil cracking processes used in oil refineries. Processes include atmospheric and vacuum distillation, catalytic cracking, HF alkylation, propane deasphalting, catalytic reforming, crude distillation with light-naptha specialties, and polymerization. Oils and oil processing effluents held for 40 days in a system of ponds reduced nearly all components to a harmless minimum. Many components took less than 40 days. Effluents discharged into the pond system were raw, untreated, full-range refinery wastes.

Peak reduction in pH and alkalinity took about 25 days. Eighty to ninety percent of the ammonia nitrogen was removed and phenol and sulfides were reduced more than 90% in about 5 weeks. Fathead minnows used in toxicity tests survived a 48-hr bioassay after about 3 1/2 wk. Chemical oxygen demand was reduced slightly more than 50% in about 5 wk. Biochemical oxygen demand was reduced 80% in 25 days under both summer and winter conditions.

Some oil refinery effluents will lose their toxicity if stored at room temperature for 32 days; others are more stable and are unaffected by storage.[36] Also, refinery effluents passing through open ditches rather quickly lose their toxicity to fishes. These effluents may have a high oxygen demand which may result in the deoxygenation of the receiving stream,[23] but the authors decided in this study that an actual toxicity was the most important effect of oil refinery effluents on receiving streams. Several cases were observed in which immediate oxygen demands had been satisfied, leaving dissolved oxygen concentrations of 4—5 ppm, and yet the effluents were still toxic.

Outboard motors with underwater exhausts may have a degrading effect on the quality of the water and cause tainting of fish flesh when the fuel use level reaches 8 gallons per million gallons of water. There is also an increase in the concentration of carbon—chloroform extractable materials as a result of outboard motor operation. These conditions are more likely to develop in small lakes used extensively for water skiing than in lakes used entirely for fishing.[29]

3. Detergents. By definition, a detergent is anything that cleanses, including ordinary soap. In popular usage, however, the term detergent is applied to washing products that exhibit "soapiness" without the disadvantages of soap when used in hard water. The use of detergents has been responsible for a marked increase in the phosphorus released in sewage effluents since the early 1950s. Detergents are composed of complex phosphates which eventually break down into phosphates usable by aquatic plants. Originally nearly all detergents consisted largely of alkylbenzene sulfonate (ABS), the so-called "hard" detergent which did not break down readily when passed through sewage disposal plants and which was responsible for unsightly cascades of foam at dams or any underwater structures that would cause turbulance. In 1966 detergent manufacturers switched from "hard" detergents to "soft" detergents, the quickly decomposable alkylate sulfonates. Although detergents are not highly toxic to fishes, they do cause damage to gills and remove protective mucus from gills, skin, and intestines.[16,62]

A concentration of alkylbenzene sulfonate (ABS) of about 18 ppm (54.8% active ingredient) will cause gill damage in pumpkinseed sunfish after 24 hr.[74] Bluegills have about the same sensitivity: A 30-day TLm* to ABS was 15.5—18.3 ppm. Bluegills appeared to show some acclimation to sublethal concentrations of ABS.[52] Soft detergents may be more toxic than ABS; Donald Mount found that LAS** compounds at concen-

---

*TLm — median tolerance limit, the effective level of any measurable lethal agent.
**LAS — linear alkylate sulfonate.

trations of less than 2 ppm affected the ability of bullheads, emerald shiners, and bluegills to reproduce. Still smaller amounts prevented eggs from hatching normally.[85]

Aquatic invertebrates also may be affected by detergents. ABS killed several species of mayfly nymphs when the nymphs were exposed to 16 ppm for 10 days. Caddis fly nymphs were more resistant than other species tested. Crayfish and sow bugs were reduced in numbers by a 2-week exposure to 10 ppm, but the snail (*Goniobasis* sp.) was apparently unaffected.[90]

Kent and Hooper[49] believe that ABS influences the mobility of iron by reducing the number of binding sites; it may thereby have an important secondary effect on primary production.

4. Insecticides. Since the advent of DDT (dichlorodiphenyltrichloro-ethane) in the early 1940s there has been a greatly expanded use of organic pesticides to control insects and other nuisance fauna that consume crops or cause other problems. Many of these chemical compounds are quite stable and some break down partially to form compounds that may be even more toxic to certain desirable fauna than were the original chemical compounds. Most pesticides used to control destructive insects are either chlorinated hydrocarbons or organic phosphorus compounds. Table 3.2 shows the 96-hr TLm* to fathead minnows of some widely used chlorinated hydrocarbon and organic phosphorus insecticides. Chlorinated hydrocarbons (DDT, endrin, toxaphene, dieldrin, aldrin) are more stable than organic phosphorus insecticides (chlorothion, guthion, parathion, methyl parathion, systox, malathion, EPN) and for that reason they may contaminate the aquatic environment with sublethal amounts which tend to accumulate in the tissues of aquatic animals.[63] This accumulation of chlorinated hydrocarbons may reach such high levels in animals at the summit of the aquatic food web that they are unable to reproduce or they may be poisoned outright. This biological concentration of pesticides is believed to be responsible for reduced numbers of grebes, herons, mergansers, cormorants, and eagles. Organic phosphorus compounds, although they may be highly toxic initially, usually disappear rather quickly.

Pickering, Henderson, and Lemke[67] found a wide range of variation in the toxicity of some organic phosphorus compounds to fathead minnows,

---

[2]*96-hr TLm — median tolerance limit, or the concentration of the tested material in a suitable dilutent (experimental water) at which just 50% of the test animals are able to survive for a 96-hr exposure (*Standard Methods for the Examination of Water and Wastewater,* 12th ed., 1965).

Table 3.1 Comparative Toxicity of Chlorinated Hydrocarbon and Organic Phosphorus Insecticides to Fathead Minnows In Hard Water At 25%C.[a]

Chlorinated Hydrocarbon		Organic Phosphorous	
Insecticide	96-hr TLm, ppm (mg/l) active agent	Insecticide	96-hr TLm, ppm (mg/l) active agent
Endrin	0.0013	EPN	0.25
Toxaphene	0.0051	Para-oxon	0.25
Dieldrin	0.016	TEPP	1.00
Aldrin	0.028	Parathion	1.60
DDT	0.034	Chlorthion	3.20
Methoxychlor	0.035	Sustox	4.20
Heptachlor	0.056	Methyl parathion	7.50
Lindane	0.056	Malathion	12.50
Chlordane	0.069	Dipterex	51.00
BHC	2.00	OMPA	135.00

a From Henderson, Pickering, and Tarzwell [41]

bluegills, goldfish, and guppies. Data on the comparative toxicity of some of these insecticides are shown in Table 3.2.

In situations where the application of an insecticide is a usual yearly procedure, such as in the cotton region of northern Alabama,[38] or the Mississippi Delta near Indianola, Sunflower County, Mississippi,[31] the fishes in adjacent waters that survive not only concentrate the chlorinated hydrocarbon insecticide in their bodies but build up a resistance to the insecticide which, in the case of gambusia, was approximately tenfold that of unexposed fishes. A single resistant female, exposed to 1000 parts per billion (ppb) endrin released sufficient endrin in 10 liters of tap water to kill five previously unexposed fishes in 38.5 hr.

Sixteen species of fishes taken from New York State waters contained from 0.2 to 7.0 ppm of DDT (fresh weight). Visceral fat, gills, eggs, and sex organs contained up to 40 ppm.[53] Burdick et al.[13] record the accumulation of DDT in lake trout in a number of New York waters. This accumulation was reflected in severe losses of lake trout fry when eggs from these fish were used in hatching operations.

Bridges, Kallman, and Andrews[10] followed the transference of DDT in a Colorado pond after a summer treatment of 0.02 ppm in kerosene. No DDT was found in the water after 3 wk or in the mud after 8 wk. A gradual increase in the DDT residues in trout occurred during the first month and these persisted at somewhat lower levels for at least a year. Residues in bullheads remained high until the second summer. Major metabolites in fish were DDD (dichlorodiphenyl dichloroethane) and DDE (dichlorodiphenyl ethane).

Table 3.2   Comparative Toxicity of Organic Phosphorus Insecticides to Different Species of Fish [a,c]

Insecticide	96-hr TLm (ppm active agent)			
	Fatheads	Bluegills	Goldfish	Guppies
Chlorthion	3.0	0.70	2.3	1.2
Co-Ral	18.0 [b]	0.18	18.0	0.56
Delnav	10.0	0.034	32.0	0.21
Dylox (Dipterex)	140.0	3.8	99.0	7.1
Di-Syston	3.7	0.063	6.5	0.25
EPN	0.25	0.10	0.45	0.032
Guthion	0.093	0.0052	1.3	0.11
Malathion	23.0	0.090	0.45	0.84
Methyl parathion	8.0	1.9	9.6	7.8
OMPA	100.0	110.0	610.0	20.0
Parathion	1.3	0.095	2.7	0.055
Systox	3.2	0.10	11.0	0.61
TEPP	1.9	1.1	21.0	1.8

[a] Under standardized conditions; soft water as diluent; temperature 25%C.
[b] Solubility in water less than 18 ppm.
[c] From Pickering, Henderson, and Lemke. [67]

Using the cladocerans *Daphnia pulex* and *Simocephalus serrulatus* as test animals, organic phosphate insecticides again proved to be more toxic immediately than chlorinated hydrocarbons.[73] DDT was the most toxic chlorinated hydrocarbon, and lindane the least. DDVP (dimethyl-2,2-dichlorovinyl phosphate) was the most toxic compound investigated. Although organophosphates usually do not persist as long as chlorinated hydrocarbons, Nicholson et al.[64] reported that parathion was present in orchard soils (pH 6.9—7.2) for at least 9 mo. Pond bottom mud contained 1.9 ppm parathion after a 5.6 in. rain washed orchard soil from the orchard into the pond, but this level persisted in the pond bottom for only a short time.

There is little doubt that use of organic insecticides will continue because of their efficiency in controlling agricultural pests. The use of more specific and less stable chemicals applied at the exact time and place at the absolute minimum dosages and only when needed will help prevent further contamination of terrestrial and aquatic environments. Stepped-up research on biological controls, including dessicants, chemosterilants, repellents, and sex attractants and the development of more resistant crops and better cultural methods will reduce the need for the more persistent organic insecticides which concern the fisheries biologist.

5. Herbicides. Herbicides cleared for use in aquatic-vegetation control are not considered as pollutants when applied at recommended dosages. Hiltibran[44] states that "recommended rates of application of aquatic herbicides, usually from 0.5 to 1 ppm for diquat, 2 ppm for 2,4-D and silvex preparations, 1-3 ppm for endothal, 10 ppm for sodium arsenite, and 10 to 20 lb/acre, for dichlobenil and fenac, would not greatly affect the survival of fish reproductive products." The uses of herbicides for aquatic vegetation control will be described in Chapter 6.

6. Radioactivity. Klement and Wallen[50] have listed researches on the biological effects of fallout and radioactive wastes released into rivers at reactor sites. Many of these studies are concerned with the evaluation of the hazards of such releases. Adsorption and absorption are of major importance in the uptake of radioisotopes by plants.[98,102] Fishes take up radioactive materials by *(1)* ingestion and assimilation with food[20] and *(2)* by absorption, but there is little agreement as to which is more important.[97,99,100] A variety of invertebrates have been labeled with radioactive isotopes and then used in feeding experiments. These experiments have helped to define various food chains. In a survey of the accumulation of radionuclides in aquatic insects in the Columbia River (Hanford Reservation, Washington) Davis[21] determined that the insects showed many times more radioactivity than the water they inhabit. The most abundant nuclides found in insects were P-32, Cu-64, Cr-51, Zn-65, and Na-24. Amounts were influenced by the food habits of the organisms, biological half-lives of the isotopes, and seasonal variation in feeding. There are various ways of treating atomic waste. Phosphorus-32 was partially removed from reactor effluents by passage through beds of aluminum turnings.[99] Oxidation ponds were functional in removing some low-level radioactive wastes, particularly when algal cells were removed once they became contaminated.[101]

Enough public reaction has developed against accidental environmental contamination through the escape of radioactive waste water from atomic energy plants that strong measures are being taken to prevent such occurrences. With the potential for increased buildup of radioactive isotopes in fishes, it is important to prevent their contamination, particulary because they may be a source of contamination for man.

Thermal Pollution

Most steam electric stations, regardless of whether they use fossil or nuclear fuel, use cooling water from rivers or lakes and discharge it directly back into the water source below the point of intake. This may not create problems in winter or during flood stages but during a half to two-thirds of the year when runoff waters and stream flows are low and at their seasonally highest temperatures, the heated water from the plants may raise temperatures in the rivers and parts of lakes above the maximum that is tenable for fishes and aquatic invertebrates. According to Stroud[81] discharge temperatures may range up to at least 115°F, often resulting in river temperatures above 95°F as far as five miles downstream from such generating installations. Some power plants now require as much as one-half million gallons of water (nearly 1 1/2 acre-feet) *per minute,* and this may be increased in future installations.

If these sources of hot water are not controlled, fisheries resources can be eliminated from sections of waterways as surely as if these sections were polluted with deleterious chemicals. It would be unrealistic to suggest permissible maximum temperature increases for streams, rivers, lakes, and reservoirs in the various sections of the country because of the differences in their physical and chemical characteristics and the varying biota they contain. Each aquatic situation where hot-water release is anticipated should be studied by a competent aquatic ecologist prior to the release of any hot water. Then the extent and schedule of hot-water release should be planned on the basis of the best estimate of its potential effects upon the aquatic ecosystem into which it is being released. This is the only approach which will minimize the possible damage and maximize the possible benefits of the hot water. Optimum and lethal temperature ranges are already known for many important fishes; similar temperature ranges for aquatic invertebrates that serve as food for fishes are less well known.

Inland trout streams, trout and salmon lakes, headwaters of salmon streams, and the hypolimnia of lakes containing salmonids should not be warmed by the addition of heated water.

Comparatively little is known about the currents produced by the introduction of super-heated water into rivers. According to Alabaster[1] there is usually a layer of warm water at the surface of rivers receiving heated effluent, leaving water of almost normal temperature beneath.

The Sanitary Water Board of Pennsylvania[4] adopted regulations preventing the discharge of any heated waste water into trout streams, if, as a result of the discharge, the temperature of the receiving stream should exceed 58°F or the normal temperature of the stream, whichever is higher.

In several locations along warmwater streams the warmwater discharge from an electric plant has improved fishing during certain months of the year. Elser[28] reported that fishing in a heated section of the Potomac River, Maryland, was better for nine months of the year (more fish caught per trip) than in the unheated part of the river. During one month in midsummer the fishing was poorer in the heated section; for two additional months in summer there was no difference. Fishes caught by paid anglers were largely channel catfish, smallmouth bass, and sunfishes.

Restrictions on volume and temperatures of cooling waters that may be discharged into rivers and lakes should result in the development of other methods for cooling stream electric stations or manufacturing processes that require cooling water. Either the heated water will need to be run through a series of cooling channels until its temperature is within a few degrees of the water source temperature before it is released into the source, or these stations may go to closed-circuit cooling using air-cooled radiators through which large volumes of air are passed, much as an automobile engine is cooled through the passage of air through the radiator (Fig. 3.1).

Fig. 3.1 The world's largest existing fossil-fuel steam electric station, being built by the Tennessee Valley Authority on the Green River near Paradise, Kentucky. When fully operational at its 2,558,000 kilowatt production capacity, it will recirculate some 4100 ft³/sec of condenser cooling water. The latter will be cooled for reuse (not discharged into the river) when completed and fully operational by means of three closed-circuit film type cooling towers, each 437 ft high and 320 ft in diameter at ground level. Interim cooling has been by the undesirable once-through diversion of Green River water. *Courtesy C. D. Durfee, Principal Civil Engineer, Steam Plant Design, TVA, and R. H. Stroud, Sport Fishing Institute.*

pH AND CHEMISTRY OF WATER

No attempt will be made here to describe variations in the mineral content of impounded waters found throughout North America; rather we are interested in waters containing abnormal amounts of certain chemicals obtained from contact with natural deposits of minerals. As is to be expected, the mineral composition of pond or lake water is roughly similar to that of the soils of the lake bottom and the surrounding basin.

Fish are able to live in water having a pH range from about 5 to 10. Although most natural waters do not contain chemicals in concentrations great enough to limit the survival of fish, according to Neess,[60] at pH 5.5 fish develop hypersensitivity to bacterial parasites and usually die within a short time if the pH is as low as, or lower than, 4.5.

Moreover, very hard waters are sometimes toxic to fish. New clear ponds, in regions where surface waters are hard, may show an upper pH range of 10 or more when, in bright sunlight, their submerged plants are active in photosynthesis. These plants use up all of the free carbon dioxide in the water and as much bicarbonate as is available to them, with the result that maximum alkalinity is attained. This, if high enough, will cause the death of fishes. In older ponds an accumulation of organic matter acts as a buffering agent against high pH.

McCarraher[55] reports that the northern pike is moderately euryhaline* and is able to survive in Nebraska alkaline lake waters at pH values of 9.5−9.8 for periods as long as 9 months. Prior acclimatization appeared to increase euryionic capacities.

In newly flooded strip-mine ponds H^+ ions that are associated with sulfate anions are responsible for acid conditions. If the strip mine is in a region where surface and groundwaters are hard, an accumulation of calcium and magnesium and organic material may counteract the acidity so that these waters will eventually support fish and other aquatic organisms. For example, Sigmoid Pond in Kickapoo State Park, a former strip-mine area located in east central Illinois, contained 1340 ppm of sulfate on May 18, 1938 (an analysis by Illinois State Water Survey, unpublished). This pond had a total hardness of 669 ppm, and contained large-mouth bass, crappies, bluegills, and green sunfish. The pH ranged between 8 and 9.

Flowing wells and springs occasionally contain high amounts of iron and sulfate, as well as methane and other gases that may make them uninhabitable by fish. Usually, however, the exposure of such waters to

*Able to live in waters of a wide range of salinity.

sunlight and aeration allows the precipitation of certain minerals and the release of gases.

EFFECTS OF WATER TEMPERATURE ON FISH

Temperature plays an important role in the aquatic environment in that certain organisms, including fish, are sensitive to water temperatures. In a broad sense, freshwater fish can be separated into cold- or warmwater species. Ordinarily, one thinks of the trout as being representative of the coldwater species and according to James, Meehean, and Douglas,[48] rainbow and brook trout thrive in water with a maximum summer temperature approximating 70°F. Under certain conditions they may tolerate higher temperatures for short periods of time, and in this the rainbow trout is more resistant than the brook trout to high temperatures. Fry[34] states that 77.5°F is the lethal temperature for brook trout upon prolonged exposure. During the summer of 1951, surface temperatures of a pond fed by a small amount of spring seepage remained between 75 and 79°F for 24 days, and no loss of trout occurred. At the same time, the maximum bottom temperature was 74° F.

Typical warmwater fishes are the largemouth bass, bluegill, black and white crappie, and black and yellow bullhead. These fishes, in ponds and lakes, are almost never killed by high temperatures alone. Intermediate between the trouts and the fishes listed above are such species as the smallmouth bass, rock bass, walleye, northern pike, and the muskellunge. There is no question but that these are somewhat more sensitive to high water temperatures than are more typical warmwater species; however, there is some evidence to indicate that factors other than temperature limit their distribution in certain types of warmwater habitats. Although temperature itself may not be a limiting factor for most species, high temperatures are usually associated with other conditions which culminate in an unsatisfactory habitat.

Water temperature influences the rate of metabolism and therefore the growth rate; it is often critical to spawning and to the development of normal embryos. A general knowledge of temperature requirements of common fishes may enable a fishery biologist to prevent the release of fish stocks in thermally unsuitable waters.

More will be said of the physiological effects of temperature changes on Fishes in Chapter 8.

EFFECTS OF TURBIDITY

When rain falling upon the lands runs off into watercourses, it mechanically transports soil with it in the form of silt and clay particles. This form of turbidity reduces light penetration and photosynthetic activity, smothers bottom-dwelling animals and plants, reduces waste-assimilation capacities, and may impair or curtail fish spawning.[95] In certain parts of the United States, clay particles are so finely divided that once they become suspended by water they fail to settle. This is because the very fine clay particles carry the same electrical charges and, therefore, tend to repel one another whenever they come close together. According to Butler[14] the electrical potential on the particles results from a double layer of charges. An inner negative layer is present around the surface of an aluminosilicate core. An outer positive layer is formed by cations that surround the core. Cations in the outer layer are exchanged with cations in the surrounding medium. Potential on a particle varies with the rate of exchange of cations. Precipitation is stimulated by an increase of other cations in a pond through, for example, the addition of gypsum or oil-field brine. Since Oklahoma contains extensive areas where these colloidal clay particles are present, the problem of pond and lake turbidity is of considerable importance within that state. Irwin,[46] writing of ponds in Oklahoma, states that in the clay-soil region, ponds had clear water for at least the first year if their basins were covered with vegetation at the time of impoundment. However, excavated ponds from which the vegetation had been removed had muddy water from the first. Also, older ponds that had been drained, had had the silt removed, and then were refilled, usually had muddy water. In contrast Butler[14] states that Esmey et al.[30] found that small, well-grassed watersheds used only for collection of water produced more turbid water than either cultivated or pastured watersheds. These contrasting observations indicate that some unrecognized relationships may be involved. All agree that ponds that received runoff from sizable feed lots or barnyards were usually clear of silt turbidity. Apparently, organic decay reduces the Brownian movements of the soil particles, probably through flocculation.

Both hay and fresh green vegetation introduced into a pond or lake caused a clearing of the silty water, but the fresh green vegetation was the more effective of the two. Commercial fertilizers containing super-phosphate produced a good precipitating agent involving phosphoric acid, and nitrate compounds also increased precipitation of soil particles.

Finely ground agricultural gypsum applied directly to turbid pond water, usually from a boat, also caused a clearing action by the flocculating effect of the gypsum on the suspended clay particles. The amount of gypsum required depended on pond depth and degree of turbidity. Dosage rate was around 12 lb/1000 ft^3 of water which might amount to about a ton of gypsum for a one-acre lake. However, requirements may vary considerably; tests in Oklahoma have shown that as little as 100—150 lb of gypsum per acre cleared some muddy ponds in about two days. The addition of gypsum does not affect the use of the water for stock-drinking purposes and it will not adversely affect plant or animal life.[79] Flocculating agents are sometimes applied using a crop-dusting plane.[18]

Colloidal clay particles are not limited to Oklahoma soils, and are probably found in greater or lesser amounts in all soils except those which are primarily organic.

In order to discover the direct effect of montmorillonite (hydrous aluminum silicate) clay turbidity on fishes, Wallen[93] performed a series of experiments exposing fishes to turbidities as high as 225,000 ppm. A total of sixteen common species were used. Most individuals of species exposed to more than 100,000 ppm turbidity had their opercular cavities and gill filaments clogged with clay particles. Some behavioral reactions were stimulated in common fishes at concentrations as low as 20,000 ppm. Very few instances of turbidities resulting from natural conditions have been recorded that exceeded the lowest lethal turbidity in these experiments. Maximum natural turbidities for several streams in Oregon and Idaho were between 137 and 395 ppm;[91] maximum for the Rio Grande was 14,800 ppm. Although Whitewood Creek (South Dakota) was polluted at the rate of 48,400 ppm[27] and Coyote Creek (Oregon) at 38,000 ppm,[94] these turbidities were not from natural causes but rather from mining operations. It must be concluded that natural turbidities are seldom, if ever, *directly* lethal to fishes.

Although high turbidities from soil particles may not be lethal to fishes, turbid waters may affect the productivity of an aquatic environment[59] and the growth of fishes. Growth of largemouth bass was considerably reduced in Oklahoma ponds that were turbid.[11] The effect on the growth of red-ears and bluegills was similar but less pronounced. Turbidity also affected the success of reproduction, particularly of largemouth bass. It was also shown that the volume of basic food in clear ponds was approximately 8 times greater than in ponds of intermediate turbidities (average turbidities 40−90 ppm) and 12.8 times greater than in the muddiest ponds (average turbidities 110−205 ppm). These studies indicate that although natural turbidities in ponds seldom if ever cause direct lethal effects, over a period of years they may be responsible for poor production of fish and indirectly for the disappearance of certain species.

OXYGEN AND CARBON DIOXIDE

Both oxygen and carbon dioxide sometimes occur in water in excessive or subnormal amounts with deleterious effects on fish. In bright sunlight abnormally high oxygen tensions (supersaturation) may occur within dense stands of submerged vegetation. On the other hand, unusually high carbon dioxide and low oxygen tensions may occur where rapid decay of organic material is taking place on the bottom of a pond or lake. Although high oxygen tensions are usually associated with low carbon dioxide tensions and vice versa, this is not always the case.

Dissolved-oxygen standards for the protection of fishes are no more easily defined today than they were twenty or more years ago[26] in spite of greatly increased knowledge on the subject. The standards of a minimum of 5 mg/liter for warmwater fish habitats and 6 or 7 mg/liter for coldwater fish habitats, which have been recommended and widely accepted for a long time, cannot be discarded in favor of anything better, although none was based originally on firm experimental evidence. In spite of this fact, they are as sound as any other figures that can be given because they are intermediate between the highest and lowest standards that might be given.[35,24] Recently some experiments have shown that for largemouth bass, fluctuations of oxygen levels, both above and below those considered desirable, have an effect on appetite, growth, and food-conversion efficiency. Growth of bass was impaired when these fishes were subjected alternately to low and high oxygen concentrations during a 24-hr day.[88]

After many years of studying the fishes of the Illinois River (extending from Chicago to Grafton where the river enters the Mississippi), a waterway that is moderately to severely polluted, Dr. William C. Starrett (personal communication) has come to the conclusion that the fishes of this river have become adjusted to life in waters where the oxygen is always comparatively low. For example, the Great Lakes shiner, *Notropis atherinoides* Raf., considered by most fishery biologists to be highly sensitive to low oxygen, was living and multiplying in a region of the river where the oxygen level ranged between 2 and 4 ppm.

Fish living in a medium in which the tensions of oxygen and carbon dioxide change gradually but markedly, either with changes in depth or with time of day, are able to make certain physiological adjustments to compensate for these changes. However, these adjustments cannot be made instantly. If forced to attempt rapid physiological adjustments to compensate for sudden severe changes in dissolved oxygen or carbon dioxide, fish may become incapacitated and die. Fish have been observed not only avoiding elevated concentrations but also reacting strongly to sudden very small changes in carbon dioxide tension.

Any fisherman who has operated trap nets in ponds or lakes during summer months knows that fish sometimes make trips into the lower waters where dissolved oxygen may be low and carbon dioxide tension high.[17] When caught in nets set in deep water, these fish may remain alive for some time at such depths, but if left too long they suffocate. Physiologists have demonstrated the presence of oxygen in the swim bladders of some fishes and have been able to measure the adjustments in alkalinity of the fishes' blood, resulting from changes in tension of carbon dioxide. The length of time a fish may survive low oxygen tension varies inversely with the tension of carbon dioxide.[9,25]

Interest in the effects of rapid change in carbon dioxide tension was stimulated by the death of fish in Norris Reservoir (Tennessee) in December of 1937.[68] Tributary rivers were pouring ice-cold water into the lake at a time when the lake level was being lowered a foot per day. This river water, which was colder than the lake water, caused a pushing up (because it was heavier) of the bottom water of the lake. This upswelling and mixing of the carbon dioxide-saturated bottom water was, according to Powers et al.[68] indirectly responsible for the death of fish. Small shad moving about in this heterogeneous mixture of waters passed from high carbon dioxide tensions at deeper levels to low carbon dioxide tension at the surface. These fish soon became affected by the rapid changes in carbon dioxide tension and died by the millions; larger fish rising to the surface from greater depths also became incapacitated by sudden changes in carbon dioxide tension. It was significant that throughout the period when fish were dying there was ample oxygen to support fish at all levels.

Investigating biologists[68] conducted laboratory experiments to determine the cause of death of the fish in Norris Lake. Rock bass were placed in a hardware-cloth cage and lowered to the bottom of a water-filled 10-gal carboy. The same number of fish were released in the carboy outside the cage. The carboy was left open so these latter fish could come to the water surface and gulp air. The water in the carboy was supplied with carbon dioxide to produce a CO_2 tension above normal. Fish that were free to come to the surface of the water died before those that were held in the cage, thus indicating that rapid change in carbon dioxide tension from high at the bottom of the carboy to low at the surface affected the fish adversely. However, rock bass in the cage were able, by adjusting the alkalinity of the blood, to counteract the ill effects of high but constant carbon dioxide tension, and thus to extract oxygen as efficiently as if the carbon dioxide tension were low. This situation held as long as the carbon dioxide tension remained fairly constant; but when the fish were forced to alternate between hgih and low tensions, they soon lost their equilibrium and died.

A repetition of these laboratory experiments[5] gave opposite results, namely fish that could come to the surface to gulp air lived longer than those confined to cages. C. L. Baker's[5] impression was that the death of the fish in Norris Lake was caused by sudden temperature changes rather than by variable carbon dioxide tensions.

The combinations of circumstances which produce the biological phenomena described above probably appear rather infrequently. More common are fish deaths occurring under ice in winter and in very weedy lakes during hot summer months.

WINTERKILL AND SUMMERKILL

The terms "winterkill" and "summerkill" are applied to sudden mortalities of fish which occur in winter or summer, usually as a direct result of suffocation. Conditions that set the stage for a winterkill are, however, very different from those which result in an oxygen deficiency in a lake or pond during the summer.

Winterkill

In the north, winter ice forms a seal over lakes and ponds which prevents the exchange of gases between the water—air interface. A more important source of oxygen is the photosynthetic activity of submersed aquatic plants in the presence of light. Although the penetration of light through ice is less than through clear water, there is sufficient light for varying levels of photosynthetic activity. Light may be blanketed out entirely by a layer of snow upon the ice. When all photosynthetic activity is stopped because of insufficient light, the source of additional under-ice oxygen is gone, and in a relatively short time the supply of oxygen may be completely used up by the respiration of living plants and animals and the demands of organic decay.[19],[37]

In 1945, Greenbank[37] published results of a study of the physical, chemical, and biological conditions in ice-covered lakes in Michigan. He measured dissolved oxygen, pH, carbon dioxide, alkalinity, biochemical oxygen demand, and light penetration in these ice-covered lakes to determine what factors or combinations of factors were responsible for the death of fishes, and to develop more effective methods of preventing winter fish kills. The amount of dissolved oxygen appeared to be the most important single factor influencing death or survival. This oxygen concentration might change gradually or rather suddenly, depending upon other conditions associated with the body of water in question. For example, at Green Lake Station 5, oxygen at the surface (under ice) changed from 1.8 ppm on February 5, 1943, to 9.8 ppm on February 8, an increase of 8.0 ppm in 3 days (a rate of 2.7 ppm/day). The most abrupt decline was noted in Pasinski's Pond Station 27, where the oxygen fell from 12.3 ppm on February 12, 1940, to 2.4 ppm on February 14, a rate of 5 ppm/day. A delicate balance often exists between the processes which produce oxygen (photosynthesis of plankton algae) and those that use it up.[37] As light is essential to photosynthesis, its transmission through the ice and snow covering a lake or pond is extremely important (Fig. 3.1). Measurements of light penetration show that about 85% will pass through 7.5 in. of clear ice, and as much as 11.5% through 15 in. of ice that is cloudy on top. However, 1 in. of crusted snow reduced the light penetration through the snow to between 10 and 17% of the light that fell on the snow's surface, and 5 in. of dry snow allowed the transmission of only 2.5% of the available light.[37] Clean fresh snow allowed the greatest light penetration, clean wet snow the next greatest, and granular snow the least (Fig. 3.2).

Although the rate of photosynthesis is dependent on many factors, it is conceivable that there is a range of light intensity sufficient to stimulate a level of photosynthetic activity during which the oxygen output will exactly equal the oxygen demands of the aquatic environment. This is a dangerous condition because it may depreciate rapidly into a situation of oxygen shortage. There is reason to assume that the amount of light that penetrates 1.5−2 ft of moderately clear ice (without snow) is enough to satisfy the requirements for photosynthesis.[37] Further, the evidence is conclusive that a heavy snow cover on ice so greatly reduces the amount

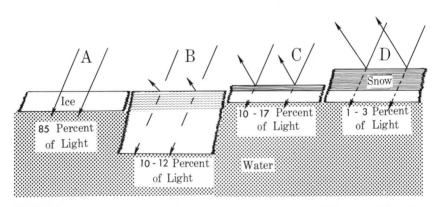

Fig. 3.2 Oxygen supply under winter ice depends upon the transmission of sufficient light for photosynthesis of plankton algae and rooted submersed plants. (A) Clear ice 5 in. thick permits about 85% of the light to pass through. (B) Cloudy ice 15 in. thick cuts out all but about 10-12% of the light. (C) One inch of snow over clear ice 3 in. thick stops all but 10-17% of the light. (D) Five inches of snow over clear ice 3 in. thick blots out almost all of the light. Some photosynthesis can go on when 10-12% of light falling on the ice passes through and reaches the water below. Five or more inches of snow stops the transmission of almost all light. Winter-kill of fishes is more common during winters when the snow on the ice persists for long periods than when it is light or melts between storms.

of light entering the water, regardless of the clarity of the ice, that photosynthesis of phytoplankton is completely stopped.

Biologists and fish culturists have tried to prevent the winterkill of fishes in various ways, most of which have been ineffectual. Some methods explored for preventing winterkill of fishes are given below:

1. Aeration of Water Under Ice. Many attempts have been made to blow air immediately under ice with pumps or blowers. This method is largely ineffectual[37] because little oxygen becomes dissolved in the water.

2. Aeration of Water Above Ice. In 1935−36, the Michigan Institute for Fisheries Research attempted experimental aeration by pumping water from a lake and spraying it into the air and allowing it to return through holes cut in the ice.[37] This improved dissolved oxygen tension, but the effect was very localized, and the oxygen disappeared within 28 hr. Improvements in this method have been made by Merna[57] and Flick[32]although the lake area affected is still relatively small.

3. Pumping of Well Water. Well water at 50°F was run through wire mesh and over an inclined trough to increase the dissolved oxygen from about 2 ppm to 4 or 6 ppm. The water was allowed to run into Pasinski's Pond (3.75 acres) through holes cut in the ice,[37] and, over a number of days, opened a hole in the pond 8 to 10 feet in diameter. However, this pumping of aerated well water proved almost useless for preventing the death of fish, because the area affected by the well water was small.

4. Snow Removal. Manual removal of snow from hatchery ponds, although frequently impractical, has caused improvement in dissolved oxygen under ice. Furthermore, pumps and other equipment may be employed. At Green Lake water was pumped onto the surface of the ice, and melted the snow to slush for a one-acre area. There was an increase in the amount of dissolved oxygen in water under the ice, even though the slush rapidly became frozen.[37]

5. Lamp Black. This substance, spread on snow-covered ice from the air, melted the snow (through absorption of heat) and thereby allowed light penetration, which resulted in improved oxygen conditions under the ice.[65]

6. Circulation of Bottom Water. A perforated plastic hose with small holes at spaced intervals was weighted and laid on the lake bottom to follow the long axis of the lake. The hose was closed at one end and fastened to an air compressor at the other. The compressor pumped air into the hose so that it bubbled out through the small holes along the entire length of the hose. These jets of air passing from the lake bottom to its surface set up currents of water which eventually carried bottom water at about 39°F to the surface.[76] This warmer water eventually melted the ice and kept a strip of open water above the hose as long as the air compressor was operated, even though the air temperature was close to 0°F. When this system was operated at intervals in a lake subject to winterkill of fishes, no loss of fishes occurred.

This method has been used to keep open water for ducks, and to prevent ice damage to piers, docks, and other installations. It may be the most practical technique yet devised for preventing winterkill,[12,69,75,77] but Patriarche[66] demonstrated that in two Michigan lakes the circulation of water resulting from the release of air from a tube on the lake bottom increased the danger of winterkill because it circulated water having a high biological oxygen demand that was immediately above the lake bottom. When this water was carried to the surface and mixed with water under the ice containing a small amount of dissolved oxygen, it used up this remaining oxygen and made conditions worse for fishes, even though this warmer bottom water melted the ice.

To prevent the upwelling of oxygen-deficient bottom water, Patriarche[66] supported an air hose at a level of 5 ft below the ice and about 5—9 ft above the lake bottom. This apparently created some turbulence which again resulted in reduced oxygen in the surface layer, and a moderately heavy fish kill occurred (mostly bluegills).

An increase in the oxygen supply of water covered by ice can come about only through photosynthesis. Thus, the maintenance of an adequate oxygen supply is dependent upon the presence and activity of green plants, composed largely of the plankton algae, and this, in turn, depends upon the transmission of light for photosynthesis. It is conceivable that most of these algae might die or go into dormant stages if forced to remain in darkness (ice covered by snow) for an extended period, so that when sufficient light for photosynthesis becomes available again, *too few phytoplankton cells* would be present to improve borderline oxygen conditions for fishes.

Results of Partial Winterkill

Seldom are all the fishes in a lake or pond killed when subjected to adverse conditions under ice. This is because some are more resistant to low oxygen tensions than others and because adverse conditions throughout a lake or pond may not be uniform, so that certain ones in more favorable locations may survive while the rest may die. However, most game and pan fishes require larger amounts of oxygen than do the coarse ones, i.e., carp, buffalo, and bullheads. For this reason, a few of the more undesirable fishes may survive to repopulate the water.

Studies of fish populations subjected to partial winterkill have been made by a number of biologists. In Michigan a partial winterkill was followed by changes in growth rate of the surviving fishes.[7] A dominant-year class of bullheads developed in Lost Island Lake (Iowa) following a partial winterkill;[58,71] this same phenomenon has been reported for Spring Lake near Savanna (Illinois).

The fish population of 10-acre Gale Lake near Galesburg, Illinois, was examined about 20 months after a winterkill had occurred during January or February of 1945.[8] Prior to the winter of 1944—45, the lake contained largemouth bass, bluegills, white crappies, carp, bigmouth buffalo, golden shiners, and catfish. When the ice melted in early March, 1945, about 4000 lb of fish carcasses were collected.

When a census of the lake was taken by treatment with rotenone on September 16, 1946, it contained white crappies, green sunfish, black bullheads, carp, buffalo, and golden shiners (Table 3.3). Approximately 106,500 fish weighing 5275 lb were collected. The larger fish shown in Table 3.3 are those which had survived the winter of 1944—45; the smaller individuals of the same species represented the young produced in 1945 and 1946. It is inconceivable that this population could have ever produced satisfactory hook-and-line fishing.

Studies of fish populations that have undergone partial winterkill illustrate well the danger of this phenomenon. Usually, it is better if the adverse winter conditions kill all the fish because the lake can then be restocked with useful kinds and numbers of fingerlings and to obtain satisfactory fishing within the second season after the winterkill occurs. Nonetheless, where the winterkill is partial and some desirable pan fish species survive, a stocking of a small number of sexually mature largemouth bass might result in the production of a dominant brood of these fish and prevent an overpopulation of the pan fish. Such a stocking probably could have been accomplished prior to the bass spawning season in a lake as small as Gale. Larger waters that have lost a part of their population from winterkill can be managed by stocking large numbers of bass fry, which are often obtainable in quantity. The rapid development of a fishable population after a partial winterkill often rests with the ability or willingness of the lake or pond owner, whether an individual, a club, or a State Department of Conservation, to appraise quickly the damage and execute a plan to rectify it before the fish surviving the winterkill have produced young. However, once a lake becomes overloaded with a super-

Table 3.3   Census Of All Fishes in Gale Lake (10.0 Acres), Gale Products Recreation Grounds, Galesburg, Illinois, September, 1946

Kind of Fish		Total Number	Total Weight (lb)	Average Weight per Fish (lb)	Percent of Total Weight
		Fine Fish			
White crappie	(large)	76	97.25	1.279	
White crappie	(small)	42,500	752.74	0.018	
Green sunfish	(large)	17	3.75	0.221	
Green sunfish	(small)	4,580	75.12	0.016	
		47,173	928,86		17.6
		Catfish			
Black bullhead	(large)	120	82.75	0.689	
Black bullhead	(small)	48,700	721.48	0.015	
		48,820	804.23		15.3
		Rough Fish			
Carp	(large)	219	1,572.75	7.182	
Carp	(small)	1,331	583.75	0.439	
Buffalo	(large)	31	626.13	20.198	
Buffalo	(small)	424	618.96	1.460	
		2,005	3,401.59		64.5
		Forage Fish			
Golden shiner		8,500	139.77	0.016	
		8,500	139.77		2.6
Grand total		106,498	5,274.45		
Per acre		10,650	527.45		

abundant population of sunfish, crappies, bullheads, carp, or buffalo fishes, much more radical measures are needed to restore fishing.

Summerkill

Summerkill, as a major catastrophe, is less common than winterkill. On the other hand, there is some evidence that more fish die naturally in the summer period (and are never observed by man) than at any other time of year. There are several records of the disappearance of relatively strong year classes of white crappies during the summer months where the only evidence of their death was the fact that they suddenly disappeared from wing net catches and never again reappeared.[39],[87] Crappies often are in their poorest condition in the summer, and many apparently fail to recover.

Summerkills comparable in extent to kills occurring under ice in winter sometimes take place in shallow weed-filled lakes during the hot, still nights of July and August. All of the summerkills that I have observed (that did not involve pollution from outside sources) occurred after periods of several days during which skies were cloudy or partly cloudy, temperatures ranged in the 80s and 90s both day and night, and winds were calm or nearly calm. Under these weather conditions, the dissolved oxygen that may be abundant in a weed-choked lake during the daytime may dissappear entirely during the calm hot nights with the resulting wholesale death of fishes. Usually, some fishes survive summer oxygen shortages, and these may be seen gasping for air at the lake surface as the first light of the approaching dawn makes them visible. Often a quiet period lasting several days and nights may be broken off by a violent storm which restores the oxygen supply, lowers the water temperature, and stops any further death of fishes. Probably, high water temperatures, darkness, and rapid organic decay in shallow weed-filled lakes combine to produce summerkills.

Swingle[92] describes summerkills in ponds caused by dense "blooms" of *Microcystis, Anabaena,* and sometimes other algae where their concentrations in the upper surface layer of a foot or more in depth causes high water temperatures near the surface, supersaturation of oxygen there, and complete shading of water beneath the algae. The water below the surface layer may be devoid of dissolved oxygen, high in carbon dioxide, and 10°F cooler than the surface layer, and over a period of days this water may develop a biological oxygen demand. Under these circumstances, any phenomenon that will cause upwelling of the subsurface water, such as supercooling of the surface, cold rain, or prolonged wind action on the surface, may create an oxygen deficiency throughout the pond resulting in the death of fishes. One solution is to kill *a part* of the algae with copper sulfate (a complete kill of the algae might reduce the oxygen throughout the pond and cause a fish kill). If this treatment is made once or twice a week the result is deeper light penetration, diversification of algal species, and deeper distribution of oxygen.

Sometimes summerkills are caused by unrecognized epidemic diseases or parasites such as the one recorded by Allison and Kelly[2] where gizzard and threadfin shad where killed in a 200-mile stretch of the Coosa River system (Alabama) by the protozoan ciliate, *Ichthyophthirius multifiliis.* These authors further point out that parasitism may be a frequent cause of fish kills that are casually attributed to other causes.

Aquatic fungi may cause fish kills, but usually these occur in spring when waters are warming rather than in summer. The genera of aquatic fungi definitely assigned to fish kills were *Saprolignia (parasitica)* and *Ferax* and *Achlya,* with *Leptomitus, Allomyces,* and *Pytheum* associated with special situations.[78]

Reid[70] described a fish kill on Lake Maggiore, St. Petersburg, Florida, in January, 1962 (winterkill only in that it occurred in winter) in which the dissolved oxygen became zero from surface to bottom as a result of the death of a "bloom" of *Anacystes*. Ninety percent of the fish killed were brown bullheads *(Ictalurus nebulosus)*, and the rest were mullet, *(Mugil cephalus)*, bluegills, and threadfin shad, *(D. petenense)*, There was no explanation as to why the algae suddenly died.

Another type of summerkill of fishes is caused by the decay of "blooms" of toxic algae (usually blue-green algae). These toxic algae are concentrated by winds[45] or they develop from the stimulus of nitrates and phosphates originating from organic pollutants. Death of fishes may be caused by oxygen deficiences, by toxic substances released from decaying blue-green algae, or both.[54] The death of domestic livestock, forced to drink the alga-filled water, has been attributed to these toxic substances.

High or low oxygen tensions produced by unusual circumstances sometimes will cause the death of fishes. During April 1940, a loss of fish was observed at the south end of Lake Waubesa (Wisconsin) and in the Yahara River below this lake.[96] At that time an algal bloom of *Chlamydomonas* was concentrated in the south end of the lake and produced oxygen to a level of 30-32 ppm at the lake surface. The death of fishes was attributed to the presence of gas emboli in the gill capillaries which blocked blood circulation. Black crappies, bluegills, northern pike, walleyes, white suckers, and carp were killed.

In October 1936, a heavy mortality of fish was reported for the Yahara River below Lake Kegonsa (Wisconsin).[54] These fish died from an oxygen deficiency caused by the decay of an almost pure culture of the blue-green alga, *Aphanizomenon flos-aquae*. The fish were crowding close to shore and were gasping at the surface until they finally expired. *A. flos-aquae*, is known to release a very toxic substance when it dies and decays, and a secondary cause of death may have been direct poisoning.

Jackson and Starrett[7] described localized kills of fishes (mostly gizzard shad) in Lake Chautauqua on July 9, 1953, that apparently resulted from localized oxygen deficiencies. At 6:20 a.m., the dissolved oxygen content at one point was only 1.6 ppm, and later several fish were observed that presumably had died of asphyxiation. The weather was hot and the lake very quiet.

The exact determination of the cause of fish mortalities can be very difficult, especially when no measurable amounts of polluting substances are evident. Also, it must be remembered that most species of warmwater fishes are relatively short-lived and death may follow a period of senile degeneration.

OTHER DANGERS AND NUISANCES

Fishes in small artificial ponds and lakes may be decimated by some "accidents" that occur because of the physical aspects of these impoundments and the fact that men are careless by nature. These "accidents" are mentioned here so that they may be recognized and avoided.

Loss of Ponds Because of Burrowing Animals

Small ponds are sometimes subjected to washouts through the activities of borrowing crayfish and of muskrats, rats, and other burrowing mammals. These animals usually work in the dam, digging tunnels above the normal water level of the pond. No damage appears until a heavy sudden rain raises the pond level well above normal, and the tunnels become water channels through which water escapes to the downstream side of the dam, usually taking with it a section of the earth fill and all of the water and fish in the pond.

It is usually impractical to bury wire mesh or metal sheeting in small dams to prevent damage from burrowing animals. The best solution is to maintain a constant vigilance and trap or poison the rodents when they appear to be damaging the pond dam. Burrowing crayfish are sometimes killed by dropping one or more crystals of crude copper sulfate in their holes or "chimneys," or by adding either one teaspoonful of carbide powder or two ounces of stock dip solution to each burrow and then tamping the burrow shut.[6] On ponds larger than 3 or 4 acres, the dams are so wide at the top that there is little danger from burrowing animals.

Wind Action

When artificial lakes and dams are too large to be subject to damage from burrowing animals, prevailing winds acting on such a wide surface can create another danger by blowing parallel to the long axes of the lakes, thus causing waves and currents that cut earth from the fills at the water line. Unless a fill is protected by rip-rapping of concrete, rocks, or by a floating boom, the action of the waves may gradually cut away the dam. Wind and wave action can occur in any part of the lake, often cutting away at one shore and filling up a nearby bay or channel. Where rip-rapping is impractical, booms or deflector structures can be used to stop severe wind and water erosions. Wind-driven ice causes considerable damage in northern lakes.

Evaporation

Evaporation of water may become a serious threat to water supplies for domestic and industrial uses in exceptionally dry years and particularly in the case of water-supply impoundments where the surface area of the watershed is comparatively small in relation to volume capacity of the lake basin.

In some instances it may be practical to use cetyl alcohol or stearyl alcohol, which, when applied from a boat, will spread rapidly over the water surface to form a layer a single molecule thick (about one-millionth of an inch thick). Field tests indicate that its use might prevent somewhat less than 70% of the potential loss from evaporation. Winds of more than 15 miles per hour will blow the protective film off, but it can be quickly replaced. These waxlike compounds do not harm fish or aquatic invertebrates, and reservoirs can be used normally for drinking water, swimming, boating, and fishing.[82]

Evaporation may cause a natural reduction of the lake surface area similar to that produced in a planned drawdown (see Chapter 6). The effects may be beneficial to fishing once the lake basin refills, provided the fish are not subject to winterkill as a result of the low water.

Mosquitoes and Other Nuisance Insects

Several kinds of aquatic insects are considered to have importance as human nuisance insects. Of these, the mosquito is the most widely distributed and most commonly associated with the aquatic habitats. However, waters that contain fishes seldom are sources of mosquitoes because their larvae are a preferred fish food and are relatively available to fishes because the larvae and pupae come to the surface to respire. While collecting material for his publication *The Mosquitoes in Illinois,* H. H. Ross,[72] found no mosquito larvae or nymphs in farm ponds except in parts containing dense stands of submersed aquatic vegetation that prevented the fish from reaching the wigglers. More common sources of nuisance mosquitoes are water-filled cans and temporary pools in ditches, woodlots, and marsh areas. Other common nuisance insects are mayflies that clog highways with their flights and bodies, biting flies of many kinds, and nonbiting midges.

The dangers of applying organic insecticides over aquatic habitats has been stressed early in this chapter. Repellents and noninsecticidal controls are used wherever possible.

An unusual biological answer to controlling mosquitoes and other aquatic invertebrates is the use of "annual" fishes.[43] These fishes have the capacity to survive and multiply in impermanent water where other fishes would perish. Annual fishes are found in a wide range of temperate and tropical habitats where the water disappears at least once a year. The fish survive until the next wet season in the form of eggs (embryos) buried in the soil. These eggs may be concentrated, transported, and dispersed in damp peat moss. After reintroduction into water, the eggs hatch within in a few hours. The young are hardy, voracious, mature quickly, and show high fertility.

Leeches

Leeches, also called "blood suckers," are rather flat, wormlike animals, tapered at one end and rounded at the other, usually colored black or brown. Most of the kind commonly encountered in freshwater lakes and ponds range from 1/2 in. up to 3 in. length. Leeches obtain their food by attaching themselves to animals in the water and sucking blood through tiny punctures which they make in the skin. When leeches are present in a farm pond, they can become so much of a nuisance as to ruin the pond's use for swimming.

Fortunately, it is a simple matter to eliminate leeches from a pond with copper sulfate. For ponds with moderately hard water, a concentration of 5 ppm is usually enough to kill all the leeches. The copper sulfate can be dissolved and distributed over the entire pond, using one of the distribution methods described in the preceding section on summerkill. Any pools or tributaries connected with the pond should also be treated.[3]

REFERENCES

1. Alabaster, J. S., 1962, "The effect of heated effluents on fish," *Air and Water Pollution* 7(6/7), 541-563.
2. Allison, R., and Kelly, H. D., 1963, "An epizootic of *Ichthyophthirius multifiliis* in a river fish population," *Progressive Fish Culturist* 25(3), 149-150.
3. Anon., 1956, *Controlling Plant and Animal Pests in Farm Ponds with Copper Sulfate*, Phelps Dodge Refining Corp., pp. 1-32.
4. Arnold, G. E., 1962, "Thermal pollution of surface supplies," *J. Am. Water Works Assoc.* 54, 1332-1346.
5. Baker, C. L., 1942, "The effects on fish of gulping atmospheric air from waters of various carbon dioxide tensions," *Tenn. Acad. Sci.* 17(1), 39-50.
6. Beall, H. B., 1959, "Death to Diogenes the digger," *West Va. Cons.*, April, 32.
7. Beckman, W. C., 1950, "Changes in growth rates of fishes following reduction in population densities by winterkill," *Am. Fish. Soc. Trans.* 78(1948), 82-90.
8. Bennett, G. W., 1948, "Winterkill of fishes in an Illinois Lake," *Lake Management Repts., Illinois Biol. Notes* 19, 1-9.
9. Black, E. C., Fry, F. E. J., and Black, V. S., 1954, "The influence of carbon dioxide on the utilization of oxygen by some freshwater fish," *Can. J. Zool.* 32(6), 408-420.

10. Bridges, W. R., Kallman, B. J., and Andrews, A. K., 1963, "Persistence of DDT and its metabolites in a farm pond," *Am. Fish. Soc. Trans.* 92(4), 421-427.

11. Buck, D. H., 1956, "Effects of turbidity on fish and fishing," *Oklahoma Fish. Res. Lab. Rept.* 56, 1-62.

12. Burdick, M. E., 1959, "Open water in winter," *Wisconsin Cons. Bull.* 24(2), 21-33.

13. Burdick, G. E., Harris, E. J., Dean, H. J., Walker, T. M., Skea, J., and Colby, D., 1964, "The accumulation of DDT in lake trout and the effect on reproduction," *Am. Fish. Soc. Trans.* 93(2), 127-136.

14. Butler, J. L., 1964, "Interaction of effects by environmental factors on primary productivity in ponds and micro-ecosystems," Thesis, Oklahoma State Univ., Stillwater, 98 pp.

15. Cairns, J., Jr., 1967, "Living with our natural water systems," *Sci. and Cit.* 9(2), 28-33.

16. Cairns, J., Jr., Scheier, A., and Hess, N. E., 1964, "The effects of alkyl benzene sulfonate on aquatic organisms," *Ind. Water Wastes.* 9(1), 22-28.

17. Carlander, K. D., 1952, "Farm fish pond research in Iowa," *J. Wildlife Management* 16(3), 258-261.

18. Clyma, W., and Broadhurst, W. L., 1961, "Clarification of Playa Lake water by aerial application of a flocculating agent," *Texas Agr. Expt. Sta. Progr. Rept.* 2168, 1-6.

19. Cooper, G. P., and Washburn, G. N., 1946, "Relation of dissolved oxygen to winter mortality of fish in Mich. lakes," *Am. Fish. Soc. Trans.* 76, 23-33.

20. Davis, J. J., 1962, "Accumulation of radionucleides by aquatic insects," *U. S. At. Energy Comm. HW-SA-2848.*, pp. 1-4.

21. Davis, J. J., and Foster, R. F., 1958, "Bioaccumulation of radioisotopes through aquatic food chains," *Ecology* 39(3), 530-535.

22. Dorris, T. C., Copelands, D. J., and Patterson, D., 1961, "The case for holding ponds," *Oil Gas J.* 30 (Oct.), 1-5.

23. Dorris, T. C., Gould, W., and Jenkins, C. R., 1959, "Toxicity bioassay of oil refinery effluents in Oklahoma," *Trans. 2nd Sem. on Biol. Prob. in Water Pollution. USPHSW60-3* pp. 1-10.

24. Doudoroff, P., 1959, "How should we determine dissolved oxygen criteria for freshwater fishes?" *Trans. 2nd Sem. Biol. Prob. Water Pollution, USPHSW60-3,* pp. 1-10.

25. Doudoroff, P., and Katz, M., 1950, "Critical review of literature on the toxicity of industrial wastes and their components to fish," *Sewage Ind. Wastes* 22(11), 1432-1458.

26. Doudoroff, P., and Shumway, D. L., 1967, "Dissolved oxygen criteria for the protection of fish," in "Symposium on water quality criteria to protect aquatic life," *Am. Fish. Soc. Spec. Publ.* 4, 13-19.

27. Ellis, M. M., Westfall, B. A., and Ellis, M. D., 1946, "Determination of water quality," *U.S. Fish Wildlife Serv. Res. Rept.* 9, 1-122.

28. Elser, H. J., 1965, "Effect of warmwater discharge on angling in the Potomac River, Maryland, 1961-62," *Progressive Fish Culturist* 27(2), 79-86.

29. English, J. N., Surber, E. W., and McDermott, G. N., 1963, "Pollutional effects of outboard motor exhaust--field studies," *J. Water Pollution Control Federation* 35,

30. Esmey, M. L., Guyer, B. E., Shanklin, M. D., and Temple, L. H., 1955, "Treatment of surface water supplies for the farm home," *Univ. Missouri Agr. Expt. Sta. Res. Bull.* 589, 1-36.

31. Ferguson, D. E., Culley, D. D., Cotton, W. D., and Dodds, R. P., 1964, "Resistance to chlorinated hydrocarbon insecticides in three species of freshwater fish," *Biol. Sci.* 14(11), 43-44.

32. Flick, W., 1968, "Dispersal of aerated water as related to prevention of winterkill," *Progressive Fish Culturist* 30(1), 13-18.

33. Fremling, C. R., 1964, "Mayfly distribution indicates water quality on the upper Missis-

sippi River," *Science* 146(3648), 1163-1166.

34. Fry, F. E. J., 1951, "Some environmental relations of the speckled trout *(Salvelinus fontinalis)*," *Proc. N. E. Atlantic Fish Cont.* pp. 1-29.

35. Fry, F. E. J., 1959, "The oxygen requirements of fish," *Trans. 2nd Sem. Biol. Prob. Water Pollution, USPHS Tec. Rept. W60-3*, pp. 106-109.

36. Gould, W. R., and Dorris, T. C., 1961, "Toxicity changes of stored oil refinery effluents," *J. Water pollution Control Federation* 33(Oct.), 1107-1111.

37. Greenbank, J., 1945, "Limnological conditions in ice-covered lakes, especially as related to winterkill of fish," *Ecol. Monographs* 15, 343-392.

38. Grzenda, A. R., Lauer, G. J., and Nicholson, H. P., 1964, "Water pollution by insecticides in an agricultural river basin," II. "The zooplankton, bottom fauna, and fish," *Limnol. Oceanog.* 9(3), 318-323.

39. Hansen, D. F., 1951, "Biology of the white crappie in Illinois," *Illinois Nat. Hist. Surv. Bull.* 25(4), 211-265.

40. Henderson, C., Pickering, Q. H., and Cohen, J. M., 1959, "The toxicity of synthetic detergents and soaps to fish," *Sewage Ind. Wastes* 31, 295-306.

41. Henderson, C., Pickering, Q. H., and Tarzwell, C. M., 1959, "Relative toxicity of ten chlorinated hydrocarbon insecticides to four species of fish," *Am. Fish. Soc. Trans.* 88(1), 23-32.

42. Hey, D., 1955, "A preliminary report on the culture of fish in the final effluent from the new disposal works Athlone, Sapica," *Proc. Intern. Assoc. Theor. Appl. Limnol.* 12, 737-742.

43. Hildeman, W. H., and Walford R. L., 1963, "Annual fishes: Promising species as biological control agents," *J. Trop. Med. Hyg.* 66(7), 163-166.

44. Hiltibran, R. C., 1967, "Effects of some herbicides on fertilized fish eggs and fry," *Am. Fish. Soc. Trans.* 96(4), 414-416.

45. Ingram, W. M., and Prescott, G. W., 1954, "Toxic freshwater algae," *Am. Midland Naturalist* 52(1), 75-87.

46. Irwin, W. H., 1945, "Methods of precipitating colloidal soil particles from impounded waters of central Oklahoma," *Oklahoma Agri. Mech. Coll. Bull.* 42(11), 1-16.

47. Jackson, H. O., and Starrett, W. C., 1959, "Turbidity and sedimentation at Lake Chautauqua, Illinois," *J. Wildlife Management* 23(2), 157-168.

48. James, M. C., Meehean, A. L., and Douglas, E. J., 1944, "Fish stocking as related to the management of inland waters," *U.S. Fish Wildlife Serv. Cons. Bull.* 35, 1-22.

49. Kent, F., and Hooper, F. F., 1966, "Sythetic detergents: Their influence upon iron-binding complexes of natural waters," *Science* 153(3735), 526-527

50. Klement, A. W., Jr., and Wallen, I. E., 1960, "A selected list of references on marine and aquatic radiobiology," *U.S. At. Energy Comm. Off. Tech. Info. Rept.*, No. TID-3930, pp. 1-42.

51. Krumholz, L. A., and Minckley, W. L., 1964, "Changes in the fish population in the upper Ohio River following temporary pollution abatement." *Am. Fish. Soc. Trans.* 93(1), 1-5.

52. Lemke, A. E., and Mount, D. I., 1963, "Some effects of alkyl benzene sulfonate on the bluegill, *Lepomis macrochirus*," *Am. Fish. Soc. Trans.* 92(4), 372-378.

53. Mack, G. L., Corcoran, S. M., Gibbs, S. D., Gutenmann, W. H., Rechahn, J. A., and Lisk, D. J., 1964, "The DDT content of some fishes and surface waters of New York state," *N. Y. Fish Game J.* 11(2), 148-153.

54. Mackenthun, K. M., and Herman, E. F., 1948, "A heavy mortality of fishes resulting from the decomposition of algae in the Yahara River, Wisconsin," *Am. Fish. Soc. Trans.* 75(1945), 175-180.

55. McCarraher, D.E., 1962, "Northern pike *Esox lucius,* in alkaline lakes of Nebraska," *Am. Fish. Soc. Trans.* 91(3), 326-329.

56. McKee, J.E., and Wolf., H.W. (eds.), 1963, *Water Quality Criteria,* Calif. State Water Quality Control Board, Sacramento, 548 pp.

57. Merna, J.W., 1965, "Aeration of winterkill lakes," *Progressive Fish Culturist* 27(4), 199-202.

58. Moen, T.E., 1960, "Bullheads by the millions," *Iowa Cons.* 19(5), 37.

59. Murphy, G.I., 1962, "Effect of mixing depth and turbidity on the productivity of freshwater impoundments," *Am. Fish. Soc. Trans.* 91(1), 69-76.

60. Neess, J.C., 1949, "Development and status of pond fertilization in central Europe," *Am. Fish. Soc. Trans.* 76(1946), 335-358.

61. Neess, J.C., Dugdale, R.C. Goering, J.J., and Dugdale, V.A., 1963, "Use of nitrogen-15 for measurement of rates in the nitrogen cycle," in *Radioecology, Proc. 1st Nat. Symp. Radioecology,* Reinhold Publishing Corp., New York, pp. 481-484.

62. Nerhring, D., 1962, "Laundry waste waters and fish," *Dent. Fisch/tg.* 9, 46-51.

63. Nicholson, H.P., Grzenda, A.R., Lauer, G.J., Cox, W.S., and Teasley, J.L., 1964, "Water pollution by insecticides in an agricultural river basin," I, "Occurrence of insecticides in river and treated municipal water," *Limnol. Oceanog.* 9(3), 310-317.

64. Nicholson, H.P., Webb, H.J., Lauer, G.J., O'Brien, E.E., Grzenda, A.R., and Shanlin, D.W., 1962, "Insecticide contamination in a farm pond," *Am. Fish. Soc. Trans.* 9(2), 213-222.

65. O'Donnell, D.J., 1947, "The use of lamp black on freeze-out lakes," *9th Midwest Wildlife Conf. Mimeo.,* pp. 1-9.

66. Patriarche, M.H., 1961, "Air-induced winter circulation of two shallow Michigan lakes," *J. Wildlife Management,* 25(3), 282-289.

67. Pickering, Q.H., Henderson, C., and Lemke, A.E., 1962, "The toxicity of organic phosphorus insecticides to different species of warmwater fishes," *Am. Fish. Soc. Trans.* 91(2), 175-184.

68. Powers, E.B., Shields, A.R., and Hickman, M.E., 1939, "The mortality of fishes in Norris Lake," *J. Tenn. Acad. Sci.* 14(2), 239-260.

69. Rasmussen, D.H., 1960, "Preventing winterkill by use of a compressed-air system," *Progressive Fish Culturist* 22, 185-187.

70. Reid, G.K., 1964, "Oxygen depletion in a Florida lake," *Quart. J. Florida. Acad. Sci.* 27(2), 120-126.

71. Rose, E.T., and Moen, T., 1951, "Results of increased fish harvest in Lost Island Lake," *Am. Fish. Soc. Trans.* 80(1950), 50-55.

72. Ross, H. H., 1947, "The mosquitoes of Illinois," *Illinois Nat. Hist. Surv. Bull.* 24(1), 1-94.

73. Sanders, H.O., and Cope, O.B., 1966, "Toxicities of several pesticides to two species of cladocerans," *Am. Fish. Soc. Trans.* 95(2), 165-169.

74. Scheier, A., and Cairns, J., Jr., 1966, "Persistence of gill damage in *Lepomis gibbosus* following a brief exposure to alkyl benzene sulfonate," *Notulae Naturae (Acad. Nat. Sci. Phila.)* 391, 1-7.

75. Schmitz, W.R., 1959, "Research on winterkill of fish," *Wisconsin Cons. Bull.* 24, 19-21.

76. Schmitz, W.R., and Hasler, A.D., 1958, "Artificially induced circulation of lakes by means of compressed air," *Science* 128(3331), 1088-1089.

77. Scidmore, W.J., 1957, "An investigation of carbon dioxide, ammonia, and hydrogen sulfide as factors contributing to fish kills in ice-covered lakes," *Progressive Fish Culturist* 19, 124-127.

78. Scott, W.W., and O'Bier, A.H.. 1962. "Aquatic fungi associated with diseased fish and fish eggs," *Progressive Fish Culturist* 24(1), 3-15.

79. Stroud, R.H., 1959, *Reducing Turbidity,* S. F. I. Bull. 94, p. 6.

80. Stroud, R.H., 1965, *Purifying Sewage,* S. F. I. Bull. 164, p. 4.
81. Stroud, R.H., and Douglas, P.A., 1968, *Thermal Pollution of Water,* S. F. I. Bull, 191, pp. 1-8.
82. Stroud, R.H., and Jenkins, R.M., 1960, *Smothering,* S. F. I. Bull. 108, pp. 7-8.
83. Stroud, R.H., and Jenkins, R.M., 1961, *Sea Frontiers,* S. F. I. Bull. 120, p. 5.
84. Stroud, R.H., and Jenkins, R.M., 1961, *Lake Erie Puzzle,* S. F. I. Bull. 121, pp. 6-7.
85. Stroud, R.H., and Massman, W.H., 1966, *Soft Detergent Hard on Fish,* S. F. I. Bull. 172, p. 6.
86. Srinath, E.G., and Pillai, S.C., 1966, "Phosphorus in sewage, polluted waters, sludges, and effluents," *Quart. Rev. Biol.* 41(4), 384-407.
87. Starrett, W.C., and McNeil, P.L., jr., 1952, "Sport fishing at Lake Chautauqua near Havana, Illinois, in 1950 and 1951," *Ill. Nat. Hist. Surv. Biol. Notes,* 30, 1-31.
88. Stewart, N.E., Shumway, D.L., and Doudoroff, P., 1967, "Influence of oxygen concentration on the growth of juvenile largemouth bass," *J. Fisheries Res. Board Can.* 24(3), 475-494.
89. Surber, E.W., 1965, "Water quality criteria for fresh-water fishes," *Proc. 16th Ann. Conf. S. E. Assoc. Game and Fish Comm.,* pp. 435-436.
90. Surber, E.W., and Thatcher, T.O., 1963, "Laboratory studies of the effects of alkyl benzene sulfonate (ABS) on aquatic invertebrates," *Am. Fish. Soc. Trans.* 92(2), 152-160.
91 Swartley, A.M., 1938, "Extracts from report on Rogue River turbidity," in H. B. Ward, "Placer mining on the Rogue River, Oregon, in its relation to the fish and fishing in that stream," *Appendix A, Oregon Dept. Geol. Mineral Ind. Bull.* 10, 26-27.
92. Swingle, H.S., 1966, "Fish kills caused by phytoplankton blooms and their prevention," *FAO World Symp. on Warmwater Pond Fish. Cult.,* No. FR:IX/ E-12, pp. 1-5.
93. Wallen, I.E., 1951, "The direct effect of turbidity on fishes," *Oklahoma Agr. Mech. Coll. Bull.* 48(2), 1-24.
94. Ward, H.B., 1938, "Placer mining on the Rogue River, Oregon, in its relation to the fish and fishing in that stream," *Oregon Dept. Geol. Mineral Ind. Bull.* 10, 4-25.
95. Wilson, J., 1959, "The effects of erosion, silt, and other inert materials on aquatic life," *Trans. 2nd Sem. Biol. Prob. Water Pollution, USPHS Tech. Rept.* No. W60-3, pp. 269-271.
96. Woodbury, L.A., 1942, "A sudden mortality of fishes accompanying a supersaturation of oxygen in Lake Waubesa, Wisconsin," *Am. Fish. Soc. Trans.* 71(1941), 112-117.
97. Foster, R.F., and McConnon, D., 1965, "Relationships between the concentration of radionuclides in Columbia River water and fish," in *Biological Problems in Water Pollution.,* Trans. 3rd Sem. Robt. A. Taft San. Eng. Cent. USPHS Pub. No. 999-WP-25, pp. 216-224.
98. Foster, R.F., and Rostenbach, R.E., 1954, "Distribution of radioisotopes in the Columbia River," *J. Am. Water Works Assoc.* 46(7), 633-640.
99. Olson, P. A. 1961, "Effect of treatment of reactor effluent on radionuclides in fish." *U.S. At. Energy Comm. Res. Devel. Rept.* No. HW-69500, pp. 147-150.
100. Schiffman, R.H., 1958, "The uptake of strontium from diet and water by rainbow trout," *U.S. At. Energy Comm. Rept.* HW-59500, pp. 16-19.
101. Steel, E.W., and Gloyna, E.F., 1955, "Concentration of radioactivity in oxidation ponds," *Sewage Ind. Wastes* 27(8), 941-956.
102. Tsiroglou, E.C., Bartsch, A.F., Rushing, D.E., and Holaday, D.A., 1958, "Effects of uranium ore refinery wastes on receiving waters," *Sewage Ind. Wastes* 30(8), 1012-1027.

4

CARRYING CAPACITY, PRODUCTIVITY, AND GROWTH

The *carrying capacity* of a container (a pail or basket) is limited by the height of its sides and its diameter. Not so well defined, however, is the ability of an environment to support life. The term "carrying capacity" was probably first used in game management to express the *maximum* population of game animals supported by a limited range during a period covering at least the four seasons of one year.[48] Before we define carrying capacity further, it is important to distinguish between this term and saturation. An adult animal population that tends to be uniform over a wide area may reach a saturation point. Saturation point is defined as a uniform *maximum density of grown individuals* attained by a species, even in the most favorable local environments. However, saturation also implies a degree of intolerance of animals to "piling up," an interaction between individuals that may have little connection with other environmental conditions. Thus, saturation should not be confused with carrying capacity, which always implies a tendency toward uniformity over a wide area.

Carrying capacity when applied to fishes in aquatic habitats may be defined as the *maximum poundage of a given species of fishes that a limited and specific habitat may support during a stated interval of time.* Since adverse environmental factors during certain seasons might actually control the maximum poundage of fish, seasonal adversity could establish the carrying capacity. However, as fishes rarely can be seen readily, or estimated by direct observation, little is known of the effects of seasonal adversity on fish populations. We believe that food is often limiting to population size in fishes, but other factors may be of equal importance. Therefore, at present the concept of carrying capacity is largely theoretical.

CARRYING CAPACITY AND STANDING CROP

In contrast to carrying capacity, which emphasizes *maximum poundage* and a *stated interval of time,* the term *standing crop* is applied to something very definite, namely, *the poundage of a given species or complex of species of fishes present in a body of water at a specific moment.* When one drains a pond and makes a census of the fish, the census total is the *standing crop* of that pond at the time it was drained. A census of the same fish in the same pond may be taken at a later date to give a different standing crop figure, influenced, perhaps, by a change in the relative abundance of various kinds of fishes present. Still, both census figures represent standing crops of this pond. In theory, the standing crop might be lower than, equal to, or in excess of the carrying capacity of the pond.

The relationship of the actual numbers of fishes to carrying capacity and standing crop is not well understood (although, in general, large numbers of fishes are usually associated with small individual sizes of those fishes and vice versa). In theory, a body of water in which the fishes represented the greatest range of species and sizes would offer the maximum in efficient utilization of available food (Fig. 4.1), although it is

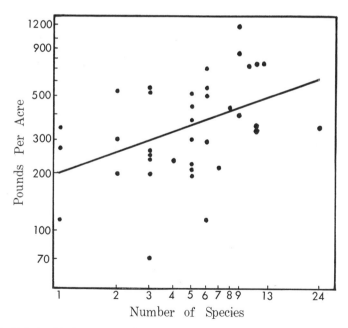

Fig. 4.1 Relationship between standing crops of fishes and numbers of species in midwestern reservoirs [from Carlander, K. D., 1955, *J. Fisheries Res. Board Can.* 12(4)].

conceivable that the kinds and relative numbers of fishes within any given size range might not be paralleled by an equal abundance of acceptable food for this size range. Thus, a part of a population representing a certain size range of one or more species might be stunted, while in the same species, other sizes might be growing rapidly.

Relation to Surface Area

The carrying capacity (in pounds) of a body of water for a specific fish population seems to be more closely correlated to surface area than depth or volume; probably the zone of light penetration at the surface produces the bulk of the food supply (directly or indirectly) for fishes. There seems to be much evidence that carrying capacity is directly related to fish food production, which, in turn, is related to the basic fertility of the water and conditions allowing the capture of this fertility by the food chain.

Experimental Testing

Little is known regarding the carrying capacity of any water for individual species of game or panfish, although European fish farmers engaged in raising commercial fishes for market have recognized that there are production limits of ponds for carp and other commercial species. It is common practice in fish farming to stock ponds with only a sufficient number of fish to produce a marketable product at the end of one or two growing seasons. Baccius[4] wrote: "It has been fully proved that a given space of earth can produce only a certain quantity; so only can a given space or quantity of water produce a certain quantity, either of vegetable matter or animalcules; and curious as it may appear, yet it is as true as curious, that by storing only the proper number of fish adapted to the water, the weight in three years will prove equal to what would have been had twice the number been placed therein, so that the smaller number produces the same weight as the larger, from a given quantity of water. By overstocking the water, the fish become sickly, lean and bony."

Swingle and Smith[71] described an experiment in which two ponds were stocked with 6500 newly hatched bluegill fry per acre in late spring, and when the ponds were drained in November, the fish had grown to an average weight of slightly less than one ounce and the total populations in each of the two ponds amounted to approximately 300 lb/acre. The fish were returned to the refilled ponds and when the ponds were drained two years later, these fish still averaged about an ounce each and the ponds' populations still weighed about 300 lb/acre.

In another series of experiments,[71] three ponds were stocked with 1300, 3200, and 6500 bluegill fry per acre. When these ponds were drained in November of the same year, the fish in the first pond averaged 4 oz, those in the second slightly less than 2 oz, and those in the third approximately 1 oz. The total weight produced was approximately 300 lb/acre in each of the three ponds.

In 1939 these same authors (Swingle and Smith[72]) published the results of other experiments dealing with the carrying capacity of waters:

"In May 1936, one pond was stocked with bluegill bream fry at the rate of 26,000 per acre, weighing 2 pounds 5 ounces. Another pond was stocked with year-old fingerlings at the rate of 13,000 per acre, weighing 180 pounds. ... When drained the following November, the former pond produced at the rate of 105 pounds of fish per acre and the latter at the rate of 92 pounds per acre. One pond gained 103 pounds per acre, while the other lost 88 pounds per acre due to overstocking."

In a second experiment, Swingle and Smith used a pond of 1.8 acres over a period of two years. In the spring of the first year (1935), they stocked 4485 fish of eight common pond species, weighing 40 lb, 9 oz. At the end of that year they collected 22,069 fish weighing 293 lb, 4 oz. Early in the spring of 1936 they stocked 236 fish of the same species in this pond, weighing 24 lb 7 oz. At the end of 1936 they collected 30,405 fish weighing 296 lb 2 oz.

In these experiments the variation in total numbers and weights of fish stocked seemed to have little effect upon the total weights of fish found in the ponds at the end of one growing season. Rather the total weights of these populations were adjusted upward or downward until they approached a rather uniform level for individual ponds, probably associated with the food-production capacities of these ponds.

More recent experiments suggested that the uniformity of the poundages of fish in the ponds reported by Swingle and Smith[72] may not always occur and that a rather wide range of variation in the poundages of fish supported by similar ponds in a given year or from the same series of ponds in successive years may be expected.

Each year, 1964—1967 inclusive, Buck and Thoits[17] stocked each of nine contiguous one-acre rectangular ponds in June with 1000 advanced carp fry from a single source and drained the ponds and took a census of the carp in October. Water was supplied to all ponds by gravity flow from the new Stephen A. Forbes Lake, Marion County, Illinois. During the first summer (1964) each of the ponds were fertilized with 450 lb of inorganic fertilizer (7-28-14) applied in small amounts at weekly intervals. No fertilizer was added in 1965 and 1966. The lack of fertilizer in 1965 and 1966 was evident in the production of carp (Fig. 4.2). In 1967, to test the potential of "maximum" fertilization for reducing variation from

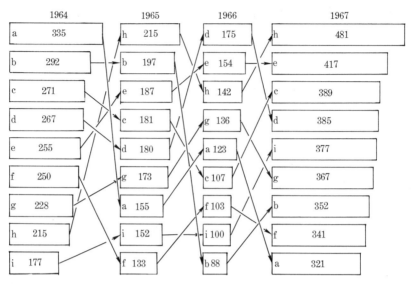

Fig. 4.2 Changing production in pounds per acre of carp in nine contiguous one-acre ponds at the Sam A. Parr Cooperative Fisheries Research Center, Marion County, Illinois. The ponds were stocked with 1000 carp fry in early summer and drained and censused in October. Ponds were labeled a, b, c, etc., in order of decreasing production in 1964, and these labels were retained for these same ponds throughout the four years of this investigation. Ponds were fertilized in 1964 and again in 1967.[17]

pond to pond, these investigators applied both inorganic (6-24-12) and organic (clover hay) fertilizers up to the maximum without creating the danger of oxygen deficiencies. This fertilization program more than tripled the poundages of carp being supported by the ponds (in October) over that of 1966, but the range of production differences in individual ponds was not reduced. The difference in the range from lowest to highest production in 1967 was 160 lb (321−481 lb); in 1964, it was 158 lb (177−335 lb), the variation about the mean in 1967 was the largest obtained in any year (standard deviation 46.9 lb). Buck and Thoits concluded that production of carp was controlled by no single dominant factor such as the relative fertility of the aquatic environment but by a complex of integrated and interacting factors. At each new season there might be entirely new combinations of random assortments of such factors. Increasing the fertility of the pond habitats to approach pollution levels, as was done in 1967, might be expected to simplify the biota by reducing it to pollution-tolerant forms. It was evident in this case that if this objective was attained it had no influence on fish-production variability.

In these experiments it was impossible to produce fish flesh to give a nearly uniform standing crop in a uniform length of time where pond basins were similar, water supply was similar, and the source and numbers of a single species were the same, with no recruitment and very little mortality. One would hardly expect to arrive at similar production and standing crops in less similar aquatic habitats stocked with varying numbers of several species of fish that were potentially more variable in recruitment and natural mortality.

When a pond is divided by a wire net that will allow the circulation of water throughout the pond but which separates the fishes to give two isolated and similar populations, the production of fishes on either side of the dividing net is more nearly similar than is to be found in two ponds of similar size separated by an earthen levee.

Wohlfarth and Moav[83] found that if the fish were at different densities on either side of the dividing fence, the denser side would produce smaller fish but higher yields. Also when the biomass (corrected for size of fish) in the two sides of the pond was unequal, the side with the higher biomass would benefit from the lower biomass of the other half. Divided ponds are also used for testing growth capacity of various stocks of fishes.

These authors recognized that the source of variation of yields of adjacent and otherwise similar ponds was the random variation in the organic development within the water.

Factors Affecting Poundage

We have seen that the poundage of fish supported by a pond or lake of constant size may vary within a range of 30 to 50% on the basis of random variation in the quality and quantity of the mass of living organisms within the water. This is only one source of variation, and the carrying capacity of a lake or pond for fish may be affected by (1) natural or artificially induced changes in the fertility of water, (2) age of water if age represents change in chemical composition, (3) fertility of watershed soil if a change brought about through erosion (reduced fertility) or artificial fertilization is carried to the pond in runoff water, (4) changes in the kinds of fishes, or in the relative abundance of certain kinds and sizes of fishes, and (5) changes in the amount of available substrate for the support of invertebrate fish-food organisms.[70]

It is well known that the highest production may be obtained by the use of those species with the shortest food chains (plant-feeding fishes).[7] However, a more efficient species at one level of management may not be more efficient at another level. For example, bluegills and channel catfish are both largely insectivorous.

"In fertilized ponds the bluegill was more efficient, yielding 560 kg/ha as compared with 370 kg for channel catfish. When placed in ponds receiving supplemental feeding, however, the order was reversed with channel catfish yielding up to 2688 kg/ha and bluegills 896 kg/ha. A partial explanation could be that the smaller mouth size of the bluegill made it more efficient in harvesting small natural foods, but this was a disadvantage when supplemental food was supplied as pellets.[70]

Fertilization. Fisheries literature contains listings of many censuses of fish populations made through the draining of ponds and lakes or through the use of rotenone. Many of these censuses have been republished by Carlander[18] in his compilations of growth and population statistics. A great deal has been published on the increase in the standing crops of fishes resulting from the use of various fertilizers.[6,16,38,67,68,73] These studies furnish evidence that various inorganic and organic fertilizers introduced into ponds will temporarily increase the standing crop of most fishes, although there is evidence that one species may be benefited through the use of fertilizer to a much greater extent than another inhabiting the same water.[38]

A pond fertilized for a period and then left without the addition of fertilizer will show a smaller standing crop of fishes each year for three or more years after fertilization is stopped.[74,17] This indicates that some of the fertilizer does not recycle in the food chain, either because it has been washed out of the pond, removed as a part of an annual crop of fish, or has become bound up in insoluble or unavailable compounds in the pond bottom. However, if the standing crop of fishes, even though reduced, is still not so low as it was prior to the beginning of fertilization, it is an indication that some of the fertilizer is still available for incorporation into the trophic cycle. This accumulation of fertilizing materials may go on as a natural process (even if a pond or lake owner adds no organic or inorganic fertilizers) through the death and decay of plants and animals in the pond, through the accumulation of dust and leaves blown in from outside sources,[35] and through the addition of nutrients leached from the soils of the watershed.

Cooper[27] has stated that the standing crops of fishes in natural lakes average 50−150 lb/acre, whereas artificial impoundments show standing crops of fishes of 200−400 lb. This difference must be related to the glacial origin of many of the natural lakes considered by Cooper, and the location of many artificial impoundments in agricultural land where natural and artificial fertilizers could collect more easily.

Chemical Basis for Fertility. Moyle[53] demonstrated a positive correlation between the presence of varying amounts of certain chemicals (total

phosphorus, total nitrogen, and total alkalinity) in the surface waters of
Minnesota lakes and the poundage of fishes supported by those lakes,
although this could be expressed as a direct relationship only in the case
of total phosphorus.

Kinds of Fishes.   Standing crops of fishes vary greatly on the basis of the
kinds of fishes making up a population and the relative abundance of each
of several kinds (Fig. 4.3). Standing crops of fishes in Illinois ponds varied

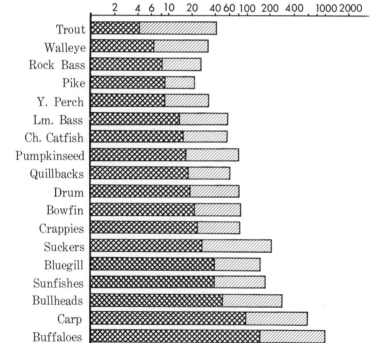

Fig. 4.3 Standing crops of named fishes in North American lakes and reservoirs. Usually
these fishes are in combination with other species. This figure furnishes a rough approximation
of the relative efficiency of the species listed [from Carlander, K. D., 1955, *J. Fisheries Res.
Board Can.* 12(4)].

from 75 lb/acre in soft-water ponds of the Ozark hills of southern Illinois, where the population was largemouth bass and green sunfish, to 1100 lb/acre in a black-soil-floodplain pond in central Illinois, where the population was composed of crappies and bigmouth buffalo. In Iowa the standing crops of fishes ranged from 28 to 1235 lb/acre.[20] Where the standing crop exceeded 300 lb, usually bullheads or buffalo were present. Populations of bluegills usually exceeded 100 lb/acre. In Kentucky, poundages ranged from 200 to 1000/acre in unfertilized ponds.[22]   In study of twenty-two Kentucky ponds containing mostly largemouth bass, bluegills, and green sunfish, Turner[78] found standing crops of these fishes varied from 70 to 770 lb/acre and averaged 385 lb. However, ponds that contained populations useful for angling averaged only 282 lb/acre of which 130 lb/acre was composed of useful-sized fish.

Jenkins[44] made an analysis of forty-two ponds in Oklahoma in which the standing crops ranged from 57 to 931 lb/acre and averaged 341 lb/acre. The average bass population was 44 lb/acre, bluegills averaged 161 lb/acre, black and white crappies 63 lb/acre, and black bullheads 161 lb/acre. Most desirable species from the standpoint of harvestable-sized fish were largemouth bass, channel catfish, and warmouths; then came redear sunfish, bluegills, and green sunfish. A number of ponds for which censuses have been taken one or more times show the influence of kinds of fish upon the standing crop. Ball,[5] repoisoning Ford Lake (Michigan) for a second time, found 2.4 times the weight of fish which had been recovered when the lake was poisoned ten years previously. In the earlier census, the yellow perch was dominant in the population whereas in the latter census, the bluegill was dominant. Ball concluded that the difference in the poundage of fish in the two censuses was due to the fact that the perch is largely piscivorous in its feeding habits, whereas the bluegill is largely dependent on invertebrates for food and thus is closer to the primary food chain.

A census of Fork Lake, a pond of 1.38 acres in central Illinois, was taken at the beginning of a cropping experiment when an undesirable population of fish was poisoned, and again four years later when the pond dam was washed out.[11] At the time of the first census, Fork Lake contained 5350 fish weighing 774 lb or 561 lb of fish per acre. By weight, carp and bigmouth buffalo made up 47.5%, bullheads (plus four channel catfish) 41.2%, and largemouth bass and panfish, 6.3%. At the time of the dam failure, an estimate of the population was 10,300 fish weighing 260.9 lb or 189.1 lb/acre. By weight, 64.7% of the population was largemouth bass and 35.3% bluegills. This population had been subjected to heavy wing net-fishing for bluegills. The earlier population containing carp, buffalo, and bullheads was 2.85 times as heavy as that composed of bass and bluegills.

Censuses of Duck Pond (3.05 acres), an isolated part of an old flooded strip-mine in Vermilion County (Illinois), were taken at two widely separated times. At the time of the first census in 1940, the pond contained 11,269 fishes of 30 species weighing 2051 lb or 672.5 lb/acre. The population was composed of 3.0% bass, 12.2% pan fish, 0.6% catfish, 23.5% coarse fish (largely quillbacks and carp), and 60.7% forage fish (gizzard shad). In a second census made in 1945, the population consisted of 3450 fishes of 18 species weighing 689.1 lb or 229.7 lb/acre. This population was composed of 2.6% largemouth bass, 33.1% pan fish, 1.3% catfish, 41.0% rough fish, and 22.0% forage fish (gizzard shad). The large difference in the total poundages of fishes in the two censuses is difficult to explain. There were more pounds of bass in the first census (62.4 lb as compared with 18.2 lb) and more pounds of pan fish (251.2 to 205.2 lb). However, the large differences were in the poundages of rough fish (479.8 lb in the first census, 282.2 lb in the second) and forage fish (1245.0 lb of gizzard shad in the first census, 150.0 lb in the second). Apparently at the time of the second census, the populations of coarse fish and gizzard shad were considerably below the carrying capacity of the pond for these species.

Arrowhead Pond, an artificial pond of 2.6 acres on the grounds of the Illinois State 4-H Club Camp, University of Illinois Allerton Estate near Monticello, Illinois, was stocked in 1948 with 22 fingerling bass, 26 adult bluegills, 7 adult warmouths, and 103 black bullheads. Censuses of this pond were taken by drainage in the springs of 1950, 1952, and 1953, and during October 1955 (Table 4.1); populations of the four species that were becoming overabundant were reduced prior to restocking.

The four censuses of Arrowhead Pond showed a range of standing crops from 164.3 to 254.5 lb/acre. The total poundage was lowest when the bass were the most numerous and highest when bluegills and bullheads were abundant. All of these fish except the warmouths appeared to be in competition, each species ready to "take over" the pond if an oppurtunity should arise.

A census of the fish population of Ridge Lake (central Illinois) has been taken by draining nine times in the past 27 yr.[12,13] Numbers and weights of fish per acre taken in these censuses are listed in Table 4.2. The time interval between each of the first six censuses was 2 yr; between the sixth and seventh censuses, 3 yr; between the seventh and eighth censuses, 3 1/2 yr; and between the eighth and ninth censuses, 3 yr (because the lake was not restocked after the fall 1959 census until the spring of 1960). Each September, 1951 through 1955 inclusive, the water level of Ridge Lake was lowered to reduce the surface area during the fall months so that the fish populations exposed in the 1953 and 1956 censuses were hardly comparable to the others. Table 4.2 shows that after 1945 the population

Table 4.1   Numbers and Weights of Largemouth Bass, Bluegills, Warmouths, and Black Bullheads Taken in Four Censuses of Arrowhead Pond, Illinois State 4-H Club Camp, Monticello, Illinois

| | 1950 Census | | 1952 Census | | 1953 Census | | 1955 Census [a] | |
	Number	Weight (lb)	Number	Weight (lb)	Number	Weight (lb)	Number	Weight (lb)
Largemouth bass	81	52.2	1057	102.1	210	60.0	1019	46.6
					728	133.8 [b]		
Bluegills	6392	395.1	2584	251.3	2108	171.6	389	38.3
Warmouths	28	3.1	417	24.7	436	42.1	546	24.6
Black bullheads	1672	211.2	63	51.2	30	14.8	2260	344.9
					7	4.8 [c]		
Totals	8173	661.6	4121	429.3	3519	427.1	4214	454.4
Per acre	3143	254.5	1585	165.1	1353	164.3	1621	174.8

[a] Outlet valve of pond inadvertently opened at night by parties unknown; fish collected from stream channel throughout several hundred yards below outlet. Probably some large bass and large bluegill taken by poachers.
[b] Smallmouth bass moved into Arrowhead Pond for wintering October 1952 to March 1953.
[c] Six green sunfish weighing 1.0 lb and 1 carp weighing 3.8 lb.

was composed largely of bass and bluegills. No bluegills were stocked until 1944, a year after the 1943 census. Warmouths were stocked in 1949 and channel catfish, in small numbers, in 1951 and 1955. Neither was numerically very abundant because of low success in reproduction; in fact, only a few young catfish were observed in the last three censuses. A few bullheads, green sunfish, carp, and minnows entered from the small feeder stream or came upstream over the spillway during floods. Hybrid sunfish were stocked instead of bluegills in 1960 after the lake was drained in the fall of 1959 and left dry over the winter of 1959—1960. Lake chubsuckers were also stocked in 1960.

Table 4.2 shows that no two censuses were very similar, either in numbers, or pounds of fish per acre. The poundage of bass in 1943 when almost no other fish were present was exceeded slightly by only two subsequent censuses. Exclusive of the drawdown period, the lowest poundages of bass appeared in the 1947 and 1959 censuses when the bluegills were most abundant, both in numbers and in pounds per acre. Bluegills larger than about 2.5 in. ranged in number from 440 to 5400/acre and in weight from 58 to 193 lb/acre.

The standing crops of fish recorded in the 1947, 1949, 1951, and 1959 censuses (which are most nearly comparable to one another, with both bass and bluegills present and no drawdowns) ranged from 140 to 256 lb/acre. The highest poundage (256) represented more than an 80% increase over the lowest poundage (140).

After each census, *all of the bass of useful sizes for angling were returned to the lake,* and the bluegill populations were drastically reduced, usually to less than 200 per acre of the larger fish. The population after two, three, or four growing seasons (1959 census) reflected the struggle for dominance between the bass and bluegills. From Table 4.2 one is led to believe that fall drawdowns of the lake affect both species: the bass through a poundage decrease with little change in numbers, the bluegills through a decrease in both numbers and poundages, but with a more severe effect on numbers. The use of the drawdown as a management practice will be described in Chapter 6.

The nine censuses of Ridge Lake paralleled the four censuses of Arrowhead Pond in exposing what appears to be competition, primarily between largemouth bass and bluegills in which the bass would rather quickly lose out except for the artificial culling of bluegills on each census. Ridge Lake is a highly favorable habitat for bluegill reproduction and survival, but poor in nutritional resources for bluegills of desirable sizes.

Table 4.2   Number and Weight of Largemouth Bass, Bluegills, and Other Fish Per Acre, in Nine Draining Censuses of Ridge Lake, Coles County, Illinois

Census Year	Largemouth Bass Number	Largemouth Bass Total Wt (lb)	Bluegills Number	Bluegills Total Wt (lb)	Other Fish Number	Other Fish Total Wt (lb)	Totals Number	Totals Total Wt (lb)
1943	265	48.2			2	0.5	267	48.7[a]
1945	91	39.6	559	7.0	42[b]	25.7[b]	692	72.3
1947	139	31.5	3702	193.3	37	31.6[c]	3878	256.3
1949	113[d]	50.4[d]	1095	86.9	6	2.9	1215	140.2
1951	84	49.9	2887	105.2	61	8.7	3032	163.8
1953[e]	116[e]	26.6	440	58.2	55	32.0[f]	610	116.9
1956[g]	132	37.5	1010	119.9	52[h]	42.1[h]	1194	199.6
1959[i]	138	31.1	5453	161.7	135[j]	54.5[j]	5724	247.2
1963	366	46.7	5031	135.4	473[k]	58.8[k]	5870	240.9

[a] Only largemouth bass stocked; other fish indigenous to Dry Run Creek watershed.
[b] Black bullheads; 19 averaging 1.2 lb each per acre; plus a few green sunfish.
[c] Nine pounds of black bullheads and about 22 lb of carp per acre.
[d] Most satisfactory bass population from the standpoint of angling.
[e] This population had been subjected to two September drawdowns to expose 69% of the surface area.
[f] Channel catfishes at 27.8 lb/acre and warmouths.
[g] This population had been subjected to three September drawdowns to expose 35% of the surface area.
[h] Mostly warmouths and channel catfishes.
[i] After four growing seasons of stable water levels.
[j] Channel catfishes, warmouths, and carp.
[k] Lake chubsuckers, warmouths, and channel catfishes.

Growing Season. Swingle and Smith[73] state: "After the fish used in stocking have spawned once, more small fish are present than can be adequately supported by the food that the pond is producing. Hence a pond rapidly reaches its maximum carrying capacity, usually within one year."

The length of the fish-growing season in the southern part of the United States may be more than 10 months, whereas in the northern states it may be less than 4 months (Fig. 4.4), and northern lakes and ponds may be covered with ice from 3 to 5 months. The length of the growing season affects the time required by a population of fishes to approach the carrying capacity of an unpopulated body of water. Ball[6]

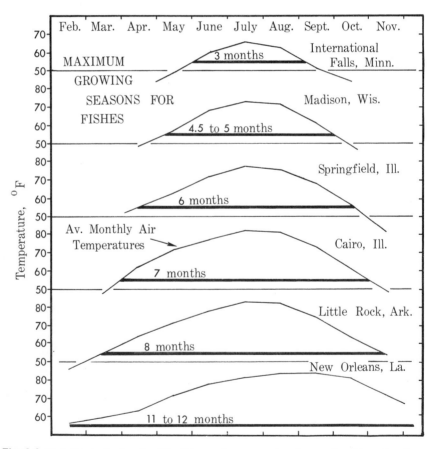

Fig. 4.4 Variation in the length of the fish-growing season, based upon the observation that growth in warmwater fishes is very slow at temperatures below 55° F (records from U.S. Weather Bureau, 5-yr average).

found that the total weight of fish recorded at the end of the third year did not vary greatly from that of the second year. This indicates that two growing seasons may be required for a population to approach the carrying capacity of a body of water in the northern part of the United States.

Other Factors Related to Standing-Crop Size. The relationships between the standing crops of fishes and certain environmental and fish population characteristics have troubled fishery biologists for years. Recently, using regression methods, Carlander[19] attempted to determine whether certain environmental factors may affect standing crops of fishes. He found *(1)* no relationship between standing crop and lake area; *(2)* an increase in standing crops with decreasing average depths (may not be entirely significant); and *(3)* a significant increase with increasing hardness of the waters. There was also an increase in standing crop with an increase in number of species present (Fig. 4.1).

As stated previously, Moyle[55] was able to show that the standing crops of fishes in Minnesota increased with increases of phosphorus, nitrogen, and total alkalinity.

Undoubtedly the standing crop of fishes is also related to the abundance of aquatic organisms acceptable for food and the availability of these organisms to the fishes. For bluegills, which are omnivorous in their feeding habits, these organisms are largely primary consumers such as the cladoceran *Daphnia* and dipterous larvae, although some amphipods, ostracods, and copepods are usually present along with all of the major lenitic insect groups.[34] Primary consumers greatly outnumber secondary consumers (such as dragonfly nymphs, water mites, and beetle larvae) in the diet of bluegills, which probably reflects the greater abundance of primary consumers. However, there may be a lack of correlation between the frequency of occurrence of specific organisms in bottom samples and their frequency of occurrence in the bluegill stomachs, suggesting that bluegills either select certain organisms or there are differences in the availability of various organisms to bluegills. Analyses of fish stomach contents suggest that most kinds of fishes have preferences for certain foods for varying periods of time, after which they make radical changes in their diets. But no one knows whether the selection of certain kinds of foods over other kinds represents choice or availability, whether the sudden changes are the result of satiation for the food or its sudden unavailability.

Fish of Useful Sizes. In passing judgment on the value of a fish population for sport angling, it becomes necessary to set up arbitrary standards for fish of useful sizes as opposed to those too small to be utilized by anglers if the fish are to be eaten. Immediately, we enter an area of controversy among fishery biologists as well as among fishermen. In 1939, Illinois biologists[15] set up arbitrary standards for useful sizes in some common panfish and catfish: "6 inches or longer for bluegills, and other sunfish, 8 inches or larger for black and white crappies, 7 inches or larger for bullheads, and 12 inches or larger for channel catfish." At that time, the length limit of 10 in. for largemouth bass was still in force in Illinois; however, a bass should be 9 in. or longer before it is large enough for table use. In some states bluegills of over 5 in.[6,68] and bass over 7.2 in. were considered of edible sizes, and bullheads were considered to be of an edible (or saleable) size in Michigan at approximately 7 in. total length.[7]

Walleyes and northern pike are too small to be useful unless the walleys are about 12 or 13 in. long and the northern pike 16 to 18 in.

The decision as to what constitutes a fish of useful size might better be made by the fishery biologist rather than the fishing public. Just because the fishing public will take 5-in. bluegills does not mean that they would still do so if enough bluegills of 6 in. or larger were available to satisfy their desire for fish. In taking 5-in. bluegills, fishermen are demonstrating that the 5-in. length is the minimum size for which they can find use. This should not be the goal of the fishery biologist.

Fish management should be able to produce fish of such sizes that the sporting aspects of fishing are satisfied and the end product (in this case the fish) is large enough for table preparation. When the head, fins, and tail are removed from a 6-in. bluegill, the part remaining is barely large enough to make an attractive morsel. A 5-in. fish would scarcely be of interest, unless bones were cooked sufficiently to be eaten without separation from the flesh. Even then the work of cleaning and scaling is large for such a small return. The only reason for recommending a minimum crappie size of 8 in. is that these fish have small bones that are almost impossible to separate from the meat in fish smaller than 8 in.

As mentioned above, the potential angling value of a fish population may be defined on the basis of numbers of fish of useful sizes that are present in a population. A large standing crop of fishes may mean nothing from the aspect of potential angling if it is divided into units too small to be usable.

FISH PRODUCTION

Definition

The term *production* may be defined as the sum of all organic matter added to a defined organic unit (a fish population, for example) in a unit of time, regardless of whether or not all of the unit remains alive at that time. Production may be expressed in various units such as wet or dry weight of biomass, nitrogen content, or calorific content, of which the latter is preferred.

Primary productivity is the total amount of plant material synthesized[64] in the form of periphyton, planktonic algae, or macrophytes, some of which cycles through the food chain until it produces fishes. During the transfer of energy through an energy cycle, only a small percentage of the food consumed is used for fish growth in each successive step. The rest may be used as an energy source or may not be used in the chain of consumers leading to fishes. Much is not consumed at all. Thus only a small fraction of primary production finds its way into fish production, which accounts for the difficulty in showing direct correlation between high or low primary production and high or low fish production.[50]

Applied to a fish population the term production generally denotes *the weight of fish flesh added during a specified period.* For example, if a new pond containing no fish were stocked in March with 1500 bluegill fry weighing a total of 1.0 lb and in November when the pond was drained 200 lb of bluegills were collected, the fish production for that period would be 199 lb plus an additional poundage of fish that had been lost through natural causes during the season. In addition, flesh added to fish that later died and decayed or were eaten by predators must be included in a total production estimate. If this same pond were restocked in March of the next season with 203 lb of bluegills and drained in November, with a population weighing 204 lb, the production the second year would be 1 lb plus a poundage lost as above.

The term "production," therefore, is more definitely associated with yield than with standing crop because the removal of fish through natural mortality and fishing leaves food and space for expansion of the population to an extent comparable to that which has been removed. This replacement comes about through recruitment of new individuals and the addition of flesh to the fishes already present. Production may be influenced by the same forces that affect the magnitude and variability of the standing crop, and for that reason production may be as variable, but where a population of fishes is exerting pressure on the habitat, the forces of expansion are almost but not quite controlled. In warmwater environments absolute control of sunfish recruitment appears impossible until a situation develops in which numbers have increased with no further expansion of biomass, and the individuals of the population are actually losing weight.[81] Under conditions of high density of individuals in limited space, production is less than at intermediate densities.[81]

Food Conversion

Various kinds of fishes are able to convert foods (of several kinds palatable to them) into flesh at various rates. Maximum efficiency in food conversion is attained when food is available for consumption at a rate between maintenance requirements and the maximum a fish is able to eat in a specified period. When food is scarce, a fish may expend too much energy in finding the food, and, therefore, be unable to approach maximum efficiency. Where food is superabundant, the fish may consume more than it can digest and assimilate so that a loss of efficiency results.

Thompson[75] stated that at 70°F, 2.5 lb of minnows are required to produce one pound of bass. When larger amounts were fed to the bass, the food was used less efficiently and conversion values were 3.8 for largemouth bass and 4.5 for smallmouth bass.[81]

Markus[49] has shown that the rate of digestion in largemouth bass is very slow at temperatures below 65°F, but that it increases rapidly between 65 and 90°F. Molnar and Tolg,[51] also working with largemouth bass, discovered that the greatest increase in rate of digestion occurred between 5°C (41°F) and 10°C (50°F) (Table 4.2), and that there was a linear relationship between the logarithms of time and temperature (Table 4.3). Thompson[75] used Markus' temperature—digestion rate curve along with mean monthly temperatures at each of seven different localities within the range of largemouth bass in the United States to compute the total quantity of minnows which a 10-in. bass could digest in a year at each of these locations. Since the maximum yield is probably proportional to the total of potential digestion, it may be possible to show the relationship between carrying capacity and potential yield at different latitudes. Carrying this idea further, Thompson published a table showing the theoretical effect of latitude on potential annual sustained yield (Table 4.4).

Relation to Standing Crop

There appears to be an inverse relationship between production and the standing crop of fishes, that is, when the standing crop is low, production is high and when the standing crop is high, production is low.

Actual data on the relationship between production (as expressed by fish yields) and the standing crops of fishes are as yet inadequate to test

Table 4.3 Relationships Between Time and Temperature in the Digestion Rate of Largemouth Bass. 51[a]

	5°C	10°C	15°C	20°C	25°C
Hours to empty stomach	110	50	37	24	19
Standard deviation	12.90	6.87	8.29	4.22	2.21
Duration of emptying stomach as a percentage	100	45.6	33.7	21.5	17.0

a From Molnar and Tolg.[51]

Table 4.4   Effect of Latitude on Annual Yield as Estimated From Mean Monthly Temperatures of Different Localities[a]

Locality	Latitude	Maximum Annual Yield as Percentage of Carrying Capacity
Vilas County, Wisconsin	46° North	21
Madison, Wisconsin	43° North	39
Urbana, Illinois	40° North	50
Cairo, Illinois	37° North	74
Memphis, Tennessee	35° North	86
Jackson, Mississippi	32° North	102
New Orleans, Louisiana	30° North	118

[a] From Needham, J.G., 1941, *A Symposium of Hydrobiology,* The Univ. of Wisconsin Press, Madison, Wisconsin.

Thompson's theories as expressed in table 4.4. Where data on yields and standing crops are available for comparison, there are other factors that obscure a clear relationship, such as fishing pressure, apparent uncooperativeness on the part of fish, known differences in food chains, etc. For example, the yields of bass at Ridge Lake were influenced by the intensity of fishing but more so by the presence or absence of available foods;[12] even in years when the highest yields were taken (about 65 or 70% of the available weight of bass in the lake), there was no indication that these yields reduced potential yields for following seasons because the rate of production or "surplus production"[28] increased to compensate for these high yields.

A recent study of a smallmouth bass population in a gravel-pit pond[14] that produced hook-and-line yields of more than 100 lb/acre for two successive years, and 80 lb/acre in the third year, suggests that the maximum annual yield of fish in the region of central Illinois may be nearer 100% of the carrying capacity than 50% as given by Thompson (Table 4.4). The smallmouth bass yield from this pond for any one season was almost wholly dependent upon fish spawned during the two preceding years. When a census of the population was taken after four years of high yields, the standing crop at the beginning of the fifth year (fish caught by fishermen in April, May, and early June plus the fish taken in a June census of all remaining fish) was approximately 100 lb/acre, which is considered relatively high for this kind of fish in this type of water (gravel pit) in central Illinois.

Largemouth bass are less predictable than are smallmouth bass. Certainly, the fishing pressure was heavy enough at Onized Lake (Illinois),[10] in 1939 and 1940 to produce a catch of fish by hook-and-line methods, large enough to tax the production capacity of that body of water. The yield of largemouth bass here was 53.0 lb/acre in 1939 and 19.8 lb/acre in 1940. The weight of bass caught in April, May, and June of 1941, when added to the weight of bass taken in the total fish census of June 24, 1941, suggested that the standing crop of bass at the beginning of 1941 may have been between 50 and 60 lb/acre or about 2.5 times the weight of bass taken in 1940 when the total fishing pressure exerted on the lake was 1647 man-hours per acre. On the basis of the 1939 yield of 53.0 lb/acre, the carrying capacity of Onized Lake for bass could be estimated to lie between 50 and 100 lb/acre, which is anything but specific. However, the fact that yields of largemouth bass are influenced largely by factors other than angling pressure makes it unsafe to estimate its turnover, production, or carrying capacity in a mixed population of fishes.

Bluegill yields from Onized Lake for 1939 and 1940 were 174 and 66 lb/acre, respectively. The estimated standing crop at the beginning of 1941 was around 153 lb/acre, which must have been considerably under the carrying capacity of Onized Lake for bluegills. More than 6500 bluegills were taken in the final census (June 24, 1941), which was more than 3200 per acre, a sufficient number of active digestive tracts to convert food to flesh quickly if an excess of food (over maintenance needs) was available.

These feeble attempts to unravel the basic relationships between standing crops, observed yields, and productive capacity in populations composed of several species of fishes emphasize the need for more data on fish populations composed entirely of one species.

Estimating Production

Many attempts have been made to estimate the fish-production potential of lakes on the basis of physical and chemical factors.[52,53,57,60,39,40,62] These attempts were based on complete censuses of the fishes of some small ponds, sport-fishermen catch data on intermediate-sized waters, and commercial fishing yields from large lakes. Production was shown to have correlation with depth, area (both positive and negative, depending on the author), carbonate alkalinity, and length of the food chain. In a recent paper Hayes and Anthony,[40] using Hayes' Productivity Index, have shown that there are significant positive relationships between production and the three factors of area, depth, and alkalinity. Ryder[62] estimated fish production of north-temperate lakes by using the regression of yield on mean depth and total dissolved solids. He related fish production in pounds per acre per year, with a morphoedaphic index (M. I. = T/D where T = dissolved solids and D = mean depth in feet) and obtained a straight-line relationship when he plotted the logs of fish production and logs of morphoedaphic indexes. Such studies are useful to estimate production on a broad basis, but can scarcely be applied to individual lakes.

For more specific information, a fairly close estimate of total production of fish flesh in small lakes may be obtained for one or two growing seasons provided the fish are tagged or marked when released at the beginning of the period, and are collected by draining for a census at the end. In the final census, marked fish are counted to determine natural mortality; fishing mortality within the period must be measured through a creel census. Marked fish in the "draining" census are weighed individually to calculate the gain in flesh made during the period. Unmarked fish are weighed, as they also represent production.

Total production equals the sum of the following: *(1)* flesh gained by recaptured marked fish; *(2)* flesh produced by new recruits entering the population; *(3)* flesh gained by fish lost through natural mortality; and *(4)* flesh gained by fish captured by anglers.

An estimation of flesh gained by marked fish eventually lost through natural causes may be made if one assumes that these fish remained alive for half the period in question. Under this assumption their gain per individual would equal one-half that of marked fish of a comparable size range. Loss of production through natural deaths among new recruits is an unknown quantity, and it might or might not represent a very large poundage of fish flesh. Estimated production in long-lived species is probably more accurate than that in short-lived species because the annual turnover (recruitment and death rate) is smaller. Using the method outlined above for bass in Ridge Lake (Illinois) with a period limit of two years, the gains are as follows: in the 1941-1943 period, 58.5 lb/acre; in the 1943-1945 period, 34.2 lb/acre; in the 1945-1947 period, 37.2 lb/acre; in the 1947-1949 period, 59.8 lb/acre; and in 1949-1951 period, 53.5 lb/acre.[10] However, these estimates of production for two-year periods cannot be used to estimate the maximum production for a single year.

RELATIVE PLUMPNESS OF FISH

In analyzing the success of a population of fish, one is struck by variations in the conditions between individuals of the same species as well as between species. This is pronounced when, for example, trout from high mountain lakes which contain rather sterile water and in which the feeding period is short are compared with trout from lower, more fertile habitats, where the feeding season is comparatively longer.

In waters which contain several species, the variation in condition or plumpness is usually greater between species than between individuals within a species; the bass in a lake may be in good flesh while the blue-gills may be thin; at any specific time the variation in condition within a species may not be large. Larger differences may be noted at other times of the year, or even over longer periods, the latter situation perhaps reflecting long-time changes in food availability, or changes in population density.

General word descriptions of condition are likely to be subjective, and not clear to others interested in this phenomenon. For this reason several methods have been devised for converting condition to a numerical value which, although it may be meaningless in itself, may present an index which allows for a more objective comparison between populations either on a geographical, time, or species basis.

Methods of Measuring Condition

All of the methods devised thus far roughly correlate the surface (as expressed in linear measurement) with the volume (as expressed in weight). By relating length to weight, formulas have been developed, the solutions of which are numbers which represent *condition factors* and which stand for a *measurement of relative plumpness*. A plump fish of a given species and length will show a higher factor than a thin individual. By calculating this factor for an adequate sample of a species under specific describable conditions, such as a limited length range, a specific body of water, and a specific time of the year, and averaging these calculations one may arrive at an *average condition factor* for the species, under the experimental conditions which pertain. This allows the fisheries biologist to make objective interspecific and intraspecific comparisons under different geographical or time situations.

All the methods thus far developed are similar, differing in such things as whether the standard length (tip of snout to base of tail excluding the tail fin) or total length is used, whether the English system or the metric system is used, and the size of the multiplying factor which is used to minimize the possibility that the solution be expressed as a decimal fraction. Hile[41] developed a *Coefficient of Condition (K)* expressed as follows:

$$K = \frac{100 \text{ x weight in grams}}{\text{length}^3 \text{ in centimeters (standard)}}$$

A system developed and used in England was invented by E. M. Corbett, and issued by the Salmon and Trout Association, Fishmonger's Hall, E.C. 4, London (undated). This method used total length in inches and weight in pounds and ounces, although fractional lengths were converted to tenths of inches, and fractional ounces to hundredths of pounds. A multiplier of 100,000 was used to eliminate completely the decimal point and give only whole numbers in the solution. This formula is as follows:

$$\text{Condition Factor, C.F.} = \frac{100,000 \text{ x weight in pounds}}{\text{length}^3 \text{ in inches}}$$

Cooper and Benson[26] developed another method in which:

$$\text{Coefficient of Condition, } R = \frac{10 \text{ x weight in grams}}{\text{length}^3 \text{ in inches}}$$

Still another method which is useful to workers in the United States develops an Index of Condition, C, using the English system of weights and measures (expressing fractional inches in tenths and fractional pounds in hundredths). Total length is used, and the multiplying factor is an intermediate 10,000.[76] This formula is expressed as follows:

$$\text{Index of Condition, } C = \frac{10,000 \text{ x weight in pounds}}{\text{length}^3 \text{ in inches}}$$

When calculations are made by this method using the lengths and weights of largemouth bass between 5 and 15 in. total length, an index of condition of 3.5 - 4.5 denotes a fish in poor flesh, 4.6 - 5.5 one of average plumpness, and 5.6 - 6.5 a very fat fish. In fish such as the bluegill which is laterally compressed and deep in proportion to length, the index of condition figures is different. In bluegills 5 to 8 in. in total length, a figure of 7.0 or below denotes poor flesh, 7.1 - 8.0 normal plumpness, and above 8.0 usually good plumpness.

Condition Cycles

There is some evidence that certain kinds of fish show annual condition cycles associated with the four seasons of the year. These may be related to reproduction, seasonal feeding cycles, or other unknown causes. If one were able to expose a "normal" cycle of condition for larval fish, immature fish, mature males, and mature females of a given species, one might compare this empirical condition cycle with the condition of a population of fish of the species in question collected from the same water in different years, or at different times of the year, or less accurately, fish of that species collected from different waters at different times of the year.

LeCren[89] calculated such an empirical condition cycle for the perch *(Perca fluviatillis L.)* in Lake Wendermere (England) which he called the

Relative Condition Factor and expressed by the formula:

$$K_n = \frac{W}{aL^n}$$

Where W is the average weight of a length group of fish, a is a constant, and n is an exponent representing the cube relationship between length and weight (usually between 2.5 and 4.0).

The length-weight relationship was first expressed graphically by plotting the observed lengths and weights as a dot diagram on double logarithmic graph paper. The points for fish having the same length-weight relationship will lie in a straight line with some scatter due to individual variation. This line represents the logarithmic form of the preceding equation, that is,

$$\log W = \log a + n \log L,$$

where n represents the slope of the line and $\log a$ its position. Changes in the value of n can usually be readily observed as changes in slope.

LeCren[89] found that upon using large samples of perch of various lengths and categories collected over the seasons, n varied with the several categories (mature males, immature fish, etc.) but appeared to remain the same for each category throughout the seasons; while the constant a varied in a uniform manner over the seasons, indicating a regular seasonal cycle.

By making use of this *Relative Condition Factor,* it was possible to distinguish between and measure separately the influences on condition of length and other factors that are not readily separated when using other types of condition factors. The seasonal cycle of perch condition showed a maximum high in September and a low in early spring; this appeared in both immature fish and in mature ones where the effects of gonad development could be cancelled out.

Cycles of condition associated with seasons have been reported for several Centrarchids. For example, the bluegills in a pond in central Illinois[11] showed high condition during May and early June at the beginning of the spawning season, followed by a gradual drop in condition throughout the summer and fall until a low point was reached in October or November. Over the winter, the condition gradually rose, but the most rapid rise took place in early spring, during the months of March, April, and May, when bluegills were feeding heavily on dipterous larvae and cladocera and their gonads were enlarging in preparation for spawning. Some of the loss in condition of bluegills, beginning in late May and extending through the summer, was undoubtedly associated with the long spawning season of this fish, which began in May and extended into early September.

A seasonal condition cycle for white crappies in a lake in the same region[37] was quite different from the bluegill cycle of condition. In Lake Decatur (Illinois), crappies of 6 to 8.5 in. usually showed their highest condition in the fall and winter, and the condition of these fish dropped sharply from early spring to June or July. Following a low point, usually in July, the condition of the crappies began to rise in August and continued to rise until winter.

Several studies on condition in largemouth bass suggest that these fish show no seasonal cycle of plumpness. There is evidence, however, that the average condition of a bass population may change rather suddenly with changing feeding conditions.[27] For example, in 1941 at the time of an extensive natural die-off of the pondweed, *P. foliosus,* in a pond,[11] the bass had an average condition of 5.00. After the plant die-off began, they became very fat and their average condition rose to 6.15.

Condition and Growth Rate

High condition of fishes is usually associated with rapid growth,[27] but this is not always so, particularly where fish are living in very soft water in which there may be such a shortage of calcium as to affect the growth of the skeleton of the fishes. In some other locations, relatively rapid growth seems to be associated with moderately low condition, at least during a part of a year.

Use of Condition in Management

An important value of condition factors is in their use in determining the well-being of a fish population in which one has a special interest, either as a sport fisherman or as a lake owner. Often, when fish are in poor condition (exclusive of lows of normal cycles), it may mean overpopulation or disease. A high condition may mean a sparse population or a high temporary food supply. When either of the extremes of condition may appear, the situation may bear investigation.

The condition of any component of a population of fishes is related to the relative abundance of food for that group and this relative abundance of food may be related to high natural food production of the aquatic habitat, but more especially to the number of individuals among which a specific quantity of food must be divided. Rapid growth, high condition, and large average size of a species may be essentially functions of natural or artificial cropping, because the type and intensity of cropping that occurs may determine the amount of food an individual fish is able to gather in a given period of time.

Average condition figures have been calculated for most species of freshwater fishes of interest to anglers.[18] These condition figures may be used by lake and pond owners, as well as fishery biologists, as a basis for comparison with the condition of fish that are members of a specific local population.

GROWTH

Most kinds of warm-blooded vertebrates (birds and mammals) attain an adult size in a rather definite length of time, after which there is little change, except for the addition of fatty tissues if feeding conditions are good. On this basis a coyote would never be expected to grow to the size of a wolf or a gray fox to the size of a coyote.

However, growth in fishes is unlike growth in most warm-blooded animals in that it is relatively indeterminate and follows no exact pattern of attaining a maximum size in relation to a specific length of time. Thus, although every species of fish probably is characterized by a maximum length and weight, this size is so much greater than the *average* attained by any given individual of any selected species in most waters that fishing contests with prizes for the largest examples of each kind of fish have flourished and will continue to flourish as long as man is interested in angling.

Growth stoppage in fishes is not associated with sexual maturity as it is in most warm-blooded animals, and fishes continue to grow throughout life, although growth is relatively slower in larger and older fishes than in smaller and younger ones.

Some fish show annual cycles of efficiency in maintenance and growth. For example, northern pike follow maintenance and growth cycles that are highest in late June [maintenance was 45 mg of minnow *(Phoxinus phoxinus)* per gram of pike], declining in August and September until a fairly stable maintenance rate of 25 mg/g is reached in October.[45] Maintenance and growth continue at low levels until April when the rates of both again increase to the June maximum rates. During peak growth periods and after the maintenance requirements are satisfied, 1 g of food will produce 0.437 g of pike. Compared to some other fish, pike show rather low maintenance requirements and relatively high conversion of food to flesh.

The question sometimes arises as to what freshwater fish grows the fastest. According to Netsch and Witt[54] , the longnose gar *Lepisosteus osseus* might be near the top of the list. Young of the year gar raised experimentally for 52 days ate and digested an average of 9.1% of their body weight each 24 hr. These fish increased in length at a rate of about 3 mm per day, and their food conversion factor was 2.34. These authors estimated that these longnose gars were growing up to six times faster than other common large freshwater fishes.

Growth of Fish in New Waters

Fish often grow rapidly and reach exceptionally large sizes when first introduced into new waters. This superior growth is largely due to an abundance of food and space and possibly an absence of parasites and other biological forces which may slow down the rate of growth in waters where these fish have been present for some years.

One of the most interesting of introductions was that of the importation of certain game and food fishes from Europe and North America into the waters of South Africa.[1,2,3] The importation of trouts into South Africa started with the brown trout in 1892 and the rainbow in 1897. Exotic fishes introduced included carp from England in 1896, European perch in 1915, and the North American largemouth bass from an English hatchery in 1927. Fish imported to South Africa from the United States were smallmouth bass from Maryland in 1937, bluegills from Maryland in 1938, and spotted bass from Ohio in 1939. The live-bearing top minnow gambusia appeared in South Africa in 1936 from an unknown source. Following are some records of catches of warmwater fishes of known ages that had been stocked in South African waters:

A largemouth bass caught on January 19, 1949, by Mr. D. S. Stewart and reported by Mr. H. Manson, Hon. Secretary to the White River Angling Society, was 23 in. long, girth 17 in. and weight 7 lb. 10 oz. Growth calculations from scale measurements indicated a growth to 9 in. the first year, then 15 in., 18, 20, 21, 22, and 23 in.; its age was 7 years plus part of an additional summer. Official record showed that largemouth bass from Paarde Vlei Lake, Somerset West, in July, 1936, weighed 5 lb, 1 oz, was 19 in. long, and was stocked in 1930 as a fingerling. These bass-growth records are similar to examples of maximum growth for largemouth bass in northern United States (increment of about one pound per year), but no example of largemouths of 8 to 10 lb, which are fairly common in the United States, has been recorded for South Africa, This may be related to the genetics of the original stock, the source of which (in the U.S.) is unknown.

A bluegill was caught on March 17, 1947, by Mr. H. F. Palmer that weighed 3 lb, 1 oz in a dam (pond) at Butha Buthe in Basutoland. "The fish could not swim upright in 9 inches of water." It could not have been more than 8 years old because the first bluegills were imported in 1938 and the first fingerlings were distributed in 1939. At least one bluegill exceeding three pounds is recorded for the United States, so here again maximum sizes may be comparable in South Africa and North America.

Effects of Starvation

Under conditions of near-starvation, fishes may remain the same size for an indefinite period, and such fish usually live longer than normal.[25] After months or years of life on a maintenance diet, they still retain the capacity to grow rapidly to large sizes should an abundance of food suddenly become available.[77] This was demonstrated with bluegills when fish 3 to 5 years old and averaging 0.08 lb each were moved into a renovated pond where food competition was probably absent (Fig. 4.5). The fish grew to an average size of about 0.40 lb each in one growing season, although they had been badly stunted in previous years.

For some unknown reason, the eyes of fishes continue to grow even when the fishes are subjected to stunting. The effect of this phenomenon is that badly stunted fish have larger than normal eyes in relation to their body size. Thus it is often possible for one who handles many fish of a selected species to tell which individuals and populations are stunted without studying growth rings on their scales. Conversely, rapidly growing fish will have eyes that appear unusually small for the size of the fish.

Factors Affecting Rate of Growth

There are many factors that affect the rate of growth of fishes. Some are very important and are quite apparent; others are integrated with several other factors so that they are much less obvious.

Population Density.   This is one of the most obvious factors related to growth (Fig. 4.6). The relationship is inverse in that an increase in population is associated with a decrease in growth rate.[32,80,27,55]

Genetic Composition.   Little is known of the genetic makeup of any kind of fish except for a few species that may be considered as domestic (goldfish, carp, etc.). Growth must have a relationship to genetics and a maximum potential rate of growth must be recognized for any species.

Length of the Growing Season.   The rate of metabolism of fishes varies with water temperature, and as the seasons change the water temperatures change and the rate of metabolism changes. In the temperate zone winter are periods of low metabolism and almost no growth for fishes. The length of the growing season for fishes, which rather closely parallels

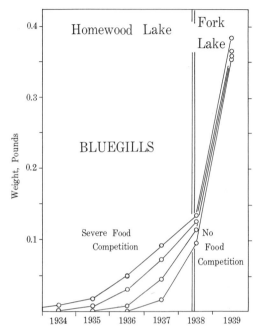

Fig. 4.5 Three to five-year-old stunted bluegills from Homewood Lake (Illinois) more than tripled their weight in one season after release in Fork Lake where adequate food was available (from Bennett, G. W., Thompson, D. H., and Parr, S. A., 1940, *Illinois Nat. Hist. Surv. Biol. Notes* 14).

the agricultural growing season but is somewhat shorter, limits the annual growth cycle to a definite period of weeks or months (Fig. 4.4). The amount of growth actually taking place during this time depends upon a combination of factors, the most important of which, is the availability of food resources. At one extreme, a fish might approach the maximum rate of gain for a given species in a location where food was abundant and the growing season was less than 3 mo; at the other extreme, a fish might remain at a constant weight throughout a growing season of 8 or 9 mo if it consumed no more than a maintenance diet. There are aspects of a short growing season that may have an important bearing on management practices. In some Michigan waters where the length of the growing season does not exceed 5 mo and ice and snow covers the lakes for 4 or 5 mo, bluegills seldom mature sexually until the third summer of life. [8] This means that all phases of management that bear any relationship to time of sexual maturity of the fishes must be adjusted accordingly.

Viosca[79] described the growth of warmwater fishes—largemouth bass, spotted bass, and crappies—in the International Paper Company reser-

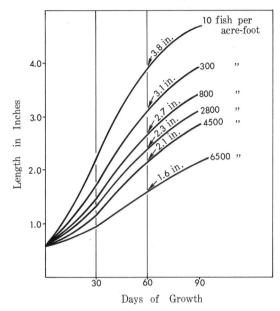

Fig. 4.6 Relationship between growth and growing time, in days, of small walleyes in ponds. Population density in fish per acre-foot is shown. The growth curves reflect in part the relative density of the fishes [from Dobie, J., 1956, *Progressive Fish Culturist* 18(2)].

voir at Springhill, Louisiana, where the growth period for these fishes is limited by draining and refilling operations rather than the length of the natural growing season. The lake basin (270 acres) is pumped full in April and May, and newly hatched fry are brought in with the water. The lake is drained in September or October to make room for waste water from the paper mill so the growing season for fry of various fishes ranges from 5.5 to 6.5 mo. Fish that enter the reservoir through the pumps as fry in April and May produce a "field day" for anglers by late summer. In 1949, largemouth bass (age group 0) ranged from 11.1 to 13.8 in. and 11.4 to 24.5 oz; spotted bass (ten times as numerous as largemouth) ranged from 6.1 to 10.6 in. and 1.4 to 11.6 oz. In 1950, crappies reached sizes as large as 9.8 in. and weights of 12 oz in 6.5 mo. These crappies averaged a weight increment of 1.8 oz per month, which must be very near their maximum rate of growth. The accumulation of nutrients from the decayed paper waste added to the productivity of this reservoir.

Water Temperatures. The effects of water temperatures on the growth rate of fishes within the growing season may be demonstrated. Total yearly growth of 3 to 5-yr-old smallmouth bass in South Bay, Lake Huron, appeared to be related to mean surface water temperatures for the period

July through September[24] although a similar relationship could not be demonstrated for bass of the same ages in Lake Opeongo, Ontario.

When fingerling largemouth bass from Iowa were transported to Florida for a comparison of growth rate with the Florida subspecies[23] the Iowa bass grew more rapidly than the Florida bass but did not mature during the experiment, while the Florida bass became sexually mature at 9 mo. Both subspecies grew rapidly under temperature conditions that allowed growth the year around.

Optimum temperatures for the growth of fishes vary with different species and when water temperatures exceed the optimum the growth rate usually decreases. For example, when the water temperature was about 55°F brook trout consumed a quantity of minnows per week about equal to half of their body weight and grew rapidly. At 63°F the rate of feeding decreased and at 70°F feeding was reduced to six percent per week of the trout body weight.[66]

Photoperiod.   The growth rate of fishes increases as the photoperiod is increased and decreases with a decrease in the photoperiod.[30] This may explain why some fishes show maximum growth rates in spring and summer and much reduced rates in late summer and early fall, at which times the photoperiod is gradually shortened but the water temperatures are still warm enough for a high rate of metabolism.

In studying the growth of largemouth and smallmouth bass in Norris Reservoir, Jones[46] concluded that although the agricultural growing season at Knoxville, Tennessee, was almost 7 mo, the bass-growing season was only 4 mo. He assumed that because the bass stopped growing they could not grow after late September or early October, even though the water was still warm. Jones may have misinterpreted the effects of a declining photoperiod and what presumably was a temporary fall shortage of bass foods in Norris Reservoir; he assumed that these effects represented a definite bass-growing season which was much shorter than the agricultural growing season. Others have shown that bass may grow rapidly during April, September, and October in waters several hundred miles north of Norris, Tennessee, provided the water is above 60°F and an abundance of food is available.[11] This indicates that growth in bass is less influenced by photoperiod than by available food.

Water Chemistry.   The chemistry of water is the basis for its fertility and productivity; therefore it must also be related to fish growth.[32]

Physiological Relationships.   Closely related to water chemistry are the physiological relationships of the various kinds of fishes in an aquatic environment in which products of metabolism of one species may inhibit or stimulate the growth rate of others.[69,17]

Oxygen. The oxygen supply available to young fishes affects their growth rate. A high constant supply stimulates the rate of growth and a low or variable supply inhibits growth.[65]

Iron. Roeder and Roeder[59] discovered that swordtail tropical fish, *Xiphophorus hellerii* and *X. maculatus,* required iron as ferrous sulphate for normal growth.

Predator—Prey Relationship. In some populations of predatory fish the abundance and growth rate of any given year class appears to be related directly to the abundance of a year class of the principle prey species. Such a relationship was observed in Oneda Lake (New York)[33] between the walleye and perch. In contrast, a lack of sufficient predators on a prey species may result in poor growth of that species. This situation was observed in the bluegill population of Reelfoot Lake (Tennessee) over a period of more than twenty years during which bird predators were much reduced and commercial fishing for bluegills was eliminated.[63]

Local Optimum Habitats with a Large Source of Available Food. High growth rates are often discovered in very localized situations where because of some unusual source of available food a local population of fishes is growing more rapidly than the same species in less favored environments. Such a situation was observed by Peek,[56] among smallmouth bass in Arkansas. It was also seen in studies of growth of largemouth bass in Wisconsin.[9]

There is evidence, both from laboratory feeding experiments and field studies,[15] that fish supplied with quantities of one or several live foods alternate between periods (weeks) of heavy feeding with rapid growth and periods of little or no food consumption with subsequent growth stoppage. Fish, like some other animals, may find a heavy diet without variety unattractive.

In the laboratory experiments cited above, bluegills that stopped feeding were being fed earthworms at the rate of 7-8% of their body weight per day. However, other bluegills receiving earthworms in smaller quantity (3-5% of body weight per day) did not stop feeding.

A continuous study of the ecology and growth of one or several species making up a small fish population will show that there are times when certain types of food are abnormally abundant and that this abundance is often reflected in unusual growth. For example, in August 1941, a sudden die-off of heavy growths of submerged aquatic plants in a pond in central Illinois[11] was followed during August, September, and October of 1941 by a rapid growth of largemouth bass. These plants were protecting a large population of small fish which suddenly became easily available. Bass that were between 10.5 and 11.0 in. before the plant die-off, averaged 13.0 in. in October; those about 7.0 - 8.0 in. before the die-

off averaged 10.5 in. in October; and the surviving members of the current year class averaged nearly 6.5 in. by October. No comparable growth
rate increase was shown among bluegills, even though the pond developed
a bloom of plankton algae following the death of the higher aquatic
plants. In this instance, a large supply of food suddenly became available to the bass with no comparable increase in food for bluegills. The
cause of death of the rooted aquatic plants was unknown, but its effect
was highly favorable to a species of fish having little direct ecological
relationship to aquatic plants.

All of these growth-controlling factors are important, but *in the production of fishes of above average size, a large source of available food
per individual fish seems to exceed in importance the length of the growing season* (Fig. 4.5). Often a large supply of available food is present for
the few fish that are restocked in renovated lakes, and they grow pheno-
menally during the first season before population expansion has reduced
the food supply per individual fish.[36]

INTERPRETATION OF GROWTH FROM FISH SCALES

Variations in growth rates and the occurrence of growth stoppage are
recorded on the scales of fishes. When a fish is growing rapidly, the circuli (fine lines of new material) laid down on the edges of the scales are
relatively coarse and spaced far apart; on the other hand, when growth
is slow, the circuli are fine and close together. A fish subjected to a period
of starvation not only loses body flesh, but erosion with resorption of
material on the edges of the scales may also take place. However, on a
maintenance diet where the condition of a fish remains constant, there
appears to be neither increment nor erosion of the scales. Thus, the correct interpretation of the marks on the scale surface will give an accurate
growth history of a fish.

The years of a fish's life are recorded as a series of annuli or distinct
rings laid down around the focus or center of the scale, each one representing a year. The circuli are between the focus of the scale and the first
annulus and are also between the other annuli. A newly hatched fish may
be scaleless, but if it is of a scaled species, the scales soon form. Once the
fish becomes covered with scales, the number remains constant throughout life, and the scales must grow as the body grows to form a covering
for the fish. Any natural or artificial phenomenon that will stop feeding
and growth of a fish for about fourteen days or longer will be followed,
once growth is resumed, by the appearance of an "annulus," on the margin of the scales. The so-called "true annulus" was first called a winter
ring because it was not visible until new circuli were laid down in the

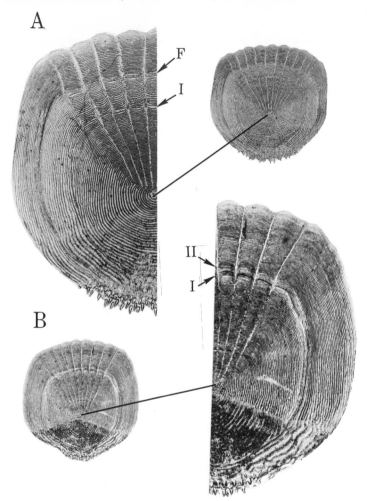

Fig. 4.7 Abnormal growth rings on fish scales. A. Yearling bluegill from Fork Lake, 1938 year class, taken September 26, 1939, age 16 mo showing well-defined annulus (I) and false annulus (F). The false annulus was formed on this scale about July. B. This female largemouth bass was 10.1 in., weighed 0.49 lb, and was taken April 20, 1941, before the 1941 annulus had formed. This is a 1938 year-class fish in which the 1939 annulus (I) and the 1940 annulus (II) are separated only in the anterior field of the scale.

spring when the fish had resumed growth. Further studies of annulus formation showed that some fishes in some locations did not begin to grow until the middle of summer[37] so that the winter ring became a summer ring. Hubbs and Cooper[43] recorded a double annulus in green and long-eared sunfishes in Michigan. They believed that the outside member of the double ring was the true annulus, whereas this outer ring

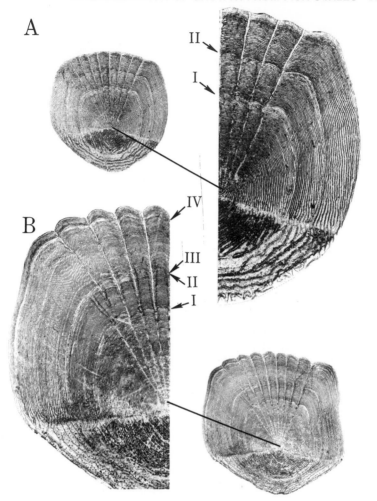

Fig. 4.8 Normal and abnormal growth rings on largmouth bass scales. A. Normal scale pattern for 1938 year-class largemouth bass in Fork Lake (Illinois) after more than two years of growth. This male bass was 9.6 in., weighed 0.45 lb, and was taken August 30, 1940. B. A 1938 year-class bass in which the second (II) and third (III) annuli coincide. This female fish was 15 in., weighed 2 lb, and was taken July 8, 1942 from Fork Lake. This could not have been a 1939 year-class fish because there was no 1939 year-class in this pond (1938 year-class original fry were sexually immature in 1939).

in actuality probably was a mark laid down during the first early peak of spawning.

The 1938-brood bluegills at Fork Lake (Illinois)[11] were growing very rapidly in 1939, and during the growing period of that year many members of this brood laid down two or three distinct "annuli" on their scales (Fig. 4.7A): formation of the true annulus was completed by the end of

May; the second annulus (false) first became visible during the latter part of June and the third annulus (false) appeared on the scales of a small percent of the population in July and August. There was no satisfactory method of separating false from true annuli,[15] other than through an intimate knowledge of the population structure. It is my belief that the false annuli appeared on the scales of the Fork Lake bluegills because they went "off their feed" for short periods.

Some abnormalities of growth, which are reflected on the scales of a fish and cause difficulty in the correct interpretation of age and growth, are:

1. False annuli. These are false rings having all of the characteristics of true annuli, but which form during the middle of the growing period and after the true annulus has formed for the current year (Fig. 4.7A).

2. Skipped annuli. The position of the annulus for one year coincides with that of the preceding year, e.g., the fish does not grow during one growing season (Fig. 4.8B).

3. Overlapping annuli. Growth in length through one growing season is very small with no corresponding increase in plumpness. The annulus for one year coincides in part with that of the next, but in part (usually in the anterior field) is separated by four or five circuli (Fig. 4.7B). Without detailed growth information, a scale reader is likely to consider the second component of the double ring as a false annulus.

4. Close spacing of annuli. Growth for one season is small and two annuli are separated entirely, but by only a few circuli. Without growth information, a scale reader is liable to consider the outer annulus as false.

Scales, spines, bones, and otoliths of fishes have been used successfully in age determinations. Studies of these parts from fishes of known ages prove that most species usually lay down a single growth ring each year. However, there are some exceptions, such as the European carp, which frequently forms extra "annuli." But even the scales of carp may be interpreted on the basis of "growth patterns" for successive growing seasons, provided a specific population is being studied intensively over a period of several years.

In the wake of the many excellent studies on the age and growth of fishes,[58,84,85,86,87,88,90] the methodology for using scales (and other structures such as ear stones, vertebrae, spines, and opercular bones that show annual rings) in an interpretation of growth, has become standardized.[18] In this chapter, *the abnormalities of growth have been stressed because the more one knows about a population of fishes the more accurate is one's interpretation of growth.* For example, Dr. R.W. Larimore found a mark on the scales of Varnard Lake warmouths[47] that corresponded in time to a period when a drag-line was dredging the shallows of the pond from which these warmouths were taken. Without a series of fish collections before and after the drag-line operation, it would have been impossible to explain the "false annulus" that appeared on the scales of many warmouths, apparently caused by the "feeding disturbance" resulting from the operation of the drag line.

There is more to reading scales than counting rings. One must become familiar with the usual variations in the marks and ridges on scales of specific species, as well as the potential for abnormalities on these scales and causes for the abnormalities.

REFERENCES

1. Anon., 1945, Inland Fisheries Department Report No. 1, Inland Fisheries Dept., Union of S. Africa, Cape Town, pp. 1-47.
2. Anon., 1947, "Claim of 'world record' bluegill," *Piscator.* 1(2), 14.
3. Anon., 1949, "Big fish records," *Piscator.* 3(9), 12-14.
4. Baccius, G., 1841, *A Treatise on the Management of Freshwater Fish,* J. Van Voorst, London.
5. Ball, R. C., 1948, "Recovery of marked fish following a second poisoning of the population in Ford Lake, Michigan," *Am. Fish. Soc. Trans.* 75(1945), 36-42.
6. Ball, R. C., 1952, "Farm pond management in Michigan," *J. Wildlife Management* 16(3), 267-269.
7. Ball, R. C., and Ford, J. R., 1953, "Production of food-fish and minnows in Michigan ponds," *Mich. State Univ. Agr. Expt. Sta. Bull.* 35(3), 384-391.
8. Ball, R. C., and Tait, H. D., 1952, "Production of bass and bluegills in Michigan ponds," *Mich. State Univ. Agr. Expt. Sta. Tech. Bull.* 231, 1-25.
9. Bennett, G. W., 1937, "The growth of the largemouthed black bass *Huro Salmoides* (Lac.), in the waters of Wisconsin," Copeia 2, 104-118.
10. Bennett, G. W., 1945, "Overfishing in a small artificial lake," *Illinois Nat. Hist. Surv. Bull.* 23(3), 373-406.
11. Bennett, G. W., 1948, "The bass-bluegill combination in a small artificial lake," *Illinois Nat. Hist. Surv. Bull.* 24(3), 377-412.
12. Bennett, G. W., 1954, "Largemouth bass in Ridge Lake, Coles County, Illinois," *Illinois Nat. Hist. Surv. Bull.* 26(2), 217-276.
13. Bennett, G. W., Adkins, H. W., and Childers, W. F., 1969, "The largemouth bass and other fishes in Ridge Lake, Coles County, Illinois, 1941 - 1963," *Illinois Nat. Hist. Surv. Bull.,* 30(1), 1-67.
14. Bennett, G. W., and Childers, W. F., 1957, "The smallmouth bass, *Micropterus dolomieui* in warm-water ponds," *J. Wildlife Management* 21(4), 414-424.
15. Bennett, G. W., Thompson, D. H., and Parr, S. A., 1940, "Lake management reports 4. A second year of fisheries investigations in Fork Lake, 1939," *Illinois Nat. Hist. Surv. Biol. Notes,* 14, 1-24.
16 Brown, W. H., 1951, "Results of varying the ratio and species combinations in stocking of largemouth black bass and channel catfish in experimental farm ponds," *Texas Game, Fish and Oyster Comm.* pp. 1-21.
17. Buck, D. H., and Thoits, C. F., and Rose, C. R., 1968, "Variations in the carp production in replicate ponds," *Am. Fish. Soc. Trans.,* 99(1), 75-79.
18. Carlander, K. D., 1953, *Handbook of Freshwater Fishery Biology with the First Supplement,* Wm. C. Brown, Inc., Dubuque, 429 pp.

19. Carlander, K. D., 1955, "The standing crop of fish in lakes," *J. Fisheries Res. Board Can.* 12(4), 543-570.

20. Carlander, K. D., and Moorman, R. B., 1956, "Standing crops of fish in Iowa ponds," *Proc. Iowa Acad. Sci.,* 63, 659-668.

21. Clark, G. L., 1946, "Dynamics of production in a marine area," *Ecol. Monographs* 16, 321-335.

22. Clark, M., 1952, "Kentucky's farm pond program," *J. Wildlife Management* 16(3), 262-266.

23. Clugston, J. P., 1964, "Growth of the Florida largemouth bass, *Micropterus salmoides floridanus* (LeSueur), and the northern largemouth bass, *M. s. salmoides* (Lacepede), in subtropical Florida," *Am. Fish. Soc. Trans.* 93(2), 146-154.

24. Coble, D. W., 1967, "Relationship of temperature to total annual growth in adult smallmouth bass," *J. Fisheries Res. Board Can.* 24(1), 87-99.

25. Comfort, A., 1963, "Effect of delayed and resumed growth on the longevity of a fish *(Lebistes retriculatus,* Peters) in captivity," *Gerontologia* 8(213), 150-155.

26. Cooper, E. L., and Benson, N. G., 1951, "The coefficients of condition of brook, brown and rainbow trout in the Pigeon River, Atsego Co., Mich." *Progressive Fish Culturist* 13(4), 181-192.

27. Cooper, E. L., Hidu, H., and Andersen, J. K., 1963, "Growth and production of largemouth bass in a small pond," *Am. Fish. Soc. Trans.* 92(4), 391-400.

28. Cooper, G. P., 1966, "Fish production in impoundments," *Mich. Dept. Conserv. Res. Develop. Rept.* 104, 1-21.

29. Cooper, G. P., and Latta, W. C., 1954, "Further studies on the fish population and exploitation by angling in Sugarloaf Lake, Washtenaw Co., Michigan," *Papers Mich. Acad. Sci.* 39(1953), 209-223.

30. Cross, W. L., Roelofs, W., and Fromm, P. O., 1965. "Influence on photoperiod on growth of green sunfish, *Lepomis cyanellus,*" *J. Fisheries Res. Board Can.* 22(6), 1379-1386.

31. Dobie, J., 1966, "Food and feeding habits of the walleye, *Stizostedion v. vitreum,* and associated game and forage fishes in Lake Vermilion, Minnesota, with special reference to the tullibee, *Coregonus* Leucichtys *artedi,*" *Minn. Fish. Invest.* (4), 39-71.

32. Eipper, A. W., 1964, "Growth mortality rates and standing crops of trout in New York farm ponds," *N.Y. State Coll. Agr. Expt. Sta. Cornell Univ. Memoir* 388, 1-67.

33. Forney, J. L., 1965, "Factors affecting growth and maturity in a walleye population," *N.Y. Fish Game J.* 12(2), 217-232.

34. Gerking, S. D., 1964, "Timing and magnitude of the production of a bluegill sunfish population and its food supply," *Verthandl. Intern. Verein. Limnol.* 15, 496-503.

35. Goldman, C. R., 1961, "The contribution of alder trees, *Alnus tenuifolia* to the primary productivity of Castile Lake, California," *Ecology* 42(2), 282-288.

36. Grice, F., 1959, "Elasticity of growth of yellow perch, chain pickerel, and largemouth bass in some reclaimed Massachusetts waters," *Am. Fish. Soc. Trans.* 88(4), 332-335.

37. Hansen, D. F., 1951, "Biology of the white crappie in Illinois," *Illinois Nat. Hist. Surv. Bull.* 25(4), 211-265.

38. Hansen, D.F., Bennett, G. W., Webb, R. J., and Lewis, J. M., 1960, "Hook and line catch in fertilized and unfertilized ponds," *Illinois Nat. Hist. Surv. Bull.* 27(5), 345-390.

39. Hayes, F. R., 1957, "On the variation in bottom fauna and fish yield in relation to trophic level and lake dimensions," *J. Fisheries Res. Board Can.* 14, 1-32.

40. Hayes, F. R., and Anthony, E. H., 1964, "Productive capacity of North American lakes as related to the quantity and the trophic level of fish, the lake dimensions, and the water chemistry," *Am. Fish. Soc. Trans.* 93(1), 53-57.

41. Hile, R., 1936, "Age and growth of the cisco, *Leucichtys artedi* (leSuer), in the lakes of the northeastern highlands, Wisconsin," *U. S. Bur. Fish. Bull.* 48(19), 211-317.

42. Hile, R., 1948, "Standardization of methods of expressing lengths and weights of fish," *Am. Fish. Soc. Trans.* 75(1945), 157-164,

43. Hubbs, C. L., and Cooper, G. P., 1935, "Age and growth of the longeared and the green sunfishes in Michigan," *Papers Mich. Acad. Sci.* 20, 669-696.

44. Jenkins, R. M., 1958, "The standing crop of fish in Oklahoma ponds," *Proc. Oklahoma Acad. Sci.* 38, 157-172.

45. Johnson, L., 1966, "Experimental determination of food consumption of pike, *Esox lucius,* for growth and maintenance," *J. Fisheries Res. Board Can.* 23(10), 1495-1505.

46. Jones, A. M., 1941, "The length of the growing season of largemouth and smallmouth black bass in Norris Reservoir, Tennessee," *Am. Fish. Soc. Trans.* 70(1940), 183-187.

47. Larimore R. W., 1957, "Ecological life history of the warmouth (Centrarchidae)," *Illinois Nat. Hist. Surv. Bull.* 27(1), 1-83.

48. Leopold, A., 1933, *Game Management,* Chas. Scribner's Sons, New York, 481 pp.

49. Markus, H. C., 1932, "The extent to which temperature changes influence food consumption in largemouth bass *(Huro floridana),*" *Am. Fish. Soc. Trans.* 62, 202-21-0

50. McConnell, W. J., 1963, "Primary productivity and fish harvest in a small desert impoundment," *Am. Fish. Soc. Trans.* 92(1), 1-12.

51. Molnar, C., and Tolg, L., 1962, "Relation between water temperature and gastric digestion of largemouth bass *Micropterus salmoides* (Lacepede), *J. Fisheries Res. Board Can.* 19(6), 1005-1012.

52. Moyle, J. B., 1946, "Some indices of lake productivity," *Am. Fish. Soc. Trans.* 76, 322-334.

53. Moyle, J. B., 1956, "Relationships between the chemistry of Minnesota surface waters and wildlife management," *J. Wildlife Management,* 20(3), 303-320.

54. Netsch, N. F., and Witt, A., Jr., 1962, "Contributions to the life history of the longnose gar, *Lepisosteus osseus,* in Missouri," *Am. Fish. Soc. Trans.* 91(3), 251-262.

55. Pardue, G. B., and Hester, F. E., 1967, "Variation in the growth rate of known-age largemouth bass [*Micropterus salmoides* (Lac.)] under experimental conditions," *Proc. 20th Ann. Conf. S. E. Assoc. Game and Fish. Comm.* pp. 300-310.

56. Peek, F., 1966, "Age and growth of the smallmouth bass, *Micropterus dolomieui* (Lacepede) in Arkansas," *Proc. 19th Ann. Conf. S.E. Assoc. Game and Fish. Comm.* pp. 422-431.

57. Rawson, D. W., 1955, "Morphometry as a dominant factor in the productivity of large lakes," *Verthandl. Intern. Verein. Limnol.* 12(1953), 164-175.

58. Regier, H. A., 1962, "Validation of the scale method for estimating age and growth of bluegills," *Am. Fish. Soc. Trans.* 91(4), 362-374.

59. Roeder, M., and Roeder, R. H., 1966, "Effect of iron on the growth rate of fishes," *J. Nutr.* 90(1), 86-90.

60. Rounsefell, G. A., 1946, "Fish production in lakes as a guide for estimating production in proposed reservoirs," *Copeia,* 1946, 29-40.

61. Rupp, R. S., and DeRoche, S. E., 1965, "Standing crops of fishes in three small lakes compared with C^{14} estimates of net primary production," Am. Fish. Soc. Trans. 94(1), 9-25.

62. Ryder, R. A., 1955, "A method for estimating the potential fish production of north-temperate lakes," *Am. Fish. Soc. Trans.* 94(3), 214-218.

63. Schoffman, R. J., 1966, "Age and rate of growth of bluegills in Reelfoot Lake, Tenn., for 1958 and 1965," *J. Tenn. Acad. Sci.* 41, 32-35.

64. Stanley, J., 1966, "Yields of California lakes," in *Inland Fisheries Management,* Calif. Dept. Fish and Game, pp. 140-143.

65. Stewart, N. E., Shumway, D. L., and Doudoroff, P., 1967, "Influence of oxygen concentration on the growth of juvenile largemouth bass," *J. Fisheries Res. Board Can.* 24(3), 475-494.

66. Stroud, R. H., 1958, *Temperature and Trout,* S. F. I. Bull. 74, p. 6.

67. Swingle, H. S., 1947, "Experiments on pond fertilization," *Alabama Polytech Inst. Agr. Expt. Sta. Bull.* 264, 1-34.
68. Swingle, H. S., 1952, "Farm pond investigations in Alabama," *J. Wildlife Management* 16(3), 243-249.
69. Swingle, H. S., 1957, "A repressive factor controlling reproduction in fishes," *8th Pac. Sci. Cong. Proc., 1953,* pp. 865-871.
70. Swingle, H. S., 1966, "Biological means of increasing productivity in ponds," *FAO World Sym. on Warmwater Pond Fish Cult., FR V/R-1,* pp. 1-14.
71. Swingle, H. S., and Smith, E. V., 1938, "Management of farm fish ponds," *Alabama Polytech. Inst. Agr. Exp. Sta. Bull.,* p. 1-6.
72. Swingle, H. S., and Smith, E. V., 1939, "Increasing fish production in ponds," *4th North Am. Wildlife Conf. Trans., 1939,* pp. 332-338.
73. Swingle, H. S., and Smith, E. V., 1947, "Management of farm fish ponds," *Alabama Polytech. Inst. Agr. Exp. Sta. Bull.* 254, 1-30.
74. Tanner, H. A., 1960, "Some consequences of adding fertilizer to five Michigan trout lakes," *Am. Fish. Soc. Trans.* 89(2), 198-205.
75. Thompson, D. H., 1941, "The fish production of inland streams and lakes," in *A Symposium on Hydrobiology,* Univ. Wisconsin Press, Madison, pp. 206-217.
76. Thompson, D. H., and Bennett, G. W., 1939, "Lake management reports 3, Lincoln Lakes near Lincoln, Illinois," *Illinois Nat. Hist. Surv. Biol. Notes,* 11, 1-24.
77. Tiemeier, O. W., 1957, "Notes on stunting and recovery of channel catfish," *Kansas Acad. Sci. Trans.* 60(3), 294-296.
78. Turner, W. R., 1960, "Standing crops of fishes in Kentucky farm ponds," *Am. Fish. Soc. Trans.* 89(4), 333-337.
79. Viosca, P., J., 1953, "Growth rates of black basses and crappie in an impoundment of northwestern Louisiana," *Am. Fish. Soc. Trans.* 82(1952), 255-264.
80. Warnick, D. C., 1966, "Growth rates of yellow perch in two North Dakota lakes after population reduction with toxaphene,"*U.S. Fish and Wildlife Serv. Res. Pub.* 9, 1-9.
81. Welch, E. B., and Ball, R. C., 1966, "Food consumption and production of pond fish," *J. Wildlife Management* 30(3), 527-536.
82. Williams, W. E., 1959, "Food conversion and growth rates for largemouth and smallmouth bass in laboratory aquaria," *Am. Fish. Soc. Trans.* 88(2), 125-127.
83. Wohlfarth, G. W., and Moav, R., 1966, "The relative efficiency of experiments conducted in undivided ponds and in ponds divided by nets," *FAO World Symp. on Warmwater Pond Fish Cult., FR,VI/E-3,* pp, 1-6.
84. Carlander, K. D., 1956, "Fish growth studies: Techniques and role in surveys and management," *North Am. Wildlife Conf. Trans.* 21, 262-274.
85. Creaser, C. W., 1926, "The structure and growth of the scales of fishes in relation to the interpretation of their life history, with special reference to the sunfish, *Eupomotis gibbosus," Univ. Mich. Mus. Zool. Misc. Pubs.* No. 17, 83 pp.
86. Gerking, S. B., 1965, "Two computer programs for age and growth studies," *Progressive Fish Culturist* 27(4), 59-66.
87. Hile, R., 1941, "Age and growth of the rock bass *Ambloplites rupestris* (Raf.) in Nebish Lake, Wisconsin," *Trans. Wisconsin Acad. Sci.,* 33, 189-337.
88. LeCren, E. D., 1951, "The length-weight relationship and seasonal cycle in gonad weight and condition in the perch (*Perca fluviatilis* L.)," *J. Animal Ecol.* 20, 201-219.
89. Van Oosten, J., and Hile, R., 1949, "Age and growth of the lake whitefish, *Coregonus clupeaformis* (Mitch.) in Lake Erie," *Am. Fish. Soc. Trans.* 77(1947), 178-249.

5

REPRODUCTION, COMPETITION, AND PREDATION

Whether or not a fish species is successful depends on its ability to reproduce itself within the limitations imposed upon it by a hostile environment. Reproduction is subject to the end results of *(1)* inter- and intraspecific competition for parts of habitats that may be in limited supply and *(2)* by actual predation between closely associated and interrelated forms. This predation may not be restricted in its direction; it may change with the ages of the organisms involved and with other factors in the environment. When populations appear to be static, reproduction and environmental demands are balanced. Only a slight change in either reproduction or environmental demands may cause a species to be eliminated or to overpopulate a habitat. Reproduction produces new individuals not only to replace the loss of mature animals but also to enter the trophic cycle, i.e., the young fishes feeding on plants and lesser animals and then in turn being devoured by other larger ones. Thus, the products of *reproduction* push the population *toward expansion.* In opposition, the forces of *competition* (interspecific and intraspecific) and *predation* tend to *counteract population expansion.* These interrelationships are normal and necessary to the well-being of the population and to its evolution to fit the aquatic habitats.

Geological evidence has shown that fishes have existed on the earth's surface for many millions of years. Yet in spite of the fact that they have furnished food for many forms of vertebrates, e.g., fishes, amphibians, reptiles, birds, and mammals including man, and many kinds of invertebrates, they must be considered as one of the more successful groups of vertebrates. A number of species of fishes alive today are scarcely changed in form from those found as fossils in deposits representing the Devonian period, 360 million years ago.

REPRODUCTION

Most of the vertebrates that prey upon fishes are more recent (geologically speaking) than their victims. As predators of fishes evolved, accumulated, and became more efficient, the reproductive potential of fishes must have evolved to produce larger numbers of young to compensate for greater and greater losses through predation until the reproductive potential became very high. Less than 100 years ago in the United States man began to dominate other vertebrates, and he purposely or inadvertently upset the normal relationships between fish and their habitats. The high reproductive potential of a fish without an accompanying high environmental demand no longer was an asset to a fish species and too many individuals survived for the habitat to support. This high reproductive potential of fishes remains unchanged; its significance must be appreciated in any plan for the management of a species.

Breeding Potential of Fishes

Leopold in his *Game Management** stated that the breeding potential of a species is dependent on its minimum breeding age and the number of young per year. Common warmwater fishes usually become sexually mature at one, two, or three years and produce numbers of eggs in an inverse relationship to the amount of protection that they give the sex products after they are released. In species such as the European carp which offer no protection to its sex products, a single female may produce several hundred thousand eggs. In contrast, the stickleback, which builds a complicated nest of plant material and then actively guards it, may lay a few hundred eggs. Between these extremes are the sunfishes depositing their eggs in depressions which they have made in the river or lake bottom and then attempting to guard against the predatory activities of their own kind and other kinds of aquatic predators. Here the number of eggs is intermediate, ranging from 5000 to 10,000 in largemouth and smallmouth basses to 20,000 to 50,000 in the crappies and larger sunfishes. Jenkins[71] cited an example in which fifty adult crappies with a breeding potential of 590,000 produced a population on one-year-olds of 200,500.

[1*]Leopold, A., 1933, *Game Management*, Chas. Scribner's Sons, 481 pp.

Actual counts of eggs produced by various kinds of warmwater fishes have demonstrated that the breeding potential of every species is more than adequate to replace the losses of the adults that produced them. For example, one pair of bluegills may easily produce 50,000 to 75,000 fertile eggs in a lifetime. The survival of only two of these embryos, through development, hatching, and growth to sexual maturity, is necessary to replace the loss of the parents and retain a static population.

In order to investigate the success of natural reproduction of some common nest-building fishes, Carbine[28] siphoned off the fry from the nests of largemouth bass, rock bass, common sunfish, and bluegills in Deep Lake, Oakland County, Michigan, and made counts of the number of fry collected from each nest. He found that numbers of largemouth bass fry varied between 751 and 11,457, with an average of 4375 per nest (5 nests); rock bass from 344 to 1756 with an average of 796 per nest (9 nests); common sunfish from 1509 to 14,639 per nest (2 nests); and bluegills from 4670 to 61,815 per nest with an average of 17,914 (17 nests). On the basis of the number of nests being used by these centrarchids during the 1938 season, the minimum number of fry produced in Deep Lake (surface area 14.9 acres) was estimated as follows: bluegill 6,610,000. common sunfish 1,518,000; rock bass 46,000; and largemouth bass 164,000. As this lake probably would not support a fish population of more than 8000 to 10,000 individuals of useful sizes, it is obvious that any one of the four species listed above produced enough young fish in 1938 to overpopulate the lake. Counts of bluegill and largemouth bass eggs made by other investigators were within the range of numbers given by Carbine.[39,81,83]

Other pan and sport fishes produce large numbers of eggs. Female warmouths ranging in size from 3.5 to 7.0 in. contained from 4500 to more than 50,000 eggs per fish.[90] The female walleyes in Lake Gogebic (Michigan)[50] ranging from 16.0 to 22.7 in. yielded from 37,000 to nearly 155,000 eggs per fish. On the average, 34 walleye females from Gogebic yielded 28,112 eggs per pound of body weight. Wisconsin muskellunge from 25 to 53 in. in length were reported to produce 22,000 to 180,000 eggs per fish at each spawning, and northern pike are known to produce about the same numbers.[107]

As mentioned above, only a small fraction of the young produced by any fish species survives. For example, in the spring of 1941, Ridge Lake, Coles County, Illinois (18 acres), was stocked with 100 sexually mature largemouth bass.[13] Thirty-eight schools of young were observed in early June, each containing at least 2000 individual free-swimming fry; a conservative estimate of the total was 76,000. When the lake was drained in March 1943, almost two years later, slightly more than 4000 of these young bass were still present, and even with this number, Ridge Lake was overpopulated with bass.

Heaviest losses of young fishes probably take place during the first few weeks of life when the fish are very small and relatively helpless. This appeared to be the case in studies on the spawning of northern pike in Houghton Lake (Michigan) in 1939 and 1940.[29] Weirs were installed to catch fish in the spawning migration of northern pike into the ditches tributary to the north bay of Houghton Lake and to trap the returning young pike from the ditches. In 1939, 125 females and 280 male adult pike migrated into the ditches, and 7239 young pike were caught migrating toward the lake. In 1940, 65 females and 81 males migrated into the ditches, and only 1495 young migrated out. In both years, newly hatched pike fry were about equally abundant in the ditches, but in 1939 minnows and perch were allowed to migrate into the ditches on only one day, while in 1940, minnows and perch could enter the ditches during the entire period of the investigation. In 1939, 58 young per spawning female returned, whereas in 1940 this dropped to 23.

Predation on young fish begins in the embryo stages and continues through one or two growing seasons for the slow-growing or small species. Predators large enough to use fast-growing large species for prey may be relatively rare after the first few months of growth.

However, predation does not always control year class strength, as was discovered by Kramer and Smith[83] in studying the early life history of largemouth bass in Lake George (Minn.). In this location the size of the surviving year class of largemouths was more dependent upon the amount of wind action that caused mechanical damage to eggs and yolk-sac fry than on any other factor.

Spawn Production and Number of Spawners

If natural reproduction of fishes is so successful, why have populations of many important game and food fishes continued to dwindle? The answer is obvious; although many more young of these fishes are produced than a body of water may support, the survival rate of these young between the time that they first begin to develop and the time when they in turn are of spawning age is inadequate to balance the natural attrition of the breeding adults. Fish embryos and newly hatched fry are vulnerable to many decimating forces: sudden temperature changes, disease, absence of adequate food, wave action, turbidity, aquatic fungi, fluctuating water levels, and a host of aquatic animals that would use them for food. The world is a hostile one for very small fish.

Carbine's study of the apparent predation by perch on the young of northern pike, described above, is a concrete example of interspecific

predation which may have been the most important cause for a reduction of northern pike in Houghton Lake. In situations where the survival of spawn of an important species of fish is inadequate to maintain a
population of these fish, no amount of stocking will help because *(1)*
hatchery-reared fish small enough to be supplied in quantity are more
vulnerable to predation than naturally spawned fish of the same sizes;
(2) fish too large to be preyed upon by most kinds of predators can be
reared in such small numbers in hatchery ponds that they are insignificant when they are released in large natural waters (Houghton Lake has
an area of 20,044 acres).

If habitat conditions are such that a species is disappearing from an
area, stocking of any size of fish will not change this habitat and will
do no good. Habitat demands may vary from very high to very low,
while breeding potentials remain uniformly high. The end result of these
counter forces is to obscure the relationship between number (or poundage) of spawning adults and the number of young produced (Fig. 5.1).
For example, suppose that in a given spawning season the survival rate
of bass fry (to a length of one inch) from 10 spawning pairs was 90% and
the average number of eggs produced was 2000 per female. Thus,

$$10 \times 0.90 \times 2000 = \quad 18{,}000 \text{ fry produced}$$

In another year, the spawn of 100 pairs of bass producing an average of
2000 eggs per female was subject to such heavy losses that the survival
rate was only 5%. Thus,

$$100 \times 0.05 \times 2000 = \quad 10{,}000 \text{ fry produced}$$

In these illustrations, twenty spawners in the first spawning season
produced more 1-in. fry than the 200 spawners in the following season.

In comparing annual estimates of schooling bass fry with the numbers
of sexually mature bass known to be present in Ridge Lake in each of
ten years (1941 - 1951), I was unable to show a correlation between number of spawners and the fry produced other than an indication of a negative relationship, e.g., in several years when the numbers of spawners
were smaller than average, the numbers of fry produced were larger
than average.[13] Others have found little correlation between the number of brood fish stocked in ponds and the strength of the resulting
year classes (Fig. 5.1).[79,101,103,131]

Age and Sexual Maturity

The age of a fish at the time of sexual maturity varies with its size and
the latitude of its habitat. According to Swingle and Smith,[140] bluegills

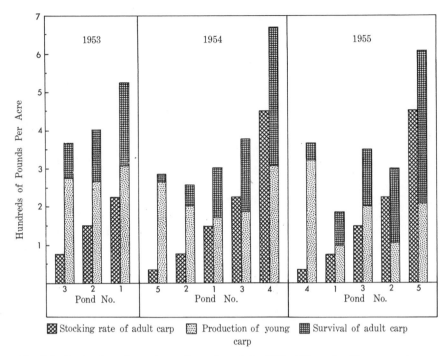

Fig. 5.1 Production of carp in small ponds at Lake Mills, Wisconsin. These experiments demonstrate that there is no consistent relationship between the number of adult fish stocked (pounds) and poundage of young carp produced. The poundage of young brought forth by the smallest poundage of adults usually equal or exceed the poundage of young produced by larger numbers of adults (pounds). Also, the total poundage of all carp produced in individual ponds is not consistent from year to year [from Mraz, D., and Cooper, E. L., 1957, *J. Wildlife Management* 21(1)].

as small as 1/2 oz have been known to spawn when 1 yr old (in Alabama) and where food was extremely plentiful, young bluegills weighing 2 oz spawned when only 5 mo old. Largemouth bass as small as 6 oz and crappies as small as 2 oz have been known to spawn when 1 yr old (Alabama).

Eschmeyer[51] stated that some of the largemouth bass taken from the Clinch River below Norris Dam (Tennessee) would probably have spawned at 1 yr of age.

Farther north in central Illinois, James,[70] making a histological study of the gonads of largemouth bass and bluegills concluded that while a few male bass produced small numbers of sperm at 1 yr, none of the females produced mature eggs. Many of the yearling bass that James studied were more than 10 in. in length and weighed 0.50 - 0.60 lb each. The larger and medium-sized 1-yr-old bluegills produced mature eggs or sperm, but those less than 2 in. contained only small oocytes, indicating that they were sexually immature.

North American centrarchids imported to South Africa have had their seasons reversed and some showed rapid attainment of sexual maturity.[59] Smallmouth bass reproduced at 17 mo and bluegills at 7 mo when their seasons were reversed south of the equator. These fish originated in Maryland and Ohio.

In the north central states, most of the common game and pan fish require one year (bluegill, rock bass), two years (crappie, largemouth, smallmouth), or three years (northern pike, walleye) to reach sexual maturity. In general young fish growing rapidly will become sexually mature sooner than those growing slowly.[52] The age of a fish at sexual maturity is important in planning stocking rates for new or renovated lakes or ponds.

Sex Ratios

Most studies of sex ratios on isolated populations of freshwater fishes have shown that more males than females are to be found among the young of the year, but among older fish the dominance of females is so great as to leave little doubt that the males die off much faster than females. This is not only true in the pike and perch families but also in some of the nest-building centrarchids.[56]

External Sex Characteristics

In many kinds of freshwater fish, secondary sex characteristics develop as the adult fishes approach the spawning season. These characteristics make it possible to separate the sexes, either through differences in coloration (Fig. 5.2) or through structural differences (such as tubercles on the heads of some male cyprinids or a complete change in body appearance in some male channel catfish and salmonids). In many species, male secondary sex characteristics are so definite as to make accurate sexing of males easy; in others only long experience can develop proficiency in sex determination.[42] An ability to separate the sexes may be useful and important when stocking new or renovated waters because it allows one to set up balanced or unbalanced sex ratios of selected kinds of fish; also, one may be relatively certain of the sex of individuals released in ponds for the production of hybrids between two closely related species.

Fig. 5.2 Sexual dimorphism in hybrid crappies. During the spawning season the male crappie (lower) becomes very dark, particularly on the head, ventral side, and fins.

Spawning

Nearly all of the warmwater fish begin spawning during the first six months of the year; some have short spawning periods lasting only a few days; others may spawn for one or two weeks, while still others may spawn intermittently over a period as long as three or four months.

Among the earliest spawners are the northern pike, walleyes, yellow perch, and muskellunge, which spawn at water temperatures of 40-60°F. Walleyes spawn at 45 - 56°F, yellow perch a little after walleyes, and muskellunge at 48-56°F.[44] Northern pike were reported by Franklin and Smith[152] to spawn at 52 - 63°F in the marshes of Lake George (Minn.). The pikes, walleyes, and perch begin spawning soon after the ice goes out in the early spring.

The nesting habits of the sunfishes (including largemouth and small-mouth basses and black and white crappies) are among the most interesting of warmwater fishes. Breder[22] described the nesting behavior of many members of this family. Some nest in groups, such as bluegills, which select areas of shallow water 1 - 4 ft in depth and exposed to the direct rays of the sun for at least a part of the day. Here they scoop out their shallow nests often located so close together that only a narrow ridge separates one nest from others surrounding it. Bluegills have a long nesting season; Fork Lake (Illinois) bluegills became ripe in late May and some ripe fish were collected every month thereafter until mid-September. Bluegills usually show two peaks of spawning activity, the first and largest at the beginning of the spawning season and a second peak a month or so later, usually in early July in the north. However, some bluegill repro-duction continued throughout most of their long spawning period. Some warmouths were found to be in spawning condition from about May 15 until August 15 in central Illinois[90] although no fish were completely spent until September 1.

Both largemouth bass and crappies have short spawning seasons com-pared to bluegills and other sunfish, although the spawning period of crappies is somewhat longer than that of the largemouths.[56,68] Crappies and largemouths begin spawning in late May or June in the north, but somewhat earlier in the south. The water temperature seems to have an important effect in initiating spawning activity of all the centrarchids. Also, sudden drops in water temperature associated with periods of cold spring weather may stop all spawning activity and sometimes kill the embryos already in the nests.

Bullheads and catfish also sweep out nests and offer protection to embryos and young fish. Channel catfish spawn during the period from late May to mid-July in Missouri,[97] with a peak occurring in early June and one in late June. Bullheads usually spawn during late May and early June as far north as central Illinois and Iowa; flathead catfish spawned during the month of May at the San Marcos, Texas hatchery[61] when the water temperature was 72 - 75°F.

Artificial inducement for spawning may be brought about by injecting pituitary extracts into fishes in near spawning condition. Clemens and Sneed[38] made extensive use of pituitary materials to spawn a number of kinds of warmwater fishes, primarily goldfish, zebra fish, and chan-nel catfish but to a lesser extent carp, green sunfish, largemouth bass, white crappie, and flathead catfish. The success of pituitary injections was indicated by stimulating ovulation or by increasing seminal plasma. Using a variety of donors, 29 interspecific and intergeneric injections and 25 interfamilial injections were successful.

Hybridization

Slastenenko[120] lists 167 known natural interspecific fish hybrids. Since his publication appeared three additional pike hybrids (Esocidae) have been identified,[41] making a total of 170. About 90% of these hybrids were found in fresh waters and approximately two-thirds of the freshwater hybrids were found in North America. Hubbs[66] believed that this high frequency of hybridization in North America was related to the recent

establishment of much of the existing fish fauna (in the Miocene, Plio-
cene, and Pleistocene epochs).

Hybrids must be considered to be potentially important because of
their physiological characteristics, which Nikolyukin[106] lists as *(1)* faster
growth rate, *(2)* greater vigor, *(3)* higher adaptive plasticity, and *(4)* more
rapid sexual maturation. Use tests for sunfish hybrids in fishing experiments indicate that they are fast growing, aggressive, and more easily
caught than the parent species.[32,34] In several sunfish hybrids soon disappeared from a mixed population of pure species bass and sunfish.
One of the factors bringing this about may have been their aggressive
biting which in one case resulted in overfishing, and/or the reduced
breeding potential of first generation (F_1) hybrids as compared with the
parent species. There also was reduced hybrid vigor of most second and
third generation (F_2 and F_3) hybrids.

Naturally produced hybrids are common among the members of the
sunfish family but their continued presence in any water depends upon
a continuing source of crosses between parent types.[33,67,85,95,115,141] Why
such interspecific crosses should occur is unknown but Dr. William F.
Childers believes that they may be related to certain suboptimum spawning conditions, which could be created by temporary high turbidity, or
they might occur when nesting is attempted in dense stands of rooted
submersed aquatic vegetation. Any situation where the participants in the
spawning act are forced to bypass preliminary and species-isolating
behavior patterns might result in hybrid production.

Natural hybrids may be produced by isolating male sunfish of one
species with females of another closely related species. Among bluegills,
green sunfish, red-ear sunfish and warmouths this is only known to occur
with certain combinations, namely, red-ear males with green sunfish
females,[34] green sunfish males with bluegill females (Fig. 5.3), and warmouth males with green sunfish females.[32] None of the other combinations of these four species produced young when pairs were isolated in
ponds, although Ricker[115] and Krumholz[85] obtained bluegill-red-ear hybrids by isolating male bluegills and female red-ears in a pond.

There is evidence that eggs of most centrarchids will develop at least
into advanced embryos if fertilized with the sperms of each of the other
species, including the largemouth, the smallmouth, and the spotted basses[33,123,150] (Fig. 5.4). Many of these crosses are completely viable and
have been made in fishery laboratories and the young raised to maturity
in ponds. Most of the hybrids are not sterile but the sex ratios of the first
generation hybrids may vary from 97% males in bluegill x red-ear crosses
to 16% males in crosses of green sunfish males with warmouth females.

Fig. 5.3 Green sunfish male x bluegill female hybrid sunfish taken from a pond near Potomac (Illinois). This fish weighed 2 1/8 lb. These hybrids were identified as bluegills by fishermen. Most exceptionally large sunfish are hybrids.

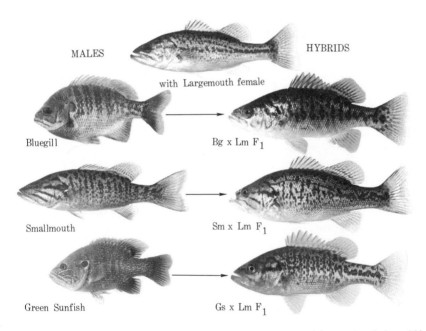

Fig. 5.4 When eggs from a female largemouth bass were separated into units of about 500
and were fertilized in the laboratory with sperms from a male bluegill, a male smallmouth
bass, and a male green sunfish, the embryos developed, hatched and grew into the hybrids
shown. Smallmouth x largemouth hybrids became sexually mature and spawned when one
year old (from an unpublished manuscript by Dr. William F. Childers).

Hybridization has been recorded in a number of families of freshwater bony fishes including several that have little or no importance to sport fishing, such as the buffalo fish and sucker family (Catostomidae), the minnows and carps (Cyprinidae), the killifishes and topminnows (Cyprinidontidae), and the livebearers (Poeciliidae). There are, however, several families that include members considered to be important game fishes in which hybrids of these game species may increase their angling values in some manner.

Disregarding the trout-salmon hybrids which will not be considered here, one of the most potentially important of .the hybrids is that produced by crossing the marine striped bass [*Roccus saxatilis* (Walbaum)] with the freshwater white bass [*Roccus chrysops* (Raf.)]. The marine species can live and sometimes reproduce in fresh water.[7,20,94] Although reciprocal crosses have been made, the more successful was that in which striped bass eggs were fertilized with white bass sperm. Individuals of this cross grew to 1.7 lb in 1 yr, 3.5 lb in 18 mo, and 4.8 lb in 2 yr. These fish may become important in large reservoirs not only as a sport fish but as a potential means of controlling excessive populations of gizzard shad and threadfin shad. In one experimental stocking of 35,000 fry it was estimated that 2,500 fish averaging more than two pounds each were taken by anglers.

Five members of the pike family, including muskellunge *(Esox masquinongy* Mitchill), northern pike (*E. lucius* Linn.), chain pickerel *(E. niger* LeSueur), redfin pickerel (*E. americanus americanus* Gmelin), and grass pickerel (*E. a vermiculatus* LeSueur), were used to make twenty reciprocal crosses of which seventeen were successful to some degree.[26] Several successful attempts have been made to cross northern pike with muskellunge. This cross grew faster than the muskellunge and the percent of hatched eggs was larger than in a pure parent fertilization made at the same time.[21,45,47] Most authors believe the muskellunge-northern pike cross is sterile.

Several catfish hybrids have been described. At least one cross, that of the channel catfish [*Ictalurus punctatus* (Raf.)] female and the blue catfish [*I. furcatus*(LeS.)] male, is potentially economically important in fish farming and in pay-fishing establishments because the hybrids grow sufficiently faster than either parent to produce fish of useful sizes in one growing season.[53]

McConnell[100] reports an interesting experiment in the production of an all-male population of the African mouthbreeder, *Tilapia mossambica* (Peters), by crossing two isolated strains. These fish have been stocked in ponds in Arizona to replace sunfish populations composed mainly of bluegills and red-ear sunfish unsatisfactory for angling. The tilapias superficially resemble the sunfishes in size and shape and like the sunfishes are prone to overpopulation.

The development of an all-male population of so-called Malacca hybrids, which eliminates the potential for overpopulation, is produced by pairing a male *T. mossambica* of the Zanzibar strain with a female of the same species but of the Java strain. The resulting progeny are all males and show more rapid growth than the parent stocks.[63,65] Once the hybrid tilapia reach a weight of 4 oz or more they are readily taken on hook and line using earthworms for bait. As will be described in Chapter 6, *T. mossambica* is very useful as a biological control for aquatic vegetation although it is killed by water temperatures below about 45°F.

Selective Breeding

Changes through selective breeding have been accomplished in carp, goldfish, and some other species of "domestic" fish raised in fish-farming operations. Most of this work has been done in Asia and Europe, where fish are raised for food or display. These fish are usually not exposed to "wild" conditions; when they escape to compete with wild fish they either die or revert to their original wild type as the European carp has done in this country.

Fish that have been raised in hatcheries for many years have probably been subjected to unintentional as well as intentional selection. Hatchery personnel may consciously choose the heaviest-bodied and fastest-growing fish for egg production; at the same time they may unconsciously select the fish that are most easily handed, e.g., those that have lost most of their "wildness." This type of selection has made hatchery trout somewhat less desirable than wild fish[146] for sport fishing and has reduced their ability to survive under "wild" conditions.

Attempts at selection for improving species of warmwater fishes apparently have accomplished little. However, unintentional selection may be operative in heavily fished, isolated, small lakes and ponds that receive no stock from outside sources. Fish in waters that receive 500 or more hours of fishing pressure per acre per season and that escape being caught are probably more wary than those that are caught. If wariness is associated with an inherited behavior pattern, it might in time become incorporated in all of the fish in this population. No one has devised a means for testing this theory, but it is conceivable that an isolated largemouth bass population exposed to this type of selection for many generations might furnish low annual production to anglers.

Unsuccessful Reproduction

Control of overproduction of young fish often is one of the major problems in fish management. In this respect, low production or nonproduction of certain hybrids may be an asset. Although most fishes have a high breeding potential, as described on page 130, this potential may not be realized, either because of unfavorable environmental conditions, actual predation, or intense intraspecific competition of young. Eschmeyer[50] described unusual concentrations of dead walleye eggs observed in 1948 in Lake Gogebic. He was unable to determine causes for the low viability of these eggs. In Fork Lake (Illinois) the production of forty bluegill nests was almost completely wiped out by predation from stunted yearling bass. Bluegills and bass often sustain severe losses of young at the time when the larvae begin to use outside sources of nutrition.[17,143] Channel and flathead catfish usually fail to reproduce in ponds.[140] Under certain contitions this inability to reproduce might be an asset, in that one could control the numbers of these catfishes in ponds through stocking, which is impossible to do when using any of the species of bullheads.

Observations of the limiting or curtailing of fish reproduction that can be traced to identifiable causes are extremely important because methods may be suggested for curtailing the survival of the young of a less desirable species while improving that of a more desirable one.

STOCKING

Prior to about 1936, the stocking of fish and the control of fishermen (daily limits, seasons, and length limits) were about the only fish-management activities known or utilized. Any time fishing was considered poor the appropriate state or federal agencies were requested to stock additional fish, the assumption being that natural reproduction of fishes was inadequate. No one had studied the natural production of young in the warmwater fishes, or the fate of the hatchery fish after they were stocked. The main emphasis was on numbers of young for stocking that could by produced in hatcheries.

With the development of methods for marking individual fish, biologists began to appraise the benefits from stocking, and the problems involved in obtaining adequate survival of fish of small sizes. Evidence was soon available that it was quite useless to stock additional fish into a fish population that had reached or was approaching the carrying capacity of the water for fish. If the stocked fishes were fry of fingerlings they would be eaten by larger fishes or placed under severe competition for food and space by native wild fishes better able to compete than the introduced hatchery fishes. If the fishes were adults, and were able to compete they added to the food competition so that all of the fish obtained less food, growth was slowed, and, in severe cases, all fish lost weight.

Stocking is far from a cure-all.[129] Examples of the futility of stocking are common. In 1952—1953, West Virginia stocked 13,651 marked and tagged smallmouth bass in the Elk River. Prior to 1961, only seven of these bass were known to have been caught, making the fish cost about $180 each to the state.[129] Similarly New Jersey stocked 16,200 marked fingerling bass into one of their bass streams between 1952 and 1955. A creel censusing system was set up to check fishermen, and the stream was seined, trap netted, and spot poisoned by state biologists. Only one marked bass was recovered, 1952 through 1958. Fish stocked in lakes were scarcely more successful. Evaluations of the stocking of millions of hatchery reared fry and fingerlings of shad, walleye, salmon, whitefish, and yellow perch have shown little or no return. Evidence accumulated over two decades as to the value of fish stocking has limited its usefulness to the following situations:[129]

1. Interim trout stocking of fish large enough to be caught immediately.

2. Stocking in newly constructed and filled artificial lakes and reservoirs.

3. Stocking in reclaimed or renovated lakes or streams where the indigenous or stocked fish population has been removed.

4. Introducing a new species to improve the ecosystem, either for sport fishing or as a "fill-in" for the food chain. Such an introduction should be preceeded by a partial poisoning of the present fish population to insure that competition for food and space is reduced before the new fish are released.

5. Stocking where conditions for growth are favorable but reproduction is uncertain or subject to predictable failure such as in shallow lakes subject to complete winterkill, or where channel catfish are released in ponds containing mixed populations of fishes.

If it were possible to list all of the fish-stocking attempts that have been made in the North American continent since 1900 one would find that almost every kind of fish of economic importance had been released in the broad spectrum of water types to be found. Often these plantings were unsuccessful because of limited habitat tolerance of the fishes involved.

Fishes often do not survive the stress of being moved from one water to another although they may appear quite normal when released. This problem is related in part to the way the fishes are handled in the process. Many years ago Plehn[111] described the damage that might occur to carp if they were taken from a warm pond and placed in cold water for holding or hauling. This sudden change in temperature caused a darkening of areas of the skin, killing the epidermis and causing it to peel off. If the temperature change was minor the fish might recover and leave no trace. If the temperature change was severe the effects might cause the fishes death, sometimes after a considerable length of time. This brought up the question of whether a carp buyer could claim compensation from the seller if the fish that he had purchased several days before, suddenly began dying.

Certain species of fish are more sensitive to handling than others that are less excitable and it seems probable that fish raised in hatcheries where they see hatchery personnel daily are less excitable when being handled than are wild fish. This must be especially true with those species that are fed on artificial or natural foods at frequent intervals, as they look to man as a source of food.

In certain years large year classes of channel catfish are produced in the upper Mississippi River, in the Illinois—Iowa section and northward. To a limited extent Illinois and Iowa have taken advantage of the excessive numbers of these fishes by trapping the catfish fingerlings in wing nets and basket traps and stocking them in inland lakes, ponds, and streams. In many instances the operation has proved to be successful; in others, the ratio of fish stocked to fish recaptured suggested a very low survival rate. In an attempt to explain this apparent low survival rate of wild catfish fingerlings Caillouet[27] studied the lactic acid content of the blood of these submature catfish taken from the Mississippi River. Unexercised catfish showed a blood lactic acid content of 2.3 to 7.6 mg/100 ml of whole blood. Under forced exercise for 5 min the amount of lactic acid increased to a maximum of 44.1 mg/100 ml and after 15 min to a maximum of 67.6 mg/100 ml of whole blood. Capturing fish in hoop nets or with an electric shocker, plus subsequent handling, elevated the lactic acid content of the blood to a greater extent than 15 min of exercise. Fatique, loss of equilibrium, and death were associated with high mean values of lactic acid in wild fish collected with hoop nets. Catish in groups were less stimulated by stresses than were individual catfish. The effects of seining and handling of catfish fingerlings raised in ponds from fish-farming parents and fed daily on prepared foods are probably less than the stresses created by the handling of wild fishes. Similar stress reactions have been observed in handling other kinds of fishes; for example, wild smallmouth bass confined in aquaria sometimes react violently, go into shock, and die when suddenly exposed to a bright light after having been in darkness.

Undoubtedly a great deal of care should be taken in moving fish from one water to another to prevent undue physical strain, exposure to low oxygen and high carbon dioxide, and sudden changes in temperature. The tranquilizers, MS-222,* methyl pentynol, or sodium amytal may be used to reduce excitement in handling and moving fish.[144] The antibiotic terramycin is sometimes used to prevent the infection of skin lesions sustained in transportation.

Many tests of stocking procedures for new or reclaimed ponds and lakes have been made since 1935. However, the recommendations of the states and provinces throughout the United States and Canada do not reveal much agreement among the fisheries biologists upon the kinds and number of fish useful for stocking new water or renovated old ones. This is due in part to dissimilarities among the fish habitats of North America, to differences in temperature ranges, to differences in the biology of certain game and pan fishes in widely separated parts of their present ranges, to regional variations in the popularity of certain fishes, and to differences in the objectives of stocking. For example, some biologists stock to produce excellent but short term angling as quickly as possible; others, to produce satisfactory angling over a longer period of time; others, to favor one species; others, to give equal status to two or more species. These variations in objectives can be accommodated only by differences in stocking methods.

Fishes Used

The Bass-Bluegill Combination. The bass—bluegill combination received much attention in the 1930s; it had been used in ponds by Dyche[44] before 1914 and by Barney and Canfield[6] before 1922. In theory, this combination seemed excellent: both largemouth bass and bluegills would be available for sport fishing; the bluegills would convert small invertebrate animals in the pond into bluegill flesh and the small bluegills would serve as food for the bass, the latter controlling excessive numbers of bluegills, so that the few that survived would grow to large average size.

As with most theories involving specific behavior patterns for animals, the bass—bluegill combination often varied from the theoretical expectation. The bass often were unable to control the expansion of bluegill numbers, and as Dyche[44] observed, the number of bass were more often controlled by bluegills than vice versa.

Later, biologists discovered that this combination furnished satisfactory fishing of both bass and bluegills as long as neither species was

*Now sanctioned for use for experimental purposes only by the Food and Drug Administration.

allowed to become overabundant. Interest was immediately directed toward stocking specific ratios of these fish because these ratios had an influence upon the length of time required for a newly stocked pond to reach overabundance, either of bluegills or bass.

In the southeast, the bluegill was more easily controlled by bass than elsewhere, and both species reproduced when one year old.[139] According to Swingle and Smith,[140] fertilized ponds should be stocked with 100 bass fingerlings and 1500 bluegill fingerlings per acre, unfertilized ponds with thirty bass fingerlings and 400 bluegill fingerlings per acre. These ratios apparently were not considered satisfactory for the southwest as Brown[23] recommended either 200 to 400 largemouth bass per acre alone or in conjunction with about the same number of bluegills or other pond fish.

In the northeast and the north central states, the bass were usually unable to attain sexual maturity at the age of one year,[113] although Clark[36] reported that they did so in Kentucky. Bluegills were sexually mature in the northern latitudes the next season after hatching. Thus, when fingerling bass and fingerling bluegills were stocked together in the same pond, the bluegills reproduced during the first spawning season, whereas the bass did not, and by the time the bass had reached sexual maturity after a second growing season, so many yearling and older bluegills were present that they limited the survival of bass embryos and fry. To prevent this early shift toward an overpopulation of bluegills, fishery biologists either stocked some other species along with largemouth bass, or used bass—bluegill ratios that gave bass a better chance to survive and reproduce, such as 100 largemouth bass fingerlings to an equal number of bluegill fingerlings. During the first season the bass fingerlings would prey upon the bluegill fingerlings, reducing their number to a low figure but still not so low as to preclude the survival of a small number of bluegills to spawn the following season. Furthermore, the pond was not so crowded with bluegills by the second season as to prevent a successful spawn of bass when they became sexually mature. Fishing for bluegills in ponds stocked originally with 100 bass fingerlings and 100 bluegill fingerlings might not be satisfactory until after individuals of the first bluegill brood spawned in the pond had reached a length of 6 in., usually late in the third summer. This process could be speeded up one full season by stocking fingerling or fry size bass at the rate of 100 per acre along with adult bluegills (that would spawn the same season as stocked) at the rate of 10 to 30 per acre. Clark[36] stated that this was the only satisfactory ratio for stocking bass and bluegills in Kentucky; more recent findings do not support Clark's specific statement for a satisfactory ratio.[55,122]

In southern Illinois, six ponds on the lands of the University of Illinois College of Agriculture Dixon Springs Experiment Station were stocked with stunted largemouth bass 6—10 in. long and with bluegill fingerlings averaging 1 in. in length.[57] Their progress was followed closely for six years. Three of the ponds scheduled to receive fertilizer were stocked with 89, 91, and 109 bass and 1127, 1250, and 1630 bluegills per acre, respectively. Three unfertilized ponds were stocked with 21, 30, and 36 bass and 310, 396, and 412 bluegills per acre, respectively. A nearly complete creel census throughout the six-year period showed that bass fishing was best during the first year. By the second season bluegills in both fertilized and unfertilized ponds were of worthwhile sizes (6 in.) and the bluegill fishing (rate of catch) improved for the next few fishing seasons, reaching a peak in about five years.

Often it is impractical or impossible to obtain enough fingerling bass for stocking new artificial impoundments of 100 to 1000 acres at rates of 100 small bass per acre. In these instances, stocking might be done by releasing bass fry or by using sexually mature bass at rates of 1 adult bass per 3—20 acres of water along with bluegills at a somewhat higher rate. Usually, after the first spawning season, young bass can be collected in numbers in all parts of the lake, and it is nearly impossible to find any bluegills. Two seasons later the lake might furnish excellent fishing for both bass and bluegills.

For artificial impoundments of intermediate sizes between farm ponds and large reservoirs, a stocking of 2 to 10 adult bass per acre, followed by a stocking of 100 small bluegills per acre after the bass had produced young, usually gives satisfactory fishing one or two seasons later.

In the northernmost states and southern Canada, the bass—bluegill combination is nearly useless because waters are infertile and growing seasons are short. Both species of fish require three growing seasons to reach sexual maturity. The bluegills show a strong tendency to overpopulate and become stunted. Rawson and Ruttan[112] stated that yellow perch grew better than bluegills in Saskatchewan and recommend stocking ponds with yellow perch and bass or northern pike. Ball[2] suggested stocking ponds in Michigan with 100 fingerling bass and 10 adult bluegills per acre. By so doing, the bass would have bluegill forage immediately instead of two or three seasons later. Later Ball and Ford[3] stated that the largemouth bass—golden shiner combination was more satisfactory for the production of bass fishing in Michigan than was the bass—bluegill combination. Regier[113] also favored the largemouth bass—golden shiner combination for New York State. Neither Brown and Thoreson[25] in the northwest (Montana) nor Saila[119] in the northeast recommended the bass-bluegill combination for ponds in these regions because results were unpredictable.

A perusal of published material on the bass—bluegill combination will show that it apparently is most successful in the southeast. Farther north, results may be good but good results are not a certainty, although records of one bass—bluegill pond in Illinois showed a high yield of both bass and bluegills for twelve years after stocking.[43] This pond of 2.5 acres was stocked originally with 100 bass fingerlings and 100 bluegill fingerlings.

In Illinois, the bass—bluegill combination usually moved in the direction of an overpopulation of bluegills. If ponds were stocked with equal numbers of bass and bluegill fingerlings per acre, this condition of overpopulation of bluegills might be delayed from five to twelve years. However, bluegills were very efficient in controlling populations of largemouth bass after bluegill numbers reach 1000 or more per acre,[13] particularly if these bluegills were small. Control was exerted through predation of small bluegills on bass eggs and fry in the nests. Stunted bluegills would gather around a bass net guarded by a male and sooner or later a bluegill would venture close enough to cause the male bass to give chase. While the male was away from the nest, other bluegills entered and fed upon bass embryos or fry. The bluegills scattered when the male bass returned, but soon the process was repeated and before long the eggs or young bass would be greatly reduced or eliminated. This was the only period in the life cycle of largemouth bass when this species was highly vulnerable to bluegill predation, but if bluegill predation on bass embryos and fry was steady and efficient for several years in succession, the bass population of a lake might dwindle to a few old fish which lived well but were unable to produce a new year class of young bass.

Small bass are also vulnerable to crappie predation where the latter are abundant. Young crappies are much more inclined to hide in aquatic vegetation than are young largemouths, and for that reason the latter are usually more vulnerable to adult crappie predation than are small crappies.

An overpopulation of stunted crappies (or bluegills), plus a few large bass unable to reproduce successfully, could be self-perpetuating and continuous until the bass are caught or die of old age. Only drastic thinning of the stunted fishes would allow the bass to bring off a successful spawn.

In contrast, an overpopulation of small bass might be controlled in a single season of fishing, provided the fishermen were educated to the necessity of taking bass of all sizes.[13]

If bass could be expected to prey upon bluegills exclusively, either through "normal" feeding habits or through a special taste for them, the bass—bluegill combination would be considerably more dependable than at present. However, largemouth bass actually select a variety of foods (including the larger aquatic insects, crustaceans, and fishes), and the evidence is that they will feed upon crayfish and their own young in preference to bluegills. Therefore, in order to control bluegills indefinitely, bass need assistance.

From the foregoing, it is obvious that the bass—bluegill combination eventually may create serious problems for the fishery manager. These problems stem primarily from overpopulation of one or the other of these two species—more often and more seriously from an overpopulation of bluegills than from largemouth bass. The stocking ratios of Swingle and Smith[140] have produced satisfactory yields in the southeast. In the central states stocking ratios must favor the rapid development of "dominant" bass populations and even then bluegills may eventually become overabundant unless placed under additional population-controlling pressures, some of which are described in Chapter 6. In the northern states this combination should be avoided because of the uncertainty of results. Combinations of largemouth bass and some other fish or fishes will produce satisfactory bass fishing and require less management effort.

Largemouth, Spotted, or Smallmouth Bass Alone. There is reason to assume that other combinations might be more satisfactory from the standpoint of angling and easier to manage than the bass-bluegill combination. Since largemouth, smallmouth, and spotted bass are fairly omnivorous in their feeding and can get along well on crayfish, large aquatic insects, and their own young, any of the three bass species stocked in a pond by itself should produce bass fishing without the complications of controlling bluegills or other fish stocked with bass. Experiments testing the ability of each bass species to survive in its own pond have proved very satisfactory, particularly if the population is set up originally by stocking several year classes to prevent the development of a dominant year class, which might become stunted. This was quite easily done by stocking an assortment of bass larger than 10 in. *in addition* to 100 fingerling bass per acre. At the first spawning season after stocking, the adult bass produced young; however, the fingerlings already present prevented the development of a dominant brood. Experiments have shown that populations of bass by themselves are as large, or larger, in pounds per acre than are bass populations in combination with other species of fish.[16]

Smallmouth bass do well in warmwater ponds if they do not have to compete with some of the more prolific warmwater fishes, such as bluegills, green sunfish, and black bullheads.[15] For example, smallmouths maintained a large population in a 14-acre central Illinois lake until excessive numbers of green sunfish prevented their successful reproduction. This lake was made by damming a pasture ravine and contained no sand or gravel in the shoal areas.

Largemouth and Smallmouth Bass with Minnows or Chubsuckers. Several fisheries biologists have tested largemouth or smallmouth bass in combination with one or several species of minnows. Ball and Ford[3] and Regier[113] tried a combination of largemouth bass and golden shiners which proved to be very successful. After five years, there were still plenty of both species present. Bluntnose minnows were able to maintain a population over at least a three-year period when confined in a very clear pond (gravel-pit) with smallmouth bass. This pond contained some rooted aquatic vegetation, smallmouths taken from this pond showed a higher average condition than others taken from a nearby pond which contained only smallmouths.

One of the most satisfactory forage fishes for bass in central Illinois is the lake chubsucker, *Erimyzon sucetta* (Lac.)[16] (Fig. 5.5). The adults are rarely more than 10−11 in. long, are round bodied and soft rayed, and are capable of maintaining a sizeable population in the presence of a dominant population of largemouth bass. This species begins to spawn in late March or early April in central Illinois and its fry are available at the time the smallmouth fry are leaving the nests. The lake chubsucker apparently fills a niche not occupied by any of the predatory or semi-predatory fishes, and its presence broadens the food web for basses (Centrarchidae) where these are dependent on crayfish, aquatic insects, and their own young for food. The lake chubsucker is a clearwater species and does not roil the pond bottom; it is so retiring and unobtrusive that it is seldom seen except during the height of the spring spawning season. This species has been stocked in ponds with smallmouth bass for as long as ten years (1958−1968). Yields of smallmouths from one pond during this period have ranged from 27 to 89 lb per acre per season (complete creel census).

The lake chubsucker ranges from eastern Minnesota to New England and south to Florida and Texas.[46] Trautman[145] listed the western lake chubsucker (subspecies *kennerlyi*) from Ohio along Lake Erie and the northern boundary of the state. Harlan and Speaker[58] doubt that the fish actually exists in Iowa; it has been reported from Missouri but seems to be rather uncommon throughout the midwest, partly, I am sure because of its retiring nature. It is the choice of fishery biologists in Illinois for stocking in combination with largemouth or smallmouth bass where bass

Fig. 5.5 The lake chubsucker is a superior forage species for largemouth and smallmouth bass in ponds and small lakes.

fishing is of primary interest. It has also been stocked with combinations of largemouth bass and hybrid sunfish.

Largemouth Bass with Red-ear Sunfish. The largemouth bass—red-ear sunfish combination has been tested extensively in Indiana[84,86] and Illinois.[12] In no case where only largemouth bass and red-ears were present has there been any evidence of overpopulation of red-ears. However, the red-ear sunfish is somewhat less desirable as a sport fish than is the bluegill because the former prefers live bait fished deep and will seldom hit artificial flies or poppers at the water's surface.

Largemouth Bass with Warmouths. Larimore[90] combined largemouth with warmouths in stocking more than fifteen ponds in central Illinois. This combination was very satisfactory. The warmouths showed little tendency to overpopulate and both warmouths and bass grew rapidly to useful sizes.

Largemouth Bass, Warmouths, Red-ear Sunfish, and Channel Catfish. Jenkins[73] concluded from his observations in Oklahoma that largemouth bass, channel catfish, warmouths, and red-ear sunfish produced more harvestable-sized fish in comparison with their total standing crops than any other warmwater fishes.

Northern Pike and Bluegills. In north central Nebraska several ponds of 5 acres or larger have been stocked with a northern pike—bluegill combination. The pike were released as fingerlings and bluegills as adults so that the latter furnished young bluegills for pike forage during the first season.[99] The combination was reported to be quite successful.

Others. Several studies have been made of combinations involving three, four, and five species of fishes, such as the bass, bowfin, and bluegill combination of Krumholz[84] or the bass, bluegill, warmouth, and channel catfish combination used in Ridge Lake.[13] The study of Thompson[142] of an unfertilized fishing-club lake in Macoupin County, Illinois, illustrates that the bass, crappie, bluegill, and bullhead combination in a lake with limited shallows may be productive of substantial annual yields, if the lake is fished intensively when the fish are biting (annual yield was about 100 lb of fish per acre of lake).

Every practicing fishery biologist will discover, sooner or later, at least one warmwater pond or lake that, although unmanaged or mismanaged, still produces as good or better fishing than any lake or pond toward which he may be directing his management efforts at that time. I have found several. In some, the high production was transitory, and ponds eventually became poor fishing waters, usually because of overpopulation. There were and are, however, a few others in which there seems to be a delicate relationship between reproductive success of the fishes and the natural food supply, perhaps through actions of predators of which I am unaware. In these waters, bluegills may range between two and three to the pound, with scarcely any of smaller sizes, or green sunfish may grow to 8 or 9 in. and may be represented by a few hundred fish instead of tens of thousands of 3 to 5-in. fish. These lakes always seem to contain many small largemouth bass, usually 6 to 9 in. There may be some unrecognized relationship between the physical environment and the fish and other aquatic organisms that inhabit it. In later chapters, we will discuss this possibility.

Walleye Stocking. The success of walleye stocking of fry or small fingerlings appears to be highly variable except in waters devoid of other fishes (new reservoirs, renovated lakes, in the northern states and Canada in winterkill lakes) and in nursery ponds where predaceous aquatic insects have been controlled. In these waters stocking is most often followed by satisfactory rates of survival. In the past forty years millions of walleye fry from hatcheries have been stocked in hundreds or perhaps thousands of lakes and rivers. In most instances there is little evidence to indicate that these plantings have been useful.

There are, however, some waters where the stocking of walleye fry has increased the yield of fish in future years. For example, the stocking of 5,000 to 9,500 walleye fry per acre in Clear Lake (Iowa) in even-numbered years resulted in larger numbers of walleye in those year classes than in the year classes of odd-numbered years.[31] Evidence obtained from seining beach areas, age determinations of walleyes caught in gill nets each year, and estimates of population made by tagging and recovery techniques all appeared to verify this assumption. In contrast, the stocking of 3,500 walleye fry per mile in Cedar River (Iowa) in 1951–1958 did not influence year-class abundance.[37]

Frank Grice of Massachusetts contacted fishery departments of fifty states and eleven provinces on the question of stocking walleyes. Forty-two states and provinces responded to the questionnaire.[130] There seemed to be a general opinion that walleye stocking was not widely successful in acid or softwater lakes.[52] Twenty-six of the agencies contacted furnished information on lakes where stocked walleyes had survived but had not become self-sustaining. Fritz H. Johnson of Minnesota produced evidence that lack of suitable spawning areas may have been responsible for the walleyes' inability to maintain populations.[76]

Other references are available that walleye stocking was useless[109] or only partly successful.

Muskellunge Stocking. The muskellunge *Esox masquinongy* Mitchill is generally recognized as the most highly prized game fish in North America. There are at least two subspecies: a northern form *E. m. masquinongy* Mitchill, and an Ohio form, *E. m. ohioenis* Kirkland, which is present in the larger streams of southern Ohio, Kentucky, and West Virginia. Since the early 1930s muskellunge have been much less abundant than they were in the preceeding century and there has been much pressure by fishermen to have state fish and game departments include them as hatchery fish. Several of the northern states have been fairly successful in the propagation of this species in ponds, and small numbers have been raised by private hatcheries and sold to lake owners (Fig. 5.6).[77]

Studies of the muskellunge have been made in Ohio, Canada, and Wisconsin,[127,128] which indicate that the cost of rearing muskellunge to fingerling size (Fig. 5.6) and the mortality rate after these fingerling have been released may be combined to produce an estimate that the cost of putting one 30-in. stocked muskellunge into a fishermans' creel may amount to approximately $200. Wisconsin reported a state-wide harvest of muskellunge in 1957 of 47,700 fish, most of which were produced naturally. Although the stocking of lakes with muskellunge has apparently won wide acceptance by sport fishermen in the Great Lakes region, it must be considered a questionable operation from the standpoint of cost accounting. John Klingbiel and Howard Snow[82] of the Wisconsin Department of Conservation concluded that the stocking of muskellunge,

Fig. 5.6 Muskellunge are sometimes stocked in small numbers in artificial lakes as a "bonus" fish and as an aid in the control of sunfish populations. Muskellunge usually do not reproduce successfully in these lakes.

northern pike, or walleyes to control sunfish populations has generally not been successful.[132]

Changes in Fishing

There are many records of highly productive lakes and ponds that lost their productiveness after a few years because of the introduction and expansion of undesirable fish or the overpopulation and stunting of desirable ones.

Krumholz[85] working on hybrid sunfish in ponds in Indiana found that 39 to 78 ponds stocked originally with hybrids and largemouth bass contained, after two years, other species of fish than were originally stocked. After questioning the owners of 29 of these ponds, 26 admitted that they had introduced other kinds of fish to make available a larger variety. Among the fish that were introduced were largemouth bass, bluegills, black and white crappies, green sunfish, orange-spotted sunfish, longear sunfish, warmouths, and in two instances, smallmouth buffalo.

Ball and Tait[4] state: "The knowledge and effort necessary to maintain, over a period of time, a pond producing fast-growing bass and bluegills are beyond the scope of the average pond owner. Consequently, it is recommended that *(1)* small ponds be stocked in such a way as to produce the species desired in the greatest edible weight in the shortest time, *(2)* these fish to be harvested, and *(3)* restocking be done instead of attempting to maintain a 'balanced' pond over a period of years." This may be a practical solution if ponds are supplied with a drain outlet and fish for restocking are readily available.

In examining the history of Fork Lake, a farm pond in central Illinois,[10] it was discovered that fishing has been considered good from 1926 to 1930 but had become poor through the development of large populations of black bullheads, carp, and buffalo fishes. A census taken in 1938 showed that Fork Lake contained 5350 fish of 16 types weighing 774 lb (539 lb/acre). Only 145 fish of the 5350 were of such species and sizes as to interest anglers.

Many combinations of fishes have been tried in ponds, small lakes and reservoirs. Some of these appear to be superior to others in the development of a population that will supply fish of desirable kinds and sizes for angling. However, the interference of man in almost all aquatic ecosystems is so pronounced that one can no longer expect to find a system of checks and balances that was once characteristic of many inland waters. It is the author's opinion that one would be naïve to expect any combination of fishes, stocked or native, in a natural or artificial lake to be productive of good fishing for an indefinite period of time. Too many of the integrated forces and counterforces that were active for promoting the well-being of a fish population in a primitive environment are absent from today's man-dominated waters.

Stocking for Improvement of a Population

Biologists are not in complete agreement on the value of adding fish stocks for the improvement of a population that, from the standpoint of fishing, is somewhat less than optimum. Viosca,[147] after taking censuses of ponds in Louisiana, concluded that the stocking of ponds which already contain fish may cause almost no change in a population of fish. He cited an example of a pond stocked with 1500 largemouth bass fingerlings which after a year or so yielded only 6 stunted individuals weighing a total of 1.85 lb as against 12,505 bluegills and green sunfish weighing 201 lb. A deeper pond nearby was stocked with 4500 largemouth bass fingerlings. Here a mixed crappie population which was already present dominated bass and other fish. When a census of the pond was taken the proportions were 8.4 lb of crappies and 1.4 lb of sunfish to each pound of bass. According to Viosca: "--this type of evidence completely discredits the idea that artificial restocking will restore the largemouth bass population of a pond dominated by other species." In contrast, Swingle, Prather, and Lawrence[138] state that "since partial poisoning is normally required in populations containing too few bass and all small bass in the pond edges are killed, marginal or sectional poisoning in the spring or summer is detrimental unless followed by restocking of bass." However, stocking of fish after a partial poisoning operation is not comparable to a situation such as Viosca described, because partial poisoning makes living space available for the stocked bass.

Lagler and DeRoth[89] came to the same conclusion as Viosca, after stocking fin-clipped bass fingerlings in the Loch Alpine ponds (Michigan); none of the 4000 bass fingerlings stocked in four years was seen again. These ponds had uncontrolled outlets, and the small bass were free to move out.

Cooper[40] says that Michigan has largely dispensed with plantings of warmwater fishes such as bass, bluegills, perch, walleyes, and northern pike. In the past, plantings of these warmwater game species were distributed among hundreds of lakes on a rather orderly schedule. Although the state-wide totals of fish stocked were large, the yearly plants to individual waters were small; bluegills were stocked at the average rate of 35 fingerlings per acre; largemouth bass at the rate of 2.4 fingerlings per acre, and smallmouth bass at the rate of 1.9 fingerlings per acre. At the same time (1947) large numbers of fingerlings of these species could be seined in most of these lakes. In twelve of these lakes, selected on the basis of public interest, intensive seining operations on shoal areas indicated populations of young fish ranging from 103 to 1760 per acre with an average of 742 per acre for the twelve lakes. This so far overshadows the maximum stocking efforts of state personnel as to make their efforts of little consequence.

By stocking 300 adult bluegills per acre in Kentucky farm ponds overpopulated with largemouth bass, Clark[36] produced satisfactory fishing for both bass and bluegills. Swingle and Smith[140] state that for ponds containing stunted bluegill populations a stocking of 100 bass fry or fingerlings per acre plus "proper fertilization" and heavy fishing for bluegills to reduce their numbers will correct this condition in a few months. This statement appears to be counter to the findings of Viosca[147] and Lagler and DeRoth[89] unless "proper fertilization" increased the available food for bluegills or at least produced enough additional plankton to allow some survival of bass.

Even with a high rate of survival of stocked fish, corrective stocking will not effectively improve a fish population unless the number of fish stocked per acre is large enough to approach that found in "superior" populations of these same fish.[31] However, this is not always easy to achieve. If bass fry were stocked at the rate of 100 per acre into a population of stunted bluegills and the survival rate of the bass was 75% (a very unlikely assumption), they soon might grow large enough to feed upon the small bluegills, reducing food competition among the bluegills and thus facilitating the growth of the larger ones to useful sizes. However, in most instances of bass-fry stocking, the evidence indicates that few survive. The larger the young fish are allowed to grow before they are stocked from a hatchery, the better are their chances of survival. The problem here is that hatchery production of large fingerlings as compared to fry might be 1 to 1000, so that the fingerling production of the hatcheries of an entire state might be able to stock only a relatively small number of ponds at the rate of 100 large fingerlings per acre.

Species of warmwater fishes that are prone to overpopulate and stunt in certain waters often may be introduced successfully into existing fish populations with the release of only a few adults. Under severe competition, these adults are incapable of producing a substantial population in one or two years, but after three or more years, they may appear in large numbers. Bluegills, red-ear sunfish, green sunfish, white crappies, and black bullheads have all been observed to increase in this manner after a small number of adult individuals were introduced into a population dominated by other fishes.

Corrective stocking is always more dependable where a part of the population has been removed by poisoning or through mechanical means (seining, etc.). This procedure should reduce the standing crop of fish to a point below the carrying capacity of the water and leave food and space for the fish that are introduced.

Corrective stocking should not be attempted unless a source of fish is available for introducing a sufficiently large number of a given species to approach the carrying capacity of the water for that species, e.g., 100 bass per acre, 300 to 1000 bluegills per acre, etc.

Stocking to Improve a Food Chain

This type of stocking is done in an attempt to improve the production of game fish in an existing fish population by increasing the forage for these game fish. The introduction of the threadfin shad into a large southern reservoir was an example of this type of stocking.[74] McCaig, Mullan, and Dodge[98] recorded that the introduction of smelt into Quabbin Reservoir (Massachusetts) furnished an improved food supply for lake trout so that the latter reached a length of 18 in. in their fourth year instead of the fifth as they had done before the smelt were abundant.

This type of stocking should be considered very carefully before it is done because: (1) food chains of fishes are very complex and the introduced species may not serve the purpose intended; moreover, (2) forage fishes that are capable of expanding their populations in the face of existing populations of predatory species already present may constitute a danger from overpopulations as the gizzard shad and suckers have done in some waters.[108]

Invertebrates such as crayfish, scuds, and insect larvae are sometimes stocked in new ponds and small lakes, and these stocking attempts are frequently successful.

Failures in Stocking Fish

Biologists in various parts of the country have developed stocking numbers and ratios of fishes intended to give satisfactory results in fishing returns. However, these stocking recommendations sometimes result in poor fishing or no fishing. There may be several reasons for these unsatisfactory results:

1. Poor fishing in new impoundments may result from unauthorized stocking prior or after the lake or pond has been stocked with tested ratios of kinds and numbers of desirable fish. Krumholz[85] mentions the problem of maintaining uncontaminated hybrid ponds in southern Indiana. In most areas there are fishermen who spend a part of their time as amateur fish managers. One of their main activities is the promiscuous stocking of small numbers of most of the kinds of warmwater fishes to be caught on hook-and-line. If one finds bluegills where red-ears were stocked or largemouth bass where there should be smallmouth bass only, one may be observing the work of an amateur fish manager. Many fishermen release leftover live minnows into streams of lakes; the contamination from the minnows may be of minor importance if none of them are goldfish, carp fingerlings, or suckers.

2. Some contamination takes place, usually in lakes or ponds near large urban centers of population, through the release of aquarium fishes when the owners tire of caring for them. Goldfish usually survive but guppies and other tropical fishes cannot live through the winter except in the deep south.

New waters that have been contaminated with local warmwater fishes soon become useless for fishing unless through accident a reasonable number of bass are also present. As discussed previously, corrective stocking of a water area that already contains fish is largely useless; it is better to kill all the fish and start again with correct numbers of selected species.

3. Poor results may be obtained because the fish stocked in new or renovated ponds died. Even though the fish released were active and swam into deep water in a normal manner, they may have sustained

injuries through handling prior to release that later resulted in their death.

For example, Brown[24] found the survival rate of bass fingerlings in bass-bluegill stocking experiments ranged from 47.1 to 83.3%. Other investigators have obtained 69.2 to nearly 100% survival[133] and a 75% survival for one pond.[121]

A striking example of this type of injury was observed by the author while tracing the fate of the original adult and yearling bass released in Ridge Lake (Illinois) in 1941.[13] These bass consisted of 58 adults from Crab Orchard Lake near Carbondale, 42 adults from Lake Chautauqua near Havana, and 335 yearlings from Lake Glendale near Robbs.

The 58 bass from Crab Orchard Lake were caught and held in wing nets, April 27 - 29 inclusive, moved into a tank truck supplied with an air compressor, and transported to Ridge Lake, a distance of 150 miles by road. The weather was unseasonably warm for April. Although the fish appeared in good condition when released, 44 of these fish (75.8%) were believed to have died soon after release from injuries sustained in capture and transportation. These 44 bass were not caught by anglers in 1941 and 1942 and were not present when the lake was drained in 1943.

The 42 adult bass from Chautauqua Lake (also caught in wing nets) were the survivors of a much larger number taken in March and April and held indoors for several weeks in aerated holding tanks. Fish injured in netting operations were removed and discarded. On May 1, bass remaining in the tanks were transported in the early morning to Ridge Lake, a distance of 145 miles. Sixteen of the 42 bass disappeared without a trace and probably died from injuries (38.1%).

The 335 Lake Glendale yearlings (5.0 - 7.0 in.) were seined on June 17, held overnight in a holding net staked out in the lake, and then were hauled in aerated tanks to Ridge Lake, a road distance of 180 miles. The weather was hot, and a few of the fish died in transit, but those released appeared to be in good shape. In this group, 317 of the 335 bass (94.6 %) disappeared. Some may have been eaten by the larger bass, but with only 100 of the larger bass released in 18 acres of water, the fish were not crowded and predation probably was not heavy. The assumption that these fish died from improper handling was further substantiated by the high survival rates of marked bass which were recorded in later years when the lake was drained in March, a census taken, and the marked fish returned immediately to the refilling lake basin. One of the Chautauqua Lake fish that survived the original road trip and stocking in 1941 later survived four lake drainings and fish censuses and was caught by a fisherman in 1949.

Stroud[126] tagged fish released in Massachusetts ponds in order to measure the recovery from angling of largemouth and smallmouth bass, pickerel, bullheads, white perch, and yellow perch. He recorded several instances of high mortality shortly after stocking, presumably from injury during handling prior to release.

PREDATION

The Role of Predation in Fish Management

At the beginning of this chapter we noted that the fishes have inhabited the earth for more than 350 million years and during this period have been relatively successful. Part of their success has been due to the development of high reproductive potential that allowed them to out-strip the predators that evolved to feed upon them. As each higher class of vertebrates appeared, certain members became predators of fishes, so that in a modern freshwater environment, fish predators are represented by a variety of invertebrates and vertebrates, each modified for predation activity in or on the water. With a little thought anyone can name at least ten common fish predators, such as:

garfishes	loons
pikes and muskellunge	ospreys
bullfrogs	cormorants
snapping turtles	gulls
alligators	terns
watersnakes	pelicans
mergansers	eagles
kingfishers	minks
ducks and geese	otters
herons	men

These predators, with the exception of man, are opportunists, willing to catch and feed upon whatever fish are available. Although most of them prefer taking fish as large as they can capture and hold, the predators of small fishes are much more numerous than those of the larger ones. In fact, only bears and men are predators of adult fishes of the largest sizes (such as the muskellunge, lake sturgeon, and salmon).

Ricker[116] distinguishes three types of numerical relationships between predators and a species of prey which they attack:

Type A. Predators of any given abundance *take a fixed number* of prey species during the time they are in contact, enough to satiate them. The surplus prey escapes.

Type B. Predators of any given abundance *take a fixed fraction* (percent) of prey species present, as though there were captures at random encounters.

Type C. Predators *take all the individuals* of the prey species that are present, *in excess of a certain minimum number.*

All of these types of predation intergrade but in certain situations they may be fairly separated.

The predation of cannibal bass on their brood mates may represent a *type A situation* in that one brood mate per twenty four hours is approximately the maximum digestive capacity of the predator bass. The number of bass fingerlings that get started as cannibals remains constant after the initial period of habit formation. After a short period of time the size relationship, between the cannibals and the surviving members of their brood mates, precludes further predation within the brood. Predation among brood mates of carp fry also has been reported.[87]

In a *type B situation* the number of prey species eaten is proportional to the abundance of predators and to the abundance of prey. Most fish-stocking ratios of predator and prey species are based on the assumption of this type of predation.

Whenever and wherever numbers of fish-eating birds are concentrated, *type C predation* probably is taking place. This type of predation commonly occurs around nesting colonies and during the migrations of such birds as herons, cormorants, mergansers, and pelicans. In type C situations the predators take all of the fish they are able to catch and swallow with limited regard to species taken; in so doing they may reduce excessive numbers of individual fishes comprising unusually successful years classes of one or several species.[34] The predators commonly involved in type C situations are highly mobile and have great capacity for taking advantage of concentrations of prey species. Their activities result in thinning populations of fishes to a point where those escaping are able to find adequate food to make rapid growth and thereby attain large sizes. When the prey population reaches a certain minimum size, the law of diminishing returns makes it unprofitable for the predators to hunt further. The reproduction potential of warmwater fishes is geared to type C predation and many problems of fish management are a result of its loss.

Invertebrate Predators of Fishes.   Many kinds of aquatic invertebrates are predators of fish embryos, larval fishes, and yolk-sac and free-swimming fish fry, and in most instances the largest reduction of numbers takes place during these early and somewhat helpless stages. Studies of cyclopoid copepods and hydras in the Dnieper River (Russia) demonstrated that 10−12% of the shad eggs and 30−40% of the larvae were damaged by copepod attacks. *Hydra vulgaris* and *Pelmatahydra oligactis,* which appeared in large numbers in the river after the construction of a power station caused severe mortality of newly emerged sturgeon larvae.[148]

Crayfishes have been known to attack fish that were injured by attacks of other predators or in rotenone treatment.[102] Occasionally so many crayfish are present in ponds containing few or no largemouth or small-mouth bass to hold them in check that none of the sunfish are able to nest successfully because of crayfish depredations on their eggs and yolk-sac fry.

Many aquatic insects are predatory on fish embryos and fry. This type of predation is often such a problem in fish hatcheries that ponds are usually treated with kerosene or light fuel oil to stop up the tracheal systems of air breathing aquatic insects or treated with 0.25 ppm ethyl parathion to kill these insects before the fish fry are stocked. Such immature aquatic insects as dragonfly nymphs, giant water bugs, or beetle larvae behave like miniature dragons ready to prey on any animal small enough for them to subdue.

Vertebrate Predators of Fishes. The high reproductive potential of fishes allows predation to reduce excessive survival of young and is an essential part of fish management. Often control is vested in the several species of fishes used in stocking new or reclaimed waters in specific numerical ratios. These have been discussed in the previous section on stocking (p. 142). Often the predatory component of a predator–prey ratio is less efficient than expected, or shows preference for some prey that was not a part of the original theoretical relationship,[93,19,72,54,131,35] and as a result, the control of numbers of the prey species is less than was expected.

In the primitive environment where man was sparsely represented, if at all, predators of fishes were much more numerous than they are now. Some idea of the extent of predation in remote regions may be gathered through estimating the food requirements of small temporary concentrations of mergansers[60] or cormorants. A single predatory species can exert an influence on certain waters. For example, about 1000 cormorants were observed to be feeding on Chautauqua Lake, a U.S. Fish and Wildlife Refuge near Havana, Illinois, during the fall of 1954. These birds were present throughout a period of three weeks. Studies of cormorants in captivity have demonstrated their voracity; an adult cormorant requires a maintenance diet of about 1 lb of fish per day, and it can eat more than 2 lb per day if the opportunity arises (Dr. Leonard Durham, personal communication). Using a food-consumption estimate of 1.5 lb of fish per bird per day, the Chautauqua Lake flock must have been consuming 1500 lb of fish per day or for the three-week period, a total of 31,500 lb or

15.75 tons of fish. Although these fish may have been mostly forage species, it is well to remember that if largemouth bass or crappies were more accessible the cormorants would have been eating bass or crappies as well.

For a long time anglers looked upon fish predators as their direct competitors for the fishes of our streams and lakes, and they destroyed garfish, watersnakes, turtles, mergansers, herons, pelicans, and other known fish eaters whenever the opportunity appeared. There is little doubt that some of these fish eaters, particularly fish-eating birds, may make serious inroads on abnormal concentrations of fish such as are found in hatchery ponds or in coldwater streams where numbers of hatchery-reared trout or salmon have been stocked.[48,91] In most other waters their impact upon fish populations is likely to be beneficial.

Man's own activities and attitudes regarding fishes are in part responsible for the poor fishing that has plagued him. This situation stems from his substitution of a new type of predation for that which occurs in nature. Man preys upon large fish, but protects and pampers small ones, which is just the opposite of what natural predators do. This new type of predation and protection, coupled with the fact that no change occurred in the fishes' breeding potential, results in excessive survival and competition among the young. In this competition bass and other game fish lose out to hoards of stunted crappies, sunfish, and yellow perch.

Thus, many of the techniques of fish management that will be discussed in Chapter 6 are substitutes for a lost natural predation and are simply methods of population control or environmental manipulation used to prevent the development of dominant populations of some kinds of fishes and to stimulate the dominance of other kinds. Many observations have been made to show that where nonpiscine predators of fish are reduced, a prey species of fish may actively control the numbers and the survival of its normal fish predator. I have produced evidence that young bluegills may control the survival of young bass.[11] Carbine[29] demonstrated that perch and minnows may control the survival of aelvins and juvenile northern pike; and Eschmeyer[50] cites several instances of yellow perch, minnows, sturgeon, catfish, and suckers eating walleye eggs and fry.

COMPETITION

Several types of competition occur among the fishes in an aquatic habitat. Although the most common rivalry appears to be for food, competition for space in specific habitats, as when sunfish vie for nesting areas, may be somewhat more obvious. Not much is known of the extent and importance of any specific type of competition comparable, for example, to bird territoriality in a specific habitat, but we can demonstrate end results by the changes that take place in crowded populations where several types of competition are severe.

Competition for Food

Most fishes depend upon wide variety of food, rather than upon a restricted diet. If a seasonal or localized shortage of one food occurs, a species may shift to another type.[88,90,43,75] Anyone who has had occasion to study the stomach contents of individuals of any single species of fish collected over a period of several months or seasons has no doubt marveled at the changes in the kinds of foods as well as in the quantities of a single aquatic organism sometimes found in a single stomach. One is almost led to believe that the taking of some foods becomes habit during certain seasons. It is often very difficult to recognize competition between two kinds of fishes for a specific food organism as was described by Johannes and Larkin[75] for rainbow trout and red-side shiners. In this case, competition was recognized only because a study had been made of the feeding of the trout before the red-side shiner had become abundant.

To what extent is an available food utilized? Patriarche and Ball[110] emphasize the importance of the "forage ratio" of Hess and Swartz[62] which is the ratio of the percentage of occurrence of a food organism in an aquatic population to its percentage of occurrence in the stomach of a fish species. If this ratio varies significantly from 1:1, it should be due to either a difference in availability or a difference in preference. Allen[1] offered an "availability factor" for forage ratio and Leonard[92] suggested that the forage ratio be used as a measure of availability only.

In many cases where a specific food organism is abundant there is little question as to its availability to fish; in others it is hard to measure the difficulty involved in the capture and ingestion of an abundant organism by a predator.

Most aquatic biologists agree that the bacteria and algae are at the base of the food chain. The bacteria use complex waste materials in the water, and the algae are able to utilize inorganic salts, carbon dioxide, and water in sunlight to make carbohydrates, fats, and proteins, which are used as a source of food by other organisms. However, the food chain from bacteria or algae to the larger fishes may not consist of a single series of links but many, and is better described as a web. A few elements of these food chains may be dominant during one season or under certain environmental conditions whereas others may replace them at another time or season. At certain times, food more suitable for one species of fish may be more abundant than at other times, and this may be reflected in changes in condition, growth rate, and in standing crop of the fish.

Larimore[90] could not show definite food competition between largemouth bass and warmouths inhabiting the same lakes, although these two species often fed on similar types of organisms. Warmouths tended to utilize organisms on soft bottoms in shallow waters and along banks, whereas largemouths fed more on surface organisms and free-swimming forms in deeper or more open parts of the lakes.

Studies of the food habits of closely related fishes may show similarities, yet with certain important differences. Ball and Tanner[5] in studying the foods of bluegills and pumpkinseed sunfish from the same waters, discovered that the pumpkinseeds selected a larger proportion of mollusks and hard-bodied insects than did the bluegills, whereas the bluegills ate larger amounts of aquatic vegetation than did the pumpkinseeds. The selection of these types of foods by bluegill x pumpkinseed hybrids was intermediate between the two parent species. Both parent types were feeding upon about the same range of foods, but distinct preferences for certain types were clearly evident.

For fishes with widely differing food habits, such as largemouth bass and bluegills, there may be some evidence of food competition at times and under certain conditions. For example, bass and bluegills in one pond competed for insects when forage fish or crayfish were not available for the bass.[17] Under these conditions, however, bass ate more flying insects and bluegills more larval aquatic forms. In this particular situation, it was impossible to evaluate the degree of food competition between these two species.

Competition for Space

When fish are forced to compete for living space, there is evidence that in some and possibly all species growth rate and reproduction are affected adversely. Anyone who has kept goldfish or tropical fish in aquaria indoors and then has placed these fish in an outdoor pool during a summer period, has had a demonstration of the change in growth rate brought about by increased space. Usually, a part of the increased growth rate is due to an improved diet, but even where aquarium fishes are receiving a completely balanced diet, their growth appears to be affected by the amount of space for each fish.

Experiments designed to expose the causes of reduced growth and reproduction in crowded fishes have furnished evidence that where adequate food was available, inhibited growth and reproduction was due to ammonia and other metabolic products excreted into the water by the fishes themselves.[80,118,136,151] In most of the experiments in which conclusive results were obtained, the fish were tropical aquarium fish, goldfish, European carp, or one of the species of buffalo fish that have a reputation for intermittent production of large year classes.

Goldfish stocked in small ponds at the beginning of the growing season at the rate of 200 4-oz fish per acre produced large numbers of young whereas those stocked at the rate of 2000 or more of 4 oz or larger produced few or no young.[136] Originally, it was thought that the goldfish ate their own eggs and young in the ponds stocked with the larger numbers of adults; however, examination of adult females showed that eggs were well formed but never laid. Later, it was discovered that each time during the summer that adult goldfish were moved from their regular ponds into new ponds freshly filled with water, the fish spawned within forty-eight hours.

On the basis of these and other experiments, Swingle[136] postulated the presence of a repressive factor composed of a secretion or excretion produced by the goldfish themselves that inhibited final development and deposition of eggs, although these eggs were already practically mature.

Additional experiments showed that the inhibitory material was excreted into the water by the goldfish and that when this water was moved into new ponds it retained its ability to inhibit reproduction, even when it was diluted 2:1 with fresh water. Similar tests using carp and bigmouth buffalo gave results comparable to those from goldfish experiments.

Swingle believed that largemouth bass were affected by an inhibitory factor. Certainly there is evidence that the production of young in this species is never directly related to numbers of spawners; usually there appears to be an inverse relationship between bass fry and number of adults available for spawning.[13]

It was also assumed that overcrowded bluegills depressed the production of largemouth bass through the secretion of a repressive factor. If this were so, the repressive factor effected the bass but not the bluegills themselves. More experimental work must be done before exact evidence is available to prove or disprove this differential action, particularly when crowded bluegills have been observed repeatedly to feed upon bass eggs and fry.

Yashouv[151] placed two small carp in each of a number of aquaria containing 26—27 liters of water. These fish were fed 10% of their body weight per day and held at water temperatures warm enough for growth. Water was changed in all aquaria at 2-day intervals throughout experiments extending from 43 to 80 days. Controls received no other treatments, but experimental aquaria received varying amounts of metabolic water obtained by stocking a small container with a large number of fish for 30 to 40 min or until they had difficulty in breathing. Fish in aquaria receiving this metabolic water gained slightly or lost weight while control fish gained 150−275% of their original weight.

As yet, there is no exact agreement among investigators as to the causative agent responsible for this inhibition of growth and reproduction. One believes it is a hormone-like substance, another a substance that creates a vitamin deficiency; when fish-conditioned water was given to rats for drinking they lost weight and died after 45 to 50 days,[151] with characteristic symptoms of vitamin B_1 deficiency.

In the Far East where fish are grown in boxes in streams there is no growth inhibition, although the density of fish in the boxes amounts to as much as 50/m.[3] Here metabolic products are carried away by the current. Yashouv[151] thinks that this action of metabolic waste may represent a mechanism for slowing numerical growth of the existing population.

Mraz and Cooper[103] found little relationship between population density of adult carp (within the range of 75 and 450 lb/acre) and the weight of young carp present with them at the end of the first summer (3 mo) (Fig. 5.1). Adult carp were stocked in May just prior to the spawning season, and the ponds were drained in August or early September. These adult fish always produced a spawn; when less than 100 lb of adult carp per acre were stocked, the fish usually gained in weight; a loss in weight of adults resulted from stocking at rates of 150−450 lb/acre. Young carp averaged from 2.7 to 5.0 in. after 3 mo, and the weight per acre of young carp ranged from 98.4 to 308.7 lb. As the carp were stocked just prior to the spawning season, there was no inhibition in spawning, but growth of adults and young may have been affected later.

Among game and pan fishes in hatchery ponds no clear effect of crowding upon growth (where adequate food was available) and reproduction has been demonstrated, although one may assume that accumulation of waste may function as a growth inhibitor.

Larimore[90] demonstrated a very significant difference in the numbers of ova carried by female warmouths living under different conditions. For example, a female warmouth of 5.3 in. from Venard Lake (Illinois) contained 40,400 ova in various stages of development, whereas a female of the same length from Park Pond contained only 12,500 ova. Venard Lake was supporting a rapidly expanding fish population, whereas the fish in Park Pond were more crowded and more heavily parasitized (Fig. 5.7).

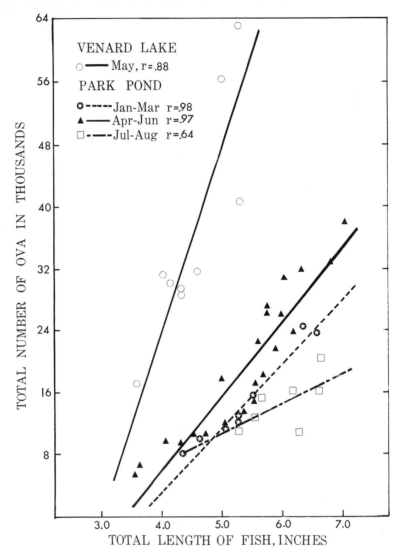

Fig. 5.7 Estimated number of ova from warmouths of various total lengths in collections from Venard Lake and Park Pond (Illinois) in 1949. Scattergram, regression line, and coefficient of correlation (r) are given for each collection group. Each graphic symbol represents one female from which the number of ova was estimated. Venard Lake warmouths belonged to a population of fish that was expanding rapidly. In Park Pond the warmouths were subjected to severe competition for food and space and many were heavily parasitized [from Larimore, R. W., 1957, *Illinois Nat. Hist. Surv. Bull.* 27(1)].

Competition for Specific Habitats

This type of competition may be more common than is the general crowding of fishes, particularly in the case of competition for spawning areas by sunfishes, or competition for limited shallow bottom areas for bottom-loving bullheads. Control of a specific habitat within an aquatic environment may allow a single species of fish to hold dominance over other components of a fish population.

Starvation

Most fishes are well equipped to withstand prolonged periods of starvation. In laboratory experiments conducted by Dr. Marian F. James[70] bass were held in aquaria at room temperature without food for several months. During this period they lost nearly half of their body weight, and some died of starvation. Some were brought back to their original weights through repeated force feeding of small amounts of food. After having been starved for two or more months, these bass were no longer interested in food and would pay little or no attention to live minnows released in the aquaria with them.

Other laboratory experiments (D. H. Thompson, unpublished) indicated that in order to maintain a constant weight bass required about 1% of their body weight per day in the form of fish. These fish were able to live for an indefinite period on a maintenance diet with no indication of ill health. It is not unlikely that food ingestion at this level may occur frequently in populations of stunted fish.

Inter- and Intraspecific Competition

In considering competition among the fishes in an aquatic habitat, one usually considers compeition between the several species first, but intraspecific competition—competition between individuals belonging to a single species—may be more continuous or severe than that between species. In describing the fish inhabiting Lake Gogebic, Eschmeyer[50] stated that walleye and northern pike dominated the game-fish population. Other species of game and pan fish were present in small numbers: largemouth and smallmouth bass, black crappies, rock bass, and, seasonally, brook trout. Young of the yellow perch were abundant, but adults were relatively scarce. On the basis of Eschmeyer's study of various phases of the life history of the walleye in this lake, it is probable that at certain periods in their life history intraspecific competition for food among walleyes was more severe than that between walleyes and other kinds of fish.

In Onized Lake (Illinois) where heavy fishing controlled the numbers of larger fish, except largemouth bass and bluegills,[9] there appeared to be severe inter-and intraspecific competition among the young of all species present. Once these small fishes reached sizes large enough to interest anglers they were thinned by fishermen.

Rose[117] recorded what appeared to be interspecific competition between white bass and walleyes in Spirit Lake (Iowa). Gill-net records over a period of nineteen years (1936—1954) indicated rather severe fluctuations in these two species in which walleyes increased when the numbers of white bass were low and vice versa.

In some locations there appears to be interspecific competition between black and white crappies, a situation in which one species is more abundant for several years and then the other replaces the first as a dominant species. Neal[104] observed such a shift in Clear Lake (Iowa) between 1950 and 1960, in which a dominant population of black crappies was replaced by one of white crappies. Increased turbidity was suggested as a cause for this shift in dominance.

Less is known of the points of conflict and the results of severe intraspecific competition for food and space. In this direction. MacPhee[96] projected a series of experiments to test quantitatively the impact of aggressive behavior and other measurable differences in the feeding success of groups of young salmon and groups of small bass fed on fruit flies. Dominance and a "peck" order among individuals of each was positively correlated with the number of flies each individual was able to capture for himself. Dominance was positively correlated with weight and aggressive action for salmon and with weight and size for bass. Intraspecific relationships observed among fishes confined in limited quarters may not be paralleled by these same kinds of fishes when they are free to move about in open waters. However we must assume that intraspecific stress under conditions of severe overpopulation must have a definite influence on behavior. Watt[149] has concluded that under conditions of intraspecific competition and a reasonably stable environment productivity can be increased greatly by the exploitation of the fish population through fishing.

REPRODUCTION, COMPETITION, AND PREDATION

In the preceding paragraphs I have attempted to illustrate several important aspects of the life cycles of fishes—reproduction, predation, and competition—which, when integrated with one another and with other forces, control the dynamics of any fish population in any body of water. Exact ecological relationships between individuals and species of fishes are obscure, largely because of the difficulty of observing what goes on below the surface of the water. We assume that fishes have habitat niches; yet one does not find a definition of the limits of a niche for any species of warm-water pond or lake fish. There is evidence that fish have "home ranges" or "territories," which, under certain circumstances, they will defend. No one can say how much intolerance there is between species of fishes or between individuals, but from the prevalence of excessive numbers of individuals in many populations of fishes intolerance between these individuals may be at a minimum. Further, excessively dense populations of fishes do not seem to do lasting damage to the aquatic habitat in any way comparable to the damage done to a deer range by excessive populations of deer. Fish populations do not seem to be self-limiting in any way except through direct predation, in some cases through metabolic secretions or excretions, or through various types of catastrophies that operate primarily on the aquatic habitat (water-level fluctuations, low dissolved oxygen and high carbon dioxide, etc.) and secondarily on the fishes. Yet with this apparent lack of many of the forces which are known to enter into the control of populations of birds and mammals there are many examples of fish populations that seem to be in a "steady state," that fluctuate very little from year to year.

Because of our inability to "see what is going on" in the aquatic habitat there has been a great tendency to resort to mathematics to define the life processes of fish populations. In an ideal situation, everything involved in life processes should be mathematically definable, but there are many pitfalls to be avoided, not the least of which is the assumption of randomness in any aspect of the distribution of any biological entity in the aquatic habitat. Fish and aquatic animals are no more randomly distributed over an aquatic habitat than are land vertebrates and invertebrates over a terrestrial one. The important question then becomes the definition of what a sample of fish, plankton, or bottom organisms represents in relation to the entire aquatic ecosystem. It is difficult to weigh variables in an aquatic environment when we probably recognize only a few of them.

In spite of the difficulties in making direct observations of fishes, it is possible to follow the results of the interaction of the forces of reproduction, competition, and predation through adequate sampling in the case of certain populations. Thompson[142] reported a population study of the fish of Lake Senachwine (Illinois) where very abundant year classes of black crappies not only controlled the survival of their own young for the next four spawning seasons, but they also controlled the survival of young of most other species of fish in this lake. During the fourth year of their dominance, the natural death rate of this year class of crappies was high. When the next spawning period arrived, the five-year-old crappies were no longer numerous enough to dominate the fish population, but there were enough of them to produce a new dominant year class of crappies.

Starrett and McNeil,[125] while studying the fish population of Chautauqua Lake (Illinois), which in some ways is similar to that of Lake Senachwine, found that the relative abundance of several species of fishes fluctuated over periods of several years, but that no one year class of any species dominated the fish population as did the black crappie broods in Lake Senachwine. In Chautauqua Lake, the 1948 year class of white crappies was much larger than any other year class of that species produced in any year from 1949 to 1961, but large year classes of other species were produced in some years.

Only occasionally are predatory fishes confronted by a shortage of prey fishes; when this does occur, it is often the result of pressure from a dominant year class of the predatory species. Such a situation occurred with largemouth bass in Ridge Lake in 1941 and 1942.[13] The 1951 angler's catch of walleyes in Clear Lake (Iowa) was unusually high, apparently because of a failure in the perch crop in 1949 and 1950, which in turn was believed to have been related to a shortage of aquatic vegetation during those years.[30]

In this same lake a very large yield of northern pike occurred in 1954 as a result of the transference in 1953 of some 17,000 young pike 10 to 16 in. long into Clear Lake from Ventura Marsh which lies adjacent to the lake. This amounted to five pike per acre, or by the spring of 1954, to 7 lb of pike per acre, a rather abrupt increase of at least 10% in the predator population of the lake. The pike caught were thin and later in the summer some were found dead along the shore.[30]

Still another type of interplay of reproduction, competition, and predation results in a progressive increase in one or two species of fishes until they become so numerous as to exceed the normal food resources for these species in their habitat. These abundant species spill over their habitat niches into those of other less aggressive species and crowd them sufficiently for food and space to prevent the survival of adequate young to maintain a level of population of the less aggressive fishes. It follows that the latter species eventually may be represented by a few old fish, and they may disappear entirely. This type of population change is nonreversible and is characteristic of fish populations subjected to limited or ineffectual predation. Only catastrophic changes in the habitat will modify the overpopulated and stunted condition of the dominant fishes.

BALANCE

Balance is a term used by some biologists to describe natural fluctuations of animal populations around a constant numerical level.[105] Other biologists have expressed the opinion that the term is inappropriate[124] because balance refers to a state of equipoise and is synonymous with equilibrium. According to Nicholson[105] "balance refers to the state of a system capable of effective compensatory reaction to the disturbing forces which operate upon it, such reaction maintaining the system in being." Beverton and Holt[18] prefer the term "steady state" to convey the meaning of general stability of populations.

Swingle[134,135,137] uses the term "balance" to define fish populations that yield satisfactory crops of harvestable fish. According to this hypothesis, fish in a balanced population *(1)* must reproduce periodically, *(2)* must produce a sustained yield (presumably by angling), and *(3)* must contain a combination of species including at least one piscivorous species. Unbalanced populations are those unable to produce succeeding crops of harvestable fish.

This concept of balance[78,135] is somewhat different from that of biologists who have applied this term previously. It visualizes a simple predator—prey relationship between carnivorous fishes (piscivorous) and their prey in which the prey species make the maximum use of the food resources to produce adults which humans consider harvestable and small fish to serve as their food. The carnivorous fishes produce young to maintain stocks of adults for fishing and to control the potential overproduction of stocks of both omnivorous and piscivorous fishes. In practice, this relationship of predator fish to prey fish may maintain itself for a number of years, but eventually it will lose this steady state and become overbalanced, usually in favor of the prey fish, and human intervention will be required to restore the original relationship. This is not the "balance" of Nicholson[105] because this system in itself is not capable of compensating for changes that may take place through natural variation of reproductive and survival rates, unless one is willing to include the management activities of man as part of the system.

The sustained yield requirement of "balance" should be based on fish of sizes large enough to interest anglers. The smaller the minimum useful size set by biologists the larger will be the number of ponds or lakes that are acceptable ("in balance"). Weights of harvestable-size fish according to Swingle[135] are given in Table 5.1 The approximate lengths of these fish have been interpolated from these weights.

Youthful fishermen are likely to accept fish of any size; adult experienced fishermen are more selective, possibly because they have to process and eat the fish. Although one may eat smelt of relatively small sizes, because their bones are fine and become soft with cooking, the same cannot be said for small crappies, bluegills, and other sunfish. Bluegills or sunfish of 0.10 lb and crappies of 0.26 lb are listed above as being harvestable. Converted to inches, these weights would represent

Table 5.1 Sizes of Harvestable Fish [135]

Fish	Minimum Weight (lb)	Estimated Length (in.)
Bluegills and other sunfish	0.10	5.0
Crappies	0.26	7.5
Largemouth bass	0.40	9.5
Bullheads	0.30	8.0
Gizzard shad	0.50	11.0
Channel cats	0.50	12.0
Gar	1.00	16.0
Buffalo	1.00	12.0
Carp	1.00	14.0

lengths of 5.0 in. and 7.5 in., respectively. For most parts of this country these minimum lengths for harvestable fish might be increased to at least 6.0 in. (0.18−0.20 lb) for bluegills and other sunfish and 8.0 in. for crappies (0.30−0.35 lb). Neither gizzard shad nor gars are usually considered utilizable in a practical sense, and buffalo cannot be harvested by hook-and-line except by special fishing methods or by accidental snagging. Disagreement on minimum harvestable (useful) sizes for bluegills and other sunfish by only one inch (5 in. to 6 in.) might make a great deal of difference in designating a population of fishes as desirable or undesirable (e.g., "balanced" or "unbalanced").

The use of the term "balance" in referring to fish populations that produce satisfactory yields has the following drawbacks:

1. Balance has been defined in more general biological terminology,[105] so that the term should not be applied with specific reference to harvestable pond-fish populations.

2. The simple predator−prey relationship which is the basis for "balance" in fish populations is an oversimplification of what actually is taking place.[17,78] Fishery biologists should be no more willing to accept such a relationship than are game biologists to accept a fox−rabbit or a prairie dog−coyote "balance."

3. Selected species, numbers, and sizes of fishes released in an artificial lake habitat represent artificial ecosystems and can hardly be expected to show any great stability of "effective compensatory reaction to the disturbing forces which operate upon it."[105] Therefore, "balance" loses its meaning when applied to such a population.

REFERENCES

1. Allen, K. R., 1942, "Comparison of bottom faunas as sources of available fish food," *Am. Fish. Soc. Trans.* 71, 275-283.
2. Ball, R. C., 1952, "Farm pond management in Michigan," *J. Wildlife Management* 16(3), 266-269.
3. Ball, R. C., and Ford, J. R., 1953, "Production of food—fish and minnows in Michigan ponds," *Mich. State Univ. Agr. Expt. Sta. Bull.* 35(3), 384-391.
4. Ball, R. C., and Tait, H. D., 1952, "Production of bass and bluegills in Michigan ponds," *Mich. State Univ. Agr. Expt. Sta. Tech. Bull.* 231, 1-25.
5. Ball, R. C., and Tanner, H. A., 1951, "The biological effects of fertilizer on a warmwater lake," *Mich. State Univ. Agr. Expt. Sta. Tech. Bull.* 223, 1-32.
6. Barney, R. L., and Canfield, H. L., 1922, "The farm pond and its productivity," *Fins, Feathers and Furs* (30), 3-7.
7. Bayless, J. D., 1976, "Striped bass hatching and hybridization experiments," *21st Ann. Conf. S. E. Assoc. Game and Fish Comm.* pp. 1-18.
8. Beers, G. D., and McConnell, W. J., 1966, "Some effects of threadfin shad introduction on black crappie diet and condition," *J. Arizona Acad. Sci.* 4(2), 71-74.
9. Bennett, G. W., 1945, "Overfishing in a small artificial lake, Onized Lake, near Alton, Illinois," *Illinois Nat. Hist. Surv. Bull.* 23(3), 373-406.
10. Bennett, G. W., 1948, "The bass-bluegill combination in a small artificial lake," *Illinois Nat. Hist. Surv. Bull.* 24(3), 377-412.
11. Bennett, G. W., 1951, "Experimental largemouth bass management in Illinois," *Am. Fish. Soc. Trans.* 80, 231-239.
12. Bennett, G. W., 1952, "Pond management in Illinois," *J. Wildlife Management* 16(3), 249-253.
13. Bennett, G. W., 1954, "Largemouth bass in Ridge Lake, Coles, County, Illinois," *Illinois Nat. Hist. Surv. Bull.* 26(2), 217-276.
14. Bennett, G. W., Adkins, H. W., and Childers, W. F., 1968, "The largemouth bass and other fishes in Ridge Lake, Illinois, 1941-1963," *Illinois Nat. Hist. Surv. Bull.* 30 (1), 1-67.
15. Bennett, G. W., and Childers, W. F., 1957, "The smallmouth bass, *Micropterus dolomieui;* in warmwater ponds," *J. Wildlife Management* 21(4), 414-424.
16. Bennett, G. W., and Childers, W. F., 1966, "The lake chubsucker as a forage species," *Progressive Fish Culturist* 28(2), 89-92.
17. Bennett, G. W., Thompson, D. H., and Parr, S. A., 1940, "Lake management reports, 4. A second year of fisheries investigations at Fork Lake, 1939," *Illinois Nat. Hist. Surv. Bio. Notes* 14, 1-24.
18. Beverton, R. S. H., and Holt, S. J., 1957, "On the dynamics of exploited fish populations," *Fish. Invest. Series* 19(2), 1-533.
19. Beyerle, G. B., and Williams, J. E., 1968, "Some observations of food selectivity by northern pike in aquaria," *Am. Fish. Soc. Trans.* 97(1), 28-31.
20. Bishop, R. D., 1967, "Evaluation of the striped bass *(Roccus saxatilis)* and white bass *(Roccus chrysops)* hybrids after two years," *21st Ann. Conf. S.E. Assoc. Game Fish Comm.,* pp. 1-17.
21. Black, I. D., and Williamson, L. C., 1947, "Artificial hybrids between muskellunge and northern pike," *Wisconsin Acad. Sci., Arts and Letters Trans.* 38, 299-314.
22. Breder, C. M., Jr., 1936, "The reproductive habits of the North American sunfishes (family Centrarchidae)," *Zool.* 21(1), 1-48.
23. Brown, W. H., 1951, "Results of stocking largemouth black bass and channel catfish in experimental Texas farm ponds," *Am. Fish. Soc. Trans.* 80, 210-217.

24. Brown, W. H., 1952, "Rate of survival of largemouth black bass fingerlings stocked in experimental farm ponds," *Progressive Fish Culturist* 14(2), 79-80.

25. Brown, C. J. D., and Thoreson, N. A., 1952, "Ranch fish ponds in Montana," *J. Wildlife Management* 16(3), 275-278.

26. Buss, K., and Miller, J., 1967, "Interspecific hybridization of esocids: hatching success, pattern development and fertility of some F_1 hybrids," *Bur. of Sport Fish. and Wildlife, Tech. Paper* 14, 1-30.

27. Caillouet, C. W., Jr., 1967, "Hyperactivity, blood lactic acid and mortality in channel catfish," *Agr. Home Econom. Expt. Sta. Iowa State Univ. Res. Bull.* 251, 898-915.

28. Carbine, W. F., 1939, "Observations on the spawning habits of centrarchid fishes in Deep Lake, Oakland County, Michigan," *North Am. Wildlife Conf. Trans.* 4, 275-287.

29. Carbine, W. F., 1942, "Observations on the life history of the northern pike, *Exox lucius* L., in Houghton Lake, Michigan," *Am. Fish. Soc. Trans.* 71, 149-164.

30. Carlander, K. D., 1958, "Disturbance of the predator-prey balance as a management technique," *Am. Fish. Soc. Trans.* 87, 34-38.

31. Carlander, K. D., Whitney, R. R., Speaker, E. B., and Madden, K., 1960, "Evaluation of walleye fry stocking in Clear Lake, Iowa, by alternate-year planting," *Am. Fish. Soc. Trans.* 89(3), 249-254.

32. Childers, W. F., 1967, "Hybridization of four species of sunfishes (Centrarchidae)," *Illinois Nat. Hist. Surv. Bull.* 29(3), 1-214.

33. Childers, W. F., and Bennett, G. W., 1961, "Hybridization between three species of sunfish (Lepomis)," *Illinois Nat. Hist. Surv. Biol. Notes* 46, 1-15.

34. Childers, W. F., and Bennett, G. W., 1967, "Hook-and-line yield of largemouth bass and redear x green sunfish hybrids in a one-acre pond," *Progressive Fish Culturist* 29(1), 27-35.

35. Clark, C. F., 1964, "Bluegill control experiment in Hamler Lake, Ohio," *Ohio Dept. Nat. Res. Publ.* W-335, pp. 1-5.

36. Clark, M., 1952, "Kentucky's farm fish pond program," *K. Wildlife Management* 16(3), 262-266.

37. Cleary, R. E., and Mayhew, J. K., 1961, "An analysis of an alternate-year walleye fry stocking program in the Cedar River in Iowa," *Proc. Iowa Acad. Sci.* 68, 254-259.

38. Clemens, H. P., and Sneed, K. E., 1962, "Bioassay and use of pituitary materials to spawn warm-water fishes," *U.S. Fish Wildlife Serv. Res. Rept.* 61, 1-30.

39. Coggeshall, L. T., 1923, "A study of the productivity and breeding habits of the bluegill, *Lepomis pallidus* (Mitch)," *Proc. Indiana Aca. Sci.* 33, 315-320.

40. Cooper, G. P., 1948, "Fish stocking policies in Michigan," *North Am. Wildlife Conf. Trans.* 13, 187-193.

41. Crossman, E. J., and Buss, K., 1965, "Hybridization in the family Esocidae," *J. Fisheries Res. Board Can.* 22(5), 1261-1292.

42. Demchenko, I. F., 1963, "On sexual differences in the pike (*Esox lucius* L.,)" *Vopr. Ikhtiol.* 3(1), 190-193.

43. Durham, L., 1949, "A study of largemouth bass-bluegill population of Martin's Pond, McLean County, Illinois," Master's Thesis, *Univ. of Illinois*, pp. 1-47 (unpublished).

44. Dyche, L. L., 1914, "Ponds, pond fish and pond fish culture," *Kansas State Dept. Fish and Game Bull.* I, 1-208.

45. Eddy, S., 1940, "Do muskellunge and pickerel interbreed?" *Progressive Fish Culturist* 48, 25-27.

46. Eddy, S., 1957, *How to Know the Freshwater Fishes*, Wm. C. Brown Co., Dubuque, Iowa, 253 pp.

47. Eddy, S., and Surber, T., 1960, *Northern Fishes,* rev. ed., Charles T. Branford Co., 276 pp.

48. Elson, P. F., 1962, "Predator-prey relationships between fish-eating birds and Atlantic salmon," *Bull. Fisheries Res. Board Can.* 133, 1-87.

49. Errington, P. L., 1956, "Factors limiting higher vertebrate populations," *Science* 124 (3216), 304-307.

50. Eschmeyer, P., 1950, "The life history of walleye *Stizostedion vitreum vitreum,* (Mitchell) in Michigan," *Mich. Dept. Cons. Inst. for Fishes Res. Bull.* 3, 1-99.

51. Eschmeyer, R. W., 1944, "Fish migration into the Clinch River below Norris Dam, Tennessee," *J. Tenn. Acad. Sci.* 19(1), 31-41.

52. Forney, J. L., 1965, "Factors affecting growth and maturity in a walleye population," *N.Y. Fish and Game J.* 12(2), 217-232.

53. Giudice, J. J., 1966, "Growth of a blue x channel catfish hybrid as compared to its parent species," *Progressive Fish Culturist* 28(3), 142-145.

54. Hackney, P. A., 1966, "Predator-prey relationships of the flathead catfish in ponds under selected forage fish conditions," *Proc. 19th Ann. Conf. S.E. Assoc. Game Fish Comm.,* pp. 217-222.

55. Hall, J. F., 1958, "Final report on the success of largemouth bass-bluegill and largemouth bass-shell-cracker rates and ratios in Kentucky farm ponds," *Proc. 12th Ann. Conf. S.E. Assoc. Game Fish Comm.,* 91-116.

56. Hansen, D. F., 1951, "Biology of the white crappie in Illinois," *Illinois Nat. Hist. Surv. Bull.* 25(4), 211-265.

57. Hansen, D. F., Bennett, G. W., Webb, R. J., and Lewis, J. M., 1960, "Hook-and-line catch in fertilized and unfertilized ponds," *Illinois Nat. Hist. Surv. Bull.* 27(5), 345-390.

58. Harlan, J. R., and Speaker, E. B., 1956, *Iowa Fish and Fishing,* 3rd ed., Iowa Cons. Comm., Des Moines, Iowa, 377 pp.

59. Harrison, A. C., 1940, "Report of the Inland fisheries advisory officer for the year 1939," *Inland Fish. Rept.* Union of S. Africa, pp. 1-19.

60. Heard, W. R., and Curd, N. R., 1959, "Stomach contents of American mergansers, *Mergus merganser* Linnaeus, caught in gill nets set in Lake Carl Blackwell, Oklahoma," *Proc. Oklahoma Acad. Sci.* 39, 197-200.

61. Henderson, H., 1965, "Observation on the propagation of flathead catfish in the San Marcos State Fish Hatchery, Tex.," *Proc. 17th Ann. Conf. S.E. Assoc. Game and Fish Comm.* pp. 173-177.

62. Hess, A. D., and Swartz, A., 1940, "The forage ratio and its use in determining the food grade of streams," *North Am. Wildlife Conf. Trans.* 5, 162-164.

63. Hickling, C. F., 1960, "The Malacca tilapia hybrids," *J. Genetics* 57(1), 1-10.

64. Hickling, C. F., 1962, *Fish Culture,* Faber and Faber Ltd., London, 295 pp.

65. Hickling, C. F., 1963, "The cultivation of tilapia," *Sci. Am.* 208(5), 143-152.

66. Hubbs, C. F., 1955, "Hybridization between fish species in nature," *Sys. Zool.* 4, 1-20.

67. Hubbs, C. L., and Hubbs, L. C., 1930, "Increased growth in hybrid sunfishes," *Papers Mich. Acad. Sci., Arts and Letters.* 13, 291-301.

68. Hunsaker, D., II, and Crawford, R. W., 1964, "Preferential spawning behavior of the largemouth bass, *Micropterus salmoides,*" *Copeia* 1, 240-241.

69. James, M. C., Meehan, O. L., and Douglas, E. J., 1944, "Fish stocking as related to the management of inland waters," *U.S. Fish Wildlife Serv. Cons. Bull.* 35, 1-22.

70. James, M. F., 1946, "Histology of gonadal changes in the bluegill, *Lepomis macrochirus* Raf., and largemouth black bass, *Huro salmoides* (Lacepede)," *J. Morph..* 79(1), 63-92.

71. Jenkins, R. M., 1955, "Expansion of the crappie population in Ardmore City Lake following a drastic reduction in numbers," *Proc. Oklahoma Acad. Sci.* 36, 70-76.

72. Jenkins, R. M., 1955, "The effect of gizzard shad on the fish population of a small Oklahoma lake," *Am. Fish. Soc. Trans.* 85, 58-74.
73. Jenkins, R. M., 1958, "The standing crop of fish in Oklahoma ponds," *Proc. Oklahoma Acad. Sci.* 38, 157-172.
74. Jenkins, R. M., 1961, *Reservoir Management—Progress and Challenge,* Sport Fish. Inst., Washington, D.C., pp. 1-22.
75. Johannes, R. E., and Larkin, P. A., 1961, "Competition for food between redside shiners *(Richardsonius balteatus)* and rainbow trout *(Salmo gairdneri)* in two British lakes," *J. Fisheries Res. Board Can.* 18(2), 203-220.
76. Johnson, F. H., 1961, "Walleye egg survival during incubation on several types of bottom in Lake Winnibigoshish, Minnesota and connecting waters," *Am. Fish. Soc. Trans.* 90(3), 312-322.
77. Johnson, L. D., 1958, "Pond culture of muskellunge in Wisconsin," Wisconsin Cons. Dept. Tech. Fish. Bull. 17, 1-54.
78. Johnson, R. E., 1949, "Maintenance of natural population balance," *Proc. 38th Conv. Int. Assoc. Game, Fish, and Cons. Comms.,* pp. 35-42.
79. Johnson, M. G., and McCrimmon, H. R., 1967, "Survival, growth and reproduction of largemouth bass in southern Ontario ponds,"*Progressive Fish Cult.* 29(4), 216-221.
80. Kawamoto, N. Y., 1961, "The influence of excretory substances of fishes on their own growth," *Progressive Fish Culturist* 23(2), 70-75.
81. Kelley, J. W., 1962, "Sexual maturity and fecundity of the largemouth bass, *Micropterus salmoides* (Lacepede), in Maine," *Am. Fish. Soc. Trans.* 91(1), 23-28.
82. Klingbiel, J., and Snow, H., 1962, *Wisconsin Cons. Bull.,* March-April, pp. 13-22.
83. Kramer, R. H., and Smith, L. L., Jr., 1962, "Formation of year classes in largemouth bass," *Am. Fish. Soc. Trans.* 91(1), 29-41.
84. Krumholz, L. A., 1950, "New fish stocking policies for Indiana ponds," *North Am. Wildlife Conf. Trans.* 15, 251-270.
85. Krumholz, L. A., 1950, "Further observations on the use of hybrid sunfish in stocking small ponds," *Am. Fish. Soc. Trans.* 79, 112-123.
86. Krumholz, L. A., 1952, "Management of Indiana ponds for fishing," *J. Wildlife Management* 16(3), 254-257.
87. Kudryns'ka, O. I., 1962, "Cannibalism among the larvae and fry of the carp," Dopovidi Akad. Nauk Ukr. RSR 1,111-113.
88. Kutkuhn, J. H., 1958, "Utilization of gizzard shad by game fishes in North Twin Lake, Iowa," *Proc. Iowa Acad. Sci.* 65, 571-579.
89. Lagler, K. F., and Deroth, G. C., 1953, "Populations and yields to anglers in a fishery for largemouth bass, *Micropterus salmoides* (Lac)." *Papers Mich. Acad. Sci.* 38, 241-250.
90. Larimore, R. W., 1957, "Ecological life history of the warmouth (Centrarchidae)," *Illinois Nat. Hist, Surv. Bull.* 27(1), 1-83.
91. Latta, W. C., and Sharkey, R. F., 1966, "Feeding behavior of the American merganser in captivity," *J. Wildlife Management* 30(1), 17-22.
92. Leonard, J. W., 1942, "Some observations on the winter feeding habits of brook trout fingerlings in relation to natural food organisms present," *Am. Fish. Soc. Trans.* 91, 219-227.
93. Lewis, W. M., Gunning, E. E., Lyles, E., and Bridges, W. L., 1961, "Food choice of largemouth bass as a function of availability and vulnerability of food items," *Am. Fish. Soc. Trans.* 90(3), 227-280.
94 Logan, H. J., 1967, "Comparison of growth and survival rates of striped bass and striped bass x white bass hybrids under controlled environments," *21st Ann. Conf. S. E. Assoc. Game Fish Comm.,* pp. 1-9.

95. Luce, W. M., 1937, "Hybrid crosses in sunfishes," *Illinois State Acad. Sci. Trans.* 30(2), 309-310.

96. MacPhee, C., 1961, "An experimental study of competition for food in fish," *Ecology* 42(4), 666-681.

97. Marzolf, R. C., 1957, "The reproduction of channel catfish in Missouri ponds," *J. Wildlife Management* 21(1), 22-28.

98. McCaig, R. S., Mullan, J. W., and Dodge, C. O., 1960, "Five-year report on the development of the fishery of a 25,000-acre domestic water supply reservoir in Massachusetts," *Progressive Fish Culturist* 22(1), 15-23.

99. McCarraher, D. B., 1959, "The northern pike-bluegill combination in north-central Nebraska farm ponds," *Progressive Fish Culturist* 21(3), 188-189.

100. McConnell, W. J., 1966, "Preliminary report on the Malacca *Tilapia* hybrid as a sport fish in Arizona," *Progressive Fish Culturist* 28(1), 40-46.

101. McFadden, J. T., Alexander, G. R., and Shetter, D. S., 1967, "Numerical changes and population regulation in brook trout, *Salvelinus fontinalis*," *J. Fisheries Res. Board Can.* 24(7), 1425-1459.

102. Minckley, W. L., and Craddock, J. E., 1961, "Predation of crayfish on fishes," *Progressive Fish Culturist* 23(3), 120-123.

103. Mraz, D., and Cooper, E. L., 1957, "Natural reproduction and survival of carp in small ponds," *J. Wildlife Management* 21(10), 66-69.

104. Neal, R. A., 1962, "White and black crappies in Clear Lake: Summer, 1960," *Proc. Iowa Acad. Sci.* 68, 247-253.

105. Nicholson, A. J., 1954, "An outline of the dynamics of animal populations," *Australian J. Zool.* 2(1), 9-65.

106. Nikolyukin, N. I., 1965, "Theoretical bases of hybridization in fish culture," in *Theoretical Bases of Fish Culture*, Nauka, Moscow, pp. 224-229.

107. Oehmcke, A. A., Johnson, L. Klingbiel, J., and Wistrom, C., 1958, "The Wisconsin muskellunge, its life history, ecology and management," *Wisconsin Cons. Dept. Pub.* 225, 1-12.

108. Olson, D. E., 1963, "Role of the white sucker in Minnesota waters," *Proc. Minn. Acad. Sci.* 31(1), 68-73.

109. Olson, D., and Wesloh, M., 1962, "A record of six years of angling in Many Point Lake, Becker County, Minnesota, with special reference to the effect of walleye fingerling stocking," *Minn. Div. of Game and Fish, Invest. Rept.* 247, 1-5.

110. Patriarche, M. H., and Ball, R. C., 1949, "An analysis of the bottom fauna production in fertilized and unfertilized ponds and its utilization by young-of-the-year-fish," *Mich. State Univ. Agr. Expt. Sta. Tech. Bull.* 207, 1-35.

111. Plehm, M., 1924, *Praktikum der Fischkranheiten,* Praktikum der Fischkrankheiten, E. Schweizerbartische Verlagsbuchandlug, Stuttgart, pp. 301-479.

112. Rawson, D. S., and Ruttan, R. A., 1952, "Pond fish studies in Saskatchewan," *J. Wildlife Management,* 16(3), 283-288.

113. Regier, H. A., 1962, "On the evolution of bass-bluegill stocking policies and management recommendations," *Progressive Fish Culturist* 24(3), 99-111.

114. Regier, H. A., 1966, "A perspective on research on the dynamics of fish populations in the Great Lakes," *Progressive Fish Culturist* 28(1), 3-18.

115. Ricker, W. E., 1948, "Hybrid sunfish for stocking small ponds," *Am. Fish. Soc. Trans.* 75(1945), 84-96.

116. Ricker, W. E. 1954, "Stock and recruitment," *J. Fisheries Res. Board Can.* 11(5), 559-623.

117. Rose, E. T., 1955, "The fluctuation in abundance of walleyes in Spirit Lake, Iowa," *Proc. Iowa Acad. Sci.* 62, 567-575.

118. Rose, S. M., 1959, "Failure of survival of slowly growing members of a population," *Science* 129(3355), 1026.

119. Saila, S. B., 1952, "Some results of farm management studies in New York," *J. Wildlife Management* 16(3), 279-282.

120. Slastenenko, E. P., 1957, "A list of natural fish hybrids of the world," *Hydrobiol. Res. Inst., Faculty Sci. Univ. Istanbul Ser. B.* 4(2-3), 76-97.

121. Smith, E. V., and Swingle, H. S., 1942, "Percentages of survival of bluegills *(Lepomis macrochirus)* and largemouth black bass *(Huro salmoides)* when planted in new ponds," *Am. Fish. Soc. Trans.* 72, 63-67.

122. Smith, W. A., Kirkwood, J. B., and Hall, J. F., 1955, "A survey of the success of various stocking rates and ratios of bass and bluegills in Kentucky farm ponds," *Kentucky Dept. Fish Wildlife Res. Fish. Bull.* 16, 1-42.

123. Smitherman, R. O., and Hester, F. E., 1962, "Artificial propagation of sunfishes with meristic comparisons of three species of *Lepomis* and five of their hybrids," *Am. Fish. Soc. Trans.* 1(4), 333-341.

124. Solomon, M. E., 1949, "The natural control of annual populations," *J. Anim. Ecol.* 18, 1-35.

125. Starrett, W. C., and McNeil, P. L., Jr., 1952, "Sport fishing at Lake Chautauqua, near Havana, Illinois in 1950 and 1951," *Illinois Nat. Hist. Surv. Biol. Notes* 30, 1-31.

126. Stroud, R. H., 1955, "Harvests and management of warm-water fish populations in Massachusetts' lakes, ponds and reservoirs," *Progressive Fish Culturist* 17(2), 51-62.

127. Stroud, R. H., 1957, *Sanctuary Muskies*, S.F.I. Bull. 62, p. 5.

128. Stroud, R. H., 1958, *Two-Hundred-Dollar Muskies*, S.F.I. Bull. 84, pp. 1-2.

129. Stroud, R. H., and Jenkins, R. M., 1961, *Stocking Story*, S.F.I. Bull. 115, p. 7.

130. Stroud, R. H., and Jenkins, R. M., 1961, *More on Walleye Stocking*, S.F.I. Bull. 117, p. 23.

131. Stroud, R. H., and Jenkins, R. M., 1962, *Bass-Shiner Combination*, S.F.I. Bull. 123, p. 6.

132. Stroud, R. H., and Jenkins, R. M., 1962, *Predator Stocking Ineffective*, S.F.I. Bull, 127, pp. 6-7.

133. Surber, E. W., 1949, "Results of varying the ratio of largemouth black bass and bluegills in the stocking of experimental farm ponds," *Am. Fish. Soc. Trans.* 77(1947), 141-151.

134. Swingle, H. S., 1945, "Improvement of fishing in old ponds," *10th North Am. Wildlife Conf. Trans.*, pp. 299-308.

135. Swingle, H. S., 1950, "Relationships and dynamics of balanced and unbalanced fish population," *Alabama Agr. Expt. Sta. Bull.* 274, 1-74.

136. Swingle, H. S., 1956, "A repressive factor controlling reproduction in fishes," *Proc. 8th Pacific Sci. Cong. (1953)*, Illa. 865-871.

137. Swingle, H. S., 1961, "Some relationships within fish populations causing fluctuations in production," *Proc. Pacific Sci. Cong. 9 (1957)*, 10, 43-45.

138. Swingle, H. S., Prather, E. E., and Lawrence, J. M., 1953, "Partial poisoning of overcrowded fish populations," *Alabama Polytech. Inst. Agr. Expt. Sta. Circ.* 113, 1-15.

139. Swingle, H. S., and Smith, E. V., 1942, "Management of farm fish ponds," *Alabama Expt. Sta. Bull.* 254, 1-23.

140. Swingle, H. S., and Smith, E. V., 1947, "Management of farm fish ponds," *Alabama. Polytech. Inst. Agr. Expt. Sta. Bull.* 254, 1-30 (rev.).

141. Thompson, D. H., 1935, "Hybridization and racial differentiation among Illinois fishes," *Illinois Nat. Hist. Surv. Bull.* 20(5), 492-494.

142. Thompson, D. H., 1941, "Fish production of inland streams, and lakes," in *A symposium on Hydrobiology*, Univ. of Wisconsin Press, Madison, pp. 206-217.

143. Toetz, D. W., 1966, "The change from endogenous to exogenous sources of energy in bluegill sunfish larvae," *Invest. Indiana Lakes and Streams* 7, 115-146.

144. Toth, R., 1966, "Fish anesthetics," in *Inland Fisheries Management,* Calif. Dept. Fish and Game, p. 148.

145. Trautman, M. B., 1957, *The Fishes of Ohio,* Ohio State Univ. Press, Columbus, 683 pp.

146. Vincent, R. E., 1960, "Some influences of domestication upon three stocks of brook trout (*Salvelinus fontinalis* Mitchell)," *Am. Fish. Soc. Trans.* 89(1), 35-52.

147. Viosca, P., Jr., 1945, "A critical analysis of practices in the management of warm-water fish with a view to greater food production," *Am. Fish. Soc. Trans.* 73, 274-283.

148. Vladimirov, V. I., 1960, "The role of predatory invertebrates in the dynamics of abundance of migratory fishes," *Ordi Khishchnykh Bespozvonochnykh V. Dinomike Chislemosti Prokhodnykh Ryb. Voprosy Ikhtiol.* 16, 55-66.

149. Watt, K. E. F., 1959, "Studies on population productivity," II, "Factors governing productivity in a population of smallmouth bass," *Ecol. Monographs* 29(4), 367-392.

150. West, J. L., and Hester, F. E., 1966, "Intergeneric hybridization of centrarchids," *Am. Fish. Soc. Trans.* 95(3), 280-288.

151. Yashouv, A., 1958, "The excreta of carp as a growth limiting factor," *Bamidgeh,* 10(4), 90-95.

152. Franklin, D. R., and Smith, L. L., Jr., 1963. "Early life history of the northern pike, *Esox lucius* L., with special reference to factors influencing the numerical strength of year classes," *Am. Fish. Soc. Trans.* 92(2), 91-110.

6

THEORIES AND TECHNIQUES OF MANAGEMENT

The objectives of management are to produce and maintain a fish population that will supply a satisfactory sustained return to those with the authority to take an annual crop. Few populations are handled with sufficient intensity to keep them producing at peak level, although many provide a fairly adequate sustained yield. Probably, private and public demand for angling would be satisfied if all available waters offered a moderate sustained yield. However, in many regions unproductive ponds and lakes (those that supply little or no fish) predominate. This is particularly true of small artificial lakes and reservoirs located near centers of population.

Most unproductive lakes or reservoirs contain "problem" fish populations. Obviously, management effort should first be directed to restoring reasonable production to these bodies of water; the application of intensive fish management can come later.

There are two methods of handling a "problem" population in a pond or lake. One is to eliminate the population entirely and start anew with fish from an outside source; the other is to change the problem population, either by direct action upon it or through indirect action, brought about by modifying the fishes' environment. Both of these approaches are in common use. However, before deciding on a management procedure, a rather careful diagnosis, requiring one or several methods of sampling the population, must be made. Following is a discussion of the uses of fish samples and some common methods of taking them.

FISH SAMPLING

The fisherman or fisheries manager can rarely see beneath the water sufficiently to identify and count the fishes in a lake or pond. Consequently, to determine the numbers and species present, he must resort to live-trapping techniques. It is seldom necessary to kill these specimens, even though their number is not large enough to have any significance in relation to the remaining population.

Reasons for Sampling Fish Populations

There are several justifiable reasons for sampling fish populations. An adequate sample allows an appraisal of the components of a population and exposes those segments of it having sizes and numbers satisfactory for angling. As described in another chapter, the main causes of poor fishing are *(1)* overpopulation and stunting of desirable species and *(2)* an overabundance of undesirable species with a concurrent shortage of acceptable ones. Once the causes of poor fishing have been exposed, it is possible to plan a method of improving the population. For example, an excessive number of stunted crappies can be thinned out by partial "poisoning;" however, if there are overabundant and stunted bullheads as well, complete elimination and restocking may be necessary. Obviously, a sampling method that will expose only the crappies does not provide a satisfactory diagnosis.

It is frequently necessary to demonstrate to fishermen and owners that lakes are not "fished out". This is commonly called for in waters close to urban centers where species exposed to heavy fishing pressures may have learned to distinguish a frog from a frog "popper" and a worm on a hook from a free one. These "fished-out" lakes are often filled with "wise" fish, and fishermen will keep trying to catch them (at the same time receiving health and aesthetic benefits) if the fishery biologist can demonstrate that desirable specimens are present.

Regular annual sampling should be done on important impoundments not only to record changes in the relative abundance of species, but also changes in their length—frequency distribution and their condition from year to year. Fish taken with various sampling techniques should be measured and weighed individually, and scale samples obtained where there is an indication of stunting or of exceptionally rapid growth. These data allow an annual appraisal of the status of all important species. When this information is integrated for several successive years, it shows unmistakable trends that may call for certain management practices.

Table 6.1 shows a hypothetical length—frequency distribution for blue-gills in an imaginary lake. In 1955, there were adequate numbers of large bluegills belonging to the 1953 year class (determined from scales). These fish showed an average Index of Condition *(C)* of 8.0 or higher, which demonstrated that the fish were relatively fat. In collections of 1955 and 1956 no excessively large year class more recent than 1954 was present although this year class was fairly well represented. However, the collections of 1957 showed very large numbers of 1956 year-class fish that, after two growing seasons, were only about 3.0 in. in length. This would indicate a dangerous situation that might mark the beginning of over-population and stunting of bluegills. Further evidence of population pressure in 1957 was found among the 1954 and 1953 year-class blue-gills which had Indexes of Condition of 7.0 and 7.4, respectively, indicating that the larger fish were thinner in 1957 than in previous years.

By September of 1958, the 1956 year class was severely stunted. After three growing seasons (summers) they averaged only 4.0 in. in length and were thin with abnormally large eyes (an indication of stunting). Blue-gills of 6 in. or larger were still fairly common, but were very thin with Indexes of Condition ranging from 6.5 to 6.9. This bluegill population needed to be drastically reduced, particularly those fish belonging to the 1956 year class. Furthermore, since the 1957 sampling disclosed an abnormally large 1956 year class, measures should have been taken then to reduce its numbers.

Table 6.1   Length-Frequency Distribution of Bluegills in Clear Lake From September Collections Taken With Wire Traps

Total Length (in.)	1955	1956	1957	1958	
3.0	13	4	256	18	
3.5	27	3	140	36	
4.0	33	63	27	216	1956 year class
4.5	12	72	47	84	
5.0	15	18	45	62	
5.5	62	17	52	14	
6.0	128	26	11	30	1954 year class
6.5	47	102	10	3	
7.0	12	13	47	4	
7.5	1	2	9	10	1953 year class
8.0	5	2	1	1	
8.5	3	1	1		
9.0	1		1		

Sampling Methods

Many types of gear have been used for sampling populations. Most of these are selective for one or more kinds of fish, and may give a faulty impression of the relative abundance of species, both those too easily caught and those not taken in proportion to their numbers.

Table 6.2 gives a rough appraisal of the efficiency of several kinds of sampling methods in relation to a number of kinds of warmwater fishes. These represent the combined experiences of Starrett and Barnickol[165] and the members of the Illinois Natural History Survey staff who have fished with these methods for many years.

Gill Nets. These nets are made with linen or nylon thread, fine enough so that fish, not seeing them, will become gilled or entangled (Fig. 6.1). Gill nets are tied to give bar measurements (one side of a square mesh) ranging from 1 to 4 in.; sometimes special sampling nets are made by splicing 50-ft sections of increasing mesh sizes from 1 in. up to 3 or 4 in. Gill nets can be set at various depths from surface to bottom. They are selective for pelagic fish such as herring and trout and are seldom used in shallow lakes.

Trammel Nets. A light gill net of small mesh is hung with plenty of extra webbing between two walls of netting consisting of very large mesh of heavy twine. A fish hitting the light net carries a pocket of this net through

Table 6.2   An Appraisal of the Efficiency of Several Fish-Sampling Methods Commonly Used in Artificial Lakes, as Related to Common Warm Water Fishes[a]

	Method of Sampling					
Kind of Fish	Trammel Nets	Wing Nets Trap Nets	Seines	Spot Poisoning	Boat Shocking	Angling
Largemouth bass	poor	poor	fair	good	fair	good
Smallmouth bass	poor	fair	fair	good	fair	good
Sunfish [b]	good	good	good	good	good	good
Crappies	good	excellent	good	good	fair	poor
Carp	good	good	good	good	fair	poor
Gizzard shad	fair	good	good	good	good	—
Gar fish	good	fair	good	good	poor	poor
Bullheads	fair	good	poor	fair	poor	good
Channel catfish	poor	good	good	good	poor	poor

[a] In part from Starrett and Barnichol.[165]
[b] Bluegills, green sunfish, red-ear sunfish, etc.

Fig. 6.1 TVA biologists use gill nets for sampling fishes in large deep reservoirs.

an opening in the larger net and so becomes trapped. Trammel nets are supplied with floats and weights; they are set across and/or floated in a current (in a river) or set around a school of fish (in a lake). These nets are selective for fish that can be frightened into hitting the net. They are commonly used for commercial fish, e.g., carp, buffalo, and catfish.

Seines. These are pieces of webbing of various mesh sizes and lengths held upright in the water by floats and weights and pulled through the water to encircle fish. They are somewhat less selective than most other types of gear. Seines can be used only where the water depth is less than the depth of the seine and where the bottom is clear of snags. When confined within a small area, certain fishes such as largemouth bass will jump over the top of a seine unless the cork line is held up above the surface of the water.[191] Other kinds of fishes attempt to go under the lead line at the bottom so that if the seine becomes snagged or rolls up, they may escape from it. Large seine hauls repeated annually on a specific lake may be used for predicting standing crops of fish in pounds per acre; isolated seine hauls are of little value in this respect.[137]

Hoop Nets, Wing Nets, and Trap Nets. A hoop net consists of a cylinder of webbing supported by hoops, open at one end and closed at the other. Inside are two funnels, one just inside the open end of the cylinder and the other midway between the open and closed ends. Hoop nets are set in rivers with the tail upstream and the open end downstream. The current keeps the hoops separated and the net stretched. Fish move into the net easily through the funnel openings, but have some difficulty in finding their way out again.[59] Usually, in swimming around inside the net after passing through the first funnel, some fish wander through the second funnel and are then inside the closed end of the cylinder called the pot. Fish are removed from the pot by releasing a drawstring after the net or pot has been lifted into a boat.

Wing nets are modified hoop nets with short wings of webbing attached to the hoop at the open end of the net. They are used in quiet water where the wings guide fish into the net opening, and are held in a stretched position by stakes or weights.[60] Wing nets are sometimes fished with a long lead net set upright between the wings at the net opening. This lead net acts as a "drift" fence and fish following it soon find themselves in the wing net.

Hansen[61] found considerable variation in the catch of wing nets at various times of the year and under varying physical and chemical conditions associated with water temperature, turbidity, dissolved oxygen, and carbon dioxide.

Trap nets are usually modified wing nets with wings arranged in loops to direct fish toward the opening of the net no matter which way they attempt to go, and with a lead net attached inside a forebay so that fish following the lead net to its proximal end are already inside of the front of the trap.

Mesh covering these nets is composed of nylon or cotton webbing squares varying in size from 1/2 in. to 4 in. Hoop diameters range from 2 1/2 to 6 ft. Trap nets of larger sizes are not used for sampling.

"Hoop nets" made of hardware cloth are more useful for fishing in ponds and small lakes than are hoop nets or wing nets made of string because the wire nets are not subject to muskrat damage. The nets are constructed of 1/2-in. hardware cloth and consist of a cylinder of wire, 2 ft in diameter and 4 or 5 ft long, with a single funnel leading into the open end and wire mesh across the closed end. Fish are removed through a small door covering an opening on one side, or through the open end of the cylinder after the funnel has been lifted out.

Baker[4] compared catches of wire traps with 1- and 2-in. mesh and discovered that 1-in. mesh traps caught 72% game and pan fish and 28% rough fish whereas the 2-in. mesh traps caught 92% rough fish and only 8% game and pan fish. However, the 1 in. mesh caught 81.5% of all of the fish caught (by number) and the 2-in. traps the remaining 18.5%.

Thompkins and Bridges[193] found that low doses of copper sulfate (0.15 ppm) in soft water irritated the fish and caused them to move about, thereby increasing the catch of wing nets set in the area of treatment.

Some fish may be attracted into a net by bait[10,32] or by the darkness of the water inside of it. Other fish, that avoid nets of small mesh, will enter those of larger mesh because their interiors are scarcely darker than the surrounding water. Certain kinds of fish such as largemouth bass will seldom enter hoop nets, wing nets, or trap nets in clear water, whether the mesh size is large or small.[145] Because these nets are attractive to certain kinds of fish and are avoided by others, they are extremely selective and samples of fish taken by them will not be representative of the fish population from which they were taken.

Minnow Seine Sampling.   Minnow seines are often used to catch the young of various kinds of fish in order to gather information on the number of species of fish present in a body of water and to determine spawning success (relative abundance of young) of the several kinds of fish present. Usually when a dominant year class of one species of fish has been spawned, it will show up almost at once in early summer minnow seine hauls.

Anyone who has made an intensive study of a fish population inhabiting a pond or lake will discover after a few years of sampling of young that total numbers and relative abundance may vary greatly from year to year. Also, the young of a given species may appear to be very abundant in the early summer when the young are small, but later, if the rate of survival is low, they may be relatively scarce.

Minnow-Seine Method of Pond Analysis.   According to the minnow-seine method of testing ponds containing largemouth bass and bluegills,[180] the condition of the fish population ("balance") may be judged on the basis of the success of reproduction of bass and bluegills for the current year and the past survival of bluegill spawn beyond the first year (3-,4-, and 5-in. length groups of bluegills). The method is based on the hypothesis that with an overabundant stunted population of bluegills, the bass (and sometimes bluegills, too) will be unable to produce enough to assure their appearance among fish caught in a reasonable number of minnow-seine hauls. On the other hand, with an overabundant stunted population of bass, there will be no intermediate-sized bluegills, and a scarcity or absence of small bluegills and perhaps small bass. These assumptions are valid if interference in spawning has not come from physical conditions such as too cold water, turbidity, or salinity, with a pH too high or low, and if there has been no great rise or drawdown of water levels at the wrong time.[180]

In 1950, an airing of conflicting ideas on minnow-seine sampling occurred when Dr. Gustav A. Swanson, editor of the *Journal of Wildlife*

Management, published some pro and con opinions of it.[2] Long-term intensive studies of populations, in which minnow-seine collections were interpreted by the minnow-seine hypothesis, often failed to define accurately the type of population present. If these studies could not demonstrate the consistent validity of the method, one may doubt the value of less intensive investigations, regardless of the number of ponds sampled and catches subjected to the test formula. As stated in 1950[2] the author has found no published information (an adequate series of experiments in which minnow-seine analyses were followed by draining or poisoning censuses of the adult fish populations) to prove the value of the minnow-seine method. Tests of the method in Iowa,[29] through use of a larger seine and age analyses of fish, demonstrated errors in interpretation of results from minnow-seine collections.

However, shoreline seining with a fine-mesh seine to catch the smaller fish in a body of water (particularly at night)[154] can furnish a great deal of information about a fish population. Some acceptable values are as follows:

1. In previously unsampled waters it will give a partial, and in some instances, a complete list of species inhabiting these waters.

2. The collection of the young of bass, walleyes, northern pike, or other game fish not only indicates their presence in the water but also their ability to reproduce under current conditions. However, their absence from waters containing adults does not necessarily mean that these populations cannot reproduce and are "on their way out."

3. The production of dominant year classes of fish may be recorded first through minnow seining.

4. Some indication of overpopulation and stunting may be gained from minnow seining, although a larger seine is much more useful for this.

Spot Poisoning. One of the more satisfactory methods of obtaining an unbiased sample of the fish population of a large lake is to poison a bay or lagoon connected with the larger body of water by a narrow channel.[156] If the bay is not too small or too shallow, it will probably contain a population fairly comparable (in composition) to that of the larger lake,[58] particularly if the fish are warmwater species and the bay is treated with the chemical during the night when they are moving about in the shallower parts of the lake.

A seine or block-off net[110] deep enough to reach from the top to the bottom of the bay is set across the channel connecting the bay with the main lake, Fish disturbed by the chemical treatment or frightened by the noises of boats are prevented from escaping by this seine. Following its placement, a canvas strip approximately the same depth as the seine can be staked across the channel adjacent to the seine. This canvas strip prevents the circulation of rotenone-treated water from the bay into the main part of the lake. The bay is then treated with derris or cube powder, 5% rotenone, or emulsifiable rotenone with a dosage of sufficient strength to kill all of the fish trapped in the bay. These poisoned fish are picked up, counted, measured, and weighed, as in a regular census. Following the rotenone treatment the seine and canvas strip are left in place until the rotenone has disappeared from the water, so that no fish are killed outside of the bay.

Spot poisoning may be done in open water by treating the circumference of an arbitrary one-acre circle and then applying the rotenone inward throughout its area. However, work in open water is not as satisfactory as in an isolated bay because in the former instance the treated water may move downwind out of the original circle, causing fish affected by the rotenone to disperse beyond the original area of treatment. In any case, it is well to pick a time when wind velocity is at a minimum to prevent, as much as possible, the mixing of treated and untreated water.

As the behavior of fishes is influenced by seasons, several spot treatments of the same bay, made several weeks or months apart, will give a better population sample than a single spot poisoning.

Boat Shocking.   In 1949, an a.c. row boat shocker was developed for the purpose of sampling fish in lakes.[113] This apparatus is useful for obtaining quickly a fish sample from lakes and ponds that are sufficiently shallow and have a water hardness of 25 or more parts per million (Fig. 6.2). If the hardness is less than 25 ppm, the effective field of the electrodes is too small for the shocker to function efficiently. A boat shocker supplied with either an a.c. or d.c. generator is often much more effective in taking fish at night, when fish are in the shallows, than in the daytime.[114] A lighting system presents no problem because lights may be powered from the generator.[127]

The boat shocker is selective in that it may stun fish attempting to hide in vegetation or on the shallow bottom, whereas fish swimming ahead of the advancing edge of the electrical field may escape unless they are cornered at the end of a bay or channel and forced to swim through the field. In general, bass tend to swim ahead of the shocker boat whereas other smaller centrarchids often try to hide in vegetation. Catfish and bullheads are seldom taken with an alternating-current shocker because they are stunned on the lake or pond bottom where they are difficult to see and pick up. With a d.c. shocker they may be led to the positive electrodes. Certain kinds of fishes attempt to escape the shocker by diving into brush and into pockets at the base of rocks, stumps, and logs lying in the water, making these ideal collecting locations. Most fishes revive

Fig. 6.2 An electric fish shocker mounted on an aluminum work boat. The biologist in the front of the boat keeps electrodes in position and picks up stunned fishes. The biologist in rear controls 220-volt generator, runs outboard motor, and cares for stunned fishes which are placed in the tank amidship.

within a period of 30 sec to 2 min. Occasionally a fish is killed by direct contact with an electrode. The shocker is not only used for sampling but also for collecting fish with "full" stomachs (food-habit studies) and for taking live specimens for stocking other waters. For some reason, many laymen have an idea that the electric shocker can be used to clear lakes of undesirable fishes. When they discover that the fish stunned by the shocker represent only a sample, they are often disappointed.

Although both direct and alternating current are used on boat shockers, alternating current appears to be more effective for collecting most kinds of fishes in shallow ponds. However, some biologists prefer a pulsating direct current to give a combination of electrotaxis and forced swimming.[26] Tests made in a webbing enclosure in a shallow lake (Minnesota) indicated that about 240 interruptions per minute was most effective for catching fishes.[163]

Angling. Fishing with certain kinds of gear (fly rod, spinning rod, etc.) and certain types of artificial or natural baits may be highly selective for certain kinds and sizes of fish. For this reason, angling is sometimes very important as a method of sampling. Largemouth bass are usually taken more readily on hook-and-line than by any known type of net or trap. Several years ago I attempted to catch largemouth bass in a lake, at a time when it contained almost no fish other than bass of about 7.5 in. total length, by using 1-in. mesh wing nets with 60-ft lead nets. Six nets were set and raised daily on six consecutive days. The catch of all nets for the 6-day period (36 net-days) was 6 of these small bass; on the last day that the nets were set I caught 47 bass on fly rod "poppers" in less than three hours.

The ability to avoid nets and seines is shared also by smallmouth bass, although they are somewhat more vulnerable than are largemouths. For sampling smallmouths, a fly rod and artificial "popper" may serve efficiently. For example, biologists captured 192 smallmouth bass (6-11 in.) in 22 hr of fishing at the rate of 8.7/hr.[16] The fish were used to restock a renovated lake. They probably could not have been taken from the source lake (a deep quarry lake) at this rate by any other method.

Hook-and-line fishing may be useful for sampling specific fishes such as male bluegills guarding nests, or for taking fishes that inhabit a certain weed bed or lie beneath a log. As a sampling method hook-and-line fishing may be no less biased than wing nets and other types of gear.

Many kinds of fishes become trap-wise as well as hook-wise, so that most types of fishing gear become less efficient with intensive use.

Probably no type of sampling technique can be relied upon to give a completely accurate, instantaneous picture of an entire fish population. As a means of testing the efficiency of common sampling techniques, Barry[9] sampled Lenape and Bischoff Reservoirs (Indiana) with electrofishing gear, gill nets, traps, and rotenone treatment of bays prior to making draining censuses of the fish in these reservoirs. In general, composite samples from gill nets, traps, and electrofishing gave a fair estimate of the relative abundance of various species, and rotenone embayment samples gave a good estimate of total pounds per acre.

If sampling is being done to appraise the general well-being of a population and its management needs (if any), as many types of sampling as are possible and practical should be used. It is the author's opinion that if only limited time is available for sampling, electrofishing with a boat shocker will give the most comprehensive sample of the fish populations of shallow ponds and reservoirs.

MANAGEMENT TECHNIQUES

Once sufficient sampling of a fish population has indicated that management is necessary, one should investigate the known techniques and decide which are applicable. Often several methods seem justifiable and one or more must be selected on the basis of expediency.

COMPLETE FISH-POPULATION REMOVAL

Complete removal of a population is usually desirable when a lake or pond becomes contaminated with species of no value for angling or fish production. Such fishes as buffalo, suckers (of several kinds), gizzard shad, and sometimes stunted black bullheads may have limited sport-fishing value. These species often crowd out more desirable game and pan fishes. Even if these undesirable fishes are present in small numbers, they are always a potential danger to the production of a high sustained yield of more desirable species because of their capacity for producing tremendous numbers of young at a single spawning and their ability to modify their environment (by stirring silt) in their search for food. These fishes, and some others unlisted, are completely under control only when they are absent.[100]

Population Removal by Draining

All artificial ponds and lakes should be built with drain outlets of suffi-cient size to allow their basins to be drained within a period of three to thirty days. If such a lake becomes contaminated with undesirable species or must be drained for any other purpose (such as the recovery of stolen goods), a Wolf-type weir (Fig. 6.3) can be placed across the outlet, the live fish separated from the water, and the valuable fish saved alive for restocking.[203] A Wolf-type weir is more satisfactory than any other type of screen because the water falls through the bottom of the wire-mesh weir instead of flowing through a perpendicular screen. The fish either are left exposed on the wire mesh of the weir bottom or they flop across the bottom screen into a holding box. This is the only type of screen that can handle a large flow of water without frequent shutoffs for cleaning the screen. A Wolf-type weir can be constructed below almost any outlet that will give six inches to two or more feet of working space below the level of the outflowing water. If it is necessary to catch very small fish or plankton organisms, such a weir may be covered with copper window screening or MS-904 Saran Screen.[23] Usually it is not desirable to use mesh of smaller than one-fourth to three-eights of an inch.

Before draining, it is necessary to make some arrangements, either temporary or semipermanent, for storing desirable fishes. The surface spillways of some artificial lakes may terminate in stilling basins of suffi-cient size and depth to hold fish. Such an arrangement was used at Ridge

Fig. 6.3 Small Wolf-type weir built across the concrete flume below drain valve for 2.5-acre pond. This weir will handle a comparatively large flow of water and allow capture of the fish alive because water drops through the bottom screen as well as flowing through the sides.

Lake where, in cool weather, all of the larger fish from 18 acres of water could be held for several days in a concrete stilling basin 70 ft wide and 30 ft long, with a maximum depth of 4 ft when the basin was pumped full.[15] Where no holding basin is available near the outlet, arrangements should be made to hold the fish in portable tanks of metal or canvas or in nearby ponds, a count being kept of the fish moved to these ponds. Later, when a small amount of water has become impounded in the drained lake basin, fish which have been held may be returned. The cool days of early spring and late fall are best for lake-draining operations, because fish can be handled at these times with a minimum of loss. Fish not saved for restocking are sorted by species (Fig. 6.4), counted, and weighed.

Most lakes and ponds will not drain completely, and it is usually neces-sary to treat the water remaining in pockets or channels in the basin with

Fig. 6.4 A sorting table for separating small fishes (dead or alive) when making a fish census. Table top consists of a sheet of galvanized metal set in an edging of 2 x 4s. Containers placed under openings in the metal sheet at the corners and in the midsection (like a billiard table) allow separated fishes to be removed from the table top. Short pieces of 2 x 2s are placed in front of the openings to prevent premature entry of live fish into them while counting is in progress.

some chemical to kill the small fish that may remain in this water and escape to the lake as the basin refills. For this purpose one can use H.T.H. powder (calcium hypochlorite) to give several parts per million* of free chlorine, or rotenone (as 5% cube powder) or emulsifiable rotenone (2—5%) to give 1 ppm or more. It is desirable to use a fish poison that disappears rapidly so that fish can be restocked within a few days.

After the fish and water have been removed from a lake basin and the water pockets and channels treated, the outlet valve can be closed so that water will collect in the basin. However, the basin may be allowed to dry for several months before reimpoundment is begun, if the fish to be restocked can be held for this length of time.

---

*Parts per million is promulgated on a weight basis, i.e., one pound of a chemical added to a million pounds of water equals one part per million. This is not too difficult to visualize if one will remember that an acre of fresh water (43,560 sq. ft), one foot deep, will weigh about 2.7 million lb. Thus, 2.7 lb of a chemical applied to 1 acre of water, 1 ft deep, (one acre-foot), will give a dosage of 1 ppm.

Population Removal With Fish Toxicants

The first highly effective material used for producing total mortality of a fish population was probably rotenone. Since the use of rotenone became general in the late 1930s, a number of other fish toxicants have been discovered and tested.

Antimycin A. This is an antibiotic which was discovered in 1945 by scientists in the Department of Plant Pathology at the University of Wisconsin.[119,120] It was purified and its chemical properties defined by the University's Department of Biochemistry. Believing that this chemical might be useful in controlling some fungus-caused diseases of plants, it was turned over to the Wisconsin Alumni Research Foundation for further testing.

In 1953, Philip Derse of the Foundation and Dr. Frank Strong of the University reported that antimycin was very toxic to fishes; yet, at the same level of dosage, it appeared to be harmless to other vertebrates and aquatic invertebrates.[39,76] Further tests were begun at the U.S. Fish and Wildlife Service Fish Control Laboratory at LaCrosse (Wisconsin) in which more than thirty species of freshwater fishes were exposed to it. These included all categories of fishes: game, panfish, rough or coarse fish, and forage species, as well as eggs, larvae, and adults in hard and soft waters at cold and warm temperatures. Later, antimycin was tested in ponds in Arkansas, Georgia, Nebraska, New Hampshire, New York, Wisconsin, and Wyoming.

Hiltibran,[81,83] working with bluegill liver cell preparations, was able to show that antimycin A inhibited the flow of energy in these preparations by completely blocking the oxygen uptake. Derse and Strong[39] had postulated that antimycin A was absorbed through the gills and interfered with the respiratory apparatus of the fish, causing its death. Hiltibran (personal communication) believes that death may result from a blocking of oxygen uptake in many systems, including the blocking of the flow of oxygen through the respiratory control center.

The action is reported to be irreversible, that is, once antimycin enters the fish's body in sufficient strength, the fish never recovers. Toxic dosages to fishes vary between 0.5 to about 80 or more *parts per billion.*[197] Perch may be killed by a dosage as low as 0.5 ppb;[153] most freshwater species die at dosages of 5–10 ppb but channel catfish and black bullheads may require 50 ppb. It degrades rapidly and usually has entirely disappeared in less than one week. Antimycin at dosages that will kill fishes is harmless to water snakes, turtles, salamanders, frogs, tadpoles, aquatic insects, and aquatic plants; also it is harmless to birds and mammals.

This material is sold under the trade name of "Fintrol." It is made up for use as a liquid or as a coating on sand which may be spread with a hand spreader from a boat or with more elaborate equipment.[121]

The wide variation in the toxicity of antimycin A to various species of fishes may make it useful for the selective removal of fishes from a population. Radonski and Wendt[153] were able to eliminate an entire perch population from Perch Lake, Oneida County, Wisconsin, with a dosage of 0.5 ppb, without killing largemouth bass, bluegills, rock bass, and golden shiners. A few bluntnose minnows were killed with the perch but many more escaped the treatment.

Rotenone.   Plants containing a chemical known as rotenone have been used for a great many years as fish killers by primitive people throughout the warmer parts of the world.[102,106,122] The common plant genera involved are *Derris, Lonchocarpus,* and *Tephrosia,* and the product is known by such names as cube; timbo, or barbasco, depending upon the locality where it is collected.

Rotenone was first used in fisheries management in the United States by Milton B. Trautman in 1934 when, at the suggestion of Dr. Carl Hubbs, he attempted to eliminate goldfish from two small ponds near Birmingham, Michigan. Little was known about dosages at that time, and the operation was only partially successful because of the light treatment used. In September of the same year, Michigan fisheries biologists attempted to eliminate a population of stunted yellow perch from a 4.3-acre lake in Ostego County, Michigan,[44] and by 1937 several states were using this material as a management tool. In 1938 biologists with the Illinois Natural History Survery made censuses of six ponds by treating them with rotenone.

Laboratory studies by Leonard[122] indicated that a dosage of 0.5 ppm of derris powder containing 5% rotenone should be lethal to all kinds of fishes, that an increase of water temperature decreased the reaction time, and that the material was somewhat more toxic in acid than in alkaline waters. Wider experience with rotenone, including newer formulations prepared by several chemical companies, has shown that it is risky to depend on a dosage of less than 1 ppm of a formulation containing 5% rotenone if a complete kill is desired. In Illinois we have used a standard dosage of 3 lb of 5% rotenone-bearing material or 3 pints of an emulsifiable concentration containing 5% rotenone for each acre-foot of water. This dosage of more than 1 ppm protects a poisoning operation from problems such as *(1)* inaccuracies in volume estimates, *(2)* fish with a high resistance, *(3)* water of high organic content or alkalinity, and *(4)* unevenness in application. It is better to use a little too much rotenone than too little, if a complete kill is desired (Fig. 6.5).

Fig. 6.5 Carp, bullheads, and green sunfish killed by rotenone treatment of a small pond.

Soon after the use of rotenone was established as a desirable management tool, it was discovered that water suspensions of rotenone were slow in penetrating deeper waters of thermally stratified lakes, and that it was possible to kill such warmwater fishes as yellow perch, rock bass, and largemouth bass in the upper, warmer layers without killing many brook or rainbow trout in the colder lower strata (Fig. 6.6).[36,90,194] Hayes and Livingstone[67] combined this technique with the stocking of brook trout and were able to increase the trout yield 230%.

If deeper waters are to be treated, a weighted hose can be connected to a tank supported a foot or two above the boat. As an outboard motor moves the boat, this motion plus gravity will feed the rotenone into these depths. However, any kind of small power sprayer can be used to force the killing agent into deep water, as well as in the treatment of the surface.

To get as even a spread as possible, a grid pattern should be followed which divides the lake surface into parallel and crossing lines of treated strips (Fig. 6.7). For complete kills, the surface waters should be 70°F or higher; if it is impossible to treat during warm weather, additional rotenone should be used, and special care exercised to spread it evenly.

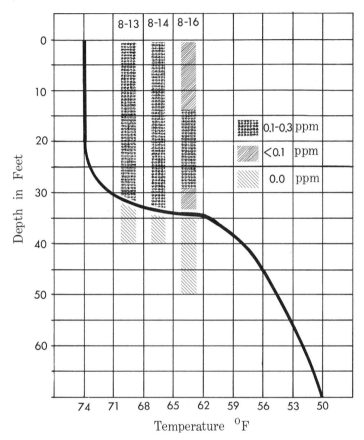

Fig. 6.6 Selective poisoning of warmwater fishes in trout ponds in Massachusetts by the use of rotenone. Tests indicated that the rotenone did not penetrate below the zone of rapid-temperature transition at 30-35 ft. Trout that remained at depths below about 35 ft were unaffected, whereas most of the warmwater fishes above 30 ft were killed [from Thompkins, W. A., and Mullan, J. W., 1958, *Progressive Fish Culturist* 20(3)].

If some fish should be saved for restocking, they can be collected by the use of a boat shocker or seines prior to the poisoning operation and stored until the rotenone has disintegrated. They then can be reintroduced into the waters. If the level of the pond or lake can be lowered, this will facilitate the collection of desirable fish as well as the treatment operation and reduce the chance that small fish will be missed.

Fish are more sensitive to rotenone than are most other aquatic organisms except Entomostraca.[21,125]

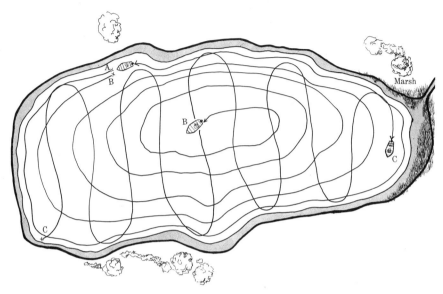

Fig. 6.7 Pattern for treating a lake with rotenone to remove all fish. (A) Boat follows shoreline, spraying a dilute solution of rotenone along water's edge. (B) Boat powered with an outboard motor makes concentric circles around the lake from shoreline to center. (C) Rotenone is released in deeper water through a weighted hose while boat makes zigzag course back and forth across the lake. Once this pattern is completed there is no place a fish can go without coming in contact with treated water.

In warm weather with water temperatures at $70-80°F$ waters usually can be restocked in four or five days. During cold weather the rotenone may remain toxic to some extent for as much as thirty days. Potassium permanganate ($KMnO_4$) or chlorine (Cl_2) will quickly oxidize the poison and hasten its disappearance.[9,116] A color test has been developed which will measure the amount of rotenone in water.[149]

Toxaphene. According to information furnished by Mr. Lynn H. Hutchens (U.S. Fish and Wildlife Service) in 1953, Messrs. Jack Hemphill and Jack Killian of the Arizona Game and Fish Commission first used toxaphene for killing fish. In the treatment of Becker Lake (Arizona) with toxaphene, several horses were deliberately allowed to drink the water and no losses resulted. No dead deer, raccoons, or other wild animals have been observed around such lakes. "As toxaphene breaks down into nontoxic substances at $190°F$, there is apparently no danger in human consumption of fish so destroyed."[69] This statement has not been entirely accepted by most other investigators. Since Messrs. Hemphill's and Killian's study in Becker Lake (Arizona) in 1953, many additional tests have been made in the U.S. and Canada. Hemphill used a dust containing 40% toxaphene, and the cost of treating a lake was found to be only about 15% of the cost of treatment with derris or cube powder containing 5% rotenone. More recently, toxaphene emulsions have become available and cost figures indicate that toxaphene treatment is about 15—30% that of rotenone. Toxaphene[53,54,72,78,85,97,98,100,140,168,206] has been applied to waters as a fish-killing agent at rates varying between 2 and 100 parts per billion. In laboratory experiments where water temperatures ranged between 70 and 80°F toxaphene disappeared in 23 days.[206] Out of doors it was reported to have persisted within a range of 20 days[53] to more than 3 years.[99] This range of difference was in part due to dosage level and in part to the method of testing: in the shorter term reporting, live fish were observed to show normal behavior in less than 4 weeks after a liquid dosage had been applied at 5 ppb. In the longer periods of reported persistence, chemical tests were used to measure the presence of toxaphene.

When dosages between 2 and 7 ppb were applied only small fish were killed. Dosages of 7 ppb and over usually killed all fishes, although some failures have been reported at dosages as high as 50 ppb.[85] Channel catfish in particular show a great deal of resistance to it.[87]

Toxaphene accumulates in fishes that are not killed, but very little information seems to be available on where it is stored, how it is stored, maximum levels of storage, and degradation. It is reported to accumulate in aquatic vegetation[99] and in lake sediments.

Toxaphene seems to have little effect on phytoplankton[140] and zooplankton, particularly rotifers, cladocera, and copepods, and normal populations usually reappear within 3 or 4 weeks after treatment.[69] Most aquatic insects seem to be quite sensitive to toxaphene[140] and bottom-living midge larvae may be killed by a dosage of 0.1 ppm.[78] This might result from the tendency of toxaphene to collect at the bottom (specific gravity 1.6). Snails appeared to be unaffected.[168] Among the invertebrate bottom organisms, dragonfly nymphs were the earliest to reappear after treatment. Chironomidae were found to be absent for more than nine months.[35,69,87,104,134,168,169]

Under alkaline conditions toxaphene is said to break down into hydrochloric acid and water, although all evidence doesn't entirely support this.[168] Alkalinity, the action of microorganisms, and turbidity[169] are important in the rate of detoxification of toxaphene.[87,134]

Most aquatic biologists have hesitated to use the newer insecticides for killing fishes because of the residual toxicity of these materials and the unpredictable length of time required after treatment before a lake or pond can be restocked.

Sodium Cyanide. Sodium cyanide is useful as a fish poison in ponds and small lakes, primarily because the poisoned fish may be revived by placing them in fresh water if the fish are removed while still active. Ponds dosed at the rate of 1 ppm sodium cyanide become nontoxic to fish in about 4 days. Fish to be revived are usually collected within the first hour or two after treatment.[20]

As cyanides can be fatal to humans, this method of fish poisoning should be done only by competent technicians. Sodium cyanide, once applied to the pond, offers little danger to wild or domestic animals. At 1 ppm, it has no noticeable effect on tadpoles, frogs, snakes, turtles, aquatic insects, or aquatic plants.

Sodium Sulfite. Sodium sulfite at a dosage of 168 ppm has been used experimentally to salvage fish in a small pond. The sulfite reduced the dissolved oxygen and forced the fish to gulp air at the surface. Fish recovered fully when placed in fresh water if they were collected when still gulping air. This method is practical only in small ponds because of the cost of the sulfite (10¢/lb).[200]

Bayer 73 or Bayluscide. This bright yellow crystalline powder known chemically as 2-aminoethanol salt of 2′,5-dichloro-4′ nitrosalicyanilide, was developed originally as a poison for snails and other mollusks and has been used in parts of the world where humans are exposed to blood flukes,[64] which depend upon snails as intermediate hosts. The recommended dosage to eliminate snails is 0.5 ppm active ingredient. This amount will kill clams as well as frogs, crayfish, and some fishes. Dosages between 0.1 and 1.0 ppm active ingredient would cover the range of toxicity for all freshwater fishes.[133] Carp and goldfish are more resistant to its effects than other species and flathead catfish were the least resistant of the eighteen species tested. This chemical has not been released for use as a fish poison but may be potentially useful. In Canada it has been applied to silt beds in streams for sea lamprey control.[174]

FISH-POPULATION ADJUSTMENT

As mentioned above, there are a number of ways that a low-producing population may be adjusted to achieve a higher yield without eliminating and replacing the entire population. These methods are applicable when:

1. A population consists of desirable fishes, but with some species stunted and others becoming scarce due to excessive competition.

2. There is high demand for one or two species and low demand for one or more other species inhabiting the same water.

3. Eliminating the indigenous population and starting over with a new one is impossible or impractical.

Use of Nets and Seines

In small ponds, wire traps or wing nets are used to reduce excessive populations of crappies, bluegills, and other sunfishes and to permit an increase in the largemouth bass. Wing nets employed in Fork Lake controlled bluegills and allowed the development of a very large bass population. The very same type of selective cropping may be done with intensive seining provided the pond or lake basin lends itself to the use of seines.[191] The main drawback to either of these methods is that they both entail a great deal of work and some rather expensive equipment. Also, relatively few lakes or ponds are well adapted to cropping with wing nets or seines, and the average pond or lake owner does not have access to this equipment.

Partial Poisoning

Soon after the use of rotenone to poison an entire population became widespread, fisheries biologists noted its differential toxicity to various species and sizes of fishes. This led to the development of the selective or partial poisoning technique with rotenone, designed to kill certain parts of a population without seriously damaging the remainder of it. This technique for removing warmwater fishes from trout lakes has been described on page 198.

In 1945 and 1946, I applied a shoreline treatment of rotenone to Park Pond, a strip-mine pond area in east central Illinois, in order to reduce an excessive population of gizzard shad and small sunfish. Later, when Dr. R. Weldon Larimore was studying the growth of the warmouth in Park Pond,[112] he found that the warmouth had made unusually rapid growth (114 and 128% of expected annual length increment) during 1945 and 1946. This he could not explain until it was discovered that the years of good warmouth growth corresponded to years of population thinning through partial poisoning.

Experience in partial poisoning operations has shown that gizzard shad are killed with lighter dosages of rotenone than almost any other warmwater fish.[18] In general most of the centrarchids (sunfishes) are moderately sensitive to rotenone, but smaller individuals of a species are generally more susceptible than larger ones. For this reason and because young fishes of many species inhabit the warm, quiet, shallow waters near the shore on bright summer days, a shoreline rotenoning operation can be used to kill numerous fish too small to interest anglers.[184]

Timing in Partial Poisoning. The timing of a partial treatment is important because the final effect may vary, depending upon whether the operation is done in the spring, midsummer, or early fall. Suppose, for example, that a lake contained an excessive number of small bass and one wished to thin this population to allow for an expansion of a relatively small population of bluegills. A partial poisoning operation in May or June, but *after* the bass had spawned, would reduce the severity of predation by young bass on newly hatched bluegills (the spawning season for bluegills lasts from late May to mid-September in the latitude of central Indiana and Illinois) and would allow a greater survival of these young in June, July, and August. Many of these bluegills might grow fast enough to exceed the size of easy predation before the next year class of bass was produced the following spring.

In another instance, a lake might contain a large population of stunted bluegills and a few large bass unable to reproduce successfully because of predation of bass eggs and fry by hoards of hungry bluegills. In such a situation partial poisoning should be performed either *(1)* immediately before the bass spawning season in the spring or *(2)* at the end of the bluegill spawning season, in September or early October. If the operation were done between these specific times, the food and space gained by the removal of a portion of the excess of bluegills would be taken up almost immediately by new hatches of young bluegills. However, population reduction by partial poisoning, just prior to the bass spawning season (and the bluegill spawning season as well), would curtail bluegill predation on the bass eggs and fry, resulting in a proportionate increase in the survival of young bass. If partial poisoning were performed in early fall after the bluegills had stopped spawning, the space gained at the expense of a part of the population could not be filled before the cold of winter, either through the production of new bluegills or growth of those escaping poisoning. Much of this space would still be available when the bass spawned the following spring, insuring improved survival of young bass. In the instances cited above, timing is of utmost importance if the desired results are to be forthcoming.

The greatest weakness of the partial-poisoning technique is that without supplementary information on the standing crop of fish, it is impossible to gauge accurately the extent of the operation in terms of the percent of a fish population removed.[101] Usually the operation is too conservative for optimum results, and a repetition may be necessary. In some instances it is useful and practical to do a partial-poisoning operation just prior to the spawning season each year for as many as five successive years. Each treatment insures the production and survival of a year class of bass for that year, and before the end of five years the bass population should be approaching the maximum that the water will support.

Swingle, Prather, and Lawrence[184] recommend the stocking of 150 to 200 fingerling bass per acre following a summer marginal-poisoning operation. Such a stocking might check the success of sunfish reproduction which could be expected to fill up the space created by the poisoning. This restocking is unnecessary if the poisoning operation can be done in spring before the bass have spawned or in the fall near the end of the fish-growing season.

Shoreline vs. Sectional Treatment.   In partial-poisoning operations one may poison completely a bay or an arm of a lake, using a dosage of rotenone of sufficient strength to kill all fish as described earlier. In such a case it may be practical to separate the rest of the lake from the treated bay by blocking the opening with a canvas strip, long and deep enough to reach across the mouth of the bay (Fig. 6.8). This strip can be hung on a wire supported by posts driven into the lake bottom.

Fig. 6.8 Canvas "fence" used in partial poisoning of a lake. Water to right of canvas was treated with sufficient rotenone to kill all of its fishes. Several fishes in the "live box" on the left side of the canvas were unaffected.

Beckman[11] demonstrated an increase in the growth rate of rock bass after he had poisoned the fish in half of a lake having a natural constriction near the center. Unless the arm or bay to be treated represents one half or more of the total lake surface area, such a fish-poisoning operation may be insufficient to reduce a stunted fish population.

Swingle, Prather, and Lawrence[184] do not favor sectional poisoning because more desirable fish are killed by this method than by marginal poisoning. This may or may not be a valid view. Sectional poisoning removes fishes in proportion to the relative abundance of kind and sizes in pond or lake, and therefore, is a useful method of cropping. It is probably the only technique short of complete poisoning that is effective in reducing stunted populations of bullheads.

It is often practical to combine marginal poisoning with sectional poisoning. In such a combined operation the section of lake receiving complete treatment should represent 20—80% of the total lake area (Fig. 6.9). In calculating the dosage of rotenone to be used, the part of the lake to receive complete treatment should be dosed at 1 ppm, the remainder being given a marginal treatment with an amount required to treat it at the rate of 0.25 ppm. This marginal amount is sprayed within a 20-ft strip parallel to the shore and completely encircling the lake exclusive of the section receiving the heavier dosage (Fig. 6.9).

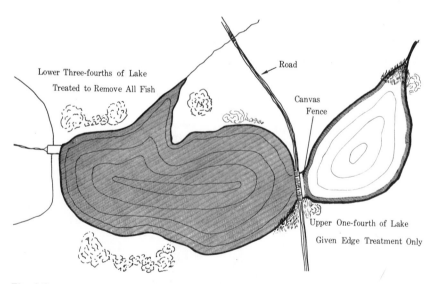

Fig. 6.9 A sectional poisoning combined with a shoreline poisoning to eliminate stunting in a fish population. Usually it is necessary to remove more than 75% of the stunted fishes before the remaining ones will grow to useful sizes.

When a sectional poisoning is combined with marginal treatment, the fish collected from the sectional part may be considered a representative sample of the entire population of the lake. From the kinds and sizes of fish in this sample it may be possible to estimate the extent of artificial cropping in the current treatment as well as to decide on further measures that may be required to thin out the more severely stunted components of the population.

In planning a partial poisoning it is well to calculate the dosage, order the chemical, and plan the mechanical aspects of the operation well in advance. If this has been accomplished, the operation can be performed on short notice, at a time when wind and weather conditions are favorable.

Selective Poisoning

Within the past ten years many bioassay tests have been made of chemicals, using fishes as test animals, in an attempt to discover new materials useful for selective poisoning of specific kinds of undersirable fishes, without causing great harm to other fishes that may be living in the same water.[128,201] Some chemicals, such as chlordane, may be dangerous to all life,[105] with others, (e.g., Aqualin[35]) the range of susceptibility of desirable and undesirable fishes may be too nearly similar. Still others may appear to be useful but need more testing.[25] A few new chemicals and new uses for old chemicals have been found that may have application in fishery management.

Copper Sulfate. Robert G. Martin has applied this old standby to greatly reduce populations of bullheads and coarse fishes with very little loss of game fishes. At the Brunswich County Fishing Lake in Virginia, he killed and removed 6000 pounds of bullheads and golden shiners with almost no loss of bass, bluegills, and black and white crappies.[173] The dosage of copper sulfate was about 2 ppm. No information was given on the hardness of the water, which is important in calculating the amount of copper sulfate to use.

Guthion. This organophosphate insecticide, that is, O,O-dimethyl S-4-oxo-1,2,3-benzotriazin-3(4)H-ylmethyl[65] phosphorodithioate, if applied at the rate of 1.0 ppm appears to be useful in removing miscellaneous fishes from populations of catfishes. Eradications of species other than catfishes were completed in forty-eight hours. The chemical was not influenced by hard or soft water or turbidity and disappeared from the water in less than two weeks. Initial tests for residues in the flesh of catfish killed with guthion indicated that they were not fit for consumption, but no residues were detectable in live fish after six weeks.[136]

Formalin. Formalin is often used in treating live fishes for parasites. According to Helms[68] it is also effective in controlling small tadpoles in fish hatchery ponds. Leopard and very small bullfrog tadpoles were killed with a dosage of formalin (commercial grade, 38% formaldehyde) of 30 ppm, while the fishes tolerated 45 ppm or more. Formalin may cause oxygen depletion in ponds by its reducing action, but 30 ppm formalin is safe to use if the water temperature is below 65°F.

Isobornyl Thiocyanoacetate. This is an insecticide manufactured and sold as a household spray under the trademark "Thanite."[123] Thanite is not soluble in water, but may be emulsified by combining 70% Thanite, 20% kerosene, and 10% Atlox (a commercial emulsifier). Bluegills, green sunfish, and rainbow trout were killed with dosages of less then 0.7 ppm, whereas goldenshiners, channel catfish, and black bullheads required at least 1.5 ppm. Fishes removed from the treated water when surfacing and placed in fresh water soon revived. In this respect Thanite is similar to sodium cyanide but is not so dangerous to handle as the latter. Cost of treatment compares favorably with rotenone treatment.

Isobornyl thiocyanoacetate has not been approved (1968) by the U.S. Food and Drug Administration for selective killing of fishes. The blood of fishes killed by isobornyl thiocyanoacetate contained cyanide concentrations which were similar to levels occurring in fishes killed with sodium cyanide. Fishes removed alive from the treated water and held in fresh water showed a rapid loss of cyanide from the blood.

Rotenone. Rotenone has been used for selective poisoning for gizzard shad, perch and small sunfish,[170] as discussed under Partial Poisoning above.

Treatment of Sunfish Nests. Bluegills and other sunfish nest in colonies so that many nests containing eggs or yolk-sac fry are readily observable, and available for treatment. Chemicals proposed for introduction into sunfish nests to kill eggs or fry and discourage renesting are pellets of sodium hydroxide[94] and crude copper sufate crystals.[1,17] Both chemicals are very effective for this purpose. Beyerle and Williams[17] consistently treated with copper sulfate crystals all the bluegill nests that they could find in four small Michigan lakes. Although this was done throughout the bluegill spawning season, seine samples taken after the season of nest treatment turned up more small bluegills than were captured with the same amount of seining in the year previous to the treatment. This suggests that unless *all* nests in a lake are found and treated (which is probably impossible) such a program may be useless.

Control of Predaceous Aquatic Insects.   Many fry-sized fish fall prey to predaceous aquatic insects such as beetle larvae, dragonfly naiads, giant water bugs, and back swimmers. When adult fish are present, numbers of the insects are low, so the problem arises when fry or very small fish are to be stocked in ponds containing no other fishes and that have contained water for a sufficient length of time to build up large populations of these predaceous insects. Obviously one method of eliminating this problem is to leave pond basins dry until a short time before the fry are to be stocked. Protozoa, rotifers, and microcrustacea, the normal foods for fry-size fish will appear within a few days after initial flooding; most insects usually require a longer time. Where flooding of pond basins cannot be timed to parallel stocking, a surface film of light oil may be applied 8 to 10 days in advance of stocking and continued until the fish are at least 2 in. long. One suggested formula is 1 qt of motor oil in 5 gal of kerosene, applied to the ponds at the rate of 1.75 gal per acre surface at intervals of 3 or 4 days. Air-breathing insects are suffocated by the oil when they come to the surface.

ARTIFICAL FLUCTUATION OF WATER LEVELS

In Chapter 4, I described certain experiments that demonstrated that the total weight of a population was related to the size of the water area it inhabits. Thus, if a body of water devoid of fish is stocked with a few sexually mature individuals, these fish will reproduce and they and their offspring will add flesh until their total weight approaches the poundage of fish that the water area will support. This process may require one or more growing seasons, but eventually the poundage of fish will fluctuate within a range related to the size of the habitat and its food-producing capacity (natural fertility). This poundage adjustment may be downward if more pounds of fish were stocked originally than the lake will support.

Various levels of population density affect food gathering, reproduction success, and growth rate of fish, and these factors may express themselves differently with different species and different sizes of individuals within a species. We know that rate of growth is often density dependent and we assume a relationship between the rate of growth and the amount of food that may be available to each individual fish. We also know that tropical aquarium fishes confined in small aquaria and given an abundant balanced food supply may grow scarcely at all after they reach a certain size; yet when placed in larger aquaria or in outdoor pools during summer months they may again begin to grow at a rapid rate. We assume that in overpopulated lakes and ponds fish are stunted because of lack of sufficient food, but in several species there is evidence of inhibitory factors affecting reproduction and perhaps growth also, factors that are easily demonstrated by moving the fish to water uncontaminated by their own kind (see Chapter 4). However, in other kinds of fishes no such inhibitory factors have been demonstrated.

As a group, the fishes have become adjusted to survive biological "adversity" and take advantage of biological "prosperity." The fact that the several species of warmwater fishes involved in management vary in their responses to biological adversity and prosperity is the key to the effectiveness of the water-level fluctuations.

Suppose then, that instead of culling the fish population of a lake by trap-netting, seining, or partial poisoning, we subject it to extreme crowding for weeks or months through the release of much of the total volume of water in the lake (Figs. 6.10 and 6.11). When the fish are thus crowded during warm weather they are forced from normal, familiar shallow water habitats that offer protective cover, into open water, away from shoreline debris and shallow-water vegetation.

During the period of lake drawdown when the water level is continually receding at a relatively slow rate, fishes, crayfishes, and a variety of motile aquatic insect larvae, snails, and other forms are moving down with the water. Frequently these animals become trapped in uneven pockets in the lake bottom or in mats of vegetation which collapse when the supporting water is removed. These trapped animals usually die before they can work their way back to the edge of the receding lake.

Shortly after a drawdown is completed the live fish may be in competition for a reduced oxygen supply due to the contact of the water remaining in the lake basin with partially decayed organic matter that had accumulated on the bottom in what was formerly deep water. Within a few days the oxygen demand may be satisfied.

Sometime during the winter or early spring the habitat is rapidly expanded by the addition of new water originating as runoff from the drainage basin. The exposed lake bottom is reflooded and there is suddenly plenty of space and an increasing food supply. All fish that have survived the period of crowding begin to grow rapidly. Under conditions of greatly expanded food and space, certain species that were adversely affected by crowding produce large broods of young. If these young are piscivorous they may actually check the expansion of some of the species formerly so successful in producing large numbers. Thus, there would be a sudden shift in dominance brought about by a drastic change in the habitat.[14] If this change is man-made, we have only taken our cue from

Fig. 6.10 Aerial view of fall drawdown shows lake surface area reduced by more than 50%.

nature where water levels are rarely stable, but are usually in a state of fluctuation, often mild, but sometimes very severe during floods or droughts. Flood-plain lakes in the valleys of rivers are subject to the rivers' fluctuations and, because these lakes are relatively shallow, changes may be extreme in them.

The sudden lowering of the water level of a lake with the accompanying reduction in water volume and surface area affects all parts of an aquatic habitat and all components of the animal and plant communities that inhabit the water.

Prior to 1920, changes in water levels similar to those described above commonly occurred as a natural cycle in many of the flood-plain lakes along the Illinois River in Illinois. Professor Stephen A. Forbes[52] de-

Fig. 6.11 Drawdown at Ridge Lake requires dropping the water level 10 ft. or more. Normal water level is evident on the outlet tower (left foreground). Laboratory pier (upper right) is completely exposed.

scribed the changes in water levels in the Havana region where in late summer the lakes, which extended over thousands of acres in spring when the river was high, covered only hundreds of acres, and many connecting channels were so low that it was often difficult to move a boat from the river into these backwaters. According to the average gauge readings at Havana, water levels were usually highest in spring, gradually diminishing throughout the summer until they reached a low point in early fall. Levels usually rose in fall and winter but floods seldom occurred before spring, although there were exceptions to the pattern.

After World War I, most of these bottom-land lakes were isolated from the river by earthen levees, pumped dry, and the basins used for farming. The few lakes that were left or reconverted after agricultural use were more or less stabilized through the construction of levees and spillways that kept the river water out, unless it rose above the spillways' crests, and held the lake water in when the river was lower than the crests.

During the pre-leveeing period of wide fluctuations of lake levels and areas, the lakes in the Havana region were famous for their fishing, particularly for largemouth bass. Presidents of the United States have fished there; fishing trains brought anglers from distances beyond the range of the horse and wagon. Records show that it was not considered unusual for fishermen to catch 100 bass in a day.

There are still plenty of fish in parts of the Illinois River and adjacent undrained bottomland lakes,[166] but the populations are composed largely of crappies, gizzard shad, bluegills, yellow bass, sheepshead, buffalo, carp, bullheads, channel catfish, and, where vegetation is abundant, yellow perch. Although largemouth bass are sometimes caught by bass-fishing experts, the average angler does not now think of the Illinois River as bass water.

Interest in the effects of fluctuating water levels upon fishes was stimulated by the late Dr. R. W. Eschmeyer and his colleagues,[45,46,47,48] through their investigations of TVA waters. In 1947, Dr. Eschmeyer stated that several permanent-level pools on TVA impoundments had provided poorer fishing than other reservoirs subjected to wide fluctuations of water levels. He suggested that "the winter drawdown apparently limits the abundance of rough fish (by limiting their food) without serious injury to the game-fish population." Drawdowns on TVA lakes followed no definite schedule, but most of the drop in level occurred in winter following needs for power.

Effects Upon the Exposed Lake Bottom

According to Neess[141] the bottom of a lake or pond is divided into regions, "an upper, loose, well aerated, and often highly colloidal layer of decomposed organic material, plant debris . . . and a lower anaerobic zone, differing widely in composition from place to place and often containing a large proportion of mineral matter." These soil layers have the ability to direct certain processes in the pond because the mineral composition of water is largely a reflection of the mineral composition of the soils of the pond bottom as well as the surrounding basin; also the colloidal fraction of the bottom materials consisting of humic substances, ferric gels, and clay is capable of absorbing certain soluble nutrient elements and governing their later release.

In a pond or lake where there is a shortage of oxygen near the bottom, decomposition of organic matter is slow and the products are reduced to incompletely oxidized compounds such as hydrogen sulfide, methane, and short-chain fatty acids. When the water is drawn off a lake bottom and the bottom is allowed to dry out and crack open, an abundance of oxygen becomes available, the processes of decomposition are stepped up, and the pH of the bottom soils is raised. Under these conditions there may be a release of certain fertilizing substances from organic colloidal systems, making available greater quantities of potassium and phosphate. In European pond culture it was once considered important to grow a crop plant or a legume on the exposed pond bottom. Later the need for this practice was questioned[38] although the crop furnished income to the pond owner when the pond was not producing fish.

Whether a lake or pond bottom exposed by a drawdown will develop a vegetative cover depends upon the length of time the bottom lies exposed and the season of the year when the drawdown is made. A winter or early spring drawdown, which is prolonged by drought or purposely extended throughout the following plant-growing season, will insure a luxuriant growth of terrestrial weeds on the exposed lake bottom. These weeds will reflect the fertility of the exposed lake bottom by their height and the density of the stand. Drawdowns made in July and August will be followed by some germination of seeds and growth of terrestrial plants, but drawdowns made as late as early September in the north are not followed by growth of terrestrial vegetation in the basin.

Whether or not plants grow upon the exposed bottom seems to be unimportant; of primary significance is the exposure of the bottom to rapid and complete oxidation.

Effects Upon Rooted Aquatic Vegetation

Most forms of submersed rooted aquatic plants in lakes are not greatly affected by a drawdown, e.g., exposure of portions of the bottom may not free this vegetation if water levels are normal by the next growing season, although the plants may be somewhat more sparse and scattered. In the North the drawdown is not an effective method of controlling submersed rooted aquatic plants.

However, Lantz, Davis, and Schafer[111] reported good success in using the drawdown for vegetation control as well as for improving fishing in three reservoirs in north and central Louisiana. In two of the lakes they obtained more than 90% reduction in potamogetons and southern naiad *(Najas guadalupensis)* after 1—4 yr of drawdowns. In a third reservoir where the vegetation was coontail, bladderwort, and duckweed, drawdowns produced a 50% reduction in plant growths. Differences in the response of these plants in relation to a drawdown in various parts of their natural range may be associated with differences in length of growing seasons or in the amount of seed produced in the north as compared with the south.

A drawdown may be responsible for the *spreading* of certain kinds of plants, because they may gain a root hold in parts of a lake when the water level is down, in areas that ordinarily are too deep for them. For example, in Allerton Lake near Monticello, Illinois, a September drawdown of 6 ft (maximum depth of lake 14 ft) was maintained throughout a long warm fall (1955). During this period, curly leaved pondweed, *Potamogeton crispus,* gained a start in parts of the lake where the water was 7—11 ft in depth when the lake was full. Then, as the lake refilled over winter and spring, this pondweed continued to grow so that in the summer of 1956 it reached the surface in all areas 7—11 ft deep. This created a severe nuisance for boating and swimming, and when the lake was drawn down again in the fall of 1956, the drawdown had a minimum effect upon small green sunfish, red-ear sunfish, and bluegills, because they were protected from bass predation by the dense mats of vegetation in the deeper waters. A fish census made by draining the lake completely a month after the drawdown exposed excessive populations of small green and red-ear sunfish and demonstrated the importance of pulling the water out of beds of vegetation if a drawdown is to be effective in ridding a lake of small sunfish.

Effects Upon Invertebrates

When water is released from the basin of an artificial lake through an outlet valve, motile aquatic animals are either stranded or forced to move down with the water. Animals that escape being stranded are concentrated and exposed to new environmental conditions. Such weak swimmers as many kinds of Entomostraca, rotifers, and small insects, particularly those that are littoral, are stranded as the water recedes. Snails and larger aquatic insect larvae, such as dragonfly and mayfly nymphs, may attempt to crawl along with the receding water, but most of them eventually are stranded and die or are eaten by birds or other vertebrates. Some crayfish may be stranded but most of them burrow into the lake bottom or move down with the receding waters. In draining Ridge Lake,[15] it was not unusual to find 200 to 300 lbs of crayfish in the stilling pit below the gate valve in the outlet tunnel after all the water had escaped from the basin. These crayfish moved down with the receding water and on through the outlet gate during the time the lake was being drained.

Effect Upon Fishes and Other Vertebrates

The receding water not only strands small invertebrates but many small fishes as well, particularly in the littoral zone where sticks, debris, and mats of rooted vegetation trap these small fishes in temporary water pockets which soon dry up. Certain kinds of small fishes are stranded more often than others. For example, small green sunfish are stranded more often than are small bluegills and small bluegills more often than small red-ear sunfish. Green sunfish are commonly found in shallow water along the lake edges, as are bluegills. The red-ear prefers deeper water and shows a tendency to move away from the water's edge as the lake level moves down. Neither young largemouth nor young smallmouth bass are ordinarily stranded with receding lake levels, although they may be trapped by dense mats of vegetation. Few large fishes are stranded unless they become trapped in shallow basins on the lake bottom and die later when the water in which they are trapped dries up.

Small fishes that are not stranded and successfully move down the lake basin with the water are forced from the protection of rooted vegetation and shallow-water debris into the open water of the lake where they are subject to predation from larger fishes, bullfrogs, and fish-eating reptiles, birds, and mammals. These forces, stranding or trapping and predation, materially reduce the populations of smaller fishes without greatly reducing numbers of the larger ones. The result is a selective culling action which is more specific for sunfish than for bass, but which may not be extensive enough to be beneficial unless the drawdown: (1) reduces the lake surface area by more than 25% and (2) forces the fishes from the protection of beds of aquatic plants. The selective culling action resulting in a reduction of sunfish may set the stage for high survival of bass at the next bass spawning season. Thus, fall drawdowns in several successive years may result in such a numerical buildup of bass that they will be of smaller average size than under more stable water levels (Fig. 6.12).

Heavy predation on the small fish during a fall drawdown may continue as long as their numbers are concentrated and the water remains warm enough for rapid digestion. When the lake cools below 55°F, digestion rate is greatly slowed and the rate of predation diminishes.

Although small fish concentrated by a drawdown are vulnerable to predation by many aquatic animals, it seems probable that piscivorous fish account for the death of more small fishes than all other predators together.

Flat areas in the bottoms of reservoirs suitable for making seine hauls are sometimes cleared of stumps and debris before the reservoirs are filled. Then, later, when the reservoirs are drawn down, seines may be used to harvest concentrations of carp, buffalo, and other commercial fish, thereby giving an additional assist in the process of population improvement.

Types of Drawdowns and Reservoir Management

From the standpoint of angling there is some evidence to suggest that prolonged droughts affect fish populations favorably. In droughts ex-

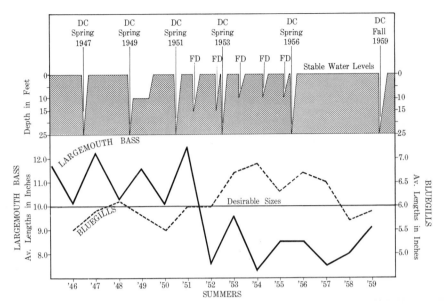

Fig. 6.12 Changes in average sizes of largemouth bass and bluegills caught by fishermen at Ridge Lake (Illinois) under several types of management: 1945-1950, biennial draining and culling of small fishes; 1951-1955, fall drawdowns with draining censuses in spring of 1953 and spring of 1956; 1956 to fall of 1959, stable water levels. DC= draining census; FD =fall drawdown. Fall drawdowns increased the numbers of bass but reduced their average size. Under stable water levels following the drawdown period, the bluegill population expanded and their average size decreased. Bass became less numerous and remained small. (Bennett, G. W., Adkins, H. W., and Childers, W. F., 1969, *Illinois Nat. Hist. Surv. Bull.* 30(1)).

tending over several years, lakes may gradually decrease in area. This gradual decrease must cause adjustment in the fish population. However, it is difficult to see how a slow drawdown would have a selective effect in eliminating excessive small fish. Yellow bass have been observed to decrease in average size during a drought period and to increase in size when a lake is refilled following a long drought.[28]

Annual cycles of water levels, such as were described above for the Illinois River and adjacent bottom-land lakes, can be shown to have a pronounced effect on the fish population. Reservoirs with the greatest fluctuations in area of water contained the largest percents (by weight) of predatory species, which included many game species.[204,205,212] Large man-made and controlled reservoirs have various types of annual cycles of water fluctuation; these cycles may be only remotely related to cycles of rainfall and runoff and not at all· to the life history of fishes. Man-made cycles may vary from one lake to the next, depending upon purposes of water release. If the reservoir is designed to control floods, water will be expelled between floods or prior to anticipated high runoff so that the lake may be partially empty for the storage of excess runoff water. However, if its purpose is to supply water for navigation, the drawdowns occur during the drier parts of the year. In most parts of North America the dry periods are in late summer and early fall. However, in some cases, where there is an irregular need for power, the water may be used to generate it, and the drawdown may conform to no schedule that relates to rainfall and runoff in the watershed or the reservoir.

As more tests of the effects of drawdowns on larger reservoirs are made, evidence accumulates that this technique is the most practical yet available for modifying the fish populations of these wide waters, particularly if drawdowns are coupled with seining operations to remove rough fish when these fish are concentrated.[91,205] Nimrod Lake on the Fourch La Fave River in Arkansas is a good example of what may be accomplished by using a drawdown in reservoir management.[91,171] This lake covered 3600 acres at conservation pool level. In the early and middle 1940s fishing was excellent, but by 1950 the rate of catch had fallen off considerably. Beginning on October 1, 1955, the lake was lowered slowly until by December 1 the level was 12 ft below the conservation pool level and the lake was reduced to 700 acres. While the lake level was down, more than 85,000 lb of fish of commercial species were harvested. Pre-drawdown sampling of fish indicated an abundance of rough fish and few game fish except white crappies. Sampling in the season after the lake had refilled exposed a large increase in game fishes, including new year classes of both largemouth bass and white bass. The transparency of the lake also had increased from around 12 in. pre-drawdown to 3–4 ft post-drawdown. Boat dock operators reported improved fishing.

Water-level fluctuations on Fort Peck Reservoir (Montana) and Fort Randall Reservoir (South Dakota) have shown promise in limiting carp reproduction in the latter by reducing the level following the peak of carp spawning in late spring[172] and improving conditions for pike spawning in the former by increasing water levels to cover recently established vegetation.[148] These fluctuations were timed in spring instead of fall and designed to affect certain species of fishes rather than to influence the entire population. If these operations become annual practices for these reservoirs, and continue to give desired results, we may expect to see the development of other drawdown techniques for specific management needs on other reservoirs.

Where fishing is an important use for a "waterfowl" lake, there has been conflict between fishermen and those concerned with waterfowl, relative to the time that a drawdown is made. Waterfowl managers usually favor a mid-summer drawdown to allow the planting of millet or other quick-maturing grain on exposed mud flats. Fishermen may wish to prolong the summer fishing period as long as possible because, once the lake is drawn down, it may be difficult or impossible to move boats across the exposed mud flats. Moreover, the basin of the lake that is left will probably slope into deep water so gradually that fishing from the bank, once the lake has been drawn down, may be impossible.

The duck enthusiast will insist that the lake must be lowered in sufficient time to absolutely insure a grain crop. The interests of these two groups could be compatible except when the lake bottom is flat and there is too little water left for the fish to survive. In states where spring fishing is permitted, a drawdown in July will have given the fishermen a season of three or four months. They may then be more likely to accede to the desires of those who would plant millet or some other duck-food crop. Fishermen not only benefit from oxidation of the bottom, but also from the mechanical action of the roots of the grain plants growing in the lake bottom and the lake fertilization resulting from the decay of plant stems and duck excrement in the lake basin.

LAKE FERTILIZATION

The fertilization of ponds and lakes for increased production of fish has its origin in antiquity, and for centuries it has been common practice in Europe and parts of Asia to fertilize carp ponds.[138] In the United States the production of fish in ponds for commercial sale is limited.

Thus primary values in pond fertilization for the improvement of sport fishing appear in the southeastern United States where soils are often infertile. Swingle and Smith[186,187] stated that fertilized ponds in Alabama support four to five times as great a weight of fish as unfertilized ones; and consequently, the former give much better fishing. They recommended the use of 100 lb of 6-8-4 $(N-P-K)$ and 10 lb of nitrate of soda per acre of pond for each application, with a seasonal schedule of eight to fourteen treatments, beginning March or April and extending to September or October. More recently Swingle[182] recommended that for old ponds, only super phosphate at the rate of 40 lb/acre/treatment, or 15 lb/acre of triple super phosphate is necessary because enough potassium is available in the pond and atmospheric nitrogen is fixed by bacteria and algae in the pond.

In Alabama such a fertilization program produces a "bloom" of plankton algae that prevents the development of filamentous algae and shades out any rooted submersed aquatic vegetation.[187]

According to Swingle,[179] the algae produced by inorganic fertilization were largely genera of the Chlorophyceae: *Scenedesmus, Ankistrodesmus, Chlorella, Staurastrum, Pandorina, Cosmarium, Chlamydomonas, Nannochloris, Pediastrum, Coelastrum,* and others. Euglenophyceae were also abundant and occasionally dominant. Dinophyceae were often present but usually not in large numbers. The blue-green algae, *Coelosphaerium* and *Microcystis,* occasionally became abundant for limited periods. Variations in kinds of algae were observed in various types of ponds.

Swingle recognized the competition between plankton algae and filamentous algae for dominance. He stated that either 6-8-4 or cottonseed meal applied in clear ponds in cold weather will stimulate the growth of filamentous algae on the bottom which will rise to the surface and shade out plankton algae. However, if these substances are applied when the water is "warm," plankton algae will be produced. Most organic material encourages the growth of filamentous algae unless it colors the water and thereby shades the bottom.

There is no question but that the application of balanced inorganic fertilizers will increase the production of fish in a pond or lake by increasing the phytoplankton and, in turn, the aquatic animals at various trophic levels between the phytoplankton and fishes.[138] However, Gooch[55] states that in spite of the fact that experiments in increasing aquatic productivity in North America have been conducted for more than 37 years (1929 to present) "no one has yet mounted an agressive and sustained attack to elucidate the role played by artificial fertilization in aquatic (vertebrate and invertebate) productivity. As a result, we are essentially no closer now to predicting results of fertilizer practices than we were 37 years ago."

"For example, the pond does not exist for which it is known how much of what kinds of fertilizer elements are necessary to maximize the fish production relative to the cost of fertilizer. And though it may be argued that such a pond can never exist, it seems reasonable to expect that we can narrow considerably the wide gap existing between what we know now and this rather ideal situation. The key to the problem lies in realizing that we must find out what happens under what conditions to the fertilizer elements after they have entered the pond."[55] The lack of specific knowledge on the behavior of potassium, phosphorus, and nitrogen as they function as fertilizer materials in an aquatic environment must be admitted. However, some information is available on these standard inorganic fertilizer materials and on other microelements such as manganese that may produce chemical changes that release inorganic fertilizers from insoluble chemical compounds in the substrate of a pond or lake.[70]

Some of the available information on inorganic fertilizer materials and trace elements is given below.

Manganese

Hasler and Einsele[65] described the use of manganese to release phosphate from iron. Thus, manganese dioxide (MnO_2) which is not a fertilizer, may release phosphate ($-PO_4$) from an insoluble bond with iron, so the effect is the same as though phosphate were added.

Also, manganese is essential for healthy plants; it plays a role in photosynthesis and heterotrophic growth as well as in other physiological processes. When manganese is added to superphosphate as a pond fertilizer, phytoplankton production is greater than when superphosphate is used alone. When manganese was added to ponds built in high phosphorus—low manganese soil, 0.89 lb of manganese per acre increased phytoplankton production 16.4%.[8]

Lime

Many authors stress the importance of lime in pond fertilization where there is a natural shortage of calcium.[19,38,63,141,158,175,198,199,207] In waters containing less that 10 ppm total hardness, the addition of lime may be followed by a large increase in fish production. When hardness equals 40 or more ppm there is no benefit in liming. Lime is believed to have many effects, particularly on the bottom mud where it changes the colloidal and adsorptive properties and creates an alkaline environment which is more suitable than an acid environment for bacteria and fungi. Thus it increases indirectly the rate of decay. It is believed to have several possible chemical actions, such as the precipitation of iron compounds, and may counteract the poisonous properties of sodium, potassium, and magnesium ions. The calcium in lime may displace other fertilizing substances from organic colloidal systems, making available K^+, and $-PO_4$.[141,198] The calcium in strip-mine waters may be responsible for the establishment of strong buffer systems that keep the high sulfate ($-SO_4$) from being toxic to fish and other aquatic organisms. Lewis and Summerfelt[124] demonstrated that the addition of lime to softwater minnow ponds containing high carbon dioxide raised the hardness of the waters from 15 ppm to 56 ppm and the buffering capacity enough to prevent the death of minnows which had been subjected to a pH range from 4.5 at night to 9.5 in bright sunlight.

In European ponds, enough lime is added to the drained pond basin to give a slight alkaline reaction and a crumbly mud structure. When unslaked lime is used on a drained pond basin, it is believed to have a toxic effect on aquatic organisms and fish parasites.

In soft water, the addition of lime may be followed by an increase in carbon dioxide storage in the form of bicarbonate. Swingle[179] believes that calcium competes with the algae for the free carbon dioxide, but Nielsen[142,143] demonstrated that aquatic plants used bicarbonate (HCO_4) directly in photosynthesis, up to one-half of the amount present. Bicarbonate was used more slowly than free carbon dioxide because the latter diffuses about eight or nine times as fast as bicarbonate.

Calcium may be applied in the form of "quick lime" (CaO) or as agricultural limestone. It should never be applied at the same time as phosphate, and quick lime should be applied two to three weeks before fish are stocked.

Potassium

Ponds with sandy bottom soils are often poor in potassium and respond markedly when this element is added. Usually it is difficult to measure the effects of adding potassium. These effects may be direct if there is a potassium scarcity or indirect if the addition of potassium displaces hydrogen from soil colloids, forming dilute acids in which phosphorus becomes soluble, i.e., potassium may indirectly make phosphorus available. German fish culturists usually mix potassium and phosphate fertilizers and apply them together.[158]

Phosphorus

Phosphorus is the most important fertilizing element in lakes and ponds, but may be easily lost through combination with an excess of calcium to form tricalcium phosphate $Ca_3(PO_4)_2$.[73] As carbon dioxide increases, the precipitated salt may be converted to the more soluble di- and monocalcium phosphates.[74] As mentioned in connection with manganese above, iron may unite with phosphate to form an insoluble precipitate. Phosphorus also may combine physically with micelles of ferric hydroxide or be absorbed directly on organic soil colloids on the pond bottom. For these reasons, phosphorus added to a lake or pond quickly goes out of solution, but still may be available on the pond bottom. It therefore follows that phosphorus applied at one time in some quantity may become available in small but useful amounts over a long period of time. European workers recommend about 17 kg/hectare (15.2 lb/acre) of phosphorus (applied as superphosphate) as an optimum dose.[158] Experiments in Israel[75] and in this country do not seem to substantiate a one-shot dosage or the 17 kg/ha amount as optimum.

Hepher[75] working in Israel developed what he called a standard dose of fertilizer for fish ponds which consisted of 53.5 lb of superphosphate and 53.5 lb of ammonium sulfate per acre, for a pond 32—39 in. deep, applied each time at intervals of two weeks. He found that neither the applications of the same amounts made at weekly intervals instead of two weeks, nor two double doses at the beginning of the season, would increase the production. This was explained on the basis that excessive fertilization increased phytoplankton production in the upper layers where favorable light conditions existed but decreased production in the lower layers because of shading by excessively dense upper layers.[75,208]

When ponds in Yugoslovia failed to respond to phosphate application it was discovered that the concentration of phosphorus in water flowing into these ponds was between 1.4 and 4 mg per liter. On the basis of yearly inflow this would amount to between 201 and 573 lb/acre.[49] Phosphorus was being trapped in these ponds; an analysis showed that water flowing out of the ponds contained 50—70% less phosphorus than that flowing in. Some phosphorus also may be available from the pond basins of old ponds that had been fertilized.[183] Phosphorus that has accumulated in the bottom muds may be circulated in summer by releasing compressed air above acidified phosphorus-rich mud. This operation may sometimes endanger fishes if it circulates water which may have a high biological oxygen demand (see Chapter 3).

Nitrogen

Inorganic nitrogen is more often used in this country than in Europe or Asia as a fertilizing material. Some algae are able to fix nitrogen from the atmosphere if phosphorus is available,[37,51,157] particularly the blue-green algae, *Anabaena* and *Nostoc*.[141] However, nitrogen in fertilizers gives a quick source of this element to the algae.

Trace Elements

Plant physiologists recognize the need for trace elements in the normal physiology of certain algae and higher aquatic plants. These micronutrients are boron, chlorine, colbalt, copper, iron, manganese, molybdenum, silicon, sodium, vanadium, and zinc. All have shown to have importance in the physiology of certain kinds of algae.[131] Several vitamins in small quantities are known to be required as growth factors by certain species of algae. Algae also produce growth-inhibiting substances, so that a plant can cause its own destruction through the production of growth-inhibiting substances that it is unable to tolerate but which may stimulate other kinds of algae.

It has been suggested by some physiologists that algae secrete several kinds of substances, some antibiotic and some stimulating. The amount secreted and the net result of the secretions would be determined by the prevalence of one group of substances over the other. Thus, sequences of algal blooms may be expected to occur under conditions of a nutrient supply in excess of critical values.

Organic Fertilizers

Organic fertilizers are used much more extensively in Africa, Asia, and the Far East than in North America.[152,195] In the Orient and Africa, fishes are raised for food and not for sport fishing and high production is necessary and desirable. Wastes from domestic animals and man are used to fertilize fish ponds and these are supplemented with grass cuttings, rice bran, soybean meal, ground nutcake, and other organic materials which may be available. The fish are selected for their high production which means their food chains are short. Brackish water species are the gray mullet (*Mugil cephalus*) and the milk fish *(Chanos chanos)*. Inland-pond species are several carps including the common carp, *Cyprinus carpio,* tilapias, primarily *Tilapia mossambica,* and the giant gourami *Osphronemus goramy.*

In this country organic fertilizers are sometimes inadvertently used in fish ponds when the latter are also serving as manure ponds for the disposal of wastes from feeding lots or "floors" for swine or cattle. Whether or not fish are able to live in such ponds depends upon the size of the pond in relation to the number of animals on the "floor." No specific information is available to the author for defining an optimum relationship between the number of domestic animals, surface area, volume of water, and kinds of fishes, but several examples of fish production in such ponds have been observed. In almost every case where fish were living in manure-contaminated ponds, the ponds were built originally for recreation and erosion control and were later used for waste disposal. Consequently, the ratio of domestic animals to pond area often was relatively low. Ratios 100 to 1000 head of domestic animals per acre of pond surface are not unusual where ponds have been built specifically for waste disposal. These ponds quickly become anaerobic and unsuitable for any fishes.

The fishes that I have observed being taken from ponds receiving organic waste were all of exceptional size and plumpness for their kind. This suggests a numerically limited population having an abundance of available food. Some fishes taken from manure-contaminated ponds were largemouth and smallmouth bass, bluegills, black crappies, and naturally produced red-ear x warmouth hybrids. There was no evidence that these fishes were dangerous to handle or eat.

Judging from their use in organically fertilized ponds in Asia and Africa, the tilapia *(Tilapia mossambica)* might be more suited to manure-contaminated ponds in this country than native sport fishes.

Other Functions of Fertilizers

There are some uses of fertilizer other than those of increasing phytoplankton. Swingle[179] mentions Irwin's work on the use of inorganic fertilizer to cause clay particles to settle out of muddy ponds (see Chapter 3). Ball[5] believed that the addition of fertilizer to the entire shoal area of North Twin Lake (Cheboygan County, Michigan) stimulated the growth of filamentous algae on the bottom; which seemed to interfere with the nest building of sunfishes.

Although no controlled experiments have been reported to date, it seems likely that undissolved salts of commercial fertilizers falling into nests of centrarchids containing developing eggs of yolk-sac fry would cause the embryos to die. Commercial fertilizer is usually broadcast in shallow water over an area that corresponds roughly with that selected by bluegills and other sunfishes for nesting. If a fertilization schedule calls for an application of fertilizer to the shoal waters of a pond at two-week intervals from early spring to September or October, it is probable that many centrarchid embryos would be killed. This might give substantial assistance in keeping the bluegills or other sunfishes from becoming overly abundant.

One of the techniques of pond management often suggested is the systematic destruction of sunfish nests (Chapter 3).

Less effort would be required to drop a small handful of inorganic fertilizer into a nest from a boat than to mechanically destroy the nest, and the former method might be more effective. If fertilizer should prove useful in poisoning sunfish embryos, pond fertilization would be serving a dual purpose.

Dangers from the Use of Fertilizers

The application of inorganic fertilizers to ponds and lakes for increasing fish production[179,187] has not been well accepted in parts of the United States outside of the southeast; there it has been applied on a wide scale, particularly in Alabama.[27] The objections to pond and lake fertilization are many, and it seems apparent that results have been variable and quite unpredictable.[5,31,62,86,155]

In the northernmost states, the suffocation of fishes under ice is common during severe winters with heavy snowfall. Fertilization of ponds and lakes in this region increases the danger of winterkill.[22,189] Ball and Tanner[7] stated that the addition of fertilizer to one of their experimental ponds was the indirect cause of winterkill, because the fertilizer stimulated the algae which later decomposed under the ice.

In all parts of the country there is the ever-present danger of "summerkill" of fishes, where calm hot weather along with an abundance of plankton algae may result in nocturnal oxygen depletion in lakes and ponds.[107] This occurrence is not uncommon in organically rich lakes which are not fertilized. Swingle and Smith[186] advise against applying fertilizer when rooted aquatic plants are decomposing. They cite an instance when an application of fertilizer was broadcast over decomposing masses of *Najas,* with the result that oxygen was depleted and bass and other fishes died.

In Michigan ponds, the use of fertilizer could not be depended upon to control higher aquatic plants,[6] and produced filamentous algae even if not applied until after the water had warmed in the spring.[6,146] This agreed with findings in Wisconsin[66] and in the hard water ponds of West Virginia.[177]

The nuisance values of algae stimulated by inorganic fertilizers are stressed by several authors. Ball and Tanner[7] state: "The appearance of the lake and its use for swimming, boating, and other recreational purposes were adversely affected by the fertilizer. The matted green scum formed by the filamentous algae around the shore and festooning the marginal vegetation was very unsightly and was a hindrance to fishermen, both in the use of their boats and by the fouling of their baits. The odor of the decaying algae was very unpleasant." Patriarche and Ball[146] warn about the unsightly condition that occurs when a growth of filamentous algae follows fertilization. Hansen et al.[62] describe a bloom of *Rhizochlonium* sp. in Lauderdale Pond (Illinois) which covered from 25 to 75% of the surface and stopped fishing except where the algae was absent.

There has been a tendency on the part of some aquatic biologists to oversimplify the problem of pond fertilization and to consider results obtained under some conditions to be universally meaningful.[141] Actually the problem of fertilization of waters is so complex that it is difficult to duplicate results from one pond to another, to say nothing of duplicating results from one research station to another.

There are dangers inherent in the fertilization of any eutrophic lake by any means.[92,189] Hasler and Einsele[65] cite the changes that have taken place in Lake Snake, Vilas County, Wisconsin; Pontiac Lake, Michigan; Lake Okoboji, Iowa; Sylvan Lake, Noble County, Indiana; and Stadlsee near Waldsee in Wuerttenberg, Germany. They also describe the possibility that fertilization may replace an efficient natural food chain with one that is much less efficient. "For example, in a natural lake, a rich growth of *Cyclotella,* a small diatom, fulfills the ideal food requirement of

Daphnia, but fertilization might encourage previously rare or nonexistent algae which are not very suitable as food for *Daphnia,* while the desirable form, *Cyclotella,* is suppressed."

Swingle and Smith[185] demonstrated that by applying inorganic fertilizer to ponds in the proper amount they could increase the standing crop of bluegills from 130 lb/acre to between 300 and 500 lb/acre. These results have not been demonstrated in Michigan,[146] in Indiana,[107] in Illinois,[62] or in any other part of the United States outside of the southeastern states.

In ponds in some of the least productive soil types in Illinois the addition of recommended amounts of inorganic fertilizer increased the average standing crop of fish by about 1.22 times.[62] The improvement in fishing was such that uninformed fishermen could not tell which ponds were fertilized and which were not; yet in terms of total yield, rate of catch, and average size, the fertilized ponds did produce better bluegill fishing than did unfertilized control ponds. In contrast, the controls usually produced a higher yield of bass 10 in. or larger than did the fertilized ponds.

The fertilization of ponds and lakes cannot be recommended as a general fish-management technique outside of the southeastern United States, because the results are too variable and uncertain. Once the fertility of small impoundments in productive soils has been built up, this fertility may manifest itself in luxuriant annual crops of filamentous algae, blue-green algae, or rooted aquatic vegetation. There are already numerous examples of such ponds, most of which are quite productive of fish, but they are problem waters because a treatment to kill rooted vegetation will be followed by obnoxious blooms of algae, which in turn may require chemical treatment. These lakes have reduced aesthetic values, and fishing and swimming are limited by plant growths of one type or another.

If fertilization appears desirable in starting new ponds of low natural fertility, the program should be stopped before undesirable plant growths are evident. New gravel-pit ponds, stone-quarry ponds, or dug ponds having basins of raw clay are often poor fish-producing waters when first formed. The addition of several hundred pounds per acre of commercial fertilizer during the first year will improve fish production without creating nuisance vegetation problems in later years.

AQUATIC VEGETATION AND CONTROL MEASURES

The vegetation that develops in an aquatic environment is as characteristic and specialized as that associated with any terrestrial habitat. How may aquatic plants suddenly appear in a new artificial lake, which a few months before was a dry valley supporting only terrestrial grasses and shrubs? Since the valley was flooded, the terrestrial plants have disappeared and have been replaced by widespread floating mats of green "scum" composed of one or several varieties of filamentous algae. Shallow water supports a few scattered plants of a fine-leaved pondweed *(Potamogeton* sp.), a higher plant that grows almost entirely below the water surface and which cannot support its own leaves when it is lifted out of water.

Undoubtedly, resting cells of various kinds of algae blow about on winds. Seeds of certain higher plants may be transported by special organs which allow them to become airborne (e.g., the feathered seeds of the cattail). Still other seeds which are covered with a very hard coat are eaten by aquatic birds and pass through their digestive tracts undigested, only to fall to the pond bottom and germinate in a new location. It is conceivable that seeds and parts of plants might become entangled with or stick to the muddy toes of aquatic birds and be carried for short distances in this manner.[159] Some seeds float from one location to another through connecting water courses. Thus, during a flood period a pond located well upstream in a watershed might furnish floating seeds to a downstream impoundment. As previously mentioned, some plants, like cattails, have wind-blown seeds. (Fig. 6.13).

Fig. 6.13 Dense stand of cattails (background) with Arrowhead *(Sagittaria)* in foreground. These are among the more common forms of nuisance emergent aquatic vegetation.

Of the submersed pondweeds, the fine-leaved varieties usually appear first, later to be followed by coarser-leaved varieties. Why this should be so is unknown, although there is evidence that the new habitat is more suitable for some species than others. This may be demonstrated by artifically introducing a variety of submersed and emergent aquatic plants into a newly-impounded water area. Usually only a few kinds will survive and these are the species that might be expected to move in naturally. Experience has shown that it is often a complete waste of money to purchase aquatic vegetation for plantings in new impoundments, particularly if these species are not common in similar waters.

Types of Aquatic Plants

Aquatic vegetation exclusive of bacteria and molds may be separated into algae and higher plants.

Algae can be further subdivided into the various categories listed below:

1. Plankton algae—free-floating cells of single or colonial habit, forming characteristic groups, short strands, or spheres with or without power of movement: *Phacus, Scenedesmus, Microcystis, Pandorina.*

2. Filamentous algae—usually form strands or threads of cells that may grow on the pond bottom but often float to the surface forming scums or floating mats (Fig. 6.14) of hairlike strands: *Spirogyra, Zygnema.*

3. Algae that grow upward from the pond bottom in a plant form not unlike that of some of the higher plants: *Nitella, Chara.*

Higher plants can be divided into the following categories:

1. Floating aquatic plants—unattached and floating about on the surface: water hyacinth *(Eichornia),* watermeal *(Wolffia),* duckweed *(Lemna),* mosquito fern *(Azolla).*

2. Submersed rooted aquatic plants—found mostly below the surface and supported by the water: pondweeds *(Potamogeton),* coontail *(Ceratophyllum),* waterweed *(Elodea),* milfoil *(Myriophyllum).*

3. Emergent rooted aquatic plants—found mostly above the surface and self-supporting: cattails *(Typha),* bulrush *(Scirpus),* arrowheads *(Sagittaria)* Fig. 6.13).

4. Woody plants and trees—not true aquatics but are usually associated with water: button bush *(Cephalanthus),* cypress *(Taxodium),* willows *(Selix).*

These plants serve the same functions in an aquatic habitat as in a terrestrial one, i.e., some are sources of food for herbivorous animals, some represent substrata upon which certain animals live, still others serve as cover and mechanical aids in escape from natural predators.

Fig. 6.14 Floating mats of filamentous algae are a nuisance to boaters and swimmers and make fishing nearly impossible.

Aquatic plants compete for space in an aquatic environment much as terrestrial plants do. However, the environment of the former is less stable than the terrestrial environments, and for this reason the plant communities are much less stable. This is particularly true of the algae, which are short lived and sensitive to minute changes in the environment, and of the submersed aquatic plants, which may be shaded out by turbid water.

Algae as Producers of Oxygen.   Plankton forms that undergo photosynthesis liberate oxygen where it may be dissolved in the surrounding water. This is the primary source of dissolved oxygen in water beneath the ice in winter.

Algae as a Basic Food.   Certain of the algae are believed to form basic foods for herbivorous animals in the aquatic environment, much as the grasses are basic foods for many of the herbivorous animals in a terrestrial habitat. In this function some species of algae are much more valuable than others just as some grasses and grains on land are more valuable than others as foods. Probably the plankton algae and bottom microflora in shallow water are more readily utilized than the filamentous forms. Actually very little is known of specific aquatic food chains and the relative values of various species of algae.

Plant cells or plant debris serve as foods for certain species of aquatic animals from protozoa to fishes. However, most of the fishes important for angling are not herbivorous, or eat only limited amounts of plant material. This is true for bluegills, which feed largely on insect larva and Entomostraca; however, at certain seasons, they apparently do feed on algae and the leaves of some submersed aquatic weeds. It has not been determined whether this vegetable matter is a selected food or taken for some other reason.

Dangerous Algae.   Several species of blue-green algae (Cyanophyceae) produce toxic substances when they die and decay. These algae have been responsible for mammalian, avian, and fish deaths.[93,109,139] The genera involved in these deaths were *Aphanizomenon, Anabaena, Nodularia, Gymnodinium, Coelosphaerium,* and *Glaeotrichia.* These algae are particularly dangerous when they appear as "blooms" on lakes and ponds and are concentrated by wind action along the downwind lake margin. Domestic stock drinking this concentration of water and blue-green algal cells rapidly show signs of acute poisoning. The toxic substance produced by the cells will cause the death of animals when algal cells are themselves excluded, and will survive the equivalent of water treatment using alum coagulation, filtration, and chlorination. However, as far as is known, no human deaths or outbreaks of human gastroenteritis have been positively traced to these algae, although unexplained outbreaks of gastroenteritis have been reported in the same areas where extensive algal blooms were present.[144]

Nuisance Algae.   Most filamentous algae are considered nuisance plants because they eventually rise to the water surface and float about as green "slime" or "scum" until they die and disintegrate (Fig. 6.12). In this position they are obnoxious to swimmers, and foul motor blades, oars, and lines of boaters and fishermen.

There are several genera of filamentous algae that grow luxuriantly on the pond surface to form a thick blanket that may almost completely cover the pond. Lawrence[115] lists *Pithophora* as a nuisance form for this reason in the southeastern states, and Hansen et al,[62] describe a pond in southern Illinois that was nearly always partly covered with a floating layer of *Rhizoclonium.* Hatchery personnel in northern states are sometimes bothered with *Hydrodictyon,* an alga in which the elongated cells are arranged in the form of a net with six sided mesh. Small fish become entangled in these algal nets and die because they are unable to escape.

Some algae that grow on rocks and submerged concrete are dangerous to bathers and wading fishermen because they create slippery footing and often cause waders to fall. One type of *Spirogyra* with very coarse filaments is notoriously slippery; I once saw a bather slip and sit down at the top of a steep, spirogyra-covered lake spillway and slide entirely to the bottom before he could stop.

Chemical Control of Algae. Algae are very sensitive to copper and for many years crude copper sulfate crystals dissolved in water and sprayed on algae or dragged in a sack behind a boat has been a standard method of algae control. In soft water, 1 ppm or less is toxic to algae, but when used in hard water the copper ions unite with carbonate in the water to form an insoluble precipitate that is useless in killing algae. Thus, it is necessary to apply a much stronger dosage (5-12 ppm) in order to control algae. In water of more than 150 ppm total hardness, dosages higher than 12 ppm of copper sulfate may become toxic to fishes. Because of the great variation in the hardness of water, it is difficult or impossible to define a meaningful dosage, and only trials will allow one to discover the amount needed for an effective treatment for a specific water.

Other chemicals used for algae control[82,129] are Dichlone (Phygon) (2,3-dichloro-1,4-naphthoquinone) applied at a rate of 6.4 oz of powder per acre-foot of water (0.15 ppm); DMC salt of liquid endothall (Hydrothal 47) [di(N,N-dimethylalkylamine)] applied at a rate of 1.5-3 Pints/acre-ft; and Dichlobenil (aquatic granules) (2.6-dichlorobenzonitrile), which is recommended for the control of *Chara* and *Nitella.* Dichlobenil is applied at the rate of 250−375 lb per surface acre[129] or at the rate of 100 lb/acre as a preemergent application only.[82]

CMU [3-(p-chlorophenyl)-1,1-dimethylurea] has been recommended as a deterrent to algal growth after an established bloom has been killed by other chemicals.[50,132]

Loss of Fish Production Through Rooted Vegetation

There is some evidence that dense stands of submersed rooted aquatic plants may bind up nutrient materials throughout the growing season,[13] so that they are not available for the production of phytoplankton and the organisms that feed upon phytoplankton. This, in turn, may be reflected upon the fish through an eventual reduction of their food supply.

An apparent relationship between fish yields and increasing stands of *Potamogeton foliosus* and *P. nodosus* is shown in Table 6.3.[13] The area of open water in this pond was reduced to 51.2% of the total surface area by a dense stand of *P. foliosus* and *P. nodosus*. The fish yield was reduced to 58.1% of the yield taken during the year when aquatic vegetation was largely absent, although during the year when the low yield of fish was taken the net-fishing intensity was increased 359% and the angling intensity was increased 157%. Swingle[179] investigated a pond that became filled with a heavy growth of naiad, *Najas guadalupensis*. He concluded that the rank plant growths did not reduce the hook-and-line yield. Evidence from the study cited above[13] indicated that the fish in that instance were actually supported in this pond at a lower poundage than they had been before the dense stand of vegetation developed.

Sudden Plant Die-offs. Occasionally progressive plant "die-offs" occur in ponds and lakes. In two instances of plant die-offs that I have observed, the deaths began at specific locations and spread to include all of the rooted vegetation in a pond. One of these occurred in early August of 1941 at Fork Lake (Illinois).[13] Here the vegetation involved was *P. foliosus*, which began to die in a small area of shallow water at the upper end of the pond and spread until all the vegetation had died and disintegrated and an algal bloom of *Aphanizomenon flosaquae* had developed.

A second example of vegetation die-offs occurred in Ridge Lake (Illinois) in 1946 when Mr. W. W. Fleming was studying plant—invertebrate relationships in dense stands of the pondweeds *P. foliosus, P. nodosus, P. pectinatus, Najas flexilis,* and *Elodea canadensis.*[15] In 1948, this die-off began about July 8 and gradually eliminated the rooted vegetation until on

Table 6.3   Reduced Yield of Fish (In Spite of Increased Fishing Pressure) Associated With the Spread of Dense Stands of Rooted Pondweeds, *Potamogeton foliosus* and *P. nodosus*, in Central Illinois[13]

Year	Yield		Area of Open Water Not Filled with Vegetation		Net-Fishing Intensity		Angling Intensity	
	lb	% of 1939 Yield	Acres	% of 1939 Area	Net-days	% of 1939 Net Fishing	Man-hours	% of 1939 Angling
1939	223.4	100.0	1.25	100.0	92	100.0	27.0	100.0
1940	200.2	89.6	0.95	76.0	182	197.8	36.3	134.4
1941	129.9	58.1	0.64	51.2	330	358.8	42.3	156.7

July 23 nothing but open water could be found at his selected sampling stations, which previously had dense stands of rooted pondweeds.

This die-off at Ridge Lake has occurred during most summers since 1946; usually when the last of the early summer vegetation is dying, a new second crop is developing in areas where the old crop died first. By early September, there is almost a complete replacement of vegetation in areas where it was present before the die-off, but the stand is somewhat less dense than was the original stand. It seems possible that this die-off is caused by some disease or parasite, but no causative organism has been isolated.

Role of Aquatic Vegetation in Management

Originally, aquatic biologists held the belief that beds of higher aquatic plants were an essential part of the aquatic environment, presumably because they were almost always present in lakes and ponds. This concept was entirely discarded by Swingle and Smith,[187] who recommended the use of inorganic fertilizers in ponds to stimulate the growth of blooms of phytoplankton to shade rooted aquatics and thereby cause them to die. These investigators demonstrated that the phytoplankton blooms stimulated a higher production of zooplankton which, in turn, raised the level of food for such omnivorous feeders as bluegills, and thereby increased the total fish production. Recently, Swingle[182] has modified this concept to recognize the potential usefulness of limited stands of rooted submersed plants.

Excessive amounts of either rooted aquatic vegetation or algae are considered undesirable in ponds and lakes used for fishing, boating, and bathing. Where there is no history of intentional fertilization, excessive vegetation may be indicative of mild or severe organic pollution from barn lots or septic tanks. One of the drawbacks to locating housing developments around lakes is that such developments often are not connected with sewage-disposal systems; rather each house is supplied with its own septic tank and tile field. If the house is close enough to the lake to benefit aesthetically from it, the field must of necessity be laid in land sloping toward the lake. Eventually effluents from these tile fields enter the lake and, because they carry phosphates and nitrates, they act as fertilizers, which stimulate aquatic vegetation and create nuisance problems. Prospective home owners who contemplate the purchase of lots for permanent homes on small lakes should insist on a sewage system which will carry all effluents away from the lake.

Control of Higher Aquatic Vegetation

Chemical Controls. For more than thirty years sodium arsenite was used for the control of submersed rooted aquatic vegetation, often with good results. The more common objections to its use are that *(1)* it is a poison which may accumulate in a pond or lake; *(2)* it is dangerous to handle and apply; *(3)* it is not very effective in the control of certain waterweeds, such as sago pondweed, *Potamogeton pectinatus,* and curly-leaved pondweed, *p. crispus.*

In the past fifteen years, many terrestrial herbicides have been tested for their potential usefulness in aquatic-weed control.[33,43,57,79,80,88,89,97,118,164,178,188,192] In 1962 Lawrence[117] summarized all available information on aquatic herbicides. At the present time there are twenty-four formulations commonly used as aquatic herbicides for the control of rooted emergent and submerged vegetation and algae. Some aquatic herbicides that are effective in controlling a variety of kinds of plants are: liquid endothall ("Aquathol"), 1,2-dicarboxy-3,6-endoxocyclohexane; granular endothall ("Aquathol granular"), potassium salt of 1,2-dicarboxy-3,6-endoxocyclohexane; 2,4-D ester or amine, liquid or granular, "Esteron 99 concentrate," Chem Pels 2,4-D; silvex, liquid ester, or potassium salt, liquid or granular ("Kuron, Aqua Vex, Chemorsel,"); and diquat ("ortho diquat"), 1:1-ethylene-2:2-dipyridylium dibromide.[129] The effectiveness of these herbicides is indicated by the frequency of their occurrence in Table 6.4, which lists various groups of common aquatic plants with dosages and application recommendations of a number of herbicides useful for their control.

In general the herbicides cleared by the U.S. Public Health Service for use in lakes, ponds, and streams are not very toxic to fishes and bottom fauna (in dosages recommended for vegetation control). Animal plankton, especially the Entomostraca, are somewhat more sensitive to these herbicides and their numbers may be temporarily reduced at the time the chemicals are applied.[34] Sometimes herbicide treatments are followed by an increase in the numbers of bottom organisms, which may parallel an increase in the organic detritus resulting from the death of plants.[63,190]

Biological Controls. Biological control of aquatic vegetation through the introduction of plant consumers is limited to relatively small waters with definite boundaries, because the numbers of organisms involved as vegetation-control agents must bear a definite relationship to the extent of the control problem. When one initiates a biological control program he probably is introducing a new and foreign, somewhat unpredictable, element into an ecosystem, an introduction that he hopes will bring about

Table 6.4   Some Common Kinds of Aquatic Vegetation with Chemicals and Dosages Recommended for Their Control[a]

Group and Species	Chemical, Active Ingredient or Acid Equivalent	Rate of Application		Specific Directions
		ppm	Other dosages	
Emergent Plants				
Arrowhead, (*Sagittaria* spp)	2,4-D			
	ester (20% G)		1 lb/440 sq ft	spread on water
	ester (4 lbs/gal)		2 oz/gal water	spray on plants
	amine (4 lbs/gal)		2 oz/gal water	spray on plants
	Silvex			
	ester (4 lb/gal)		2 oz/gal water	spray on plants
	potassium salt (6 lb/gal)		2 oz/gal water	spray on plants
	potassium salt (20% G)		1 lb/440 sq ft	spread on water
	Diquat cation		4 oz/gal	wet foliage
Bullrush (*Scirpus* spp)	2,4-D			
	ester (20% G)		100 lb/acre or 1 lb/440 sq ft	wet stems
	ester (4 lb/gal)		4 oz/gal	spray on plants
	Dichlobenil (aquatic G)		100 lb/acre or 1 lb/440 sq ft	apply in March to exposed bottom soil
	Diquat cation		2 lbs/3 gal + wetting agent	saturate foliage
Cattails (*Typha* spp)	Dalapon		4 oz/gal + 3 caps detergent	wet foliage
	amino triazole		2 oz/gal + 3 caps detergent	wet foliage
	2,4-D			
	ester (4 lb/gal)		4 oz/gal + 3 caps detergent	wet foliage
	Diquat cation		2 lbs/3 gal + 1 tsp nonionic wetting agent	wet foliage

Table 6.4 cont'd.

Water primrose (Jussiaea diffusa var. glabrescens)	2,4-D		
	ester (20% G)	100 lb/acre	spread on water
	ester (4 lb/gal)	1 oz/gal	wet foliage
	amine (4 lb/gal)	1 oz/gal	wet foliage
	Silvex		
	ester (4 lb/gal)	1 oz/gal	wet foliage
	potassium salt (6 lb/gal)	1 oz/gal	wet foliage
	potassium salt (20% G)	200 lb/acre	spread on water
	Diquat cation	1 oz/gal	wet foliage
Water willow (Justicia americana)	2,4-D		
	ester (20% G)	100 lb/acre	spread on water
	ester (4 lb/gal)	1 oz/gal	wet foliage
	amine (4 lb/gal)	1 oz/gal	wet foliage
	Silvex		
	ester (4 lb/gal)	1 oz/gal	wet foliage
	potassium salt (6 lb/gal)	1 oz/gal	wet foliage
	potassium salt (20% G)	100 lb/acre	spread on water

Submersed Plants with Alternate Leaf Attachments

Potamogetons				
Curly-leaf pondweed (P. crispus)	Endothall			
	sodium salt (2 lb/gal)	1		apply on or below the surface
Leafy pondweed (P. foliosus, P. pusillus)	potassium salt (2 lb/gal)	0.5 – 1.5		same as above
	Diquat cation	0.5		same as above
	Dichlobenil (aquatic G)		1 gal/acre 100-300 lb/acre	preemergent appl.

Table 6.4 cont'd.

Sago Pondweed (*P. pectinatus*)	Fenac sodium salt of 2,3,6-trichloro-phenylacetic acid 10% G		10-13 gal/acre 150-200 lb/acre	on exposed bottom soil on exposed bottom soil
Buttercup (*Ranunculus spp.*)	Diquat cation	0.5		apply below surface
Cabomba (*Cabomba caroliniana*)	Hydrothol 47 di(*N,N*-dimethylalkylamine) salt of endothall, L or G	2.0		apply below surface
Coontail (*Ceratophyllum spp.*)	2,4-D ester (4 lb/gal)	2.0		apply below surface
Watermilfoil (*Myriophyllum spp.*)	ester (20% G) Endothall sodium salt (2 lb/gal)	2.0 3.0		apply below surface

Table 6.4 cont'd.

Plant	Treatment		Rate	Application
	sodium salt (10% G)	3.0		spread on water
	Diquat cation	1.0	2 gal/acre	apply below surface
	Silvex			
	ester (4 lb/gal)	2.0		apply below surface
	potassium salt[c] (6 lb/gal)	2.0		apply below surface
	potassium salt[c] (20% G)	2.0		spread on water
	Dichlobenil[c] (4% aquatic G)			spread on water
	Fenac			
	sodium salt (10% G)		240-375 lb/acre	apply to exposed pond bottom
			150-200 lb/acre	
Slender naiad (*Najas flextilis*)	Diquat cation	1.0	1.5 gal/acre	apply below surface
Southern naiad (*Najas guadalupensis*)	Dichlobenil (aquatic G)		200 lb/acre	preemergent appl.
Potamogetons Floating-leaved (*P. nodosus*) (**P. illinoensis**) (*P. natans*) (*P. amphfolius*) (*P. diversifolius*)	Endothall (10% G)	1.0		spread on water
	sodium salt (2 lb/gal)		4 oz/gal	apply to leaves
	potassium salt (2 lb/gal)	1.0-2.0		apply to leaves
Free-Floating Aquatic Plants				
Duckweed (*Lemna minor*)	Endothall		2 oz/gal	apply to leaves
	Diquat cation		2 oz/gal	apply to leaves

[a] Hiltibran, 1967a; Lopinot, 1968.   [b] L – liquid form; G – granular form.   [c] Watermilfoil only.

the desired modification of that ecosystem. This "foreign element" may have a potential for creating problems greater than the one that it was introduced to solve.

The simplest and most logical approach to an excess of aquatic vegetation is to introduce some animal that will graze upon that vegetation to a point where the latter is no longer a problem; then the animal may have to move out or change its feeding habits. Some of the eaters of aquatic plants in fresh water that have been considered for vegetation control are sea-cows, *Trichechus manatus,* nutrias, *Myocastor coypu,* ducks and geese, a number of species of fishes, a snail, and several insects that attack aquatic vegetation. Sea-cows appear to be impractical because of their large size, temperature limitations, and slow reproduction.

Nutrias, the large muskrat-like rodents of South America, have been tried in Poland and Israel.[40] In one shallow lake that was rapidly filling with aquatic plants, a stocking of eleven nutrias per hectare (2.47 acres) greatly increased the extent of open water and the lake depth.[42] In another experiment the addition of nutrias to a marshy lake used for carp increased the annual production (weight) of fish by 20%.[41] However, excessive numbers of nutrias eventually damaged the pond habitat by breaking down the banks.

Ducks and geese graze to some extent on aquatic vegetation. According to Grizzell and Neely,[56] six or more muscovy ducks per acre will control duckweed. Excessive numbers of ducks in a pond will result in damage to the banks.

Several species of fish are vegetation feeders. The ones that have been used to control vegetation are the white Amur or grass carp, *Ctenopharyngodon idella,* a native of China, the tawes, *Puntius javanicus,* indigenous to Indonesia, at least four species of tilapias (Cichlids) found in tropical parts of the world, the goramy, *Osphronemus gorami,* and the common carp, *Cyprinus carpio,* particularly the variety called Israeli carp. Of all the herbivorous fishes, the grass carp is considered the best for vegetation control in ponds. A grass carp will eat 40–70% of its body weight of vegetation in a day; by comparison, a cow will eat a maximum of 10–12% of its weight in twenty-four hours. Twelve grass carp, weighing one to two pounds each per acre will control most kinds of vegetation; forty per acre will totally eradicate all vegetation.[147,161] These fish have been exposed without losses to a low temperature range of 32 to 39°F under ice for five weeks and summer temperatures as high as 96°F.[112,172]

The tilapias useful for vegetation control are *T. mossambica, T. melanoplura, T. nilotica,* and *T. zillii.*[84] Unless bred to produce one sex,[135] tilapias stocked alone in ponds are liable to overpopulate and produce an overabundance of fish too small for food. They are found in tropical climates and if used for vegetation control in the temperate zone they must be brought indoors during winter.[30]

The common carp, *C. carpio,* will control vegetation by uprooting plants in its search for bottom organisms and thereby create such high turbidities that further plant growth is shaded out. In many situations the high turbidities resulting from carp feeding activity are considered more undesirable than an excessive amount of aquatic vegetation. However certain strains of mirror carp (called Israeli carp in the U.S.) appear to be superior to the common wild carp in the actual consumption of vegetation.[3]

Another fish important as a vegetation feeder is the tawes, *P. javanicus,* [77,126,181] indigenous to Indonesia but introduced into a few other Southeast Asian countries. This fish is said to be almost as efficient as the grass carp. Gouranies are less useful in vegetation control than carp.

Other vegetation control agents that have been suggested are a South American snail, *Marisa cornuarietis,*[160] which appears to be quite efficient in eating potamogetons, other common aquatic plants and algae; and a number of insects including a Russian chrysomelidan beetle, *Galerucella nymphaeae.*[162]

At present, the Chinese grass carp, the tawes, and, to a lesser extent, tilapias appear to be the most suitable weed-control agents for Asia and the Far East.[147] In North America, the grass carp, Israeli carp, and several species of tilapia are now being tested for potential use in vegetation control,[30,135,181] not only in the deep South but in regions where winter temperatures are severe. The tilapias present no dangers to native fishes in the North, but whether grass carp will be released for distribution depends on the results of behavior and ecological studies now in progress.

REFERENCES

1. Allison, D., 1964, "Copper sulfate used in bluegill population control," *Ohio Dept. Nat. Res. Publ.* W-10, 1-6.
2. Anonymous, 1950, "Minnow seine sampling," *J. Wildlife Management* 14(1), 85-88.
3. Avault, J. W., Jr., 1965, "Biological weed control with herbivorous fish," *Proc. 18th Weed Control Conf.,* pp. 19-21.
4. Baker, C., 1963, "Fish harvest by wire nets in a stream impoundment," *Ohio Dept. Nat. Res. Publ.* W-323, 1-14.
5. Ball, R. C., 1950, "Fertilization of natural lakes in Michigan," *Am. Fish. Soc. Trans.* 78, 146-155.
6. Ball, R. C., 1952, "Farm pond management in Michigan," *J. Wildlife Management* 16(3), 266-269.

7. Ball, R. C., and Tanner, H. A., 1951, "The biological effects of fertilizer on a warm-water lake," *Mich. State Coll. Tech. Bull.* 223, 1-32.

8. Banerjee, S. M., and Banerjee, S. C., 1966, "Fertilization of fish ponds with trace element manganese for increased production of plankton," *FAO World Symp. Warm-Water Pond Fish Cult., FR,II/E-6,* pp. 1-21.

9. Barry, J. J., 1967, "Evaluation of creel census, rotenone embayment, gill net, traps and electro-fishing gear samples, by complete drainage of Lenape and Bischoff Reservoirs," *Ind. Dept. Nat. Res. Div. Fish and Game, Fish. Res. Section,* pp. 1-18.

10. Beall, H. B., and Wahl, R. W., 1959, "Trapping bluegill sunfish in West Virginia ponds," *Progressive Fish Culturist* 21(3), 138-141.

11. Beckman, W. C., 1941, "Increased growth rate of rock bass, *Ambloplites rupestris* (Raf.) following reduction in the density of the population," *Am. Fish. Soc. Trans.* 70(1940), 143-148.

12. Bennett, G. W., 1943, "Management of small artificial lakes," *Illinois Nat. Hist. Surv. Bull.* 22(3), 357-376.

13. Bennett, G. W., 1948, "The bass-bluegill combination in a small artificial lake," *Illinois Nat. Hist. Surv. Bull.* 24(3), 377-412.

14. Bennett, G. W., 1954, "The effects of a late summer drawdown on the fish population of Ridge Lake, Coles County, Illinois," *Trans. 19th North Am. Wild. Conf.* pp. 259-270.

15. Bennett, G. W., 1954, "Largemouth bass in Ridge Lake, Coles County, Illinois," *Illinois Nat. Hist. Surv. Bull.* 26(2), 217-276.

16. Bennett, G. W., and Childers, W. F., 1957, "The smallmouth bass, *Micropterus dolomieui,* in warm-water ponds," *J. Wildlife Management* 21(4), 414-424.

17. Beyerle, G. B., and Williams, J. E., 1967, "Attempted control of bluegill reproduction in lakes by the application of copper sulfate crystals to spawning nests," *Progressive Fish Culturist* 29(3), 150-155.

18. Bowers, C. C. 1955, "Selective poisoning of gizzard shad with rotenone," *Progressive Fish Culturist* 17(3), 134-135.

19. Bowling, M. L., 1965, "The effects of lime treatment on benthos production in Georgia farm ponds," *Proc. 16th Ann. Conf. S.E. Assoc. Game and Fish Comm.,* pp. 418-424.

20. Bridges, W. R., 1958, "Sodium cyanide as a fish poison," *U.S. Fish Wildlife Serv. Spec. Sci. Rept. Fisheries* 253, 1-11.

21. Brown, C. J. D., and Ball, R. C., 1943, "An experiment in the use of derris root (rotenone) on the fish and fish food organisms of Third Sister Lake," *Am. Fish. Soc. Trans.* 72(1942), 268-284.

22. Brown, C. J. D., and Thoreson, N. A., 1952, "Ranch fish ponds in Montana," *J. Wildlife Management* 16(3), 275-278.

23. Buck, D. H., and Whitacre, M., 1960, "A new method and a new material for screening fish," *Progressive Fish Culturist* 22(3), 141-143.

24. Burdick, G. E., Dean, H. J., and Harris, E. J., 1955, "Toxicity of emulsifiable rotenone to various species of fish," *N.Y. Fish and Game J.* 2(1), 36-67.

25. Burmakin, E. V., 1958, "Ichthyotoxic substances and their utilization in the control of undesirable fish," *Biol. Abstr.* 47(12), 55661 (1966).

26. Burnet, A. M. R., 1959, "Electric fishing with pulsatory direct current," *New Zealand J. Sci.* 2(1), 46-56.

27. Byrd, I. B., and Crance, J. H., 1965, "Fourteen years of management and fishing success in Alabama's state-owned public fishing lakes," *Am. Fish. Soc. Trans.* 94(2), 129-134.

28. Carlander, K. D., 1963, "Yellow bass comeback at Clear Lake?" *Iowa Cons.* 22(6). 44-45.

29. Carlander, K. D., and Moorman, R. B., 1957, "Some experiments in changing population balance in farm ponds," *Progressive Fish Culturist* 19(2), 92-94.

30. Childers, W. F., and Bennett, G. W., 1967, "Experimental vegetation control by large-mouth bass - tilapia, combinations," *J. Wildlife Management* 31(3), 401-407.
31. Clark, M., 1952, "Kentucky's farm pond program," *J. Wildlife Management* 16(3), 262-266.
32. Cobb, E. S., 1954, "The use of fish traps in the management of farm ponds," *J. Tenn. Acad. Sci.* 29(1), 45-54.
33. Cortell, J. M., 1961, "Progress report on the field testing of various herbicides for aqutic weed control," *Proc. N.E. Weed Control Conf.* 15, 532-538.
34. Crosby, D. G., and Tucker, R. K., 1966, "Toxicity of aquatic herbicides to *Daphnia magna,*" *Science* 154(3746), 289-290.
35. Cushing, E. E., Jr., and Alive, J. R., 1957, "Effects of toxaphene and rotenone upon the macroscopic bottom fauna of two northern Colorado reservoirs," *Am. Fish. Soc. Trans.* 86(1956), 294-301.
36. Davis, H. S., 1940, "A review of aquicultural investigations of the Bureau of Fisheries," *Progressive Fish Culturist* 50, 1-13.
37. De, P. K. 1939, "The role of blue-green algae in nitrogen fixation in rice fields," *Proc. Roy. Soc. London, Ser. B.* 127, 121-138.
38. Demoll, R., 1925, "Teichdungung," *Handb. der Binnenfischerei Mitteleuropas* 4, 53-160.
39. Derse, P. H., and Strong, F. M., 1963, "Toxicity of antimycin to fish," *Nature* 200, 600-601.
40. Ehrlich, S., 1961, "Experiments in reversion of the filling up processes in fish ponds," *Hydrobiol.* 18(1/2), 136-154.
41. Ehrlich, S., 1964, "Studies on the influence of nutria on carp growth," *Hydrobiol.* 23(1/2), 196-210.
42. Ehrlich, S., and Jedynak, K., 1962, "Nutria influence on a bog lake in Northern Pomorze, Poland," *Hydrobiol.* 19(3), 273-297.
43. Eipper, A. W., 1959, "Effects of five herbicides on farm pond plants and fish," *N.Y. Fish and Game J.* 6(1), 46-56.
44. Eschmeyer, R. W., 1937, "Some characteristics of a population of stunted perch," *Papers Mich. Acad. Sci.* 22, 613-628.
45. Eschmeyer, R. W., 1942, "The catch, abundance and migration of game fishes in Norris Reservoir, Tennessee, 1940," *J. Tenn. Acad. Sci.* 17(1), 90-115.
46. Eschmeyer, R. W., and Jones, A. M., 1941, "The growth of game fishes in Norris Reservoir during the first five years of impoundment," *6th North Am. Wildlife Conf. Trans.* (1941), 222-240.
47. Eschmeyer, R. W., Manges, D. E., and Haslbauer, O. F., 1947, "Trends in fishing on T.V.A. storage waters," *J. Tenn. Acad. Sci.* 22(1), 45-56.
48. Eschmeyer, R. W., Stroud, R. H., and Jones, A. M., 1944, "Studies of fish population on the shoal area of a T.V.A. main-stream reservoir," *J. Tenn. Acad. Sci.* 19(1), 70-122.
49. Fijan, N., 1966, "Problems in carp fish pond fertilization," *FAO World Symp., Warm-Water Pond Fish Cult., FR,II/E-4,* pp. 1-10.
50. Fitzgerald, G. P., 1957, "The control of the growth of algae with CMU," *Trans. Wisconsin Acad. Sci.* 46, 281-294.
51. Fogg, G. E., 1942, "Studies in nitrogen fixation by blue-green algae," I, "Nitrogen fixation by *Anabaena cylindrica* Lemm," *Brit. J. Exptl. Bio.* 19, 78-87.
52. Forbes, S. A., 1895, "Biennial report of the director of the State Laboratory of Natural History, 1893-1894," in *Rept. of Board Illinois State Fish. Comm., Oct. 1, 1892 to Sept. 30, 1894,* Springfield, pp. 35-52.
53. Fukano, K., and Hooper, F. F., 1958, "Toxaphene (chlorinated camphene) as a selective fish poison," *Progressive Fish Culturist* 20(4), 189-190.

54. Gaylord, W. E., and Smith, B. R., 1966, "Treatment of East Bay, Alger County, Michigan, with toxaphene for control of sea lampreys," *Wisconsin Bur. Sport Fish. Wildlife, Fish Control Lab., Res. Pub.* 11, 1-7.

55. Gooch, B. C., 1966, "Appraisal of N. American fish culture fertilization studies," *FAO World Symp. Warm-Water Pond Fish Cult., FAO Fish. Rept.* 44(3), 13-26 .

56. Grizzell, R. A., Jr., and Neely, W. W., 1962, "Biological controls of waterweeds," *Trans. 27th North Am. Wildlife Nat. Res. Conf.* pp. 107-113.

57. Guse, L. R., 1961, "Aquatic weed control research in Indiana," *18th North Cent. Weed Control Conf.* 102.

58. Hall, J. F., 1956, "A comparative study of two fish sampling methods in a small Kentucky impoundment," *Trans. Kentucky Acad. Sci.* 17(3-4), 140-147.

59. Hansen, D. F., 1944, "Rate of escape of fishes from hoopnets," *Illinois Acad. Sci. Trans.* 37, 115-122.

60. Hansen, D. F., 1951, "Biology of the white crappie in Illinois," *Illinois Nat. Hist. Surv. Bull.* 25(4), 211-2 65.

61. Hansen, D. F., 1953, "Seasonal variation in hoop net catches at Lake Glendale," *Illinois Acad. Sci. Trans.* 46, 216-266.

62. Hansen, D. F., Bennett, G. W., Webb, R. J., and Lewis, J. M., 1960, "Hook-and-line catch in fertilized and unfertilized ponds," *Illinois Nat. Hist. Surv. Bull.* 27(5), 345-390.

63. Harp, G. L., and Campbell, R. S., 1964, "Effects of the herbicide silvex on benthos of a farm pond," *J. Wildlife Management* 28(2), 308-317.

64. Harrison, A. D., and Rattray, E. A., 1966, "Biological effects of mollusciciding natural waters," *S. African J. Sci.* 62(7), 238-241.

65. Hasler, A. D., and Einsele, W. G., 1948, "Fertilization for increasing productivity of natural inland waters," *13th North Am. Wildlife Conf. Trans.* pp. 527-555.

66. Hasler, A. D., and Jones, E., 1949, "Demonstration of the antagonistic action of large aquatic plants on algae and rotifers," *Ecology* 30(3), 359-364.

67. Hayes, F. R., and Livingstone, D. A., 1955, "The trout population of a Nova Scotia lake as affected by habitable water, poisoning of the shallows and stocking," *J. Fisheries Res. Board Can.* 12(4), 618-635.

68. Helms, D. R., 1967, "Use of formalin for selective control of tadpoles in the presence of fishes," *Progressive Fish Culturist* 29(1), 1-7.

69. Hemphill, J.E., 1954, "Toxaphene as a fish toxin," *Progressive Fish Culturist* 16(1), 41-42.

70. Henderson, C., 1949, "Manganese for increased production of water-bloom algae in ponds," *Progressive Fish Culturist* 11(3), 157-159.

71. Henderson, C., Pickering, Q. H., and Tarzwell, C. M., 1959, "Relative toxicity of ten chlorinated hydrocarbon insecticides to four species of fish," *Am. Fish. Soc. Trans.* 88(1), 23-32.

72. Henegar, D. L., 1966, "Minimum lethal levels of toxaphene as a pesticide in North Dakota lakes," *U.S. Fish Wildlife Serv. Res. Publ.* 7, 1-16.

73. Hepher, B., 1958*a*, "On the dynamics of phosphorus added to fishponds in Israel," *Bamidgeh* 10(1), 3.

74. Hepher, B., 1958*b*, "The effect of various fertilizers and the methods of their application on the fixation of phosphorus added to fishponds," *Bamidgeh* 10(1), 4-18.

75. Hepher, B., 1963. "Ten years of research in fishpond fertilization in Israel," II, "Fertilizers, dose and frequence of fertilization," *Bamidgeh* 15(4), 78-92.

76. Herr, F., Greselin, E., and Chappel, C., 1967. "Toxicology studies of antimycin, a fish eradicant," *Am. Fish. Soc. Trans.* 96(3), 320-326.

77. Hickling, C. F., 1962, *Pond Culture,* Faber and Faber, London, 295 pp.

78. Hilsenhoff, W. L., 1965, "The effect of toxaphene on the benthos in a thermally stratified lake," *Am. Fish. Soc. Trans.* 94(3), 210-213.

79. Hiltibran, R. C., 1961*a*, "The chemical control of some aquatic weeds," *Illinois Nat. Hist. Surv. Mimeo.* A-5, 1-18.

80. Hiltibran, R. C., 1961*b*, "Weed control research in central Illinois," *18th North Cent. Weed Control Conf. Res. Rept.*, pp. 102-103.

81. Hiltibran, R. C., 1965, "Oxidation of succinate by bluegill liver mitochondria," *Illinois Acad. Sci. Trans.* 58(3), 176-182.

82. Hiltibran, R. C., 1967*a*, "The chemical control of some aquatic weeds," *Illinois Nat. Hist. Surv. Mimeo.*, pp. 1-8.

83. Hiltibran, R. C., 1967*b*, "Oxidation of alpha-ketoglutarate by bluegill liver mitochondria," *Illinois Acad. Sci. Trans.* 60(3), 244-249.

84. Hofstede, A. E., and Botke, F., 1950,"*Tilapia mossambica* Peters as a factor in malaria control in the vicinity of Djakarta," *Overdruk Landbouw,* 22, 453-468.

85. Hooper, F. F., 1959, "Population control by chemicals and some resulting problems," *Trans. 2nd Sem. on Water Pollution,* USPHS, 241-246.

86. Hooper, F. F., and Ball, R. C., 1964, "Responses of a marl lake to fertilization," *Am. Fish. Soc. Trans.* 93(2), 164-173.

87. Hooper, F. F., and Grzenda, A. R., 1957, "The use of toxaphene as a fish poison," *Am. Fish. Soc. Trans.* 85(1955), 180-190.

88. Houser, A., and Gaylor, J. Y., 1962, "Results of endothal and two formulations of silvex for the control of aquatic plants in Oklahoma," *Proc. 15th S. Weed Conf.,* pp. 244-253.

89. Hughes, E. C., 1961, "Aquatic weed control," *Res. Rept. W. Sect. Nat. Weed Commit., Can.,* pp. 107-113.

90. Huish, M. T., 1958, "Studies of gizzard shad reduction at Lake Beulah, Florida," *Proc. 11th Ann. Conf. S. E. Assoc. Game and Fish Comm.* (1957), 66-70.

91. Hulsey, A. H., 1956, "Effects of a fall and winter drawdown on a flood control lake," *5th Ann. Meet. S. Div. Am. Fish. Soc. Mimeo.,* pp. 1-7.

92. Hynes, H. B. N., 1960, *The Biology of Polluted Waters,* University Press of Liverpool, Liverpool, England, 202 pp.

93. Ingram, W. M., and Prescott, G. W., 1954, "Toxic freshwater algae," *Am. Midland Naturalist* 52(1), 75-87.

94. Jackson, C. F., 1956, "Control of the common sunfish or pumpkinseed, *Lepomis gibbosus* in New Hampshire," *New Hampshire Fish and Game Dept. Tech. Circ.,* No. 12, pp. 1-16.

95. Jackson, D. F., 1957, "Detoxification of rotenone-treated water," *New Hampshire Fish and Game Dept. Tech. Circ.* No. 14, pp. 1-28.

96. Jenkins, R. M., 1959, "Some results of the partial fish population removal technique in lake management," *Oklahoma Acad. Sci. Proc.* 37(1956), 164-173.

97. Johnson, M. G., 1965, "Control of aquatic plants in farm ponds in Ontario," *Progressive Fish Culturist* 27(1), 23-30.

98. Johnson, W. C., 1966, "Toxaphene treatment of Big Bear Lake, California," *Cal. Fish and Game* 52(3), 173-179.

99. Johnson, W. D., Lee, G. F., and Spyridakis, D., 1966, "Persistence of toxaphene in treated lakes," *Air Water Pollution Intern. J.* 10(8), 555-560.

100. Kallman, B. J., Cope, O. B., and Navarre, R. J., 1962, "Distribution and detoxication of toxaphene in Clayton Lake, New Mexico," *Am. Fish. Soc. Trans.* 91(1), 14-22.

101. King, J. E., 1954, "Three years of partial fish population removal at Lake Hiwassee, Oklahoma," *Oklahoma Acad. Sci. Proc.* 35, 21-24.

102. Kirharo, J., Guichard, F., and Bonquet, A., 1962, "Ichthyotoxic plants," III, "Second part of an inventory of fish poisons (conclusions)," *Bull. Mem. Fac. Med. Pharm. Dakar* 10, 223-242.

103. Kiser, R. W., Donaldson, J. R., and Olson, P. R., 1963, "The effect of rotenone on zooplankton populations in freshwater lakes," *Am. Fish. Soc. Trans.* 92(1), 17-24.

104. Kiyoshi, G. F., and Hooper, F. F., 1958, "Toxaphene (chlorinated camphene) as a selective fish poison," *Progressive Fish Culturist* 20(4), 189-190.

105. Konar, S. K., 1968, "Experimental use of chlordane in fishery management," *Progressive Fish Culturist* 30(2), 96-99.

106. Krumholz, L. A., 1948, "The use of rotenone in fisheries research," *J. Wildlife Management* 12(3), 305-317.

107. Krumholz, L. A., 1952, "Management of Indiana ponds for fishing," *J. Wildlife Management* 16(3), 254-257.

108. Kuronuma, K., and Nakamura, K., 1958, "Weed control in farm-pond and experiment by stocking grass carp," *Proc. Indo-Pac. Fish. Coun.* 7(2), 35-42.

109. Lackey, J. B., and Clendenning, K. A., 1963, "A possible fish-killing yellow tide in California waters," *Quart. J. Florida Acad. Sci.* 36(3), 263-268.

110. Lambou, V. W., 1959, "Block-off net for taking fish population samples," *Progressive Fish Culturist* 21(3), 143-144.

111. Lantz, K. E., Davis, J. T., Hughes, J. S., and Schafer, H. E., Jr., 1967, "Water level fluctuation its effects on vegetation control and fish population management," *Proc. 18th Ann. Conf. S.E. Assoc. Game and Fish Comm.* pp. 483-494.

112. Larimore, R. W., 1959, "Ecological life history of the warmouth (Centrarchidae)," *Illinois Nat. Hist. Surv. Bull.* 27(1), 1-83.

113. Larimore, R. W., Durham, L., and Bennett, G. W., 1950, "A modification of the electric fish shocker for lake work," *J. Wildlife Management* 14(3), 320-323.

114. Latta, W. D., and Myers, G. F., 1961, "Night use of a direct-current electric shocker to collect trout in lakes," *Am. Fish. Soc. Trans.* 90(1), 81-83.

115. Lawrence, J. M., 1954, "Control of a branched alga, *Pithophora,* in farm fish ponds," *Progressive Fish Culturist* 16(2), 83-86.

116. Lawrence, J.M., 1956, "Preliminary results on the use of potassium permanganate to counteract the effects of rotenone on fish," *Progressive Fish Culturist* 18(1), 15-21.

117. Lawrence, J. M., 1962, *Aquatic Herbicide Data,* U.S. Dept. Agr. Handbook 231, p. 133.

118. Lawrence, J. M., Beasley, P. G., and Funderburk, H. H., 1963, "Water investigations on herbicidal activity of casoron, banvel D, chlorophenoxy, and other compounds alone and in combinations on alligator weed," *Proc. 16th S. Weed Conf.* pp. 368-369.

119. Lennon, R. E., 1966a, "Antimycin-a new fishery tool," *Wisconsin Cons. Bull.* 31(2), 4-5.

120. Lennon, R. E., 1966b, "Antimycin-a new fishery tool," *Izaak Walton Mag.* 31(7), 16-17.

121. Lennon, R. E., Berger, B. L., and Gilderhus, P. A., 1967, "A powered spreader for antimycin," *Progressive Fish Culturist* 29(2), 110-113.

122. Leonard, J. W., 1939, "Notes on the use of derris as a fish poison," *Am. Fish. Soc. Trans.* 68(1938), 269-280.

123. Lewis, W. M., 1968, "Isobornyl thiocyanoacetate as a fish drugging agent and selective toxin," *Progressive Fish Culturist* 30(1), 29-31.

124. Lewis, W. M., and Summerfelt, R. C., 1961, "Adjustment of alkaline reserve of lakes by the addition of hydrated agricultural lime," *Illinois State Acad. Sci. Trans.* 54(3/4),168-174.

125. Lindgren, P. E., 1960, "About the effect of rotenone upon benthonic animals in lakes," *Fish. Board Sweden, Inst. Freshwater Res. Rept.,* No. 41, pp. 172-184.

126. Ling, S. W., 1960, "Control of aquatic vegetation," *3rd Intern. Inland Fish. Train. Cent., FAO and Indo-Pac. Fish Council,* pp. 1-12.

127. Loeb, H. A., 1957, "Night collection of fish with electricity," *N.Y. Fish Game J.* 4(1), 109-118.

128. Loeb, H. A., and Kelly, W. H., 1963, "Acute oral toxicity of 1,496 chemicals to force-fed carp," *U.S. Fish Wildlife Serv. Spec. Sci. Rept., Fisheries* 471, 1-124.

129. Lopinot, A. C., 1968, "Aquatic weeds their identification and methods of control," *Illinois Dept. Cons. Fish. Bull.* 4, 1-53.

130. Louder, D. D., and McCoy, E. C., 1965, "Preliminary investigations of the use of aqualin for collecting fishes," *Proc. 16th Ann. Conf. S.E. Assoc. Game and Fish. Comm.,* pp. 240-242.

131. Mackenthun, K. M., and Ingram, W. M., 1966, "Algal growth aqueous factors other than nitrogen and phosphorus," *U.S. Dept. Int., Fed. Water Pollution Cont. Admin. Bull.,* pp. 1-41.

132. Maloney, T. E., 1958, "Control of algae with chlorophenyl dimethyl urea," *J. Am. Water Works Assoc.* 50, 416-422.

133. Marking, L. L., and Hogan, J. W., 1967, "Investigations in fish control 19, Toxicity of Bayer 73 to fish," *Bur. Sport. Fish and Wildl. Res. Publ.* 36, 1-13.

134. Mayhew, J., 1959, "The use of toxaphene as a fish poison in strip mine ponds with varying physical and chemical characteristics," *Proc. Iowa Acad. Sci.* 66, 512-517.

135. McConnell, W. J., 1966, "Preliminary report on the Malacca *Tilapia* hybrid as a sport fish in Arizona," *Progressive Fish Culturist* 28(1), 40-46.

136. Meyer, F. P., 1965, "The experimental use of guthion as a selective fish eradicator," *Am. Fish. Soc. Trans.* 94(3), 302-309.

137. Moody, H. L., 1958, "An evaluation of fish population studies by Florida haul seine," *Proc. 11th Ann. Conf. S.E. Assoc. Game and Fish Comm.,* pp. 89-91.

138. Mortimer, C. H., and Hickling, C. F., 1954, *Fertilizers in Fishponds,* Her Majesty's Stationery Off., Colonial Off. Fish. Publ. 5, pp. 1-155.

139. Muncy, R. J., 1965, "Observations on the factors involved with fish mortality as the result of dinoflagellate 'bloom' in freshwater lake," *Proc. 17th Ann. Conf. S.E. Assoc. Game and Fish Comm. (1963),* pp. 218-222.

140. Needham, R. G., 1966, "Effects of toxaphene on plankton and aquatic invertebrates in North Dakota lakes," *U.W. Fish Wildlife Serv. Res. Publ.* 8, 1-16.

141. Neess, J. C., 1949, "Development and status of pond fertilization in central Europe," *Am. Fish. Soc. Trans.* 76(1046), 335-358.

142. Nielsen, E. W., 1944, "Dependence of freshwater plants on quantity of carbon dioxide and hydrogen in concentration," Dansk Botanisk Ark. 11(8), 1-25.

143. Nielsen, E. W., 1947, "Photosynthesis of aquatic plants with special reference to the carbon sources," *Dansk Botanisk Ark.* 12(8), 1-71.

144. Palmer, C.M., 1959, *Algae in Water Supplies,* U.S. Public Health Serv. Publ. 657, p.61.

145. Parker, R. A., 1958, "Some effects of thinning on a population of fishes," *Ecology* 39(2), 305-314.

146. Patriarche, M. H., and Ball, R. C., 1949, "An analysis of the bottom fauna production in fertilized and unfertilized ponds and its utilization by young-of-the-year fish," *Mich. State Coll. Agr. Expt. Sta. Tech. Bull.* 207, 1-35.

147. Philipose, M. T., 1966, "Present trends in the control of weeds in fish cultural waters of Asia and the Far East," *FAO World Symp. on Warmwater Pond Fish Cult., FR, VII/R-O,* pp. 1-26.

148. Posewitz, J., 1966, "Big change in the big pond," *Montana Wildlife,* July, pp. 19-22.

149. Post, G., 1955, "A simple chemical test for rotenone in water," *Progressive Fish Culturist* 17(4), 90-191.

150. Prevost, G., 1960, "Use of fish toxicants in the province of Quebec," *Can. Fish Culturist* 28, 13-35.

151. Prevost, G., Lanouette, C., and Grenier, F., 1948, "Effect of volume on the determination of DDT or rotenone toxicity of fish," *J. Wildlife Management* 12(3), 241-250.

152. Prowse, G. A., 1966, "A review of the methods of fertilizing warm-water fish ponds in Asia and the Far East," *FAO World Symp. on Warmwater Pond Fish Cult., FR,II/R-2* pp. 1-6.

153. Radonski, G. C., and Wendt, R. W., 1966, "The effects of low dosage application of fintrol (active ingredient antimycin A) on the yellow perch *(Perca flavescens),*" *Wisconsin Cons. Dept. Fish Management, Div. Manage. Rept.,* No. 10, pp. 1-9.

154. Ridenhour, R. L., 1960, "Development of a program to sample young fish in a lake," *Am. Fish. Soc. Trans.* 89(1), 185-193.

155. Saila, S. B., 1952, "Some results of farm pond management studies in New York," *J. Wildlife Management* 16(3), 279-282.

156. Sanderson, A. E., Jr., 1960, "Results of sampling the fish population of an 88-acre pond by electrical, chemical and mechanical methods," *Proc. 14th Ann. Conf. S.E. Assoc. Game and Fish Comm., (1960),* pp. 185-198.

157. Sawyer, C. N., 1952, "Some new aspects of phosphates in relation to lake fertilization," *Sewage Indt. Wastes* 24(6), 768-775.

158. Schaeperclaus, W., 1933, *Textbook of Pond Culture, Rearing and Keeping of Carp, Trout and Allied Fishes,* Paul Parney, Berlin, 289 pp.

159. Schlichting, H. E., Jr., 1960, "The role of waterfowl in the dispersal of algae," *Trans. Am. Microscop. Soc.* 79(2), 160-166.

160. Seaman, D. E., and Potterfield, W. A., 1962, "Feasibility of controlling aquatic weeds with snails," *Proc. 15th S. Weed Conf.,* pp. 256-257.

161. Singh, S. B., Sukumaran, K. K., Pillai, K. K., and Chakrabarti, P. C., 1967, "Observations on efficacy of grass carp, *Ctenopharyngodon della* (Val.) in controlling and utilizing aquatic weeds in ponds in India," *Proc. Indo-Pac. Fish. Coun.* 12(11), 220-235.

162. Smirnov, N. N., 1960, "Nutrition of *Galerucella nymphaeae* (Chrysomelidae), mass consumer of water lily," *Hydrobiol.* 15(3), 208-224.

163. Smith, L. L., Jr., Franklin, D. R., and Kramer, R. H., 1959, "Electro-fishing for small fish in lakes," *Am. Fish. Soc. Trans.* 88(2), 141-146.

164. Snow, J. R., 1958, "A preliminary report on the comparative testing of some of the newer herbicides," *Proc. 11th Ann. Conf. S.E. Assoc Game and Fish Comm.* pp. 125-132.

165. Starrett, W. C., and Barnickol, P. G., 1955, "Efficiency and selectivity of commercial fishing devices used on the Mississippi River," *Illinois Nat. Hist. Surv. Bull.* 26(4), 325-366.

166. Starrett, W. C., and McNeil, P. L., Jr., 1952, "Sport fishing at Lake Chautauqua near Havana, Illinois, in 1950 and 1951," *Illinois Nat. Hist. Surv. Biol.* Notes 30, 1-31.

167. Stevenson, J. H., 1965, "Observations on grass carp in Arkansas," *Progressive Fish Culturist* 27(4), 203-206.

168. Stringer, G. E., and McMynn, R. G., 1958, "Experiments with toxaphene as fish poison," *Can. Fish Culturist* 23, 39-47.

169. Stringer, G. E., and McMynn, R. G., 1960, "Three years' use of toxaphene as a fish toxicant in British Columbia," *Can. Fish Culturist* 18, 37-44.

170. Stroud, R. H., 1956, *Selective Poisoning,* S.F.I. Bull. No. 53, p. 2.

171. Stroud, R. H., 1957a, *Water-Level Control,* S.F.I. Bull. No. 63-64, p. 2.

172. Stroud, R. H., 1957b, *Improvement,* S.F.I. Bull. No. 69, p. 2.

173. Stroud, R. H., 1963, *Selective Control,* S.F.I. Bull. No. 136, p. 3.

174. Stroud, R. H., 1967, *New Lampricide,* S.F.I. Bull. No. 189, p. 6.

175. Stroud, R. H., and Jenkins, R. M., 1960, *Increasing Pond Productivity,* S.F.I. Bull. No. 103, p. 7.

176. Surber, E. W., 1931, "Sodium arsenite or controlling submerged vegetation in fish ponds," *Am. Fish. Soc. Trans.* 61, 143-147.

177. Surber, E. W., 1945, "The effects of various fertilizers on plant growths and their probable influence in the production of smallmouth black bass in hard-water ponds," *Am. Fish. Soc. Trans.* 73(1943), 377-393.

178. Surber, E. W., 1961, "Improving sport fishing by control of aquatic weeds," *U.S. Fish Wildlife Serv. Circ.* 128, 1-37.

179. Swingle, H. S., 1947, "Experiments on pond fertilization," *Alabama Polytech Inst. Agr. Expt. Sta. Bull.* 264, 1-34.

180. Swingle, H. S., 1957a, "Determination of balance in farm fish ponds," *21st North Am. Wildlife Conf. Trans.*, pp. 298-322.

181. Swingle, H. S., 1957b, "Control of pond weeds by the use of herbivorous fishes," *10th Ann. Weed Control Conf. Proc.*, pp. 11-17.

182. Swingle, H. S., 1965, "Fertilizing farm fish ponds," *Auburn Univ. Agr. Expt. Sta. Highlights of Agr. Res.* 12(1), 11.

183. Swingle, H. S., Gooch, B. C., and Rabanal, H. R., 1965, "Phosphate fertilization of ponds," *Proc. 17th Conf. S.E. Assoc. Game and Fish Comm.*, pp. 213-218.

184. Swingle, H. S., Prather, E. E., and Lawrence, J. M., 1953, "Partial poisoning of overcrowded fish populations,"*Alabama Polytech. Inst. Agr. Expt. Sta. Circ.* 113, 1-15.

185. Swingle, H. S., and Smith, E. V., 1939, "Fertilizers for increasing the natural food for fish in ponds," *Am. Fish. Soc. Trans.* 68(1938), 126-135.

186. Swingle, H. S., and Smith, E. V., 1942, "Management of farm fish ponds," *Alabama Agr. Expt. Sta. Bull.* 254, 1-23.

187. Swingle, H. S., and Smith, E. V., 1947, "Management of farm fish ponds," *Alabama Polytech. Inst. Agr. Expt. Sta. Bull.* 254, 1-30 (revised).

188. Switzer, C. M., 1961, "Control of aquatic weeds," *E. Sect. Nat. Weed Comm. Can. Res. Rept.*, pp. 105-114.

189. Tanner, H. A., 1960, "Some consequences of adding fertilizer to five Michigan trout lakes," *Am. Fish. Soc. Trans.* 89(2), 198-205.

190. Tatum, W. M., and Blackburn, R. D., 1965, "Preliminary study of the effects of diquat on the natural bottom fauna and plankton in two subtropical ponds," *Proc. 16th Ann. Conf. S.E. Assoc. Game and Fish Comm.*, pp. 301-306.

191. Therinen, C. W., 1956, "The success of a seine in the sampling of a largemouth bass population," *Progressive Fish Culturist* 18(2), 81-87.

192. Thomaston, W. W., 1962, "Results of experimental weed control experiments in Georgia farm ponds using simplified gravity flow techniques," *Proc. 15th S. Weed Control Conf.*, pp. 234-243.

193. Thompkins, W. A., and Bridges, C., 1958, "The use of copper sulphate to increase fyke-net catches," *Progressive Fish Culturist* 20(1), 16-20.

194. Thompkins, W. A., and Mullan, J. W., 1958, "Selective poisoning as a management tool in stratified trout ponds in Massachusetts," *Progressive Fish Culturist* 20(3), 117-123.

195. Van der Lingen, M. I., 1966, "Fertilization in warmwater pond fish culture in Africa," *FAO World Symp. on Warmwater Pond Fish Cult.*, FR,II/R-5 pp. 1-11.

196. Viosca, P.,Jr., 1945, "A critical analysis of practices in the management of warmwater fish with a view of greater food production," *Am. Fish. Soc. Trans.* 73(1943), 274-283.

197. Walker, C. R., Lennon, R. F., and Berger, B. L., 1967, "Preliminary observations on the toxicity of antimycin A to fish and other aquatic animals," *Bur. Sport Fish. Wildlife Circ.* 186, 188.

198. Waters, T. F., 1957, "The effects of lime application to acid bog lakes in northern Michigan," *Am. Fish. Soc. Trans.* 86(1956), 329-344.

199. Waters, T. F., and Ball, R. C., 1957, "Lime application to a soft-water unproductive lake in northern Michigan," *J. Wildlife Management* 21(4), 385-391.

200. Westman, J. R., and Hunter, J. V., 1956, "Preliminary observations on the lowering of dissolved oxygen by sodium sulfite and its effects on certain fishes with particular reference to problems in fish management," *Progressive Fish Culturist* 18(3), 126-130.

201. Willford, W. A., 1967a, "Investigations in fish control 18. Toxicity ot 22 therapeutic compounds to six fishes," *Bur. Sport Fish. Wildlife Res. Publ. 35, 1-10.*

202. Willford, W. A., 1967b, "Investigations in fish control 20. Toxicity of dimethyl sulfoxide (DMSO) to fish," *Bur. Sport Fish Wildlife Res. Publ.* 37, 1-8.

203. Wolf, P., 1951, "A trap for the capture of fish and other organisms moving downstream," *Am. Fish. Soc. Trans.* 80(1950), 41—45.

204. Wood, R., 1951, "The significance of managed water levels in developing the fisheries of large impoundments," *J. Tenn. Acad. Sci.* 26(3), 214-235.

205. Wood, R., and Pfitzer, D. W., 1958, "Some effects of water-level fluctuations on the fisheries of large impoundments," *7th Tech. Meet. Intern. Union for Cons. of Nature and Natural Res. Anthens-Delphi,* pp. 1-29.

206. Workman, G. W., and Neuhold, J. M., 1963, "Lethal concentrations of toxaphene for goldfish, mosquitofish and rainbow trout with notes on detoxification," *Progressive Fish Culturist* 25(1), 23-30.

207. Wunder, W., 1949, *Fortschrittliche Karpfenteichwirtschaft,* E. Schweitzerbart'sche Verlagsbuchhandlung, Erwin Nagele, Stuttgart, 386 pp.

208. Yashouv, A., 1963, "Increasing fish production in ponds," *Am. Fish. Soc. Trans.* 92 (3), 292-297.

7

FISHING AND NATURAL MORTALITY

FORCES ACTING UPON A FISH POPULATION

Each year, in every pond or lake containing fish, thousands of fish eggs are deposited, and many of these hatch into small fishes. Because they are very numerous and very vulnerable, many of these embryonic fishes die from predation, accidents, and disease before becoming free swimming: more expire before they reach fingerling sizes. It has been estimated that in one lake the loss of bluegills between free-swimming fry and fingerling stages was 86%.[40] Fingerling fishes are not only subject to death by accident and disease, they also may be decimated by predation. A few survive and grow to sexual maturity and old age, eventually succumbing to disease or, probably rarely, to senile degeneration. Whether an individual fish reaches maturity and produces progeny is unimportant to a population as long as total recruitment and growth in that population equals total losses from various causes. If such is the case, the population will continue to be numerically healthy.

That part of the population composed of kinds and sizes of fishes large enough to interest anglers will either *(1)* survive to the end of the year, having grown in the interval, or *(2)* be caught with a growth increment proportionate to the length of time they survived, based on the growth rate potential for that species in the habitat under consideration, or *(3)* die in some other way from natural causes. To the catchable stock will be added the juvenile fishes that have grown to catchable sizes during that period. Fishes already of desirable sizes that reach advanced ages for the species during the period may become senile and die from a variety of causes.

Thus, the forces that are responsible for *increasing populations* of catchable sport fishes are *recruitment* and *growth,* and those responsible for *decreasing populations* are *fishing* and the *natural mortality* which combines all other decimating factors.

Fishing mortality may be modified by changes in fishing practices, which increase in effectiveness as a result of man's inventiveness; however, this increased efficiency in taking fish is curtailed by legal restrictions to prevent overexploitation. Thus legal restrictions and fishing methods directly affect fishing mortality and indirectly natural mortality (by upsetting interspecies relationships within an ecosystem).

Thus, much of fishery management is involved with modifying rates of fishing and natural mortality for the overall improvement of angling.

Natural mortality operating with catch mortality can be constant or it can vary considerably from season to season with the various age components of the several species of fishes making up a population. For this reason, natural mortality may be difficult to evaluate except by direct methods.

In this chapter we are primarily interested in forces which cause the reduction of fishes, i.e., the catch in total amount and rate, and the natural death rate.

THE CREEL CENSUS

According to Lambou[41] a creel census is a "survey where a complete check of all sport fishing is made, that is, where a 100 percent sample is taken" Fig. 7.1). Lambou proposed the term "creel survey" for an intermittent check, made during randomly selected times while anglers are in the process of fishing. Later, these samples of fishing are expanded to estimate the total seasonal fishing pattern on the water being surveyed.

Creel surveys are substituted for creel censuses when costs of the latter are prohibitive and when the survey is expected to give no more than a reasonably accurate appraisal of an extensive sport-fishing resource. Some fishing waters are so large and there are so many points of ingress and egress that it would be impossible to gather a complete record of fishing. On these waters a creel survey is the only way to obtain a valid estimate of the sport-fishing operation.

In either a creel census or survey the objective is to collect information on *(1)* the *quality of sport fishing,* expressed as to kinds, numbers, and weight of fish per unit of effort; *(2) fishing pressure in man-hours* for a whole or section of a body of water to be expressed as man-hours of fishing for a specific kind of fish, if possible on a unit of water surface area; *(3)* total *yield* in kinds, numbers, and weights for a limited period or an entire season; *(4) composition of the catch* as percents of total numbers and weights of various species and classes of fish comprising the total yield; *(5) characteristics of the fishery,* which might include the percent of the total man-hours of fishing for various classes of fish (a difficult statistic to get). It also might include data on age, sex, geographic distribution of fishermen with the type of gear each uses, and other items of information, depending upon the needs of individual states; *(6) statistics about the fish population* such as the annual exploitation rate of various year classes of selected species, an appraisal of new year classes appearing in a fishery, length of life and turnover rate of various species, disappearance of year classes of certain species resulting from natural mortality or migration, and population estimates from hook-and-line recaptures of fish previously marked; *(7)* a variety of *miscellaneous data* decided upon prior to the beginning of the creel.

Lambou[41] lists fifty-nine references dealing with creel-survey methods and the problem of sampling and sample expansions to estimate the fishing statistics for a season on a specific water or waters. Some of these are included in the literature cited at the end of this chapter.[13,15,50,56,57,84] There are many problems in sampling for fish surveys and too few actual tests of such surveys where data from a complete creel census are selected and expanded to test the potential for accuracy of hypothetical systems.

This was done by Johnson and Wroblewski[34] who described a method of sampling which allowed one operator to sample the fishing success on two nearby lakes and to extrapolate a yield estimate that was very close to the results of a creel census made on these same lakes in the same year. The five basic statistical components to be obtained are *(1)* periodical boat counts, *(2)* average number of fishermen per boat, *(3)* average trip length in hours, *(4)* average number of fish taken per trip by species, and *(5)* average weight of fish, by species, taken per trip.

Where creel censuses or surveys are made year after year in connection with other fish-management or research studies, they have been found to be useful in several categories:

They show the range of variation in the catch from a specific water that may take place from year to year, a statistic that may be much more variable than would be expected. They expose gradual expansions in numbers of some species, perhaps to the point of overpopulation and stunting, and the gradual reduction in numbers of others, possibly to the point of expiration of the species from that water. They can be used to measure the effects of management techniques, such as drawdowns or partial

Fig. 7.1a A creel census differs from a creel survey in that in the former all fishermen are contacted. In this creel census all fishing is done from boats available only at this pier. After a period of fishing anglers return to the pier with boats and fish.

poisonings, as they are reflected in the catch. They can be used to esti-mate the fishing potential for the following season, particularly if coupled with other sampling methods, such as the use of a boat shocker, and to ascertain whether fishermen are cropping all components of a population. From reports of small fish observed or released by fishermen, a creel census may expose the presence of large new year classes of such species as crappies, bluegills, or white bass that may be expected to grow enough before the next season to make a strong showing in a fishery. They may also expose the loss of a dominant year class of these same species that is suddenly removed by natural mortality.

Creel censuses are therefore important in producing evidence of the need for the application of some phase of fish management. Long-term changes in the relative abundance of various sport fishes, such as have been recorded by long-term commercial fishing statistics on commercial species[62] may appear in creel censuses carried on for a sufficiently long period of time. Such data are not often available for sport fisheries, but if they were, they would be as useful as data on commercial species.

Fig. 7.1b Fish are measured and weighed and a scale sample is taken for age determination. After the fisherman has been interviewed as to time spent in fishing and kind of bait used his fish and fishing license are returned and he can make arrangements for a future fishing trip.

And finally the creel census or survey furnishes information of interest to fishermen and helps him to decide where he wants to fish. Creel information disseminated currently through public information channels (papers, radio, television), stimulates lagging enthusiasm among sportsmen which results in increased participation in angling, purchases of licenses and fishing equipment, and health benefits in the form of exercise and relaxation.

State-Wide Fishing Surveys

Fish and Game Departments sometimes have need for estimates of statewide seasonal catches of fish, and the numbers of various categories of anglers participating in fishing activity. Such surveys would be most difficult to make through creel censuses or surveys and are usually made by sending postcard inquiries to license holders in the fall and winter after most of the fishing season is over, asking them for such general information as the number of times they went fishing, the number and kinds of fish caught, distance traveled to reach the fishing water and return, etc. Such state-wide surveys have been made by many states. In a recent California survey,[45] postcard questionnaires were sent to 0.8% of California licensed fishermen. Thirty-seven percent of these cards were returned, giving a 0.3% random sample. In an Illinois survey[42] names of Illinois fishermen were selected from the first entry in 17,325 books of twenty-five license stubs. Fifty-one percent of these fishermen returned the questionnaires sent to them. People are seldom eager to fill out questionnaires, and to get substantial returns it often is necessary to send a follow-up letter and duplicate question sheet.

Fishermen show a strong tendency to exaggerate, as was demonstrated when oral interviews based on memory were compared with creel-card records of actual catches made. There appears to be no easy solution for the problem. Fishermen who return postcard questionnaires probably are somewhat more emotionally involved in their own fishing activities than is the average angler and are more likely to remember at least their successful fishing trips.

State-wide mail surveys are of value primarily from the standpoint of publicity, which, as mentioned above, is important in stimulating interest in fishing.

FISHING MORTALITY

The angler does not think of himself as a mortality factor for fish. What he takes he assumes is justifiable, particularly if he is operating within the law. Such an attitude may be reasonable because in many situations he is simply substituting himself for other mortality factors that might remove the same or greater quantities of fish.

As discussed in Chapter 5, many species of fish have been subjected to high mortality rates for almost as long as they have existed on the earth's surface, and it must be assumed that high mortality rates are normal and beneficial.

Angling Compared to Natural Predation

Most methods of angling are not only very inefficient for taking warmwater fishes, but are also highly selective for certain species and sizes. Unless many natural predators are present, this inefficiency and selectivity creates a problem in the management of small artificial lakes because pole-and-line fishing permits the survival of too many small fish.[6]

Under a system of population control through natural predation, fish populations are more likely to be cropped in relation to the relative abundance of the component species in the habitat. This type of cropping tends to hold down the numbers of all species. Also, since there are more predators of small fish than of large ones, a severe culling of small fish is continuously taking place.

Man has yet to devise a cropping system comparable to a natural system of population control. His nearest approach in artificial waters has come from artificial drawdowns and from stocking predatory fishes in sufficient numbers to dominate momentarily the aquatic environment.

Yields and Standing Crop

It is logical that a yield of fish, if it has been sustained over a period of years, must bear some definite relationship to the population of fish (poundage) that the body of water supports and to the rate of their replacement. As the crop is taken, increased food resources become available for the potential replacement of fish-flesh removed, and this replacement must depend upon (1) the efficiency of food gathering, (2) the replacement time available, and (3) the ability of the number of digestive tracts uncaptured and those added through new recruitment to convert the food into flesh, to replace that taken.

Usually when one speaks of a sustained yield, he is talking about a yield level or range of levels repeated in each successive season for a period of years. He probably is not speaking of the *maximum* poundage of fish that may be replaced in each growing season. Rather, he may be thinking of some poundage below the absolute maximum that may be taken by a reasonable amount of effort on the part of the fishermen. Thus, there are many levels of so-called sustained yields, none of which, in reality, may be the maximum.

In small lakes and ponds containing a limited number of kinds of fishes, it is sometimes possible to demonstrate competition between species and individuals for food and space. One may suspect that the same factors are active in larger waters with a greater variety of species, but direct observation is difficult or impossible. Complexity in the environment increases exponentially with increased numbers of species.

In the Great Lakes, for example, yields were higher before 1920 than they have been since. According to Van Oosten[82] the annual yield of fish before 1920 varied around 100 million lb; from 1920 to 1947 it ranged around 78.5 million lb., a reduction of 22%. Van Oosten believed that factors leading to the decline of this fishery were (1) increased fishing pressure, (2) improvement in fishing methods, (3) extension of fishing grounds, (4) replacement of better classes of fishes with poorer types, and (5) (a variation of 4) the introduction of the smelt.

In considering the factors that reduced the standing crop of the more desirable fishes, Van Oosten hesitated to place major importance either on interspecific competition as such or on partial loss of competitive ability due to selective cropping, but looked for causes in pollution, change in the habitat, and disease. However, the fact that in Lake Michigan a big increase in the 1945—47 yield of ciscoes followed the almost complete disappearance of smelt in 1943 suggests that changes in the population might be due to interspecific competition, even in waters as large as the Great Lakes. Within the 1940—1960 period the sea lamprey (*Petromyzon marinus* L.) has been responsible for the appearance of a rapid sequence of dominating species and has greatly reduced the yields of certain Great Lakes food fishes.[62] With the reduction of the larger predatory fishes, intermediate-sized species of fishes were attacked by the sea lamprey, and in Lakes Michigan and Huron the alewife [*Alosa pseudoharengus* (Wilson)], because of its small size, was able to increase rapidly and become a dominant species of fish. With the reduction of the sea lamprey, lake trout are increasing, and chinook salmon [*Oncorhynchus tshawytscha* (Walbaum)], coho salmon [*O. kisutch* (Walbaum)], and kokanee salmon [*O. nerka* (Walbaum)] have been introduced with considerable success.

In small lakes, direct competition plays an important role in the size of the standing crop of catchable fishes. However, larger waters are not so easy to evaluate. For example, the spawning site of a species may be far removed from its feeding grounds; also, competition on the spawning grounds might be intensive with little competition on the feeding grounds. Competition for spawning space might result in a smaller number of individuals of a desirable species and, if food gathering could not be accelerated in proportion to this decrease in the number of individuals, the fish would show no growth compensation.

Several authors have attempted to predict a sustained yield in relation to the standing crop of fish. Swingle and Smith[80] estimated that 50% of the total weight of fish in a pond could be removed each year by angling. At this point, the number had been reduced sufficiently so that those remaining found plenty of natural foods and consequently did not bite well. Crance and McBay[23] demonstrated a relationship between the numbers of channel catfish stocked and the catch of these fish in the first and second years following. Because of the aggressive biting of hybrid sunfish, there was always a positive relationship between numbers of hybrid sunfish available and the rate of catch.[16,17] Catfish stocked in excessive numbers and fishable populations of hybrid sunfish were special situations, and when more "normal" mixed populations of warmwater fishes were subjected to angling at levels below 500 man-hours per acre per season it was impossible to demonstrate any very definite relationship between the number of catchable fish per acre (useful sizes) and the rate of catch.[8,9]

In their study of Sutherland Reservoir fishing (California) LaFaunce et al.[38] concluded that overall catches per unit of effort from a heterogeneous sport fishery were not meaningful indexes of population size. In this respect, a sport fishery differs from a commercial fishery in that in the former the fish exerts some choice in taking a bait and getting caught, whereas in a commercial fishery, the fish are subject to entrapment without the same degree of choice.

Maximum Yields and Length of Growing Season

Thompson[81] on the basis of digestive rates of fish at different temperatures and on the lengths of warm seasons at various latitudes in North America, calculated the maximum annual yields (based on theoretical replacement of protein) that could be taken at latitudes from 46°N to 30°N. These ranged from 21% of the standing crop in northern Wisconsin to 118% in southern Louisiana. Thompson's figure for central Illinois was 50% of the carrying capacity. Cropping tests of Fork Lake (central Illinois), a small pond of 1.38 acres, appear to substantiate a 50% yield potential.[7] Here the 1939 catch of bass and bluegills was equivalent to 934 fishes, or 162 lb/acre, a yield of "about half of the theoretical carrying capacity of the lake for hook-and-line fish." These fishes were taken in 1-in. mesh wing nets and by hook-and-line, and all were removed from the lake regardless of size. In 1940 and 1941 the yield was reduced in spite of more intensive net fishing[7] but the reduction in fish was attributed to the trapping of nutrient materials by dense stands of submersed rooted vegetation.

A later investigation, involving the cropping of smallmouth bass from another central Illinois pond, did not bear out Thompson's estimate of maximum production.[10] In this pond of 1.42 acres, the annual yields of smallmouth bass for four successive years were 78.0, 119.0, 123.0, and 81.3 lb/acre. In June of the fifth year the pond was treated with rotenone and a census was made of the remaining smallmouth bass. The total bass population, exclusive of the 0-age class (1−1.5 in. total length) amounted to 52.3 lb/acre. Previous to this census (from April 11 to June 6) fishermen had taken 48 lb of bass per acre. Together, the census and the precensus catch amounted to 100.3 lb of smallmouths per acre, a figure that must include the flesh added to individuals of the population that were alive during April and May. On the basis of this experiment, the replacement potential for fish flesh at the latitude of central Illinois and under conditions of high cropping may approach 100% during a single growing season. Although this high level of cropping over four seasons must be accepted as a sustained yield, the future yield capability of this population of smallmouths was precarious in that a reproduction failure for a given season probably would have seriously reduced the yield for the fishing season two years hence. Since individuals in this population were converting food into flesh with some efficiency, any severe reduction in the number of digestive tracts might be followed by a reduction in food conversion.

Certain species of warmwater fishes cannot be depended upon for a high sustained yield because they do not produce new year classes every year. This production of intermittent year classes may block the annual entrance of new recruits into the fishable population as the older fish are taken, until the latter become scarce and the yield is forced downward. Failure to produce annual year classes may be associated with the collection of metabolic products or other environmental conditions (Chapter 5). Yields from fish populations including several species usually are more constant, because failure of a year class in one species may be compensated for by high production in other species.

In Chapter 5, I expressed certain relationships between carrying capacity, productivity, and growth. In populations of fishes composed of one, two, or several kinds, a substantial sustained removal of one species should result in (1) increased growth rate and improved reproduction success of uncaptured individuals of that species and/or (2) an expansion of the population of some other species to use the vacated environment created by the removal of the first species, with the final result that the population of the first species might level off at a much lower point than formerly. This may have happened to many of the more desirable fishes inhabiting the Great Lakes prior to 1947 before the sea lamprey became numerous.

Underfishing

In artificial ponds and lakes where natural predators are limited, severe competition among fishes may take place because of a scarcity of adequate mortality factors (Fig. 7.2). This competition results in poor growth and eventual stunting and often causes a gradual change in population composition.

Most artificial impoundments, large or small, are underfished, i.e., usually hook-and-line fishing is not intensive or diversified enough to replace the normal system of natural predation which is usual for "wild" waters beyond the influence of human populations. Also, some individuals of certain species apparently become wary of baited hooks or artificial lures.[85]

Fishing pressures and the degree of stunting caused from overpopulation may vary from one body of water to another. The advent of stunting

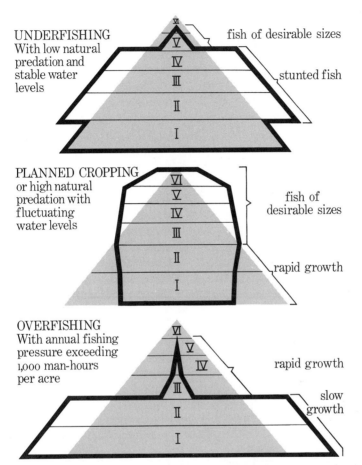

Fig. 7.2 Diagrams representing theoretical fish populations superimposed on segmented triangles proposing the first six year classes of fish populations reduced (space) on a 50% mortality rate. *Underfished population* is characterized by high survival of all year classes and by stunting; few fish attain desirable sizes. *Planned cropping* and/or high natural predation with fluctuating water levels produces a population whose members grow rapidly to large average sizes. Overpopulation is prevented, and therefore an abundance of food is usually available. *Overfished population* is characterized by overabundant year classes of very young fish showing slow growth until they reach sizes large enough to interest anglers. At this point they may be removed from the aquatic environment and the few that escape grow rapidly to large average sizes.

is purely arbitrary, and has been defined on the basis (and perhaps falsely) of average growth rates of a selected species taken from specific waters in a limited region. One might determine that the average rate of growth of largemouth bass in northern Illinois and southern Wisconsin produced fish that were 4.0 in. long the first year, 8.3 in. the second, 10.6

in. the third, and 12.0 in. the fourth. These averages might not be at all representative of bass growth in this region if the population of bass inhabiting the lakes from which samples were taken were unusually fast growing. Yet, it would seem logical to assume that fish that grew faster than these averages were living in a better environment and those that grew more slowly were stunted.

Underfishing, at least in angler-fished small waters, can be defined as *all levels of fishing pressure that, when operating in conjunction with the forces of natural mortality, cause insufficient total mortality to prevent excessive survival of juveniles and moderate to severe food competition among adults.* It becomes obvious that fishing mortality and natural mortality combine to produce the total mortality. Where natural mortality is high or variable, underfishing cannot be defined in specific terms. For example, the seasonal fishing pressure exerted by resident Indians on a Canadian lake might be no more than 2 man-hours per acre, whereas that of farm families on an Ozark hill pond might be 30 man-hours per acre. In spite of the fact that the Ozark pond might receive fifteen times the fishing pressure of the Canadian lake, the former could be underfished and the latter not. Underfishing can be explained only through a consideration of all mortality factors. In the Canadian situation, Indians might be a mortality factor of minor importance compared to predatory fish and fish-eating birds. In the Ozark pond, perhaps fish predation was limited largely to humans engaged in fishing.

The fact that fish have the potential to live for a long time on a maintenance diet makes mass mortality through starvation very rare. Barring some catastrophe, such as the drying up of a pond or the freezing of the water to the bottom, stunted populations of fishes may remain so indefinitely. These populations are rather easily indentified, because individuals usually are thin and their eyes are disproportionately large for the size of the body. As mentioned in Chapter 4, the eyes of a fish continue to grow even if the body does not.

Overfishing

When more pounds of fish are removed from a body of water in a single season than can be replaced through growth and recruitment, before the following season, the body of water is said to be overfished (Fig. 7.2). According to James, Meehean, and Douglas,[33] waters located near centers of population frequently are overfished, but their concept of overfishing may deal with selected species rather than the complex of all species present in a body of water.

Fish populations show considerable resistance to intensive angling and are not easily decimated. This point was made by Viosca[83] who stated:

"...when a body of water is said to have been fished out by angling, only a relatively small percentage of the fish have actually been removed. ... Apparently the majority of fish in a body of water cannot be taken by angling because of the automatic increase in their prey resulting from the removal of part of the stock by the very act of angling." Swingle and Smith[80] made essentially the same statement. Through fishing experiments using largemouth bass populations of known numbers per acre, Lagler and DeRoth[39] concluded that fishermen angling in experimental ponds could scarcely be induced to fish for this species when it was represented by a population density as low as 6 legal bass per acre (at this population level the rate of catch was only 0.04 legal fish per man-hour). The interest in fishing waned completely among cooperating fishermen and the impression was general that the ponds had been "fished out."

One of the first comprehensive studies of the overfishing of warmwater fishes in ponds became possible because of a complex of several favorable circumstances. A conscientious custodian at the Owens-Illinois Glass Company recreation area collected information on the fish yield of Onized Lake (Illinois), a two-acre pond that was overfished, largely because picnicking and fishing could be combined.[4] Here family groups came for picnics, but brought fishing equipment and baits too, because it was possible to watch a bobbing cork while otherwise occupied at the picnic table. With these "double" recreation facilities, many man-hours of fishing were logged because, with the stimulus of the hamburger and hot dog, the low catch rate lost its importance as a fishing deterrent. The result was that during two successive years the fishing pressure on Onized Lake exceeded 1400 man-hours per acre; the catch amounted to 350 lb/acre for the first year and then dropped to 142 lb/acre the second. This drop in yield suggested overfishing. When a complete census of the pond was made in June of the third year (after a spring catch of 71 lb/acre had been taken by a fishing pressure of 634 man-hours per acre), it contained 9171 fish (exclusive of the young of the year, which were largely lost or eaten by larger fish), but only 481 of the larger fishes were of desirable* sizes. The lake contained largemouth bass, black crappies, bluegills, green sunfish, yellow bass, black and yellow bullheads, golden shiners, and a few fishes of several other kinds. Of the important fishes in the hook-and-line catch for the preceding two years, the black crappies had been reduced to 22 fish, the yellow bass to 4, and the black bullheads to 2 fish. There were 275 bass, of which 12 fish ranged from 3 to 6 lb each. At the time of the census there were 23 bass of at least

---

*Desirable sizes were arbitrarily set as follows: at least 10 in. for largemouth bass (legal limit); 8 in. for crappies; 7 in. for yellow bass, bullheads, and golden shiners; and 6 in. for bluegills, warmouths, and green sunfish.

10 in. in length per acre. Bluegills were represented by 6545 fish, warmouths by 1638, green sunfish by 245, yellow bullheads by 347, and golden shiners by 90. Fishes grew at moderately slow rates until they reached desirable sizes and then very rapidly because of population thinning through angling. If fishing had been continued at this rate for another season, the populations of black crappies, yellow bass, and black bullheads might have disappeared entirely. However, the census gave evidence that largemouth bass, bluegills, warmouths, green sunfish, yellow bullheads, and golden shiners might be able to maintain populations indefinitely, either because of high reproductive success with high survival of young or because of increased resistance to capture, or for both of these reasons. One season with reduced fishing pressure would have allowed the population to expand to approach the carrying capacity of the pond and obscure all evidence of overfishing.

Fishing Pressure Versus Yield

In 1950 and 1951, Barnickol and Campbell[3] studied the fish yields of many small impoundments located on the August A. Busch Memorial Wildlife Area near St. Louis, Missouri. These ponds were fished at rates ranging from about 300 to 4000 man-hours per acre per season, and yields varied from as low as 20 to as high as about 300 lb of fish per acre. In 1959, Gilbert F. Weiss, Fishery Biologist for Missouri, furnished additional data on fishing pressures and yields from the Busch ponds as well as from several other Missouri lakes that were fished less heavily.

The twenty-six impoundments of one to 20 acres on the Busch Memorial Wildlife Area were not all in use during all years between 1949 and 1959, but sufficient records were available to furnish data on more than 100 pond-seasons.* Some stocking of ponds was done during the period but the numbers of fishes released were usually insignificant in relation to the fishing pressures and yields and no measurable effect of stocking could be demonstrated in the rate of catch.

Data on rates of catch for various fishing pressures on the Busch ponds and several other Missouri impoundments were combined with similar information from some lakes and ponds in central and southern Illinois.[8,30] All of the ponds contained largemouth bass and bluegills and sometimes, in addition, redear sunfish, green sunfish, bullheads, and channel catfish. These pond-season records were plotted in Figure 7.3[11] as symbols and a line drawn by inspection, representing the average

---

*A pond-season is one pond fished for one season.

relationship between man-hours of fishing per acre and rate of catch in pounds of fish per man-hour.

Figure 7.3 shows that the seasonal rates of catch from 4000 man-hours per acre to about 300 man-hours per acre were averaging about 0.10 lb/hr of fishing, and that within this range of pressures there was no change with increasing man-hours per acre. Very few fishermen will continue to fish if their catch rate does not exceed 0.10 lb/hr unless a fishing trip is combined with some other advantage such as picnicking or escape from an unfavorable environment produced by the heat and noise of a big city.

With decreasing fishing pressures from 300 down to 130 man-hours per acre the rate of catch increased gradually and at a rather slow rate, i.e., from 0.10 to 0.23 or 0.24 lb/man-hour. Below a seasonal pressure of 130 man-hours per acre the rate of catch increased very rapidly until in the best ponds at fishing pressures of 40 to 60 man-hours per acre the rate of catch averaged 1.0–1.5 lb/hr. These very high rates of catch were attained only where populations contained a high percentage of fish of useful sizes.

If it is assumed that the curve in Figure 7.3 represents a reasonably

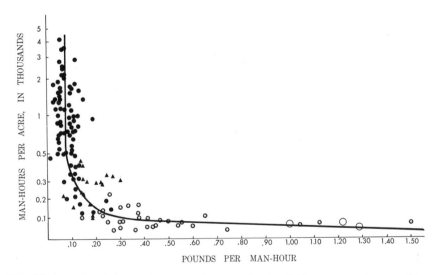

Fig. 7.3 Rate of catch in pounds per man-hour as related to fishing pressure. Sources of information were ponds and small artificial lakes in Missouri and Illinois. Missouri ponds, ● ; Ridge Lake (Illinois), ▲; Southern Illinois ponds, ★ ; Big Pond (Illinois), ο .

accurate inverse relationship between a building-up of fishing pressure and a depreciating rate of catch for largemouth bass and bluegills (or other sunfish), the curve can be used to estimate the hours of productive fishing that a lake of a given surface area may furnish each season. Also, an owner of a private lake might employ it in maintaining the proper level of fishing pressure for a high catch rate. In reverse, it could be used to calculate the size of an artificial impoundment needed to satisfy the fishing-pressure level of a fishing club of predetermined membership.

For example, if the estimated total annual fishing pressure for the members of a club approximated 8000 man-hours and they wished to maintain a catch rate of 0.50 lb/hr they would need to construct a lake of about 107 acres:

(1) Figure 7.3: For an average catch rate of 0.50 lb/hr the fishing pressure should be about 75 man-hours per acre per season.

(2) 8000 ÷ 75 = 106.6 acres. A lake of this size might cost $1000−1500 per acre or $110,000−160,000.

Types of Fishing

The total hours of fishing and the fishing schedule vary greatly from lake to lake. For example, a lake open to the public may be fished at a high rate during May and June and then chiefly on weekends during July, August, and early September. Where both boat and bank fishing are permitted, the daily pressure may be very high, as much as 50 man-hours per acre per day if the fishing is good. But at this level of fishing, the rate of catch will drop off very markedly in four days or less.

At Ridge Lake (Illinois) where bank fishing was not permitted and only seven boats were available on 18 acres of water, the approximate rate of accumulation of fishing hours was 9 or 10 per day. As the lake was open five days per week, we can estimate a fishing pressure of about 45−50 man-hours per week during the first week; later in the season the pressure was less.[8]

Many private lakes and farm ponds are fished in a leisurely manner: on one day three fishermen fish for a total of twelve hours, but the pond is not visited by fishermen again for several days or weeks. The accumulation of fishing hours is so slow that only fifty hours per acre are logged for an entire season. The same may be true for large reservoirs but for a different reason: Some artificial reservoirs are so large that the fishing pressure of all available fishermen builds up a seasonal pressure of only a few dozen hours per acre.

As fishes react in different ways to various levels of fishing, the schedule and intensity of fishing affects the yield. The bass in Ridge Lake showed a much reduced catch rate after the morning fishing period of the opening day (Fig. 7.4), and by the end of the third day, the rate had nearly reached a low point for the summer—after only about 25 hr of fishing pressure per acre.[8] Creel censuses on three Kentucky lakes demonstrated that 70% of all largemouth bass caught during the first week were taken in the first 30 hr of fishing.[14]

Records of the largemouth bass catches from relatively infertile unmanaged waters in Virginia indicated that about nineteen trips per acre removed the "harvestable surplus" of these fish, amounting to 3.6 bass per acre averaging approximately a pound each.[44] According to Martin[44] there is an easily harvested segment of any bass population which can be readily taken at a high rate of catch by light fishing pressure; after the

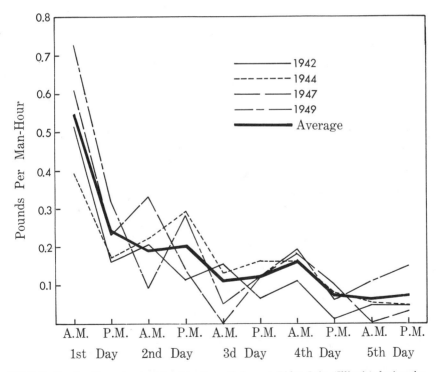

Fig. 7.4 Decelerating rate of catch of largemouth bass at Ridge Lake (Illinois) during the first week of public fishing in each of the named years, and the average rate of catch for all of these years. The first 5 days of fishing usually showed an accumulated fishing pressure of less than 40 man-hours/acre [from Bennett, G. W., 1954, *Illinois Nat. Hist. Surv. Bull.* 26(2)].

easily harvested segment has been removed, additional fishing has little effect upon further harvest and the rate of catch declines rapidly.

Several common warmwater fishes are rather seasonal in their biting habits and fishermen increase fishing pressure at these times because they know that their chances of catching fish are improved. For example, both white and black crappies bite best in the early spring before water temperatures rise into the 70°F range. Warmouths bite much better in late spring and early summer than in late summer. Also, some fish bite well under the ice in winter, whereas other common species are scarcely ever caught through ice fishing.

Fishing intensity for certain species may be increased with changes in weather conditions because fishermen know that rising waters, for example, stimulate certain species of fish to move about and feed. Most sight-feeding fishes become inactivated by rising waters because increased turbidity limits their vision. Returns from angling effort directed toward species of warmwater fishes other than largemouth bass indicate that intensive fishing pressure also depresses the rate of catch but not so rapidly as with the largemouth. Thus it is safe to state that a leisurely pattern of angling over a season is more conducive to satisfactory fishing than is an alternation of relatively intensive angling with periods of complete rest.

There are several specialized types of fishing that are of particular interest to anglers. A few of these are described below.

Tailwater Fishing. Many species of fishes react positively to current; some respond to current at all times during the year and some are stimulated only to move against the current during the normal period of reproduction. These upstream movements of the fishes produce concentrations of several species in the river channels immediately below the dams of large reservoirs where the release of water through the dam gates produces a strong current. The fishes concentrated there below the dam seem to be somewhat more vulnerable to angling than are those in the lake above (Fig. 7.5).

Fishing in the tailwaters of Table Rock, Taneycomo, and Clearwater reservoirs in Missouri received seven, ten, and sixteen times more fishing pressure per acre respectively, than did the reservoirs themselves and the Taneycomo and Clearwater tailwaters provided greater total harvest (by weight) than did their respective reservoirs.[27] In the early years of impoundment the reservoir fishing may be about equal to that of the tailwater[25,26] but in later years the tailwater fishing is usually better in rate of catch and size of fish.

Tailwaters of mainstream reservoirs are more popular than those of

Fig. 7.5 Marinas are sometimes built on the tailwaters of reservoirs to supply boats and fishing supplies and equipment for anglers. This one is located on the tailwater of Greer's Ferry Reservoir in Arkansas.

storage reservoirs because of the fast, turbulent waters below the former.[46] A January creel census by fishery biologist Ned Fogle on the Oahe Dam tailwaters (South Dakota) showed that 2829 anglers caught 3202 fish weighing over 12 tons and averaging 12.5 lb/fish.[76] This catch included paddlefish, northern pike, saugers and walleyes. The average rate of catch was one fish in three hours of angling, but this rate was also equal to 4 lb of fish per hour.

Sometimes fishing piers are constructed above the tailwaters to mitigate the dangers associated with the fishing of these areas (Fig. 7.6).[74]

Ice Fishing.   Fishing through the ice in winter continues to increase in popularity.[77] Most ice fishing is done on large lakes in the northernmost tier of states and in southern Canada, where small ice shanties are permitted on the ice so that the fishermen are protected from the cold. On some lakes, the take of fish through ice fishing may exceed that from all summer angling. For example, Holder[31] reported more than 4000 fishing huts on Lake Simco (Ontario), and Kenneth E. Christensen estimated that 70,600 ice fishermen on Houghton Lake (Michigan) took 250,000 fish during December, January, and February of 1957.[69] The catch of fishes for four summer months on this lake was estimated at 174,000 fish taken by 126,000 anglers. Stroud[70] estimated a total of 3.7 million ice fishermen in the northeastern and north-central states and 100,000 in Ontario.

A good deal of ice fishing takes place on lakes in states below the northern tier whenever the ice is thick enough to hold the fishermen. Usually fishing shanties are not used (Fig. 7.7).

Fig. 7.6 Fishing pier on the east bank of the Tennessee River below the Kentucky Dam. The circular structure is an old bridge pier which was enclosed with a fence. This pier allows bank anglers to enjoy the benefits of tailrace fishing. *Courtesy R. H. Stroud, Sport Fishing Institute.*

Fishes more commonly caught in ice fishing are bluegills and other sunfish, crappies, northern pike, yellow perch, walleyes, largemouth bass, white bass, and yellow bass. The main problem in ice fishing is in finding the fish, which are often concentrated in large schools near the lake bottom.

Spear Fishing. The sport of underwater fishing with a spear or speargun has migrated inland from the clear waters of the oceans shallows. The origin of this type of fishing probably dates back to the time of the Greeks. With the development of self-contained underwater breathing apparatus in the 1930s, a scuba diver was provided with greater lateral and vertical freedom and mobility than he had had formerly. Spearfishing and underwater observations in shallow water are usually done with a face mask and snorkel (a tube held in the swimmer's mouth and extending above the water surface); these allow the swimmer to see well to depths down to six feet or more in clear water.

As scuba diving and spearfishing in inland waters has become more widespread, a rather natural controversy has developed between the

Fig. 7.7 Ice fishing is very popular in the northern states. On some lakes more pounds of fish are taken through the ice in winter than in all of the summer fishing. *Courtesy Wisconsin Natural Resources Department, Madison, Wisconsin.*

angler and the spear fishermen. Each believed that the other would ruin his sport.

Returns from a questionnaire sent out in 1960 to various states[53] indicated that thirty-five states (73%) allowed general underwater spearfishing. Of the thirteen states that did not permit general underwater spearfishing, one allowed spearfishing for carp only, one allowed spearfishing for suckers by permit only, and one allowed spearfishing for rough fish only under the supervision of state personnel. Most of the fish that could be taken legally were coarse species, or fish of species not considered game or pan fish; one state permitted spear fishermen to take white bass, yellow bass, bluegills and four other sunfish, crappies, paddlefish, several kinds of herring, and Rio Grande perch.

Restrictions prohibiting the use of artificially propelled spears in fresh water (explosive propellents, compressed air or carbon dioxide, springs, or elastic bands) are quite general and are justified because the varying turbidity of waters which make the use of such devices dangerous to bathers and to other divers beyond the fisherman's clear vision.

The unsettled controversy between spear fishermen and hook-and-line fishermen may not be so serious as is sometimes alleged.[35] In one case where a strip-mine pond (Illinois) was set up for the exclusive use of scuba divers operating hand-held spears, hook-and-line fishermen "poached" so many of the fish that the divers were usually unsuccessful in taking anything.

Factors Related to Rate of Catch

An exact relationship between the number of fish per acre or per acre-foot of water and the rate of catch is usually obscured by various factors, some of which have been discussed previously. Quite obviously there must be some relationship between numbers of fish available and the catch rate, but often the relationship is clear only when numbers of fish are reduced to a very low figure.[39]

Stroud[66] studied the recovery of marked "salvaged" fishes released in Massachusetts lakes and ponds to gain information on the relationship between available fishes and angling returns. He could estimate only roughly the population density of the various marked species recovered, but calculated an overall harvest of 9% (from ten ponds) for marked largemouth bass, with a somewhat higher return for smallmouth bass, whereas marked chain pickerel ranged from 15% to 59%. Recaptures of other warmwater pond fishes were usually between those for bass and pickerel, although in some instances a large percent of the salvaged fishes did not survive.

The presence of more pan fishes, such as bluegills, crappies, yellow perch, or bullheads, per unit of water, could conceivably mean better fishing. One reason for poor fishing in unfertilized Alabama ponds given by Swingle and Smith[80] is that the "water is too poor to support many legal-sized fish." However, Hansen et al.[30] were unable to show that the rate of catch in fertilized ponds (which contained somewhat higher pound-ages of fish than the control ponds) was consistently better than in the control ponds.

Lux and Smith[43] attempted to discover which of a number of physical, chemical, and biological factors bore a relationship to seasonal changes in the angler's catch in a Minnesota lake. They concluded that as the available food supply increased after the middle of June, the fishing became progressively poorer. This may explain a seasonal cycle, but cannot be used to explain trends extending over several seasons.

Evidence shows that rate of growth of fishes and rate of biting are often in direct relationship. In fact, anyone fishing a new impoundment will probably discover the excellent fishing typical of an expanding population.[86] Fishing during the early years of impoundment in most water-supply reservoirs is better than in later years, and most of these reservoirs go through a predictable cycle.[5,86] Exceptions seem to be those reservoirs having large annual water-level fluctuations, which prevent the development of over-abundant, stunted fish populations. One possible explanation for the excellent fishing in new reservoirs is that the fish have an unlimited supply of available food, develop the habit of feeding for long periods each day, and bite readily at almost any time.

The situation may be contrasted with one where inter- and intraspecific competitions are moderately keen and food is more readily available at certain periods of the day than at others, and where growth is slower and fish no longer have the opportunity of gorging themselves. This may lead to the development of feeding cycles related to periods of the day when certain foods are more readily available than at other times. During these periods the fish are caught more readily by anglers, but the catch may show little relationship to the relative abundance of fish.

When fish have been crowded for a season or more and inter- and intraspecific competitions are very severe, they become thin and stunted and their growth may practically stop. Under these conditions, they bite very poorly[79] and give the impression that few or no fish are present. One explanation for this behavior pattern is that these fish are living on a subsistence diet of small aquatic organisms and are not conditioned to utilize foods as large as most live or artificial baits.

In summary, the evidence seems to favor the assumption that, within limits, there is a positive relationship between good fishing and rapid growth and an expanding population of fish, and an inverse relationship between good fishing and population density, although these relationships are not always clear.

Role of Commercial Fishing in Sport-Fish Management

When angling becomes temporarily or permanently poor in waters where commercial fishermen are operating nets, the commercial operators are usually blamed for the poor angling, even though they may not be taking the same species which the anglers take.

Although commercial fishermen compete with anglers for such fishes as walleyes and lake trout in low-producing northern lakes, no valid evidence exists that commercial fishing in shallow warmwater lakes provides competition for the angler,[36,37] even when commercial fishermen are permitted to take all sizes and kinds of fish.

An experiment involving the use of illegal-meshed commercial gear in a small pond clearly demonstrated the effects of intensive fishing with fyke or wing nets for largemouth bass and bluegills.[7] Six 1-in. mesh wing nets with leads were set across a 1.38-acre pond in two gangs so as to completely block the pond at two points (Fig. 7.8). These nets were fished for from 96 to 149 hr each month, from March to November of each year for two and one-half years, and all fishes captured were removed, regardless of size or species. These nets held bass as small as 9 in. and bluegills as small as 5 in. The catch consisted largely of bluegills, as the bass soon avoided the nets. Supplementary cropping was done by hook-and-line. At the end of the study period the bluegill population amounted to about 67 lb/acre and the bass to over 120 lb/acre. The netting operation unquestionably was a major influence in the buildup of a very large population of bass.

In some states commercial fishermen have been forced out of business except on the major rivers, and the state fisheries departments have had to assume the task of controlling rough fish. This is an expensive neverending job, and when commercial fishing is outlawed, rough-fish removal must be paid for by the sport fishermen. However, in states where commercial fishing is legal, rough-fish removal is self-sustaining and the commercial man may operate at a profit.

Many studies show that removing large crops of coarse fish with commercial gear is beneficial or at least not harmful to sport fishing. This is universally true in large shallow lakes and reservoirs containing substan-

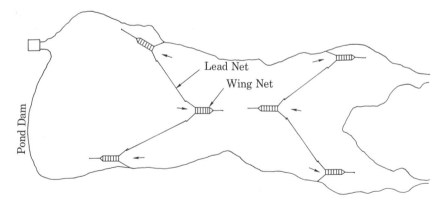

Fig. 7.8 Outline map of Fork Lake (Illinois) showing the customary arrangement of wing nets and lead nets for cropping studies. No fish could swim for any great distance in this 1.38-acre pond without running into a lead net or wing net. Arrows mark openings of wing nets [from Bennet, G. W., 1948, *Illinois Nat. Hist. Surv. Bull.* 24(3)].

tial numbers of coarse fish which are not cropped by hook-and-line.[66] Here commercial fishing is about the only means (except through natural predators) of reducing competition among species.

Originally the scope of operation of the angler and commercial fisherman widely overlapped. They both took any and all species on the basis of their ability to capture them. Gradually the angler was able to restrict the commercial fisherman to "rough" species (carp, buffaloes, and catfish), while reserving for himself all the "fine" fish (crappies, bluegills, white bass, etc.) and game fish (largemouth bass, northern pike, pickerel, and often walleye). These restrictions on the commercial fisherman did not benefit the angler, for the quality of the fishing became worse.

In the 1930s an interesting relationship existed between anglers, commercial fishermen, and natural fish predators at Reelfoot Lake (14,500 acres, Tennessee). Here anglers made an average catch of 0.89 lb of fish per hour. Largemouth bass *averaged* 1.91 lb each, crappies 0.70 lb, sunfish 0.37 lb, and catfish 2.39 lb.[36] The total anglers' yield in 1936 was 22,124 lb. At the same time, commercial fishermen were taking 529,093 lb plus an additional estimated 95,000 lb of small fish killed in netting operations.[36] Commercial fishermen were not restricted to any species, i.e., they were taking the same kinds of fishes as the sport fishermen. More obvious fish predators on Reelfoot Lake were 4000 egrets, 1500 cormorants, and 500 Ward's herons, plus smaller numbers of 7 other species of fish-eating birds. These birds were taking more than 400,000 lb of fish of kinds and sizes related to their ability to capture them. The total number of fish taken by birds, commercial fishermen, and anglers in 1937 was 1,046,133 lb or about 72 lb/acre. On the basis of rate of catch for angling and sizes of fish taken, the fishing in 1937 was excellent.

Soon after this, Tennessee began restricting commercial fishing. First, the state prohibited the commercial fishing of largemouth bass, then regulations on other species became increasingly restrictive until in 1955 commercial fishing was abolished.[59]

During the period from 1937 to 1958, as small fish were given more protection in Tennessee, the growth rate for bluegills and other centrarchids at Reelfoot Lake decreased. By 1953, anglers had increased almost 100-fold, yet they were catching only about 21 lb of fish per acre.[20] However, had they been taking as many pounds per fisherman as in 1937, their catch would have approached 153 lb/acre. The commercial fishing yield in 1953 was 21 lb/acre instead of the 1937 yield of about 36.5 lb/acre. No report is available on numbers of fish-eating birds on the lake in 1953, but since the number of fishermen increased 100-fold, it is doubtful that cormorants, egrets, and herons were as abundant as in 1937. It seems probable that the total yield of fish in 1953 was considerably less than in 1937 but more selective for larger fish.

From the standpoint of the angler, the relationship in 1937 between anglers, commercial fishermen, and fish-eating birds was nearly ideal, as the combined action of these cropping agencies was taking a reasonable annual fish crop. Thus the benefits of an expanding population were evident: fish had food and space to grow. Because the total annual mortality of fish in this lake appeared to be nearly optimum (72 plus pounds per acre), fishing remained good. Without the help of the commercial fishermen, the fish-eating birds and other natural predators available in 1937 could not have kept up with the reproductive potential of the fishes. What happened to the population is fairly evident, for the number of fish caught per fisherman in 1953 remained about the same as in 1937,[20] yet the weight of fish taken was less than one-third that of the earlier year. Recent studies[59,60] of the fishes of Reelfoot indicate that catches are poorer than in 1953.[59,60]

NATURAL MORTALITY

Natural mortality includes all causes of death of fish exclusive of pollution, angling, and commercial fishing. Deaths may result from predation, injuries received through unsuccessful attempts at predation, competition for food and space resulting in fatal injury or starvation, disease or excessively heavy infestations of parasites, catastrophes such as adverse weather conditions, floods, etc., as well as from senile degeneration.

Causes of Natural Death

Important causes for the deaths of fish change with a fish's age and size as related to its normal life span. In the embryo and early free-swimming stages when fish are very small, high mortality rates are probably caused by predation from aquatic insects and larger fish.[40]

The approximate numbers of largemouth bass fry in enumerated schools at Ridge Lake (Illinois) were compared with the bass taken by lake draining at the end of the second succeeding growing season. It was estimated that the survival rate of schooling bass fry ranged from 1 in 29 to 1 in 195.[8] These bass fry were exposed to very favorable conditions because many potential predators in the form of small bluegills, large predaceous aquatic insects, and crayfish had been removed from the lake prior to the bass spawning season. A survival ratio of at least 15 to 1 between schooling bass fry and yearlings was attained by the first year class of bass spawned in Ridge Lake after water was first impounded. Predation rates on embryos and fry of other nest-building centrarchids may be higher than on largemouth bass because the former produce larger numbers of eggs and probably offer less protection to their young.

If the young fishes of the larger species such as carp, bass, or channel catfish escape predation and can find sufficient food, they may survive the first growing season and be well on their way to adulthood. Many of the smaller species such as minnows or sunfish reach sexual maturity and spawn during the early part of the second summer of life. These yearlings may still be small enough to be preyed upon by some kinds of fishes and nearly all of the predaceous amphibians, reptiles, birds, and mammals; however, they are beyond the size for predation by most aquatic insects. By the end of the second growing season, direct predation may become a minor cause of death and other mortality causes may take over.

Ricker[55] investigated the natural mortality rate among the fishes of several Indiana lakes and concluded that once the fish reached sizes larger than 5 in., senility must account for most of the natural mortality. Ricker believed that senility in fish was active over a wide range of ages, relatively much wider than that of domestic animals and man. He based this assumption on his discovery that natural mortality in the bluegill was rather constant in fish from three to six or seven years, the approximate maximum age of this species.

Once a fish reaches a size beyond that of "easy" predation its death may result from a combination of several factors. A 5-in. green sunfish may fall prey to a 16-in. bass because a bacterial infection of the sunfish's fins has caused it to swim in such an abnormal manner as to attract attention. The internal parasites of a minnow may reduce its swimming activity so greatly that it cannot avoid being captured by a crappie or a heron. Senility may bring about predation, disease, or parasitism before the individual fish has time to die from organic degeneration.[47]

When Do Fish Die?

Fish may die at any time of year but it is probable that most of them expire during spring, summer, and fall (one must discount deaths caused by suffocation under ice resulting from unusual circumstances). However, Snieszko[63] believes that winter conditions are responsible for reducing the resistance of fish to bacterial diseases in the spring and that reported deaths associated with rising water temperatures are due to a deficiency of antimicrobial components in the fish's blood; the studies of carp blood by Schaeperclaus[58] and Plancic[52] substantiate this hypothesis. There is little question that many fish die in the spring, a large number of which appear to be diseased or infested with aquatic fungi (Saproligniales). In the case of fungus infestations, it is believed that injuries acquired by fish might heal during other times of the year. In the spring, however, conditions are optimum for the growth of aquatic fungi, and they readily gain entrance through skin abrasions and produce a toxin that causes the death of the fish. *Achlya* sp., one of these fungi, is reported to attack healthy fish without breaks in the skin.

Biologists active in state fisheries departments learn to anticipate a spring period each year when many phone calls and letters report deaths of fish in various state and private waters. Part of these originate directly from winterkill: the fish that have died over the winter start to decompose and float to the surface in spring soon after the ice goes out. Other spring reports of dead or dying fish can be assigned to disease or fungus infestations. Usually, nothing can be done to stop the fish from dying and the situation must be left to run its course. In no case that I know of has a partial loss of fish had serious consequences, unless severe winterkill was the cause of death. When fish suffocate under the ice, a partial kill may have serious consequences on later fishing (see Chapter 3).

Many fish die during the summer and fall. Usually these never appear at the surface or else float up in numbers too small to receive attention. The complete disappearance of a year class of crappies during summer is not unusual. In one instance where 1-in.-mesh wing nets with leads were used at 30- to 40-day intervals over a period of years for catching crappies, a year class was followed from the time its members were first large enough to be caught until they suddenly and permanently disappeared, indicating a complete mortality for that year class.[29] Angling returns of marked crappies in Lake Chautauqua (Illinois) showed that fishermen were taking less the 5% of the available large fish; thus, about 95% of the large crappies were dying for other reasons. Most of these deaths apparently occurred during the warm months.[64]

Scavengers

As a result of pollution, many fish die at about the same time, making available a large amount of carrion for such scavengers as survive in the lake. However, these remaining scavengers are unable to assimilate such an abundance of protein. As a result, the fish decay and float to the surface where they may be consumed by terrestrial scavengers and blow-fly larvae.

Underwater scavengers are probably not so efficient as terrestrial carrion feeders. However, they do well enough to consume a seasonal quantity of carrion of as much as 100 lb/acre in some waters without allowing any of these fish to appear on the surface. Crayfish are important as underwater scavengers and will attack injured or disabled fish before they are dead (Fig. 7.9).[47] Certain kinds of turtles also act as scavengers.

Fig. 7.9 Crayfish are important scavengers of dead and dying fishes and are a staple item in the diet of largemouth and smallmouth bass. This crayfish, *Procambarus blandingii*, is a common pond species in Illinois.

Length of Life of Fishes

Growth studies based on scale analyses furnish valuable information on the length of life of fishes. Most species do not live as long as is popularly believed, but those species inhabiting the cooler northern sections of the country live longer than the same ones in the warmer southern and central sections. Largemouth bass in northern Wisconsin may reach ages of 14 to 15 yr; in central Illinois, 500 miles south, these fish seldom live longer than 10 to 11 yr.

The natural death rate (as a percent of total numbers) from disease and accidents undoubtedly varies with age and size, being very high in juvenile fishes, low from the time the fish reach sexual maturity until they begin to approach the "old" category for that species, and then again high in the "old" fish. At Ridge Lake (Illinois) where the lake was completely drained at 2- or 3-yr intervals (1941–1963) and only marked largemouth bass put back following a draining, it was possible to define losses of marked bass from nonfishing causes.[9] Table 7.1 shows the "natural mortality" rate for bass between about 7 in. and 23 or 24 in. for 2- or 3-yr periods. High natural mortality rates for 1- to 3-yr-old bass at Ridge Lake may have been due to predation by larger bass or their movement out of the lake, because of the opportunity that these small bass were given to swim over the surface spillway in times of floods. The natural mortality rate of bass between 3 and 6 or 7 yr of age (0.75 and 4.00 lb in weight) probably was less than 10% per year. As the bass became older the natural mortality rate again increased, indicating that

Table 7.1 Natural Mortality Rates of Marked Largemouth Bass in Ridge Lake (Illinois)[a]

Weight Range (lb)	Age Range (yr)	Natural Mortality (average %)
0.15-0.75	1-3	33.0
0.76-2.50	3-5	13.4
2.51-4.00	5-6	14.6
4.01-5.00	7-8	39.0
5.01-6.00	more than 8	72.9

[a] Based on complete inventories at beginnings and ends of six 2-yr periods and three 3-yr periods, 1941-1963. Mortality rates for the three 3-yr periods were not significantly different from those of the 2-yr periods.[9] Percentages for natural mortality of 4- to 6-lb bass are less meaningful than those for smaller sizes because total numbers of these fishes are smaller.

these bass were removed from the population rather rapidly at ages beyond 8 yr.

As a rule, the species that attain the largest sizes live the longest, although in any single species, individuals that grow rapidly and gain exceptional sizes are usually short-lived for their species. For example, when I was investigating the ages and growth rates of largemouth and smallmouth bass in Wisconsin, I found that bass of 5 lb or more were often not more than 5−7 yr old. In contrast, the bass that showed 14 or 15 annuli on their scales (14+ to 15+ yr) seldom exceeded 4−4.5 lb in weight; none of the fishes of exceptional sizes for these species were slow-growing individuals. It was as if a fish were "wound up" like a mechanical toy when small, with the potential to run down rapidly or slowly depending upon its individual genetic makeup, the available food, and the forms of competition encountered.

Aquarium fishes given optimum care and a balanced diet probably live much longer than these same fishes in the wild. Of some interest are the records of longevity kept by Director William Braker of the Shedd Aquarium in Chicago.[75] The oldest fish in 1959 were some carp that were brought into the aquarium in 1929 (30 yr of age in 1959). Two alligator gars were more than 28 yr old and two Australian lung fish more than 26 yr; two tarpon were still active and healthy after 24 yr.

The longest record of life for any fish was for that of a sturgeon in the Amsterdam Aquarium that had lived for 70 yr.

However, we are interested in the approximate average maximum ages of wild fish of value in fish management. Table 7.2 gives approximate ages for some common fishes of interest to anglers.

Table 7.2 Approximate Life Spans of Some Sport Fishes

Kind of Fish	Regions	Life Span in Years
Largemouth bass	north,	14 to 16
	central, and south	9 to 12
Smallmouth bass		same as largemouth
Walleye	north	15 to 16
	south	10 to 12
Northern pike	north	16 to 17
Muskellunge	north	16 to 17
Crappie		4 to 7
Bluegill		5 to 8
White bass		2 to 5

Problems of Measuring Natural Mortality

It is usually quite impossible to observe much more than casual activities of the larger aquatic animals in the smallest and clearest ponds; therefore, direct observation is presently of little importance for obtaining information on numerical changes in a fish population. This does not minimize the value of underwater observations for many other purposes.

A comprehensive measurement of fish mortality, however, requires either complete inventories of a fish population at specific intervals (which is usually impossible), or a mathematical approach, either where returns from marked fishes over several seasons are employed to estimate natural losses for the entire population during that time, or where numbers of fish caught (separated into age classes) are used with data on effective effort to estimate natural mortalities.[51] A dependable creel census or survey is essential for furnishing information on fishing mortality.

If successive annual broods of young of a given kind of fish were nearly the same size, a comparison of the numerical sizes of all of the year classes present in a lake in any year would give acceptable information on total annual mortality over the life span of that species. Thus a consideration of the relative abundance of successive year classes of a species in any mixed population *may* show total mortality, although it probably shows little more than length of life of that species in the lake in question, because the numerical strength of new broods is seldom similar from year to year.

If fish could be marked in sufficient numbers, a measure of the returns from fishing for these marked fish over a period of several years would give an estimate of total mortality. This method was developed by Ricker,[55] who investigated the mortality rates of bluegills in several Indiana lakes by marking the fins of these fish prior to the opening of the fishing season (June 16) in two or more successive years. Catch records of marked fish over a period of two or more years furnished data on rate of exploitation. The relationship between the number of fish captured and marked the first year, and recaptured in the first and second years, allowed calculations of total mortality, from which angling mortality could be subtracted to give natural mortality.

His estimates of total mortality for bluegills in three Indiana lakes ranged from 60 to 77% per year. Of this range, fishing accounted for 19−36%, leaving 40 to about 50% for natural mortality. Ricker's calculations for total annual mortality, rate of exploitation, and natural mortality (two methods of calculation) are shown in Table 7.3.

It is somewhat of a problem to separate fishing mortality and natural mortality. Certainly, some of the fishes that fall prey to anglers would die during the same period from other causes, and some fishes might be caught by anglers if they had not previously died from natural causes. The mortality rate could be as high with no fishing as with the exploitation rates shown in Table 7.3. However, it probably would not be so high because fish populations that are not fished tend to become numerically overabundant sooner than those subjected to a substantial annual cropping.

The fish population of Sugarloaf Lake (Michigan), which was studied intensively from 1948 through 1952,[21,22] was found to remain quite constant for five consecutive years; this meant that recruitment and total mortality were nearly equal during those years.

Under these conditions the assumption was made[22] that survival could

Table 7.3 Calculations of Rates of Total Annual Mortality, Exploitation and Natural Mortality for Bluegills in Muskellunge, Shoe, and Wawasee Lakes (Indiana) [a]

Lake and Year (beginning June 16)	Total Annual Mortality a	Rate of Exploitation μ	Natural Mortality Rate	
			First Method n^1	Second Method n^2
Muskellunge 1942-43	0.60	0.19	0.51	0.47
Shoe 1941-42	0.76	0.36	0.62	0.52
Shoe 1942-43	0.71	0.24	0.62	0.56
Wawasee 1939-43	0.77	0.20 [b]	0.71 [b]	0.66 [b]

[a] From Ricker.[55]
[b] Based on an estimated rate of exploitation of 20%.

be expressed by the ratio of the number of fish in a particular age group divided by the number in the next younger age group, thus:

$$\text{S (survival)} = \frac{II + III + IV + ...}{I + II + III + ...}$$

From the rate of survival, it was possible to figure total mortality and, by subtracting the fishing mortality from this total, natural mortality could be calculated. These investigators calculated that the total mortality for bluegills was 66%. As the annual fishing mortality was 21%, the natural mortality rate was 45%. This was a little less than Ricker calculated for Indiana lakes, but still in the same general range.

Statistics on the catches of marked largemouth bass at Ridge Lake (Illinois) and the survival of marked fish from one draining census to another (usually 2 yr) gave information on fishing mortality and total mortality of the 1941 year class from 1943 to 1951.[8] Similar (but previously unpublished) data on the 1947 and 1949 year classes of bass are included with data for the 1941 year class in Table 7.4. In this table the number of fish shown opposite each period listing was the number put back following the census at the beginning of the period. The fishing mortality rate (exploitation rate) for the first year was the fraction of the fish put back after the March census that were caught during the fishing season (June, July, and August) of that year.
Thus:

$$\text{Exploitation rate (1st yr)} = \frac{C_1}{N_1}$$

where $N_1 =$ number of marked fish returned following census and C_1 = number of marked fish caught during summer of census year. Some fish might be expected to die of natural causes during this period.

The fishing mortality rate (exploitation rate) for the second year was figured in the same way except that the calculation of available fish was based on the number of fish returned following the census of March of the first year, minus the fish caught during the first year, minus one-half of the fish that disappeared between censuses (natural mortality):

$$\text{Exploitation rate (2nd yr)} = \frac{C_2}{(N_1 - C_1) - \left[\dfrac{N_1 - C_1 - C_2 - N_2}{2}\right]}$$

Table 7.4   Exploitation Rates and Mortality Rates for Largemouth Bass in Ridge Lake

Mark and Period	Number of Fish	Rate of Exploitation			Losses for 2- or 3-yr Period			Av. Annual Natural Mortality Rate	Av. Weight at Beginning of Period (lb)
		1st Year	2nd Year	3rd Year	Total Mort. Rate	Fishing Mort. Rate	Natural Mort. Rate		
LP. and RP., 1941 year class									
1943-45	1500	— [a]	0.370	—	0.638	0.309	0.329	0.164	0.17
1945-47	638	0.628	0.431	—	0.870	0.776	0.104	0.052	0.77
1947-49	81	0.259	0.227	—	0.605	0.469	0.136	0.068	2.44
1949-51	32	0.469	—	—	0.813	0.469	0.344	0.172	3.96
Av. per year		0.452	0.342		0.366	0.253	0.114		
Dorsal, 1947 year class									
1949-51	917	0.482	0.372	—	0.811	0.643	0.168	0.084	0.51
1951-53	170	0.688	0.046	—	0.818	0.700	0.118	0.059	1.97
1953-56	31	0.387	0.389	0.100	0.742 [b]	0.645 [b]	0.097 [b]	0.032	3.16
Av. per year		0.519	0.269		0.339	0.284	0.055		
L Pect., 1949 year class									
1951-53	619	0.590	0.596	—	0.929	0.794	0.135	0.067	0.59
1953-56	44	0.477	0.600	0.000	0.932 [b]	0.750 [b]	0.182 [b]	0.061	1.98
Av. per year		0.534	0.598		0.372	0.309	0.063		

[a] Lake not opened to fishing.
[b] Three years combined in these figures instead of two years.

where, C_2 = number of marked fish caught during the second summer and N_2 = number of marked fish in a census following the second summer.

The total mortality for any two-year period was the difference between the number of marked fish restocked after a draining census and the number bearing the same mark that were captured in the next succeeding census. These ranged from 60 to a little more than 90% (Table 7.4) for two years, averaging around 35% for a single year. When the fishing mortality of 25—30% per year was subtracted from total mortality, the remainder, natural mortality, averaged from 5 to 11%. This 11% calculation was the average of four two-year periods, all part of the life span of the 1941 year class.

Table 7.5 shows the annual mortality rates of bluegills and largemouth bass described above, together with those of largemouths, smallmouths, walleyes, and several kinds of pan fishes of other investigators. There is some evidence that the annual mortality rates for the longer-lived species are usually lower than those for the bluegill and other pan fishes, which are relatively short-lived fishes.

Table 7.5   Annual Mortality Rates for Some Common Hook-and-Line Fishes

Kind of Fish	Total Mortality (%)	Fishing Mortality (%)	Natural Mortality (%)	Location	Source
Bluegills	60 to 77	19 to 36	40 to 54	Indiana Lakes	Ricker
Bluegills	66	21	45	Sugarloaf L., Michigan	Cooper and Latta
Largemouth bass	35 to 40	25 to 30	5 to 11	Ridge L., Ill.	Bennett
Largemouth bass	56	20	36	Clear L., California	Kimsey
Largemouth bass	70	26	44	Sugarloaf L., Michigan	Cooper and Latta
Smallmouth bass	58	22	36	Lake Michigan, Michigan	Latta
Walleye	31	27	4	Many Point L., Minnesota	Olson
Rock bass	85	15	70	Sugarloaf L.	Cooper and Latta
Pumpkinseed	81	21	60	Sugarloaf L.	Cooper and Latta
Warmouth	70	5	65	Sugarloaf L.	Cooper and Latta
Black crappie	81	20	61	Sugarloaf L.	Cooper and Latta

Fishing Mortality, Natural Mortality, and Recruitment

Among warmwater fishes, evidence is rare that a high mortality rate, either from natural mortality or fishing mortality or both, will seriously reduce the angling potential of a fish population. This is because the number of embryos produced during each spawning period is so large, and the number that can find room to grow is so small, that a large reserve is always available from which a population can recoup its most severe losses. As mentioned in Chapter 5 our information on warmwater fishes fails to demonstrate a relationship between the number of spawners and the number of embryos surviving to reach the catchable stock.

Many common warmwater species have short lives and high natural mortality rates. Broods of such fishes as crappies and the sunfishes, the white and yellow basses, and the several kinds of bullheads live but a few years and are replaced. These fishes are subject to wide fluctuations in abundance and in growth rates, and should be cropped when they are available. With some exceptions, short-lived species are responsible for many of the problems of fishery management.

Angling mortality is probably far less important in the dynamics of sport-fish populations than most fishermen are led to believe. This is illustrated by the disproportionate number of fishes lost to natural causes in relation to the angler's catch.

Legal Restrictions on Angling Related to Mortality

The history of the use of the fisheries resources of North America follows the pattern of man's misuse of other renewable natural resources. At first there is open exploitation, followed by a gradual increase in restrictions until a maximum number are imposed. Then as more information becomes available on the correct management of this resource, unnecessary or useless restrictions are gradually removed.

A maximum of restrictions was imposed upon the warmwater fisheries resources by about 1935; since then, a gradual understanding of fish-population dynamics in warmwater lakes and ponds resulted in an almost complete reversal, once it became appreciated that fish would hatch, spawn, and die in spite of restrictions on angling.

Early restrictions on fishing were based on fair play and false or ambiguous biological concepts which seemed reasonable in the absence of contradictory data. These ideas were that *(1)* each angler should have a fair opportunity to take his share of the crop of fish (fair play); *(2)* fishes should be allowed to reach maturity and spawn at least once before they are caught (a false biological concept); *(3)* an ample brood stock must be carried over into the following year (a questionable concept because of the indefinite interpretation of "ample"); *(4)* fishes must be allowed to spawn unmolested by man (false); *(5)* the harvest of fishes must be so unselective as to forestall an overabundance of less desirable species (fair play).

With the advent of studies of entire fish populations and the related type of fishing produced by these specific populations, fishery biologists began to doubt the premises upon which most of the restrictive regulations were based. The first break with the restrictive idea came in 1944 when Tennessee, on the recommendation of R. W. Eschmeyer, liberalized fishing regulations on the TVA's Norris Reservoir.[78]

The State of Ohio soon followed this lead,[19] removing in 1945 all closed seasons, length limits, and creel limits for angling in an 80-acre lake in southern Ohio, and from eight other lakes in 1946 through 1948. Another thirty lakes were added in 1951 and by 1952 all Ohio waters under control of the Division of Wildlife were opened to almost unrestricted angling. Comparative yields and catches made before and after restrictions were removed indicated an improvement in fishing. Other states adopted the idea of year-round fishing,[28,48,68,71,72,73] but most retained some limits on the total number of fishes to be allowed per day, particularly on largemouth and smallmouth bass and other large game fishes. Some states retained minimum length limits on largemouth and smallmouth bass, walleyes, northern pike, and muskellunge, although there was no biological evidence that such restrictions were useful or necessary. Most states came to believe the closed season was unnecessary.

We will now consider in more detail the theoretical basis for biological justification of removal, or retention, of restrictions.

Size Limits. There are several assumptions upon which the idea of a minimum size limit is based. One of the most common is that each fish should have an opportunity to reproduce before it is caught. This assumption might be valid if one could demonstrate a shortage of spawn or show a relationship between abundance of spawn and number of spawners. When growth rate shows an inverse relationship to population numbers, a size-limit restriction on a short-lived species may make certain that most of a crowded population of these fish will die before they are large enough to be taken legally. For example, an 8-in. minimum limit governing the take of crappies would allow from 50 to 90% of them to die unused.

There is a further belief that each small fish returned to the water will grow to a catchable size and increase fishing success in future years. When Escanaba Lake (northeastern Wisconsin) was opened to unrestricted hook-and-line fishing, 1946 through 1956, there was no evidence of depletion after ten years.[18] More than 50% of the fishes taken from this lake by anglers during the test were illegal elsewhere in Wisconsin because of their size. Eighty percent of the catch consisted of walleyes and perch.

In contrast to the situation occurring in warmwater species with high reproductive potential, there is some evidence for retaining size limits for species living in cold water and having lower reproductive capabilities.[1] Shetter, Whalls, and Corbett[61] were able to demonstrate that protection of brook trout in a part of the Au Sable River (Michigan) by a length limit that allowed them to spawn at least once was followed by an increase in fingerlings present. This protection, plus a "flies only" regulation, allowed a buildup of the brook trout population. If warmwater species were as low in reproductive potential and as vulnerable to angling as are trout, size restrictions might certainly be reasonable.

The question of a minimum length limit on largemouth and smallmouth bass of 9, 10, 12, and 14 in. total length has been discussed for the past twenty years. In many small artificial lakes largemouth bass are the main source for control of sunfish populations. Theoretically, if the small bass below a minimum length of 12 or 14 in. are released when caught, greater control of small sunfish would be assured,[71] assuming that mortality rates due to having been hooked will be low or negligible. Low mortality rates might follow if single barbless hooks were used on all bass plugs and lures, but this would allow the escape of many bass larger than the 12-in. limit. With a 12-in. minimum length limit, how does a lake owner legally thin an overpopulation of small bass that become stunted and practically stop growing after reaching sizes of 7 to 9 in.?

At Ridge Lake (Illinois) larger yields of bass and larger individual fish were caught during a 10-yr period when small bass were removed from the lake at two-year intervals (along with small bluegills) than during the other 12 yr of this 22-yr study. With an annual fishing pressure of between 200 and 320 man-hours per acre, the larger bass that escaped were those which became "hook-wise." The proof of the need for and benefit from length limits on largemouth and smallmouth bass is not persuasive.

Creel Limits.   The purpose of a bag or creel limit may be to conserve breeding stock where fish are highly vulnerable to angling. In addition, however, justification for a creel limit is based on the assumption that the limit will reduce the creels of the more successful anglers and thereby make more fish available for the less successful anglers, and that a creel limit may prevent an individual from taking more fish than he can use.

Where creel limits are thought to be necessary, permission to change these limits should not be vested in a legislative branch of the government, otherwise adjustments cannot be made to deal with fluctuations in the stock.[1,2]

Many states retain daily creel limits on important game-fish species to conserve the breeding stocks, or, more often, to "spread the fish around" among a maximum number of anglers. There is evidence to show that the skilled fisherman still catches more than his share of fish.[67,71]

Closed Seasons.   For many years closed seasons were the rule for most species of sport fishes during their spawning season until studies began to indicate that fishing had little or no effect upon the production of young.[4,24,49] Murphy[49] set up two areas along the shore of Clear Lake, Lake County, California, one of which was opened to fishing and the other closed, and studied the production of bass fingerlings in these areas. Fingerling production was not greater in the closed area than in the area open to fishing. In later years when both areas were opened to fishing, more bass fingerlings were produced in each than in the year of the test. Murphy felt that the only times a closed season might be useful were *(1)* when the fishing pressure was extremely high, *(2)* when a lake had low productivity due to low average annual temperatures, *(3)* when fishing for a highly-prized species was excessive and *(4)* when nongame fish were crowding out game fish. In every case, he was in doubt that the closed season would accomplish the desired results.

After studying the catch of smallmouth bass in the Niangua River (Missouri) with a spring closed season for several years, Funk and Fleener[28] removed this restriction for another period of several years, and then compared the catch for these two time periods. The bass were less abundant during the period of year-round fishing but these authors noted that factors other than angling held down the numerical size of the year classes of smallmouth produced. However they did admit to the possibility that some more heavily fished streams might be overfished with a year-round season.

Sometimes, closed seasons have been set at the wrong time to give protection. From 1939 to 1949 the closed season on bass for central Illinois was April 1 or 15 to June 1. This season protected the nest-guarding bass in only about six years out of ten. There were no more young bass in years when bass nested early and were protected by the closed season than in years when they were still guarding eggs after June 1.

In general the controls imposed upon fishermen with the objective of benefiting the fish are far from realistic. Warmwater fish populations are generally controlled by interspecific competition and such catastrophies as pollution; not by angling.

POPULATION ESTIMATION

The exposure of the fishes in a lake population for direct counting requires drastic methods such as draining of the lake or poisoning of the fishes. In large lakes the performing of these operations is impossible or impractical.

The disadvantages involved in direct counting have stimulated mathematicians to develop techniques for indirect estimates. As a result, the number of animals in a specific habitat can now be calculated, at least theoretically, on the basis of recaptures of previously marked individuals.

Marking of the fishes can be accomplished by the removal of all or part of a fin or by the application of a tag. The fishes must be captured originally and recaptured by different methods or by a combination of methods that will reduce the chances of a biased selection for certain kinds, sizes, or other classifications of individuals.

The principle of indirect enumeration is as follows: In a randomly collected sample of individuals, each member is marked and released alive, and within a short period of time after the marked sample has had opportunity to mix with the unmarked population, another random sample is taken. In this second sample some marked individuals appear. The proportion of recapture of the total number of fishes taken in the second sample should be the same as the proportion initially marked to the total population.[32]

$$\text{total population} = \frac{\text{total marked x total caught when recapturing}}{\text{recaptures}}$$

If the calculation is to approach a reasonable degree of accuracy, no individuals must be any more likely than others to appear in the catches at the time of recapture. From what is known of the selectivity of fishing gear and the nonrandom distribution of fishes, it becomes obvious that this poses a real problem in fish-population estimation unless the method is used with a knowledge of its shortcomings, since fish behavior (and catchability) is modified by species, size, sex, season, environment, and many other factors.

It is important that the date of recapture be close to the date of marking, so that there is a minimum of replacement of marked individuals through death and recruitment; however in some situations replacements may occur at a fairly constant rate in relation to time, and adjustments can be made to compensate for them.

For those who have a special interest in the methods of fish-population estimation, I have listed a few references dealing with this subject.

A PARTIAL LIST OF PAPERS ON FISH-POPULATION ESTIMATION

1. Adams, L., 1951, "Confidence limits for the Peterson or Lincoln index used in animal populations studies," *J. Wildlife Management* 15(1), 13-19.
2. Allen, K. R., 1966, "Some methods of estimating exploited populations," *J. Fisheries Res. Board Can.* 23(10), 1553-1574.
3. Cole, C. F., 1966, "Virtual population estimations of largemouth bass in Lake Fort Smith, Arkansas, 1957-1960," *Am. Fish. Soc. Trans.* 95(1), 52-55.
4. Cooper, G. P., 1952, "Estimation of fish populations in Michigan Lakes," *Am. Fish. Soc. Trans.* 81(1951), 4-16.
5. Cooper, G. P., 1953, "Population estimates of fish in Sugarloaf Lake, Washtenaw County, Michigan, and their exploitation by anglers," *Papers Mich. Acad. Sci.* 38(1952), 163-186.
6. Davis, W. S., 1964, "Graphic representation of confidence intervals for Peterson population estimates," *Am. Fish. Soc. Trans.* 93(3), 227-232.
7. DeLury, D. B., 1947, "On the estimation of biological populations," *Biometrics* 3(4), 145-167.
8. DeLury, D. B., 1951, "On the planning of experiments for the estimation of fish populations," *J. Fisheries Res. Board Can.* 8(4), 281-307.
9. Fredin, R. A., 1950, "Fish population estimate in small ponds using the marking and recovery technique," *Iowa State J. Sci.* 24(4), 363-384.
10. Hatcher, R. M., 1965, "The estimation of channel catfish *(Ictalurus punctatus* Refinesque) populations in farm ponds from catch statistics," *Proc. 16th Conf. S.E. Assoc. Game and Fish Comm.*, pp. 270-276.
11. Jackson, C. H. N., 1939, "The analysis of an animal population," *J. Animal Ecol.* 8(2), 238-246.

12. Krumholz, L. A., 1944, "A check on the fin-clipping method for estimating fish populations," *Papers Mich. Acad. Sci.* 29(1943), 281-291.

13. Omand, D. M., 1951, "A study of populations of fish based on catch effort statistics," *J. Wildlife Management* 15(1), 88-98.

14. Ricker, W. E., 1937, "The concept of confidence or fiducial limits applied to the Poisson frequency distribution," J. Am. Statistical Assn. 32: 349-356.

15. Ricker, W. E., 1940, "Relation of 'catch per unit effort' to abundance and rate of exploitation," *J. Fisheries Res. Board Can.* 5(1), 43-70.

16. Ricker, W. E., 1942, "Creel census, population estimates and rate of exploitation of game fish in Shoe Lake, Indiana," *Invest. Indiana Lakes and Streams* 2(1942), 215-253.

17. Ricker, W. E., 1944, "Further notes on fishing mortality and effort," *Copeia,* (1), 23-44.

18. Ricker, W. E., 1945, "Abundance, exploitation, and mortality of the fishes in two lakes," *Invest. Indiana Lakes and Streams* 2, 345-448.

19. Ricker, W. E., 1954, "Stock and recruitment," *J. Fisheries Res. Board Can.* 11(5), 559-623.

20. Ricker, W. E., 1958a, *Handbook of Computations for Biological Statistics of Fish Populations,* Queen's Printer and Cont. of Sta. Bull. 119, Ottawa, pp. 1-300.

21. Ricker, W. E., 1958b, "Some principles involved in regulation of fisheries by quota," *Can. Fish Culturist* 22, 1-5.

22. Robson, D. S., and Regier, H. A., 1964, "Sample size in Peterson mark-recapture experiments," *Am. Fish. Soc. Trans.* 93(3), 215-226.

23. Rose, E. T., 1949, "The population of yellow pike perch *(Stizostedion v. vitreum)* in Spirit Lake, Iowa," *Am. Fish Soc. Trans.* 77(1947), 32-41.

24. Schaffer, M. B., 1951, "Estimation of size of animal populations by marking experiments," *Fisheries Bull. Fish and Wildlife Serv. 69,* 52, 191-203.

25. Schnabel, Z. E., 1938, "The estimation of the total fish population of a lake," *Am. Math. Monthly* 45(6), 348-352.

26. Schumacher, F. X., and Eschmeyer, R. W., 1943, "The estimate of fish populations in lakes or ponds," *J. Tenn. Acad. Sci.* 18(3), 228-249.

27. Waters, T. F., 1960, "The development of population estimate procedures in small trout lakes," *Am. Fish. Soc. Trans.* 89(3), 287-294.

28. Zippin, C., 1958, "The removal method of population estimation," *J. Wildlife Management* 22(1), 82-90.

REFERENCES

1. Allen, K. R., 1954, "Factors affecting the efficiency of restrictive regulations in fisheries management," *New Zealand J. Sci. Tech. Sect. B* 35(6), 499-526.

2. Allen, K. R., 1955, "Factors affecting the efficiency of restrictive regulations in fisheries management," II, "bag limits," *New Zealand J. Sci. Tech. Sect. B* 36(4), 305-334.

3. Barnickol, P. G., and Campbell, R. S., 1952, "Summary of selected pond studies in Missouri," *J. Wildlife Management* 16(3), 270-274.

4. Bennett, G. W., 1945, "Overfishing in a small artificial lake, Onized Lake near Alton, Illinois," *Illinois Nat. Hist. Surv. Bull.* 23(3), 373-406.

5. Bennett, G. W., 1946, "Pond talk—II," *Illinois Wildlife* 1(2), 8-10.

6. Bennett, G. W., 1947, "Fish management—a substitute for natural predation," *12th North Am. Wildlife Conf. Trans.,* pp. 276-285.

7. Bennett, G. W., 1948, "The bass-bluegill combination in a small artificial lake," *Illinois Nat. Hist. Surv. Bull.* 24(3), 377-412.

8. Bennett, G. W., 1954, "Largemouth bass in Ridge Lake, Coles County, Illinois," *Illinois Nat. Hist. Surv. Bull.* 26(2), 217-276.

9. Bennett, G. W., Adkins, H. W., and Childers, W. F., 1969, "Largemouth bass and other fishes in Ridge Lake, Illinois, 1941-1963," *Illinois Nat. Hist. Surv. Bull.* 30(1), 1-67.

10. Bennett, G. W., and Childers, W. F., 1957, "The smallmouth bass, *Micropterus dolomieui*, in warm-water ponds," *J. Wildlife Management* 21(4), 414-424.

11. Bennett, G. W., and Weiss, G. F., 1959, "Fishing pressure and the empty creel," *Illinois Wildlife* 14(3), 8-9.

12. Bennett, G. W., Thompson, D. H., and Parr, S. A., 1940, "A second year of fisheries investigations in Fork Lake," *Illinois Nat. Hist. Surv. Biol. Notes*, 14, 1-24.

13. Best, E. H., and Bales, H. D., 1956, "An evaluation of creel census methods," *Calif. Fish and Game* 42(2), 109-115.

14. Bowers, C. C., and Martin, M., 1956,"*Results of an Opening Week Creel Census and Tagging Study on Three State-Owned Lakes,*" Kentucky Dept. of Fish and Wildlife Res., Fish. Bull., No. 20, 13 pp.

15. Carlander, K. D., DiCostanzo, C. J., and Jessen, R. J., 1958, "Sampling problems in creel census," *Progressive Fish. Culturist* 20(2), 73-81.

16. Childers, W. F., 1967, "Hybridization of four species of sunfishes (Centrarchidae)," *Illinois Nat. Hist. Surv. Bull.* 29(3), 159-214.

17. Childers, W. F., and Bennett, G. W., 1967, "Hook-and-line production of largemouth bass and redear x green sunfish hybrids in a one-acre pond," *Progressive Fish Culturist* 29(1), 27-35.

18. Churchill, W., 1957, "Conclusion from a ten-year creel census on a lake with no angling restrictions," *J. Wildlife Management* 21(2), 182-188.

19. Clark, C. F., 1965, "Importance of angling regulations—liberalized angling," *Proc. 32nd Ann. Meet. Assoc. Midwest Fish & Game Comm.*, pp. 174-180.

20. Cobb, E. S., 1953, " The status of commercial and sport fishing on Reelfoot Lake," *Progressive Fish Culturist* 15(1), 20-23.

21. Cooper, G. P., 1953,"Population estimate of fish in Sugar Loaf Lake, Washtenaw County, Michigan, and their exploitation by anglers," *Papers Mich. Acad. Sci.* 38, 163-186.

22. Cooper, G. P., and Latta, W. C., 1954, "Further studies on the fish population and exploitation by angling in Sugarloaf Lake, Washtenaw County, Michigan," *Papers Mich. Acad. Sci.* 39(1953), 209-223.

23. Crance, J. H., and McBay, L. G., 1966, "Results of tests with channel catfish in Alabama ponds," *Progressive Fish Culturist* 28(4), 193-200.

24. Eschmeyer, R. W., 1942, "The catch abundance and migration of game fishes in Norris Reservoir, Tennessee, 1940," *J. Tenn. Acad. Sci.* 17(1), 9x-115.

25. Fritz, A. W., 1967, *1966 Carlyle Reservoir and Tailwater Sport Fishing Creel Census,* Illinois Dept. Cons. Spec. Rept. 17, 29 pp.

26. Fritz, A. W., 1968, *1967 Carlyle Reservoir and Tailwater Sport Fishing Creel Census,* Illinois Dept. Cons. Div. Fish. Spec. Rept. 21, 31 pp.

27. Fry, J. P., 1965, "Harvest of fish from tailwaters of three large impoundments in Missouri," *Proc. 16th Conf. S.E. Assoc. Game and Fish Comm.*, pp. 405-411.

28. Funk, J. L., and Fleener, G.G., 1966, *Evaluation of a Year-Round Open Fishing Season Upon an Ozark Smallmouth Bass Stream, Niangua River, Missouri,* Missouri Dept. Cons., Div. Fish. D-J Series No. 2, 21 pp.

29. Hansen, D. F., 1951, "Biology of the white crappie in Illinois," *Illinois Nat. Hist. Surv. Bull.* 25(4), 211-265.

30. Hansen, D. F., Bennett, G. W., Webb, R. J., and Lewis, J. M., 1960, "The effect of pond fertilization on angling for largemouth bass and bluegill," *Illinois Nat. Hist. Surv. Bull.* 27(5), 345-390.

31. Holder, A. S., 1965, "Ice fishing in Lake Simcoe," *Fish and Wildlife Rev.* 4(1), 13-17.

32. Jackson, C. H. N., 1939, "The analysis of an annual population," *J. Animal Ecol.* 8(2), 238-246.

33. James, M. C., Meehean, O. L., and Douglas, E. J., 1944, "Fish stocking as related to the management of inland waters," *U.S. Fish Wildlife Serv. Bull.* 35, 1-22.

34. Johnson, M. W., and Wroblewski, L., 1962, "Errors associated with a systematic sampling creel census," *Am. Fish. Soc. Trans.* 91(2), 201-207.

35. Kempenger, J. J., 1968, "Impact of underwater spearfishing on a mixed warmwater fish population," *Wisconsin Dept. Nat. Res. Rept.* 30, 1-10.

36. Kuhne, E. R., 1939a, "The Reelfoot Lake creel census," *Tenn. Acad. Sci. Reelfoot Lake Biol. Sta. Rept.* 3, 46-53.

37. Kuhne, E. R., 1939b, "Preliminary report on the productivity of some Tennessee waters," *Tenn. Acad. Sci. Reelfoot Lake Biol. Sta. Rept.* 3, 54-60.

38. LaFaunce, D. A., Kimsey, J. B., and Chadwick, H. K., 1964, "The fishery at Sutherland Reservoir, San Diego County, Calif." *Calif. Fish and Game* 50(4), 271-291.

39. Lagler, K. F., and DeRoth, G. C., 1953, "Populations and yield to anglers in a fishery for largemouth bass, *Micropterus salmoides* (Lac.)," *Papers Mich Acad. Sci.* 38, 235-253.

40. Lagler, K. F., Hazzard, A. S., Hazen, W. E., and Tompkins, W. A., 1950, "Outboard motors in relation to fish behavior, fish production and angling success," *15th North Am. Wildlife Conf. Trans.*, pp. 280-303.

41. Lambou, V. W., 1963, "Recommended methods for reporting creel survey data for reservoirs, prepared for the reservoir committee," *Paper for Southern Div. Am. Fish. Soc.*, pp. 1-30.

42. Lopinot, A. C., 1967, *The Illinois Angler—a Survey of 1965 Illinois Licensed Fishermen,* Illinois Dept. of Cons., Springfield, Ill., 81 pp.

43. Lux, F. E., and Smith, L. L., Jr., 1960, "Some factors influencing seasonal changes in angler catch in a Minnesota lake," *Am. Fish. Soc. Trans.* 89(1), 67-79.

44. Martin, R. G., 1958, "Influence of fishing pressure on bass fishing success," *Proc. 11th Ann. Conf. S.E. Assoc. Game and Fish Comm.*, pp. 76-82.

45. McKechnie, R. J., 1966, "California inland angling survey for 1964," *Calif. Fish and Game* 52(4), 293-299.

46. Miller, L. F., and Chance, C. J., 1954, "Fishing in the tailwaters of T.V.A. dams," *Progressive Fish Culturist* 16(1), 3-9.

47. Minckley, W. L., and Craddock, J. E., 1961, "Active predation of crayfishes on fishes," *Progressive Fish Culturist* 23(3), 120-123.

48. Mraz, D., 1964, "Evaluation of liberalized regulations on largemouth bass, Browns Lake, Wisconsin," *Wisconsin Cons. Dept. Tech. Bull.* 31, 1-25.

49. Murphy, G. I., 1950, "The closed season in warm-water fish management," *15th North Am. Wildlife Conf. Trans.*, pp. 235-251.

50. Overton, W. S., 1954, "Game and fish survey methods," *Proc. S.E. Assoc. Game and Fish Comm.*, pp. 102-104.

51. Paloheimo, J. E., 1959, "A method of estimating natural and fishing mortalities," *J. Fisheries Res. Board Can.* 15(4), 749-758.

52. Plancic, J., 1956, "Enfloss der Winterung auf den Hamoglobingehalf bein Laichkarpfen," *Deut. Fischerei Zeitung* 3(12), 373-375.

53. Poole, R. L., Kuester, D. R., and Witt, A., Jr., 1963, "The status of spearfishing and the use of scuba in fish management programs in the freshwaters of the United States," *Am. Fish. Soc. Trans.* 92(1), 30-33.

54. Ricker, W. E., 1945a, "Causes of death among Indiana fishes," *10th North Am. Wildlife Conf. Trans.* pp. 266-269.

55. Ricker, W. E., 1945b, "Natural mortality among Indiana bluegill sunfish," *Ecology* 26(2), 111-121.

56. Robson, D. S., 1960, "An unbiased sampling and estimation procedure for creel censuses of fishermen," *Biometrics* 16(2), 261-277.

57. Robson, D. S., 1961, "On the statistical theory of a roving creel census of fishermen,"

Biometrics 17(3), 415-437.

58. Schaeperclaus, W., 1956, "Bekampfung der infektiosen Bauchwassersucht des Karpfens durch Amtibiotika," *z. Fischerei* 5(1-2), 3-59.

59. Schoffman, R. J., 1959, "Age and rate of growth of the bluegills in Reelfoot Lake, Tennessee, for 1950 and 1958," *J. Tenn. Acad. Sci.* 34(1), 73-77.

60. Schoffman, R. J., 1962, "Age and rate of growth of the largemouth black bass in Reelfoot Lake, Tennessee, for 1952 and 1961," *J. Tenn. Acad. Sci.* 37(1), 1-4.

61. Schetter, D. S. Whalls, M. J., and Corbett, O. M., 1954, "The effect of changed angling regulations on a trout population of the Au Sable River," *19th North Am. Wildlife Conf. Trans.*, pp. 222-238.

62. Smith, S. H., 1968, "Species succession and fishery exploitation in the Great Lakes," *J. Fisheries Res. Board Can.* 25(4), 667-693.

63. Snieszko, S. F., 1958, "Natural resistance and susceptibility to infections," *Progressive Fish Culturist* 20(3), 133-136.

64. Starrett, W. C., and Fritz, A. W., 1957, "The crappie story in Illinois," *Outdoors in Illinois* 4(2), 11-14.

65. Starrett, W. C., and McNeil, P. L., Jr., 1952, "Sport fishing at Lake Chautauqua near Havana, Illinois, in 1950 and 1951," *Illinois Nat. Hist. Surv. Biol. Notes* 30, 1-31.

66. Stroud, R. H., 1955, "Harvests and management of warm-water fish populations in Massachusetts lakes, ponds and reservoirs," *Progressive Fish Culturist* 17(2), 51-62.

67. Stroud, R. H., 1957a, *More on Skill,* S.F.I. Bull. 66, p. 8.

68. Stroud, R. H. 1957b, *Wisconsin Liberalization Test,* S.F.I. Bull. 68.

69. Stroud, R. H., 1958, *Year-Round fishing,* S.F.I. Bull. 77, p. 6.

70. Stroud, R. H., 1963, *Ice Fishing,* S.F.I. Bull. 137, p. 4.

71. Stroud, R. H., 1964a, *12-inch Bass Limit,* S.F.I. Bull. 147, p. 3.

72. Stroud, R. H., 1964b, *Liberalized Bass Fishing,* S.F.I. Bull. 156, p. 5.

73. Stroud, R. H., 1965, *Liberalized fishing—again,* S.F.I. Bull. 161, pp. 6-7.

74. Stroud, R. H., and Jenkins, R. M., 1959a, *Tailwater Fishing Pier Mitigates Losses,* S.F.I. Bull. 97, pp. 1-2.

75. Stroud, R. H., and Jenkins, R. M., 1959b, *Aquarium Fish Longevity,* S.F.I. Bull. 97, p. 2.

76. Stroud, R. H., and Jenkins, R. M., 1961a, *Winter Tailwater,* S.F.I. Bull. 113, p. 6.

77. Stroud, R. H., and Jenkins, R. M., 1961b, *Ice Fishing,* S.F.I. Bull. 113, p. 2.

78. Stroud, R. H., and Jenkins, R. M., 1962, *Year-Round Fishing,* S.F.I. Bull. 123, p. 2.

79. Swingle, H. S., 1956, "Determination of balance in farm fish ponds," *North Am. Wildlife Conf. Trans.* 21, 298-322.

80. Swingle, H. S., and Smith, E. V., 1947, "Management of farm fish ponds," *Alabama Polytech. Inst. Agr. Expt. Sta. Bull.* 254, 1-30 (revised).

81. Thompson, D. H., 1941, "The fish production of inland streams and lakes," *A Symposium on Hydrobiology,* Univ. of Wisconsin Press, pp. 206-217.

82. Van Oosten, J., 1949, "The present status of the United States commercial fisheries of the Great Lakes," *14th North Am. Wildlife Conf. Trans.* pp. 319-330.

83. Viosca, P., Jr., 1945, "A critical analysis of practices in the management of warm-water fish with a view to greater food production," *Am. Fish. Soc. Trans.* 73(1943), 274-283.

84. Van Geldern, C. E., Jr., 1961, "Application of the DeLury method in determining the angler harvest of stocked catchable sized trout," *Am. Fish. Soc. Trans.* 90(3), 259-263.

85. Witt, A., Jr., 1948, "Experiments in learning of fishes with shocking and hooking as penalties," unpublished m.s. thesis, Univ. of Illinois Library, 60 pp.

86. Wood, R., 1951, "The significance of managed water levels in developing the fisheries of large impoundments," *J. Tenn. Acad. Sci.* 26(3), 214-235.

87. Zippin, C., 1958, "The removal method of population estimation," *J. Wildlife Management* 22(1), 82-90.

FISH BEHAVIOR AND ANGLING

Water is so different from air in the conductance of light, sound, and chemical stimuli that the behavior and responses of fishes diverge considerably from those of terrestrial vertebrates. Although the eyes, "ears," olfactory, and other sensory organs of the former are adjusted to function under water, the relative importance of these organs is not the same as for terrestrial animals.

The differences in the media of air and water can be appreciated by the skin diver. Near the surface of the lake, he can see at best but a few feet in fresh water, and can scarcely detect his outstretched hand in turbid water. Moreover, if he descends to depths greater than a dozen or more feet, he enters a twilight zone where he can see little, even when the water is clear. He cannot talk to his diving partner because of the mouth-blocking air hose, but even were he unencumbered, he could not be heard for more than a few inches. Although most of the diver's sense organs are of limited use to him when submerged, this does not mean that submerged vertebrates lack acute sensory perception, but rather that the organs of submerged animals are adapted to function under water, and the interrelationships of various types of sensory perception for aquatic animals are simply quite different from those of terrestrial ones.

An angler who has never been submerged often assumes that the sensory organs of fishes are similar in function to his own. Thus, if he sees a fish in the water, he may take it for granted that the fish views him as an upright land animal, or that it is too low in the vertebrate scale to recognize him as a potential danger (which probably is a mistake).

A nominal amount of research has been done on the sensory organs of fishes and their relationship to behavior. This chapter reviews these studies and attempts to develop reasonable concepts of the functioning of sensory organs in circumscribing the normal behavior of fishes.

VISION

Most fishes have functional eyes. All of the so-called game fishes and pan fishes have well-developed ones and use them in finding and capturing their foods. Color vision has been tested in a number of species, all of which appear to be color perceptive.

Color Vision

Investigations of color vision in largemouth bass[21] indicated that bass vision was similar to that of a man looking at objects through a strong yellow filter, i.e., the yellow filter made it difficult for the man to separate colors at the blue end of the spectrum. Tests of color vision in bluegills using red and green lights at variable intensities demonstrated the ability of these fish to distinguish these colors. After 100 practice trials, bluegills made 94 correct selections out of 101 tests.[67] Other investigations indicated that various fishes differed in their ability to separate colors although they had little difficulty in separating colors from shades of gray of equal intensity.[86] The elritze (a minnow) could distinguish blue from green but confused red with yellow. The stickleback could discriminate red from green, but not blue from yellow.[122]

Most of the kinds of fishes tested seemed to respond well to red, and either to shun or prefer it. In one series of experiments, untrained mud minnows and common shiners were stimulated by red. In daylight the mud minnows had a respiratory rate of 30 per minute. When a ruby glass was placed over the source of light, the fishes settled to the bottom, had fits of trembling, and more than doubled their rate of opercular movement. The common shiners "breathed" 60 times per minute in diffuse daylight, 85 times per minute when a carbon filament light was turned on in addition, and 150 times per minute when a ruby filter was placed over the light.

When trained to feed in response to a definite color, small fishes that were offered a whole spectrum on the wall of the aquarium gathered in the particular region of color to which they had been conditioned, and followed the movement of the spectrum. Carp were trained to give a positive response to a violet disc but a negative one to a blue disc, and to move to a white triangle in preference to a white square. When confronted with a violet square and a blue triangle, these fish went to the violet square in preference to the blue triangle, suggesting that the stimulus of color was stronger than the stimulus of shape.

These laboratory experiments indicate the importance of color in the vision of fishes. Most fishermen are aware of the reaction shown by largemouth bass to red, orange, and yellow. In an Illinois lake, studies made in the daytime indicated that red and white casting baits had a catch rate for largemouth bass of 3.5 times that of the next most often listed color, which was black.[32,33] Among fly rod lures, yellow seemed to be the color most acceptable to the largemouths; white or combinations of white and other colors caught the second greatest number of fish. Black lures were important in both casting and fly rod sizes; some fishermen believe that fish strike black lures because they see these baits poorly and strike out of curiosity. Black plugs that create a disturbance at the surface of the water are often very effective for night fishing. Fish swimming below such a surface lure at night follow the water disturbance and may see the indefinite outline of the lure.

Underwater observations of the behavior of smallmouth bass in a quarry lake supported the idea that colors of lures were important. Smallmouths lying in several feet of water along a steep bank were presented with variously colored floating fly rod "poppers" of cork and hair by a fisherman operating from a boat. A diver equipped with scuba* watched the behavior of fish as the "poppers" were moved overhead. Red and yellow "poppers" obviously excited the fish and even when they did not strike they often made short runs under the baits. They were particularly excited by "gantron" baits (covered with paints having high reflecting qualities) in very bright yellow. Poppers of blues, greens, white, and black seemed to stimulate very little interest in this species.

Tests of the effectiveness of various colored gill nets in catching European perch, *Perca fluviatilis,* indicated a decreasing efficiency sequence of green, red, brown, black, blue, white, yellow.[90]

Underwater Vision

A description of a fish's underwater vision is given by Walls[122] as follows: "... if a fish looks slantingly upward at the water surface, he cannot see through it, but instead sees mirrored upon it objects which are on the bottom at a distance (Fig. 8.1). If he looks more directly upward, he sees into the air. In effect there is a circular window in the surface through

---

[1]*Self-contained underwater breathing apparatus.

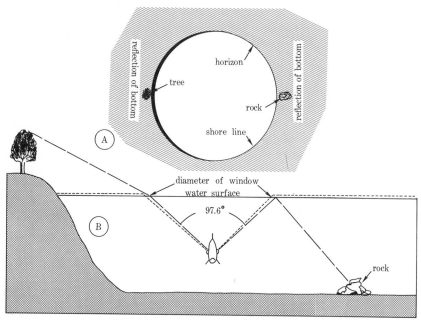

Fig. 8.1 (A) Visual field of a fish looking upward. (B) Horizontal view of the visual field (from Walls, G. L., 1942, *The Vertebrate Eye and its Adaptive Radiation,* Cranbrook Institute of Science Bulletin 19, Bloomfield Hills, Michigan).

which he can look. This window enlarges if he sinks, shrinks if he rises, but always subtends an angle of 97.6° (in fresh water) at his eyes (Fig. 8.1B). If the bottom is distant, the surface outside the window is silvery with the reflection of the light scattered in the water, and this light of course always washes over and dilutes the image of the bottom, even when the latter is close enough to the surface to be seen reflected from it.

"Through his surface window the fish sees everything from zenith to horizon in all directions. This hemispherical aerial field is not narrowed or widened according to the size of the window and depth of the fish. It always contains everything above the plane tangent to the water surface at the rim of the window, but the distortion and brightness of objects within it do vary. The objects seen proportionately largest are those directly overhead. If an object should swing down a semicircle from the zenith toward the horizon, along a meridian of the aerial hemisphere, it would get shorter and shorter in its meridional length and in its width measured parallel to the surface. Thus, even though its linear distance from the fish were constant, its apparent size would become smaller, the closer it approached the horizon. It would be seen more and more dimly, too, for light rays which make small angles with the water are largely reflected, and but little of such light is refracted down through the surface to enter the eye of a fish.

"The entire circumference of the 'horizon' which a swimming man could see by treading water and rotating 360° on his axis, is, for the fish, contracted to the few inches or feet of circumference of his surface window (Fig. 8.1A and B). It follows that a man standing on the bank of a pool is seen as a tiny doll by a fish which is a few yards away and only a few inches below the surface. Our tendency is to suppose that the fish will see us more poorly still, just as we see him less well, if he drops deeper in the water, but since dropping lower enlarges his window, it magnifies objects on the shore—magnifies them, that is, as compared with their apparent size when the window is smaller. To see the fishermen optimally, then, the fish must seek a depth from which the improvement of visibility through enlargement is not cancelled by the loss of light through the greater distance of water through which the rays must travel to his eyes. The poor fish is thus fated never to see us as we are—even through the flat glass side of an aquarium tank" (figure references in parentheses mine.)

A system of signalling by "visual images" is common to the majority of fishes as well as to many mammals and birds.[88,102] Some of these "visual images" are postures of nutrition, of danger, of passive defense, of fear, of defeat, of aggression, and of female attraction. Although these displays are largely visual, they sometimes involve other sensory organs in combination with vision, such as in the fright reaction described by von Frisch[39] (p. 306). Signalling by visual posturing is highly developed among the nest-building sunfishes (Centrarchidae) and will be described later in this chapter.

The eyes of most kinds of fish protrude enough and are located on the body in a position to give a full visual field. This is necessary because a fish has no neck, a situation that is not compensated for by his buoyancy and ability to rotate on his vertical axis.

Changing Pigmentation

Many years ago while stationed at the Rock Creek Hatchery in south central Nebraska, I observed some very large *black* rainbow trout in the small spring-fed rocky stream that meandered through the hatchery grounds. The hatchery superintendent told me they were blind "spawners" (fish used for stripping eggs and sperm in artificial trout propagation) that had been injured and later released in the creek. For something to do on a Sunday afternoon, four of us decided to catch one of these black trout; using two minnow seines, one above and one below a fish, we tried to trap him in the bag of one or the other of the seines. He always escaped, usually by finding an opening under the seine when a rock caused a momentary lifting of the lead line. The fish was as capable of avoiding capture as if it had functional eyes, except that once it escaped the net it did not seek cover as a normal trout would do. The dark color of these trout is characteristic of fish that are totally blind.

The relationship of light to the intensity of a fish's pigmentation is described by Walls:[122] (1) when no light is striking a fish (with or without functional eyes) the melanophores (dark pigment cells) "contract." (2) When light strikes only the skin (whether the eyes are present or not) the melanophores "expand." (3) If more of any light entering the eye strikes the upper part of the retina, the melanophores "contract" despite the tendency mentioned in (2). (4) If more of the light entering the eye strikes the lower part of the retina, the inhibitory effect of the tendency given in (3) upon the tendency in (2) is ineffective and the melanophores expand. Thus the extent of pigmentation depends upon a combination of stimuli upon the skin and eyes. A fish that is completely blind darkens in the light because there is no functional eye to inhibit the innate tendency of the illuminated melanophores to expand. Fish taken from muddy water are usually light in color because they are exposed to limited light.

Direct Observation and Sun Orientation

Sun orientation consists of a change in angle of an animal's directed movement in relation to position of the sun throughout the daily cycle. This rhythmic orientation may be evident in a fish's daily behavior pattern.[108]

According to Hasler et al.[57] the eyes of fishes are useful in orientation. These investigators demonstrated that white bass in Lake Mendota (Wisconsin) moved in a definite direction when transported from one part of the lake to another on clear days, but when displaced on cloudy days, or if blinded by eye caps, they moved at random. These invesitgators demonstrated in laboratory experiments that the sun was a source for orientation (whether the "sun" was natural or "artificial") and that the fish had a biological "clock" that operated in combination with the sun to allow compensation of movement for changing sun angles at different times of day.

In some earlier experiments, Hasler[53] had discovered that the elritze (a European minnow) used minute marks on the wall and floor of its tank for orientation rather than the presence of an artificial "sun." It was only after removing all visible marks in the tank during training over a long period of time that these fish were taught to associate a 90° angle of a "sun" to a feeding position. Even sunfish trained to artificial light cycles showed evidence of effective orientation.[109]

Green sunfish and post-cichlids were trained to compass directions under the sun at Madison, Wisconsin, in the Northern Hemisphere, and then were flown south to the equator and on into the Southern Hemisphere.[58] At the new experimental locations a green sunfish continued to change its angle of movement in the same direction as in the original northern latitude even though the sun at the equator was much higher than at Madison. However, these tests under a high sun caused fish to become disoriented during the afternoon of the first day. Both fish eventually became adapted to the change from north to south.

With a combination of sun orientation and/or the demonstrated ability of a fish to orient through observation of inconspicuous "landmarks" under water, it is little wonder that they show considerable ability to return to "home" territory after having been displaced. As will be described later, other sensory organs aid in "homing."

Light Sensitivity

The eyes and other light-sensitive organs of fishes control to some extent the relative position of fish in a body of water. Fish placed in a tank containing a light gradient selected the level of illumination most satisfying to them and were restricted in their movements by light above a certain intensity.[131] Light affects many activities of fishes: feeding, defense, daily and seasonal vertical migrations, reproduction, and general activity.[83] Reaction to light also may change as a fish grows from fry to adult size.[100] An important reason why electrofishing at night is so much more efficient than in daytime is because certain kinds and sizes of fishes usually found in deep water move into shallow water with the coming of darkness.

Many kinds of fishes show diurnal rhythms associated with the changing intensity of light. Elritze kept in a tank were active during the day and quiet at night, but their behavior was reversed if they were given hollow bricks in which to take cover and thus avoid bright light.[70] When cover was available, they were active at sunrise and sunset. Minnows kept in continuous darkness showed no rhythm of locomotor activity. Blinded minnows responded to daily variations in light intensity and were more active at night than during the day. These and many other laboratory experiments demonstrate the high light-sensitivity of most kinds of fishes.

Some species prefer semidarkness and are so sensitive to light that they exhibit extreme agitation if forced to swim in illuminated clear water.

Walleyes in Lake Gobegic (Michigan) were so sensitive to an automobile floodlight at close range that they would collide with rocks or beach themselves in their attempts to escape.[34]

Fingerling channel catfish being reared in turbid river water in wooden hatchery troughs exhibited extreme fright when clear water was turned on them while the troughs were being cleaned. When black bullheads are placed in an aquarium in strong light they tend to pile up, each fish trying to hide under the others. Smallmouth bass, redear sunfish, and grass pike in laboratory tanks have been observed to die of shock when the lights in the aquarium room were turned on at night.

HEARING

Laboratory experiments using modern equipment have established that all species studied have the ability to hear. The range of tone perception is believed to vary from 8 to 22,000 cycles per second (cps). The "ears" of fishes are internal and consist of a sacculus and lagena *(pars inferior)* believed to be responsible for hearing, and a utriculus and semicircular canal system *(pars superior)* concerned with equilibration. In some species the *pars superior* may take part in the perception of tones. In the Ostariophysi (examples are goldfish and yellow bullhead), the connection of the air bladder with the "ear" by Weber's ossicles increases the ability of fish to hear. Perception of very low frequencies is generally attributed to sensory organs in the skin.

Various species of common warmwater fishes have different ranges of sound perception; for example, the range of the bluegill is 35—9860 cps,[115] for the yellow bullhead 210—1840 cps.[72] and for the carp 8—22,000 cps.[105] These ranges cover a part of the range of human speech, but a great deal of intensity is lost between air and water, so that it would be difficult for a fish to hear a fisherman talking. This is not true for vibrations transmitted through the bottom of a boat or from walking with "heavy feet" along the water's edge. The disturbance caused by rowing or paddling where the oarsman is careless about letting oars or paddle hit or scrape the edge of the boat is undoubtedly heard by fishes.

Sound Location

Fish can learn to distinguish between tones of different intensities and are able to distinguish a change in frequency (one-fifth of an octave) in a continuously sounding source.

According to Kleerekoper and Chagnon,[71] creek chubs were able to locate a source of vibration and move toward it along curved pathways which probably represented fields of higher intensity such as are produced by the crests of interfering waves or by a standing wave.

Sound Production

Many kinds of fishes are capable of producing sounds, but production in the range audible to humans appears to be limited to the bony fishes (Teleostei). The sounds may be pinging sounds, thumpings, or stridulations made by rubbing together parts of the skeleton, or by vibrating an elastic spring muscle over the swim bladder.[85] Fish emit different sounds during different activities and can use their hearing as a kind of radar to detect the location of food and to avoid obstacles.[1]

Noises made by fishes are associated with spawning, danger, the presence of food, rivalry between males, schooling, and territorial behavior.[72,101,103]

Among freshwater fishes known to produce sounds are the sheepshead or drum, several kinds of minnows (Cyprinidae),[31,126] several kinds of cichlids,[93] and the catfishes. Others probably produce vibrations of various frequencies beyond the ability of the human ear to hear.

Records of sound produced by freshwater drum were made in Lake Winnebago (Wisconsin) using a Type H-11 hydrophone (U.S. Navy).[107] The sheepshead started "drumming" in early May and continued at a decreased intensity until the end of August. Drumming began about 10 a.m., and continued until sunset; highest drumming activity occurred during the afternoon. Sounds were produced by sexually mature males only and appeared to be for communication during the spawning season.

The drumming sound of the sheepshead is produced by muscular contractions which actuate a tendon-like structure across the swim bladder. The frequency spectrogram of the sounds produced covers a broad range of frequencies between 150 and 2000 cps, with the largest relative amplitudes within the range of 250 to 400 cps.

In the blacktail shiner and the red shiner only the ripe females produced sounds. These sounds were useful in attracting ripe males of their own species.[31] The satinfin shiner is reported to make a sound similar to the sound made when one strikes wood with his knuckles. These sounds were produced when males fought and when males and females courted. Isolated females also produced fainter, less frequent knocks than males, so that it was impossible to positively identify the source of the sound when males and females were together. Males also made a purring sound when actively courting females.[126]

Many species of marine fishes are known to produce sounds, and some deep-sea forms are believed to use their sound-producing apparatus to engage in echo-sounding.[48]

ODOR PERCEPTION AND TASTE

Fishes demonstrate an ability to taste and "smell" substances dissolved in water. In fact the sense of "smell" appears to be very highly developed and probably has many functions other than that of food finding. The catfishes are largely dependent upon the sense of smell in many of their biological functions,[10] and they are even able to identify other individual fishes by odor.[120] Fishes living in the pools of a small stream apparently orient themselves to these locations by a combined use of sight and odor perception.[49,117] It is of some interest to note here that detergents are damaging to the chemoreceptors of the catfishes *(Ictalurus)*.[9]

Terrestrial animals are able to detect an odor when (according to one theory) minute particles of a substance are dissolved on membranes associated with sensory cells of olfactory nerves. These minute particles are carried on air current and are, in some instances, subject to dessication. One modern theory of odor perception suggests that substances having odor interfere with enzyme-catalyzed reactions in the receptors. The fact that enzymes are affected in their action by minute amounts of many substances may explain the wide range of compounds that possess odors. The ability of animals, including man, to recognize faint odors in the presence of a constant strong odor is explained by the rapid reversibility of inhibitory effects on enzymes of odors continuously applied at a constant level. The strong odor of a soybean processing plant (although not unpleasant to many people) does not obscure a weaker but more delectable odor of broiling steak.

There is no indication that the acuity of olfaction in fishes is any less than that of terrestrial animals.

Location of Taste Organs

In many fishes, taste buds occur on the outer surface of the body as well as in the mouth. This is often demonstrated by lowering a piece of raw meat on a string into an aquarium so that it approaches the tail of a black bullhead. The fish will immediately turn and grasp the meat. Experiments have shown that taste buds are most abundant in the barbels of the bullhead but lesser numbers are scattered over the surface of the body and tail.[65]

This wide distribution of taste buds is characteristic of fishes that normally live in turbid waters such as bullheads and other catfishes, carp, and some of the other fishes that live and feed on the bottom. Fishes such as bass and sunfish (Centrarchidae) that feed primarily by sight have less well developed and less widely distributed taste buds. However, observations substantiate a general hypothesis that the outer surface of most fishes are sensitive to a variety of mild chemical stimuli.

Bullheads and other fishes that have taste organs scattered over the outer surface of the body use their olfactory organs for locating food at a distance.[52] Tests of bullheads with barbels removed (taste) and others with olfactory tracts severed (odor perception) demonstrated that odor perception was more important than taste in locating earthworms in a cheesecloth sack.

Olmsted[94] tested bullheads with many natural substances to determine which ones proved stimulating to them. Using thirty pairs of fish throughout a fairly long period of time, he charted the number of bites made by each pair during the trials extending for one-half hour. Materials used for testing the fish were graded by using an arbitrary scale from 100 to 0; most stimulating materials were rated near 100 and lesser ones accordingly lower. In these experiments he discovered that human saliva rated below earthworms and liver, but was rather high in its overall rating. Thus the custom of "spitting on one's bait" is apparently more than a superstition.

Some Uses of Odor Perception

Odor perception is less limited by water than is vision and hearing. For this reason the olfactory organs of fishes are highly developed and extensively used for many purposes.

Schooling. Wrede[132] discovered that schools of elritze were held together by a substance in the mucus of that species; the introduction of mucus from these minnows into a part of an aquarium would cause the minnows in the aquarium to congregate there. Vision appeared to be important in schooling during daylight hours, but the stimulus of odor held the schools together in darkness. "Both blinded and hind-brain-extirpated fish could be trained to these substances, indicating chemoreception, although animals with nose intact responded best."[132] Schools of young silver salmon in an aquarium remained intact as long as the room was lighted, but when the light was extinguished and infrared substituted, dispersal of the school was complete in a matter of a few seconds, indicating that in this case, schooling depended entirely upon vision.[5]

Fright Reaction. Blinded elritze that did not respond to pike mucus were placed in an aquarium with a pike that captured some of them.

When those remaining were tested with a combination pike and elritze odor, they gave a severe fright reaction. Thus, when these minnows show a reaction to odors of several other fishes, it may be that the reaction is due to past experience with these fishes and is a learned rather than an innate response.

In a long series of experiments, von Frisch[39] tested a substance exuded by an injured elritze minnow which he called "Schreckstoff" (alarm substance). This material would cause an alarm reaction (Schreckreaktion) when released in a school of uninjured minnows. Quantitatively, when 100 ml of this solution was poured into aquaria of 25- to 150-liter capacity, the minnows gave pronounced fear reactions. The alarm-causing material was mostly in the skin, because extracts from minnow intestine and liver gave no reaction, and extracts from gills, muscle, and ovaries were from one-tenth to one-hundredth as active as skin extracts. Minnows with severed olfactory nerves would not respond to the substance; for this reason von Frisch concluded that the alarm substance was odoriferous. Huttel[68] pointed out that the alarm substance of the elritze was a purin- or pterin-like substance.

That the alarm reaction may be transmitted by sight alone was demonstrated by Verheijen[121] when he placed two aquaria containing elritze side by side and dropped tissue juice into one aquarium to produce typical fright reactions. Minnows in the adjacent aquarium eventually huddled together in a tight "fright" school, but were about 10 sec slower in their reaction than were the minnows stimulated with "fright" juice.

Forrester[38] described an unsuccessful attempt to drive young pink salmon to the lower end of a long channel where they were to be surrounded by a seine for tagging. The plan was to have men start at the upper end of the channel and wade down, beating the water as they moved to drive the fish ahead of them. When the seine closed the escape route almost no salmon were trapped. They had escaped the drive by moving lateraly instead of downstream.

On a second attempt the beaters were supplied each with a paw of a freshly killed bear which they periodically dipped in the water. The salmon became violently agitated and the majority turned from facing the current and bolted downstream to lower end of the channel where they were easily surrounded by the seine. In the succeeding few days this method was used several times with great success. Forrester concluded that bear odor was an extremely effective repellent for pink salmon.

Identification of Common and Uncommon Odors.   Fisheries researchers at the University of Wisconsin[52] demonstrated that blinded bluntnose minnows, after a training of 2.5 months, were able to distinguish between odors of the plants, water milfoil, *Myriophyllum exalbescens,* and coontail, *Ceratophyllum demersum,* when rewarded with food and punished with electric shock. These minnows were able to detect a water rinse of a sprig of these aquatic plants diluted 1:10,000. Hasler and Wisby[59] found that bluntnose minnows could detect phenols at concentrations of 0.01 ppm and could discriminate between phenol and p-chlorophenol at concentrations of 5×10^{-4} ppm.

These studies suggest that olfaction in fishes (at least in some species) may be as important in the routine of day to day existence as is olfaction in dogs. Fish may not be so obvious in their use of the sense of smell as are dogs, but there is little doubt that they may recognize a "home" environment, identify individual fishes of their kind, as well as those of other kinds, and perform other functions through the use of olfactory organs. Further experiments indicate that some fishes are "blood-hounds" in their use of the sense of smell. This is particularly true of fishes that make long migrations.

Odor as an Aid in Migration. Biologists have long searched for an explanation for the return migration of salmon to a specific location in a home stream. These fish are spawned in freshwater streams, usually many miles from the oceans. After spending several months in the stream where they were spawned, they gradually work seaward, finally leaving fresh water, for a period of several years in the ocean. When they reach sexual maturity, they return to the stream system where they were spawned, migrate upstream, always selecting the right branch or tributary until they return to the location of their origin, where they in turn spawn. Hasler and Wisby[60] have postulated that salmon must find the way back to their place of origin through their retention of olfactory impressions of the stream. In order for such a hypothesis to be true, investigators would have to be able to give an affirmative answer to the following questions: *(1)* Do streams have characteristic odors to which fish can react, and, if so, what is the nature of the odor? *(2)* Can salmon detect and discriminate between such odors if they do exist? *(3)* Can salmon retain odor impressions from youth to maturity?

They began by testing unconditioned salmon fry with odoriferous substances[127] to find ones that the salmon fry gave evidence of liking or disliking. Salmon fry were placed in a central water-filled compartment of an apparatus and a test substance was introduced into one of four tributary arms through which water flowed to supply the center compartment. Gates at the openings of the tubes were opened and the fry were allowed to enter the tubes of their choice. Their distribution after the test was recorded and compared with the distribution obtained when no odor was introduced.

Many organic odors were tested in this manner. None was found which would attract salmon, but morpholine seemed to fit the necessary requirements; it was soluble in water permitting accurate dilutions, detectable in very low concentrations (easily detected at 1×10^{-6} ppm) making the treatment of large volumes of water feasible, and chemically stable under stream conditions. At low concentrations, morpholine was neither an attractant nor repellent, so that salmon could be conditioned to it in either direction. Thus salmon fry which hatched in a stream treated with a low concentration of morpholine should associate that odor with the spawning site when they returned several years later. This would give the stream a characteristic odor [and satisfy condition *(1)*]. Salmon have already shown evidence of detecting this odor at concentrations as low as 1×10^{-6} ppm [condition *(2)*], and if they were able to retain odor impressions from youth to maturity they should have no difficulty in arriving at the original spawning site. A further and a very crucial test would be an attempt to decoy the salmon conditioned to morpholine up the wrong stream branch by treating that branch with morpholine. If the salmon entered the wrong branch, it would be certain proof that they were migrating entirely by odor impressions. However, if they did not enter the wrong branch, the odor theory would not necessarily be disproved because the odor impression of the "home" stream might consist of a complex of odors including morpholine, and the salmon might not have accepted the other components making up the odor complex (excluding morpholine) of the wrong stream branch. Salmon could be expected to enter a "wrong" stream branch when the odor impression for morpholine completely subordinated other stream odors. Field tests to measure the possibilities given above have not been completed.

In further experiments on odor recognition in salmon, sexually ripe coho salmon were captured in each of two branches of the Issaquah River in Washington, and marked and returned downstream below the junction of the two branches to remake the upstream run and reselect the correct branch.[128] In one half of the fish the nasal sac was plugged with cotton. Most of the normal fish repeated their former stream choice upon reaching the fork while the plugged-nose fish selected one or the other of the branches in nearly random fashion. Although the pressure of the cotton plugs in the nasal sacs of the plugged-nose salmon may have influenced their behavior (and no similar pressure was applied to the normal fish), the experiment is indicative of the importance of the olfactory system in the migration of these fish.

Brett and MacKinnon[20] made a series of tests to explore the sense of smell in migrating coho and spring salmon. When dilute solutions of various chemicals were introduced in the path of salmon moving up a fish ladder, they caused no significant change in migration rate. However, a dilute rinse of mammalian skins had a distinct repellent action, suggesting that the salmon may have been conditioned against such odors.

These experiments with salmon indicate that the olfactory organs are very important in orientation and migration of these fishes. The long migrations of salmon are necessary in order that the fish complete its life cycle; therefore one might expect that sensory development of organs useful in making the long journey might be more highly developed in salmon than in fishes living a fairly localized existence.

Odor as an Aid in Homing. Homing, home range, and territoriality of fishes will be discussed later in Chapter 8. Displaced fishes find their way back to home areas by using a combination of sensory organs. However, Gunning[49] was able to show that odor orientation was more important than vision in the rapid return of a fish to its home area. In fact, blind fishes with unimpaired olfactory organs were able to return to a home range, after being displaced experimentally, as quickly and accurately as control (normal) fishes.

More detailed and technical information on the functioning of the sensory organs of fishes may be found in the book *The Physiology of Fishes,* Vol. 2, edited by Margaret E. Brown.[22]

TEMPERATURE RECEPTION AND RESPONSES

The body of a fish is almost uninsulated from the temperature of the water surrounding it and does not maintain a constant body temperature. This does not mean that they are insensitive to temperature changes or cannot be killed by high or low temperatures. Fishes frequently expire through exposure when they are moved from extremes of heat and cold within the north-south range of a species. For example, red-ear sunfish transferred from northern Texas to central Illinois lived during the summer but died over the first winter, in all probability from the cold. There is also a likelihood that bluegills from northern Michigan would die from high water temperatures if moved to southern Alabama or Georgia. However, through a series of transplants, gambusia, a live-bearing top minnow indigenous to the southern United States, was purposely moved northward from its normal range nearly 700 miles during a period of about twenty years. This was accomplished in four or five stages: offspring of the fishes that survived one or more winters at one stage were in turn moved northward to the next stage until they were thriving in southern Michigan.[74] These fish are now being successfully established as far north as Winnipeg, Manitoba, Canada.[112]

Sensitivity to Temperature Change

Variations or changes in temperature affect production of carp[6] and may block simple reflexes.[104] Also affected are swimming ability of smallmouth fry[79] and speed of perch swimming.[63] Temperature along with other factors may influence depth distribution of perch and crappies throughout the seasons;[117,118] it is also believed to be the final triggering mechanism for spawning of many fishes.[69] Cold temperatures make all fish sluggish, and brown bullheads react still further by burying themselves in lake bottom sediments[81] when water temperatures are below 65°F.

Although temperature receptors have not been discovered in a fish's skin, there is little doubt that fish are capable of feeling relatively slight changes in temperature. Sullivan[119] and others[23,24] describe experiments in which fish were fed at the same time that the temperature was slightly raised so that feeding became associated with small rises in temperature. After a training period, a temperature rise as small as 0.03–0.1°C would produce a feeding reaction. By the direct approach, employing electrophysiological equipment, it has been demonstrated that a rising temperature (within a range of 4 to 17°C) increased the frequency of rhythmic impulses in trunk lateral line nerves, with about a twofold increase in frequency for each 4° temperature rise.

After fish were shown to be sensitive to small changes in temperature, the next approach was to see how they were affected by rapidly increasing temperature. There was no response until a specific "response temperature" of 27°C (80.6°F) was reached, when the fish suddenly began vigorous swimming movements.[106] In reverse, fish plunged into cold water reacted immediately with violent bursts of activity followed by benumbed inactivity.[19]

Changes in temperature of a few degrees Centigrade, with time for the body of the fish to equilibrate with the water (20 min), resulted in a little movement at low temperatures, increasing as the temperature was raised to a peak which occurred at the temperature that the species normally selected in a temperature gradient. If the temperature were raised further, activity decreased reaching a second low several degrees below the lethal level.[19] If the temperature were increased further, movement again increased to a second peak, after which activity stopped abruptly and the animal died. These experiments demonstrate the relationship of temperature to activity levels in fishes. Peaks of activity were modified to some extent by exposure to low or high temperatures for extensive periods prior to testing.

Mortalities Caused by High Temperatures

Fishes are occasionally killed by high water temperatures even when out of doors in natural waters (see Chapter 3, p. 70), for example, Bailey[7] recorded such a mortality of fishes in a part of Bass Lake, Livingston County, Michigan, that had become separated from the main lake by a gravel ridge. At the time of the kill the pond was about one-fourth acre with a maximum depth of five inches.

On the afternoon of July 12, 1952, the water in this pond reached a temperature of 38°C (100.4 °F) and fish began to die without showing symptoms of oxygen shortage. Not all of the fishes died, and several days later there were still live killifish and gambusia (a southern species), as well as bluegills, pumpkinseeds, longear and green sunfish, all apparently in good condition. Most of the mud minnows, chubsuckers, golden shiners, blacknose shiners, blackchin shiners, sand shiners, and bluntnose minnows were dead, as were the brown and yellow bullheads, stonecats, madtoms, and Iowa darters. Among the minnows, catfish, and madtoms, the smaller individuals survived while the longer ones died.

Even fishes normally living in tropical climates may be killed by high water temperatures not greatly exceeding those reported by Bailey.[7] Lethal temperatures for tilapias, *T. mossambica*, acclimated to 30°C (86°F) were killed at temperatures of 38.25°C (102°F).[3]

The interpretations of all temperature reactions, including lethal reactions, are complicated because they are dependent upon the previous acclimation of test animals, are affected by diet, length of photoperiod, and probably by other factors related to the physiology of the fish. Thermal deaths may be complicated by oxygen and carbon dioxide tensions, mineral content, and salinity of the water.[41] When high temperature mortality occurs out-of-doors, as described by Bailey above, one can hardly explain why some fish died and others survived.

Temperature Acclimation

Fish in pools that are drying up may die of high water temperatures or high or low dissolved oxygen tensions. The temperature at which a fish dies (both high and low) is affected by the temperature to which the fish was acclimated prior to exposure. Brett[19] lists upper and lower lethal temperatures for a number of freshwater fishes when these fishes previously had been acclimated to various temperatures. Lethal temperatures for three warmwater fishes listed by Brett are given in Table 8.1.

The changes in a fish's ability to tolerate low or high temperatures resulting from a change in acclimation temperature probably do not have a great deal of survival value under natural conditions. It has been shown by Brett and others that the rate of increase in ability to tolerate higher temperatures is relatively rapid, requiring twenty-four hours at temperatures above 20°C (68°F). Conversely the loss in this increased tolerance to high temperatures and a gain in resistance to low temperatures is much slower, requiring as much as twenty days to approach complete acclimation in some species. Thus, sudden drops in air temperatures that cause rapid and abnormal cooling of natural waters might cause the death of fishes acclimated to warm waters, whereas warm air temperatures resulting in rapid and abnormal warming of cold waters might have little effect because the fish could become acclimated to higher temperatures almost as fast as the water temperature could increase.

The relationship between acclimation temperatures and lethal temperatures in fishes is undoubtedly a factor in the survival of fishes transported overland in tanks, particularly where fish are cooled abnormally through the use of ice or refrigerated tanks.

Preferred Temperatures

Anglers have shown considerable interest in the temperatures which sport fishes of various species prefer during summer months. They be-

Table 8.1   Lethal Temperatures for Three Warmwater Fishes

	High Temperatures		Low Temperatures	
	Acclimation Temp.	Lethal Temp.	Acclimation Temp.	Lethal Temp.
Largemouth bass	20°C (68°F)	32.5°C (90.5°F)	20°C (68°F)	5.5°C (41.9°F)
	25°C (77°F)	34.5°C (94.1°F)		
	30°C (86°F)	36.4°C (97.5°F)	30°C (86°F)	11.8°C (53.2°F)
Bluegill	15°C (59°F)	30.7°C (87.3°F)	15°C (59°F)	2.5°C (36.5°F)
	20°C (68°F)	31.5°C (88.7°F)	20°C (68°F)	5°C (41°F)
	30°C (86°F)	33.8°C (92.8°F)	25°C (77°F)	7.5°C (45.5°F)
			30°C (86°F)	11.1°C (51.9°F)
Yellow perch	5°C (41°F)	21.3°C (70.3°F)	10°C (50°F)	1.1°C (34°F)
	10°C (50°F)	25°C (77°F)	25°C (77°F)	3.7°C (38.7°F)
	15°C (59°F)	27.7°C (81.9°F)		
	25°C (77°F)	29.7°C (85.5°F)		

lieve this knowledge will help in locating these fishes, which, of course, is the first step in catching them. Ferguson[36] made laboratory studies of the preferred temperature of yellow perch and compared his results with fishery biologists. He used Fry's definition of preferred temperature:[40] "The region, in an infinite range of temperature, at which a given population will congregate with more or less precision—a temperature around which all individuals will ultimately congregate, regardless of their thermal experience before being placed in the gradient."

The level of thermal acclimation influences the preferred temperature. In general, the preferred temperature is considerably higher than the acclimation temperature for fish that are acclimated to low temperatures.

The differences decrease up to the final preferendum where they coincide. In nature a fish may be prevented from selecting its true preferred temperature by light, feeding routines, social behavior, and dissolved gases.

Table 8.2 shows the preferred temperatures of some sport fish. This table represents a part of the table given by Ferguson.[36] Preferred temperatures for four species have been collected from two or more investigations, for regions that are often widely separated. For example, the preferred temperatures of walleyes in Norris Reservoir, Tennessee, are

Table 8.2   Field Observations of Some Species of Sport Fish and Temperatures Associated with Them. August Distributions and Temperatures Were Used Whenever Possible [a]

Species	Temperature °C	°F	Water	Location	Author
Largemouth bass	26.6-27.7	79.9-81.9	Norris Reservoir	Tenn.	Dendy, 1948
Spotted bass	23.5-24.4	74.3-75.9	Norris Reservoir	Tenn.	Dendy, 1948
Walleye	20.6	69.1	Trout Lake	Wis.	Hile and Juday, 1941
Walleye	22.7-23.2	72.9-73.8	Norris Reservoir	Tenn.	Dendy, 1948
Rock bass	14.7-21.3	58.5-70.3	Lakes	Wis.	Hile and Juday, 1941
Yellow perch	21.2	70.2	Lake Opeongo	Ontario	Ferguson, 1958
Yellow perch	21.0	69.8	Costello L.	Ontario	Ferguson, 1958
Yellow perch (small)	12.2	54.0	Muskellunge L.	Wis.	Hile and Juday, 1941
Yellow perch(large)	20.2	68.4	Muskellunge L.	Wis.	Hile and Juday, 1941
Yellow perch	20.2	68.4	Silver Lake	Wis.	Hile and Juday, 1941
Yellow perch	21.0	69.8	Nebish Lake	Wis.	Hile and Juday, 1941
Smallmouth bass	20.3-21.3	68.5-70.3	Nebish Lake	Wis.	Hile and Juday, 1941
Brook trout	14.2-20.3	57.6-6̄.5	Moosehead L.	Maine	Cooper and Fuller, 1945
Brook trout	12.0-20.0	53.6-68.0	Redrock L.	Ontario	Baldwin, 1948
Lake trout	10.0-15.5	50.0-59.9	Cayuga L.	N.Y.	Galligan, 1951
Lake trout	14.0	57.2	White L.	Ontario	Kennedy, 1941

a   From Ferguson.[36]

several degrees higher than those for walleyes in Trout Lake, Vilas County, Wisconsin, which is more than 1000 miles farther north. This is probably true also for largemouth and spotted bass although no information is at hand for bass in more northern locations. Fishes shown in table 8.2 are arranged in order of descending (higher to lower) temperature preferences.

There are a number of records of fish acclimated to low temperatures which have invaded warm water in spite of a lethal effect;[44,50] also, a concentration of fish (mostly white crappies) apparently caused by a temperature gradient of only 1 to 2°F has been recorded.[50]

Rising water temperatures in spring and early summer would eventually force species of fish preferring cool waters out of the upper layers of a lake. For example, the lake trout and walleyes of Trout Lake, Vilas County, Wisconsin, had always left the surface waters by the time spring was well advanced and successful fishermen caught these species after May by trolling with baits at depths of 25—100 ft.

BEHAVIOR PATTERNS

Fishes have many behavior patterns that are well known, partly because they are common to many species. Other behavior patterns of a more specific nature are familiar to many because the fish are common and widely distributed. Each group of fishes has its own characteristic reproductive pattern,[125] but the discussion in this chapter will be of more general types of activities.

Some Types of Behavior Patterns

Fishes are so often referred to as "schooling," that one may be led to believe that this is the normal social grouping for these animals. Although not all fishes show schooling tendencies, almost all display some sort of social behavior.

Social Groupings. Breder[18] recognized four degrees of social groupings among fishes: solitary, aggregating, schooling, and podding. Some kinds of fishes show more than one of these grouping classifications in relation to seasonal or sexual behavior. Breder's grouping classifications are defined as follows:

1. Solitary. Fishes that show zero or negative attraction toward others of their kind.

2. Aggregating. Fishes attracted to their kind by favorable temperature, local abundance of food, or other environmental detail, but which show no particular polarity as a group, nor is the group capable of any specific

directional movement. These fish are oriented without reference to other individuals.

3. Schooling. Fishes sufficiently attracted to one another to impel them to swim in substantially similar paths and perform as a troupe of like-acting individuals in which independence of action is reduced to near the vanishing point. Such a group of fishes is polarized and capable of forward movement as a unit.

4. Podding. Fishes packed so closely in groups as to leave no swimming clearance, i.e., these fish are actually in contact with one another. The individuals may or may not be polarized.

Schooling in fishes appears to be the result of a combination of visual and olfactory responses and these are of varying importance within the range of species that form schools.[62] Fish in schools exhibit less movement and consume less oxygen than do isolated individuals of the same species,[82] partly, no doubt, because schooling fishes appear to be under stress when isolated. Hergenrader and Hasler[63,64] in studying the schooling of perch in Lake Mendota (Wisconsin) discovered that the fish in the schools were more compact in summer than in winter, individuals being usually less than 1.5 ft apart in summer and more than 2.0 ft apart in winter. This was believed to be an effect related to greater visibility in winter even though the ice was often 50 cm (20 in.) thick. There was also a negative correlation between water temperature and school size ($r = -0.89$).

Among warmwater species, solitary and aggregating fishes are more common than schooling or podding fishes. Most species of centrarchids (sunfishes) are solitary or aggregating, although crappies might be considered as schooling under certain conditions. White bass and many kinds of minnows show well-defined schooling, as do bullheads, although under certain conditions the latter form pods. Aggregations, schools, and pods are, in general, without obvious leadership and may shift first in one direction and then in another. Leadership may be evident in schooling fish where a female is followed by a number of males. Schooling may have survival value in that the "confusion effect" of a large school of fishes may reduce the precision of a predator's attack.

Seasonal Rhythm. Most warmwater fishes have a fairly constant seasonal rhythm of activities. Being adapted to warm water, their movements tend to be inhibited by low water temperatures. Some forms such as the smallmouth bass spend the winter in a quiescent state in schools or groups. Others, such as the northern pike, are quite active in winter and move about constantly. Greenbank[45] set trap nets facing in both directions across the opening into Target Lake, a backwater area of the

Mississippi River (Wisconsin), during 40 days of winter and caught 3328 fish, most of which were black crappies, yellow bullheads, and bowfin. He found a positive correlation between total fish movement and the amount of snow cover on the ice. This movement was more related to reduced light conditions than to current, temperature, or dissolved oxygen.

Breder[17] in his treatise on the reproductive habits of North American sunfishes (Centrarchidae) stated that "hibernation" in most species was broken up at about 10°C (50°F), with a general movement from deep water to inshore areas. But not all of the centrarchids are quiescent in winter. Hansen[51] found that the crappies in Lake Decatur in central Illinois were more readily trapped in nets in fall, winter, and spring than in summer. The poorest trapping season for crappies in this lake was from about mid-July to late September. Other warmwater fishes also show a tendency to be less active during the hottest part of the summer than in spring and fall.

Daily Activity.   There are many records of daily activity patterns of warmwater fishes. Carlander and Cleary[25] describe three types of diurnal movements of fishes that they observed through the use of gill nets: *(1)* more activity at night than in the daytime; *(2)* more activity in daylight than in darkness; and *(3)* activity that resulted in movement from one habitat to another at different periods of the day. These authors listed walleyes and tullibee as being more active at night than in daytime, and perch and northern pike as being more active in the daytime. They stated that common suckers moved into shallow water at night and into deep water during the day, whereas carp and yellow bass moved into shallow water during the daytime and into deep water at night. Spoor and Schloemer[113] had previously reported an inshore and offshore movement of common suckers at Muskellunge Lake, Vilas County, Wisconsin, associated with darkness and daylight (No. *3* above). They could demonstrate no such directional movement in rock bass, but the peaks of activity (catches) for this species were at dusk and dawn, with considerable activity during the night. Hasler and Bardach[56] discovered an interesting daily migration of the perch in Lake Mendota (Madison, Wisconsin) beginning about the end of May and continuing into October. These fish moved toward shore in certain areas in the hours before sunset and, to a lesser degree, before sunrise. Once they reached the 18-ft (6-meter) contour they changed direction and cruised along parallel to the shore. With the coming of darkness these fish appeared to disperse rather suddenly. Fish caught at sunset were gorged with freshly ingested water fleas *(Daphnia),* which suggested that this movement may have been a feeding migration.

The difference in activity periods of closely related species is illustrated by laboratory experiments of Childers[27] using white and black crappies. These two species were placed in separate large aquaria and supplied with a known number of minnows. As the minnows were eaten, they were recorded and others were added to replace them. Both kinds of crappies consumed more minnows during the 2-hr dawn period and more food was consumed at night than during the day; however, the black crappies ate 2.5% of their food during daylight hours and the white crappies consumed 14.8% of their food in daylight. A similar difference in feeding habits of the two kinds of crappies is suggested by a trapping study conducted by David H. Thompson[51] in which 31% of the white crappies netted in Meredosia Bay (Illinois) were caught during the day and 69% at night. By comparison, 11% of the black crappies were caught during the day and 89% at night. "Night" included dusk, darkness and dawn.

Behavior of Individual Fish Species. Miller[88] made a very comprehensive study of the behavior of the pumpkinseed sunfish and compared this species with several other members of the genus *Lepomis,* including the orangespotted sunfish, bluegill, redbellied sunfish, *(auritus),* longeared sunfish, green sunfish, and pigmy sunfish, *Elassoma evergladei.* She described antagonistic behavior associated with nest guarding, and defined more than ten behavior patterns related to contacts between males or between females over territories, or related to the "peck order" of dominance where fishes were confined to aquaria.

Sunfishes appear to "sleep" in darkness and show a variety of "comfort" movements which Miller believes "occur with greater frequency when the animal is under stress caused by social or other environmental conditions." Some of the more common comfort movements are yawning, body bending, chafing (rubbing the body against a stick, stone, or the bottom), jerking, mouth snapping, and fin quivering.

The detailed behavior of other kinds of warmwater fishes is not as well known as is that of the sunfishes, but each species undoubtedly has very characteristic behavior patterns. In their work with the "natural" production of sunfish hybrids, Dr. William F. Childers and John Tranquilli (personal communication) believe that differences in the prespawning behavior of the several species of sunfishes that inhabit the same aquatic environment prevent hybridization between these species, and that interspecies crossing occurs only when visual prespawning behavior has been bypassed, such as might take place in a permanently turbid pond where a ripe female of one species might blunder into the nest of a ripe male of another species.

The details of behavior of species of game and pan fishes are of interest to fishery biologists because they sometimes suggest new approaches to fishery management; to anglers they are important because they may suggest new points of vulnerability.

Responses to Specific Stimuli

Many instances of fish activity resulting from a combination of stimuli have been recorded in fishery literature. Eschmeyer[35] found that when the fall drawdown of Norris Reservoir was begun in September (1942), the white bass, yellow bass, and sauger migrated upstream from Watts Bar Reservoir into the mouth of the Clinch River and upstream to Norris Dam. These fishes represented the larger individuals of the 1942 year class (the first) produced in Watts Bar Reservoir. The distance from Watts Bar Dam to Norris Dam is about 118 miles by water (river channel, 38 miles to the mouth of the Clinch, and about 80 miles up the Clinch), fishes appeared below Norris Dam. Apparently the stimulus for this unusual migration was the arrival of cooler water at Watts Bar Reservoir. Later, largemouth bass appeared in considerable numbers. A few largemouth bass were present in the river between the reservoirs, but white bass, yellow bass, and saugers were relatively scarce.

Fishes are sometimes stimulated to move by violent storms or in spring by the entrance of warm surface water into cold ponds or lakes. For example, wing nets set on March 9, 1942, in Fork Lake (Illinois) caught few fish until a warm rain of about one inch fell during the night of March 16. When this water drained into the pond, the fish were stimulated to move and when the wing nets were raised on March 17, they contained many more than the March "quota" of bluegills and some were released.[12]

Wood[130] assigns to Dr. C. M. Tarzwell the observation that largemouth bass move into newly flooded backwater areas with rising waters in less than 48 hr after flooding has begun and are the first to leave when waters begin to fall.

Whitmore, Warren, and Doudoroff[124] used a "channeled avoidance tank" to test the reaction of small largemouth bass, bluegills, and several kinds of juvenile salmon to various levels of oxygen tension. Marked avoidance of 1.5 mg/l dissolved oxygen was observed in tests of largemouth bass and some avoidance reaction was evident even with dissolved oxygen as high as 4.5 mg/l. In bluegills, avoidance reactions were definite at oxygen concentrations of about 1.5 and 3.0 mg/l, although the reaction at the latter concentration was not very pronounced. These experiments furnish proof that warmwater fishes are capable of adjusting their movements to avoid low concentrations of dissolved oxygen in the aquatic habitat. In contrast to the above Pearse and Achtenberg[98] believed that perch would enter deep stagnant waters of Lake Mendota where dissolved oxygen was very low.

Hyperactivity as a Lethal Factor

Under certain conditions death may follow violent muscular activity, such as struggling of fishes in a live box, responding to vigorous chasing, swimming through swift passages of water, or struggling on a trolling line.[15] Although death from exertion is more characteristic of trouts and salmon than of warmwater fishes, it may occur in certain of the more sensitive warmwater fishes such as gizzard shad, some minnows, and occasionally smallmouth bass.

The precise cause of death is unknown, but it is likely that the main cause is a severe acid—base disturbance following a large accumulation of lactic acid. The acid concentration becomes great enough to reduce the oxygen-combining power of the blood, reduce its alkali reserve or carbon dioxide-combining capacity, and alter the shape and probably the volume of the red cells.

Mortalities of fishes resulting from hyperactivity during handling and transportation might contribute to oxygen deficiencies in holding basins and tank trucks. This suggests the value of a tranquilizer in reducing oxygen requirements during fish-moving operations.

"Stay-at-Home" Fish

Largemouth bass were reported to rove over the entire water area of Third Sister Lake (Michigan) and showed almost no tendency to remain in one location.[8] In contrast some other fishes showed strong tendencies to remain within 30 yards of the point of original capture.[8] The same was true of bullheads where 39% were recaptured within 15 yards of the point of release and 81% within 100 yards. In other tests all of the bullheads recaptured more than once were taken at the same location each time, even though the time intervals between recaptures were several weeks or months.[110] Walleyes marked or tagged on their spawning areas were recaptured at the same locations in successive years.[34,29,95,30,37] Walleyes may be less restricted in their movements later in the season, although fishermen have discovered that these fish are often found in about the same location day after day.

Newly stocked fish may or may not move about, depending on the kind of fish and various other factors. Smallmouth bass (from ponds) stocked in a stream showed tendencies to either "stay put" or move upstream.[77] Stocked northern pike moved to all parts of 3643-acre Clear Lake (Iowa) within six months.[26]

Homing and Home Range

In general terms, homing is the ability of an animal to return, when displaced, to an area which may be considered its home range.[43,61] This home range may or may not be the location where the fish was spawned. The return of smallmouth bass to home pools in Jordan Creek (Illinois) is an example of a generalized type of homing.[76] Marked smallmouths were moved by tank truck to locations upstream and downstream from their home pools and many of them were able to find their way back to the pool from which they were taken originally. Some of these bass were even moved from their home stream into another tributary of the same river system several miles distant. At least one fish found its way back to its home pool although to do so required that it move down the stream in which it was released until it reached the larger river, then up this river to the mouth of the home creek, and finally upstream to its home pool. Once the fish reached the larger river it might be possible for it to identify the odor of water flowing from the home creek because the mouth of the creek to which it was taken was downstream from the home stream.

Displaced longear sunfish returned readily to home locations in an Indiana stream.[49] They moved both upstream and downstream to return to their home ranges, although those released in the stream below returned more rapidly than those released upstream from their home ranges. As mentioned previously, further tests demonstrated that olfactory organs were more important than vision in homing of longears released downstream from their home pools.

Investigations of homing of fishes in streams have brought to light the presence of a roving population that apparently does not show homing tendencies.[42,43,76,78] These roving fish are important in repopulating streams that have lost their fish populations through temporary but lethal pollution, or through severe drought. There is also some evidence for the presence of homing and roving populations in lakes.[96,97] Parker[96] found that approximately 31% of the smaller centrarchids (sunfishes) and 18% of the largemouth bass in Flora Lake (Wisconsin) "homed," as did 25% of the bass in nearby Dadik Lake.

Gerking[43] compiled a table of the species of marine and freshwater fishes that have shown homing capabilities. In the reproduction of this table (Table 8.3) marine fishes have been omitted.

Table 8.3 Species of Fish Known to Have Restricted Movement, not Associated with Spawning [a]

Species	Reference
Salmonidae: salmon family	
Brown trout	Schuck, Allen, Stefanich
Brook trout	Shetter, Stefanich, Newman
Rainbow trout	Stefanich, Holton, Newman
Cutthroat trout	Miller
Coregonidae: whitefish family	
Mountain whitefish	Stefanich
Catostomidae: sucker family	
Golden redhorse	Gerking
Hog sucker	Gerking
White sucker	Stefanich
Ictaluridae: catfish family	
Yellow bullhead	Shoemaker, Ball, Funk
Channel catfish	Harrison
Percidae	
Fantail darter	Winn
Iowa darter	Winn
Rainbow darter	Winn
Orangethroat darter	Winn
Greenside darter	Winn
Centrarchidae: sunfish family	
Bluegill	Ball
Longear sunfish	Gerking, Funk
Rock bass	Scott, Gerking, Funk
Green sunfish	Greenberg, Gerking
Largemouth bass	Parker and Hasler
Smallmouth bass	Larimore, Gerking, Funk
Spotted bass	Gerking
Pumpkinseed	Shoemaker
Spotted sunfish	Caldwell, Odum, and Hellier

[a] From Gerking[43] and others, but including only freshwater fishes.

There is a great deal of evidence that a fish which shows homing tendencies recognizes the area in which it lives and orients itself accordingly. Some fish also show territoriality, represented by an area which it will defend, and hierarchy of peck-order among its closest associates. These hierarchies develop very quickly with sunfish in aquaria.[46] According to Gerking[43] species which exhibit marked aggressive tendencies will show sedentary populations. Both Larkin[80] and Miller[89] recognize the importance of space requirements in determining population density and growth.

Some investigators wish to set aside the use of the term "homing" for the movements of those fishes which make long migrations to spawn in locations where they themselves were hatched. Well-known examples are the salmon and the eel. This point of distinction based on distance is probably a somewhat unnecessary refinement.

Parts of home ranges may be considered territories which the residents defend against all encroachment insofar as they are physically able. This is particularly true during the spawning season among fishes that build nests.

No one has yet described the roles of hearing, the sensory perception of semicircular canals, the kinesthetic senses, and the lateral line senses in orientation or homing, although auditory organs and the lateral line organs are believed to supplement vision and olfaction in helping to locate objects at a distance. These objects may be moving and thereby create mechanical disturbances and their presence and location may be perceived and accurately computed from the time relations of reflected water waves set up by the swimming movements of the fish itself. In moving water the presence of deflecting objects is readily recorded. This type of sensory perception is extremely important in turbid water where vision is impaired.

Theories of Migration in Fishes

It has been shown that vision and olfactory senses have a role in orientation and home-range recognition. Hasler et al,[57] have modified the classification of Griffin[47] to define the types of abilities required by fish that return home from varying distances.

Type I. The ability of an animal to find its way home by relying on local landmarks within familiar territory and the use of exploration in unfamiliar areas.

Type II. The ability to maintain a constant compass direction in unfamiliar territory.

Type III. The ability to head for home from unknown territories by true navigation.

The homing movements of displaced warmwater fishes are operative over relatively short distances as compared with the spawning (homing) migrations of such fishes as salmon, eel, and some other marine fishes. These fishes are able to migrate many thousands of miles and return with great precision to specific spawning locations where they themselves were hatched. Such migrations may involve the three types of homing abilities listed above: identifying local landmarks and exploring, maintaining a fixed direction in unfamiliar territory, and true navigation.

The migrations of the salmon have been studied more than those of any other fishes and serve to illustrate the complexity of these spawning movements. Salmon are spawned in coldwater streams tributary to the oceans and move downstream into salt water where they spend two to seven years at sea depending on the species. When they reach sexual maturity, they return to the same rivulet so consistently that populations in streams not far apart follow distinctly separate lines of evolution. Salmon belonging to the genus *Oncorhyncus* die after spawning, while those belonging to the genus *Salmo* may return to the home stream on several annual spawning trips.[54] Many salmon have been marked, either as young on their seaward migrations or as adults at sea. A few have been marked in the home stream, caught and remarked at sea, and then recaptured once more in the home stream.[16,66,99] These tag returns show that some salmon may migrate 1200 to 1700 miles to return "home."

A salmon approaching sexual maturity and stimulated by an urge to spawn is confronted by two problems: *(1)* finding the mouth of the river to which the salmon's home rivulet is tributary and *(2)* finding the actual location in the rivulet that will satisfy the homing urge.

The theory of odor recognition may be adequate to explain an upstream migration to specific spawning grounds, but it can hardly be very useful for finding the mouth of a home river from a distance of hundreds of miles. However, the fact that on sunny days white bass were able to return to their spawning area in Lake Mendota after having been caught in fyke nets, tagged, and released at one of several release stations, indicates that some kinds of fishes have a type of sun-orientation ability.[57] On cloudy days the white bass swam randomly. Perhaps salmon are also capable of finding their way by sun orientation (Type II, a method for maintaining fixed direction). Yet some observations have been made that suggest true navigation. Salmon are known to migrate at night in the sea and gill-net fishermen make night sets for them. Hasler[55] reports an observation of Clifford Barnes (University of Washington) who saw salmon migrating at night at right angles to his oceanographic research vessel. Because of a luminiscent sea, the school of large salmon was easily observed. The fish swam on a fairly straight course until out of sight.

Adult American eels, *Anguilla rostrata,* caught on their spawning migration downriver and placed in circular tanks oriented southward when allowed a view of only the sky, a direction representing their supposed breeding area in the region of the Saragasso Sea.[87] The southward orientation continued even if the eels were denied a view of the sky as long as they were exposed to the dual rhythm of light—dark. This appears to indicate that the eel seems capable of noncelestial orientation.

The migration of salmon, eels, and other migratory species over long distances of open ocean certainly demands an ability to navigate. How else could fishes keep from becoming "lost" and how else could they pinpoint an ocean location or the mouth of a specific river along a thousand miles of shoreline?

No warmwater fish shows migration habits and abilities for homing comparable to that of some marine fishes. The objective of summarizing homing in the salmon is to illustrate the extent of development of the sensory organs in fishes and to emphasize the complexity of their instinctive behavior patterns.

Responses of Fish to Angling

Angling is a mortality factor along with natural predation, diseases, old age, and other factors (Chapter 7). Angling might be called unnatural predation. A natural predator (man) causes the death of a fish through the degradation of a natural function of that fish (the fish engulfs an insect larva containing a hook and is caught, or strikes an artificial lure that imitates some natural food, and is hooked). This seems like a method of predation that is foolproof, i.e., the fish does not know that it is being attacked until it is on the hook and therefore has less than the usual warning that a predator is attacking.

Why then are not all fish of desirable kinds and sizes removed from heavily fished waters?

In part, the answer lies in the ability of all living organisms to develop greater or lesser awareness of forces in their environment that would cause their death. Thus, in spite of the fact that angling is a "refined" mortality factor in fishes, many of the fishes subjected to angling are able to adjust to this factor and avoid being caught.

Why do fish attempt to capture a natural or artificial bait or lure? No one except a fish can know exactly, but fishermen assume that they bite because they are hungry, "angry," inquisitive, or are protecting a home territory, a nest, or a hierarchy that is broken by the audacious action of a plug.

Why then do fish refuse to bite? They may fail to come within striking distance of the bait, may be unconvinced that the bait is a natural food organism, or be frightened by unusual noises made by the fisherman or by the bait. There is evidence also that fish may become conditioned to avoid a bait through seeing one of their members being caught,[28] much as minnows are observed to give a fear reaction to pike after one of their members has been captured and eaten.

In this chapter I have attempted to describe the limits of sensory perception in some freshwater fishes and a few behavior patterns related to their success as animals inhabiting an aquatic environment. In the next few pages I will attempt to establish a relationship between fishermen and certain factors that are believed to influence the rate of catch of fish.

Factors That Influence Biting

Factors that influence the angler's rate of catch can be conveniently divided into several categories: *(1)* physical—those such as climate, season, time of day, etc., that influence the general and nonspecific behavior of fish in their contacts with fishermen; *(2)* human—those, such as degree of care in presenting baits, that are controlled almost entirely by the fisherman; and *(3)* fish response—factors controlled almost entirely by specific fish behavior patterns. These factors may work separately or in combination.

Water Temperatures. Changes in water temperature associated with the cycle of seasons affect the response of fish to the feeding stimulus. As water temperatures drop below 18.3°C (65°F) warmwater fishes become slow moving and sluggish and their rate of digestion becomes proportionately slowed.[84] However, the fact that most species of warmwater fishes may be caught in winter through the ice suggests that they are attracted by food, even though the digestion of any food material ingested may require days. Because of a sluggishness of movement and a tendency to congregate in deep water, the fish may be difficult for the winter angler to find. Once a concentration of fish is located, they are often caught at a relatively high rate and fishermen tend to congregate at points where a few good strings of fish have been taken.

For some unknown reason the catch of fish through the ice is usually more rewarding in fish per man-hour during late January and February than during the early part of winter. It has been conjectured that fat stored during fall may be reduced by the latter part of winter so that the fish become more interested in taking food.

Of all the warmwater fishes, the crappies are more associated with early spring fishing than any other kinds. Hansen[51] showed that the larger white crappies in Lake Decatur (Illinois) reached peak weight in fall, winter, or early spring and lost weight during the spring months. The period of good crappie fishing was usually correlated with the period of weight decline.

Largemouth and smallmouth bass will begin to feed actively in early spring when the water is at a temperature below 15.6°C (60°F), but their movements are so sluggish that an artificial lure moved at "normal" speed for summer bass fishing is too "fast" for the bass to capture. This is also true for various pan fish, e.g., bluegills, red-ears, pumpkinseeds, and warmouths. Yellow perch and yellow bass are often taken in numbers in early spring and they are more active at colder water temperatures than are most sunfish.

Walleyes, northern pike, and muskellunge are quite active during early spring when the water is still relatively cold.

Except for the high rate of catch sometimes recorded for ice fishing the catch rate for most anglers' species is highest in the spring months, beginning in March in the south, in late April and early May in the mid-states, and in late May and early June in the northernmost states and southern Canada. The phenomenon of good spring fishing is probably due to a combination of factors including a warming of waters, a sex stimulus, and a scarcity of small fish upon which to feed. This high catch rate may continue until spawning is completed and summer water temperatures are attained. At this time a maximum of foods is available both in quantity and variety and surface water temperatures that exceed $23.9-26.9°C$ ($75-80°F$) cause fish to seek locations where they may find cooler temperatures and adequate oxygen.

Most small ponds and lakes are thermally stratified during summer months (see Chapter 2, p. 44). The warm upper layer of water is often above the optimum for warmwater fish, but cooler water may be found at greater depths. When a fish moves downward from the warm upper epilimnion into the transition zone (metalimnion), it gradually enters cooler water and the amount of dissolved oxygen decreases until at some level it may disappear entirely. The optimum temperature—oxygen relationship may be at a level where the water is as cool as the fish can find with still sufficient dissolved oxygen for the fish to carry on respiration without discomfort. Here the fish may remain, except during periods of active feeding. If a fisherman can locate this level and keep his bait (whether artificial or natural) within this stratum of water, he may often catch fish when others fishing the surface or at other depths may catch little or nothing. Even bluegills may be caught by trolling a worm in this stratum when the shore shallows are devoid of them.

Some improvement in feeding activity and rate of catch occurs during fall months, but less fishing is done in fall than during any other season. There are some exceptions; most active fishing for muskellunge takes place after waters have cooled from summer temperatures.

Thus, water temperatures affect the behavior of fishes, and the successful angler adjusts his fishing operations to conform to these temperature effects.

Water Transparency. Most game and pan fishes important for angling find their food more readily through sight than through taste. This is why artificial lures are very effective in taking these fish. Thus, within limits there is a positive correlation between an increasing clearness of water and increasing catch. This was demonstrated at Fork Lake (Illinois) using surface fly rod lures for bass and bluegills. When the transparency of this pond (Secchi disk) was 0.5—2.0 ft the catch rate was 2.4 fish/man-hour; with transparencies of 2.1—2.5 ft the catch rate was 2.86 fish/man-hour; and at 3.5—4.5 ft the catch was 6.59 fish/man-hour.[14]

In most waters, turbidity is caused by suspended particles of clay or silt stirred up by the action of bottom-feeding fishes or wind, or carried into the lake with inflowing water. Turbidity may also result from a "bloom" of plankton algae stimulated by fertilization of the water. This nonsilt type of turbidity has less of an effect upon rate of catch than turbidity caused by clay or silt particles. In lakes and ponds containing carp, suckers, or bullheads, a more-or-less constant turbidity may result from the rooting and stirring of the bottom of these fishes. Impoundments that are "muddy" during periods of dry weather are often kept so by these fish, and this type of turbidity is usually as bad for angling as is silt brought in by floods.

In most small lakes and ponds, fishing is poor if the transparency of the water is less than two feet (Secchi disk). Fly casting is probably best when the transparency of the water ranges between 3.5 and 6.0 ft. When the transparency is greater than 6.0 ft, fish are able to see the angler for some distance and unless long casts are made to place the angler beyond the fishes' vision, or extreme care is taken to shield his movements from the fish, the rate of catch will decrease as the water becomes clearer.

Diurnal Effects.   Alternate periods of darkness and daylight affect the feeding and therefore the catch rate of fishes. Often diurnal movements of certain species develop in certain lakes and these movements are usually associated with feeding. Such movements[27,56] have been described under a preceding section *(Daily Activity).*

It is impossible to say that the stimulus for feeding is entirely one of the changes in light intensity even though periods of feeding in many lakes appear to be associated with dawn and dusk.

Rising and Falling Water Levels.   Most artificial lakes are built to store water temporarily during heavy runoff from the watershed. This storage capacity represents the vertical distance within the lake basin between a lower normal spillway crest and a higher large surface floodway. Once the lake level rises to the crest of the floodway, several hours may elapse before the stored water has time to pass over the lower normal spillway outlet to bring the lake back to "normal" level. This capacity for storage reduces the size (and cost) of spillway structures and assures that sudden rises in water level in the lake are common. The extent of these rises may vary, but in most artificial lakes the range of vertical distance for storage between the normal spillway crest and the flood spillway crest is from 1 to 6 ft.

A sudden inflow of water may stimulate fish to move and feed, particularly in early spring when runoff water from a warm rain may bring in water at a temperature above that of the lake. Fish may feed actively as long as silt brought in by the runoff does not cause the lake to become turbid.

Channel catfish are always stimulated to feed on rising water levels; in fact, it is almost the only time they bite well in lakes.

Flood waters almost always carry a load of silt, and the fishes that depend upon sight for feeding may have difficulty in finding food. This was illustrated during the 1943 early summer flood on the Salt Fork of the Vermilion River (east central Illinois) when the river overflowed certain strip-mine lakes. Those who fished the strip-mine lakes during the flood period of several weeks caught almost nothing. After the high water has subsided so that it no longer entered the lakes, and after the lakes had cleared, largemouth bass were caught in large numbers in all parts of the area. This very unusual fishing lasted for about a week, after which bass fishing dropped to the "normal" low rate of catch. The exceptional fishing may have been due to the fact that bass had trouble finding sufficient food in the highly turbid flood waters.

During the months of May, June, July, and August, the catch of fish per fisherman-day in Lake Chautauqua, a 3600-acre lake in the floodplain of the Illinois River (Illinois), paralleled rather closely the highs and lows of the lake level (Fig. 8.2).[114] Here the catch was composed largely of yellow bass, black and white crappies, bluegills, channel catfish, and freshwater drum, and all of these species apparently were stimulated to bite by a rise in lake level. This was not true for largemouth bass; greater numbers were caught when the lake level was low than when high.

Barometric Pressures and Fishing Tables. There is a great deal that is inexplicable about the biting of fishes, and it is natural that man should develop a wide variety of theories to rationalize the catches he may or may not make. So far, none of these theories has been substantiated by scientific testing.

Several years ago fishermen were interested in barometric pressures because fish were supposed to bite best when the barometric pressure was rising or high and poorest when it was falling or low. In order to test this theory Dr. David H. Thompson compared a ten-year fishing record of the Rinaker Lake Fishing Club near Carlinville, Illinois, with baromet-

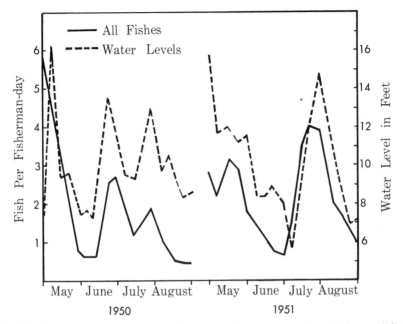

Fig. 8.2 Weekly average water levels and corresponding average catches of fishes per fisher-man-day (all species) at Lake Chautauqua during May, June, July, and August of 1950 and 1951 (from Starrett, W. C., and McNeil, P. L., 1952, *Illinois Nat. Hist. Surv. Biol. Notes* 30).

ric records from two nearby weather stations. Fishermen making the record were not aware of the theory that the fish were supposed to be influenced by barometric pressures. Thompson found periods of high, intermediate, and low rates of catch, but they could not be correlated with any levels or changes of barometric pressures. He concluded that the change in pressure on a fish moving from the surface to the bottom of a pond was so many times greater than the effect of changes of atmospheric pressure that the latter certainly might be hidden. However, stormy weather (usually associated with low barometric pressure) might keep fishermen from going out on large lakes.

Tests of the solunar tables theory of John Alden Knight[73] showed that catches made with hook-and-line and with gill nets[111] were not demonstrably better during solunar periods than at other times.

Several investigators have tested the effect of moonlight on rate of catch of fish,[91,92,133] and their reserved conclusions were that fishing usually was better in darkness.

Other fishing tables and fads have come and gone without serious damage to fish populations or the fishing public; there is no danger in these proposals and they add a speculative interest to the age-old question of why fish bite when they do and why they do not bite at other times.

Resistance of Fish to Being Caught. All successful living organisms show ability to counter decimating forces in their environments by developing resistance or immunity to disease, by instinct, or by learned avoidance reactions. In angling, the fish may be confronted by a food item presented in a particular manner, such as a worm on a hook, by an object that is supposed to look and act like some natural food, such as a crippled minnow lure, or by an object that attracts because of its movements and lack of identifying characteristics, which the fish is supposed to strike to find out what the object is. The fish has the choice of striking or ignoring the bait. Whether or not he strikes depends upon the behavior of the fish.

Laboratory experiments at the Illinois Nautral History Survey, Urbana, demonstrated that fish were quite capable of learning and that certain species were more easily taught than others. Mr. Lynn Hutchens and later Dr. Arthur Witt[129] tested the ability of common warmwater fish to learn to avoid an earthworm impaled upon a hook; at the same time these fish were being fed on free earthworms. Largemouth bass learned quickly, but were sometimes daring, as they evidently realized they would be hooked. Bluegills learned quickly and were much less bold than were the bass. Warmouths were difficult to impress with the danger of being hooked and learned very slowly. Even an electric shock applied to the warmouth when it bit the hooked worm did not always deter it from biting the next one presented. The fish that "learned" to avoid being caught retained this learning for several days.

Lagler and DeRoth[75] discovered that the bass in Lower Lock Alpine (Michigan) could not be "fished out." When the population of this lake had been reduced to 6 legal bass per acre the rate of catch was 0.04 legal fish per hour (25 hr to catch one legal fish). At this time the fishermen had the impression that the lake was "fished out."

Westman, Smith, and Harrocks[123] describe a "die-away curve" in fishing success for largemouth bass which was the same when captured fish were returned to the water as when they were removed from the water.

The largemouth bass of Ridge Lake (Illinois) always exhibited resistance to being caught (Fig. 7.3).[13] In 1949, for example, the lake contained 1027 marked bass large enough to catch. These fish were returned to the lake basin after the lake was drained in March and a small amount of water had collected behind the dam. By June 1, when the lake was opened to fishing, it had refilled only to the 11-acre contour; when at spillway level the lake area was 18 acres. Thus, all of the larger bass that had developed in 18 acres were concentrated in a much smaller volume of water supporting subnormal populations of small fish and crayfish because of a reduction in numbers of these food organisms during the March drainage. In spite of these adverse conditions for bass, after 220 hours of angling per acre, fishermen were able to catch only 595 bass or only 67.1% of the weight of bass returned.

Anderson and Heman[4] found a marked difference in vulnerability to angling of bass 9 in. (23 cm) or longer from fished and unfished populations. Tests were run with tagged fish in ponds and in Little Dixie Lake (Columbia, Missouri). They estimated that the loss of vulnerability might be retained for at least six months. Bennett[13] reported a rapid decline in the catch rate of bass from morning to afternoon of the first day of public fishing at Ridge Lake (Illinois) after about 6 or 7 man-hours of fishing per acre, and by the fourth day of fishing, after approximately 25 man-hours per acre, the rate of catch of bass was as poor as at any time during the summer fishing season. During winter these bass seemed to become less wary so that at the beginning of a new fishing season in June at least some of the bass larger than 9 in. were vulnerable to capture.

The experience at Onized Lake (Illinois) where 275 bass were present in a 2-acre pond after more than 3000 hours of angling points up the futility of fishing for bass after they have become "conditioned" to angling.[11]

Aldrich[2] describes some observations made on largemouth bass at Spavinaw Lake (Oklahoma): By sitting quietly and flipping pebbles into the water dozens of bass were attracted to the boat. Minnows flipped overboard were seized at once and "the congregated bass remained to see how long our generosity would last." A fly or spinner flipped among them resulted in a strike immediately, but once the unlucky individual was hooked, the rest vanished. Continued casting was useless until the boat was moved to a new location. This type of observation could be made almost anywhere on Spavinaw Lake on days when few fishermen were present.

"Records reveal that on days of heavy fishing, Friday, Saturday, and Sunday, the catch per person was very low. This poor catch is not the result of an abundance of poor or mediocre fishermen. The best anglers have learned that they cannot always catch fish, particularly bass, when there is a crowd on the lake. Everyone reports seeing plenty of bass, but few catches are made on weekends."

Ciampi,[28] after testing fish at the Shedd Aquarium (Chicago), concluded that the largemouth bass demonstrated the highest level of "intelligence" in avoiding artificial baits; the smallmouth bass followed close behind. Along with the muskellunge, largemouths were the only species that would not take an artificial bait after any other fish in the same tank had hit it. On the basis of his experiments, Ciampi ranks the "intelligence" of fish studied in the following order: *(1)* largemouth bass, *(2)* smallmouth bass, *(3)* muskellunge, *(4)* northern pike, *(5)* rainbow trout, *(6)* bluegills, *(7)* crappies, *(8)* gar.

Fisherman "Know-How." A fisherman must realize, that if he is to be successful in catching the more wary fish he must introduce himself and his fishing lure into the fishes' environmental background without causing undue alarm. At this point many would-be fishermen are failures, because they assume that they are operating mostly in one medium, air, while the fish are operating in another, and because they cannot see, hear, smell, or feel the presence of fish in the water below, that the fish cannot see, hear, smell, or feel their presence above. Usually a fish is made wary of impending danger or at least of an abnormal addition to its environment before the lure has even been presented. Under these conditions a fisherman places himself under a severe handicap that must be overcome before he can expect a strike. A quiet fisherman in a slow-moving boat propelled by quiet oars in well-oiled oarlocks, or a sculling paddle, may bring himself within casting distance of a bass without alerting the fish to his presence. On heavily fished waters where noisy fishermen are the rule rather than the exception, a quiet approach may catch a fish "off guard."

Creel records on heavily fished waters have shown that more than 80% of the fish are caught by less than 50% of the fishermen; in the case of largemouth bass the catch usually is made by about 25% of the fishermen.

The best way to learn how to fish is to go fishing with a successful angler and try to copy his methods. There are experts in all types of fishing, from trotliners to fly fishermen. These anglers have special methods that usually bring results and often may be unwilling to divulge their secrets to anyone except their closest friends.

Underwater observations of the behavior of bass in relation to lures presented to them has led us to believe that there are rather small differences in the way a bait is "fished" which determine whether a bass strikes or simply follows without striking. The successful fisherman knows how to give the lure that extra something that makes the difference; this ability is an art and not a science.

REFERENCES

1. Ahemanskiy, Yu.A., 1958, "Fishing with sound (lov ryby no zvuk)," *Priroda* (2), 104-105.
2. Aldrich, A. D., 1939, "Results of seven year's intnsive stocking of Spavinaw Lake; an impounded reservoir," *Am. Fish. Soc. Trans.* 68, 221-227.
3. Allanson, B. R., and Noble, R. G., 1964, "The tolerance of *Tiapia mossambica* (Peters) to high temperature," *Am. Fish. Soc. Trans.* 98(2), 317-320.

4. Anderson, R. O., and Heman, M. L., 1969, "Angling as a factor influencing catchability of largemouth bass," *Am. Fish. Soc. Trans.* 98(2), 317-320.

5. Anonymous, 1956, "Schooling of fish," *Progressive Fish Culturist* 18(3), 142.

6. Backiel, T., and Stegman, K., 1966, "Temperature and yield in carp ponds," *FAO World Symp. on Warmwater Pond Fish Cult, FR,V/E-2*, pp. 1-9.

7. Bailey, R. M., 1955, "Differential mortality from high temperature in a mixed population of fishes in southern Michigan," *Ecology* 36(3), 526-528.

8. Ball, R. C., 1947, "A tagging experiment on the fish population of Third Sister Lake, Michigan," *Am. Fish. Soc. Trans.* 74(1944), 360-369.

9. Bardach, J. E., Fujiya, M., and Holl, A., 1965, "Detergents: Effects on the chemical senses of the fish *Ictalurus natalis* (LeSueur)," *Science* 148(3677), 1605-1607.

10. Bardach, J. E., Todd, J. H., and Crickmer, R., 1967, "Orientation by taste in fish of the genus *Ictaluris*," *Science* 155(3767), 1276-1278.

11. Bennett, G. W., 1945, "Overfishing in a small artificial lake, Onized Lake near Alton, Illinois," *Illinois Nat. Hist. Surv. Bull.* 23(3), 373-406.

12. Bennett, G. W., 1948, "The bass-bluegill combination in a small artificial lake," *Illinois Nat. Hist. Surv. Bull.* 24(3), 377-412.

13. Bennett, G. W., 1954, "Largemouth bass in Ridge Lake, Coles County, Illinois, *Illinois Nat. Hist. Surv. Bull.* 26(2), 217-276.

14. Bennett, G. W., Thompson, D. H., and Parr, S. A., 1940, "Lake management reports (4): A second year of fisheries investigations at Fork Lake, 1939," *Illinois Nat. Hist. Surv. Biol. Notes* 14, 1-24.

15. Black, E. C., 1958, "Hyperactivity as a lethal factor in fish," *J. Fisheries Res. Board Can.* 15(4), 573-586.

16. Blair, A. A., 1956, "Atlantic salmon tagged in east coast Newfoundland water at Bonavista," *J. Fisheries Res. Board Can.* 13(2), 225-232.

17. Breder, C. M., 1936, "The reproductive habits of the North American sunfishes (family Centrarchidae)," *Zoologica* 21(pt. 1), 1-48.

18. Breder, C. M., Jr., 1959, "Studies on social grouping in fishes," *Am. Museum Nat. Hist. Bull.* 117(6), 393-482.

19. Brett, J. R., 1956, "Some principles in the thermal requirements of fishes," *Quart. Rev. Biol.* 31(2), 75-87.

20. Brett, J. R., and MacKinnon, D., 1954, "Some aspects of olfactory perception in migrating adult coho and spring salmon," *J. Fisheries Res. Board Can.* 11(3), 310-318.

21. Brown, F. A., Jr. 1937, "Responses of largemouth black bass to colors," *Illinois Nat. Hist. Surv. Bull.* 21(2), 33-55.

22. Brown, M. E., 1957, *The Physiology of Fishes,* Vol. 2, Academic Press, Inc., New York, Chap. 2, pp. 121-210.

23. Bull, H. O. 1928, "Studies on conditioned responses in fishes," Part 1, *J. Marine Biol. Assoc. U.K.N.S.* 15, 485-533.

24. Bull, H. O., 1936-37, "Studies on conditioned responses in fishes, part VII," "Temperature perceptions in teleosts," *J. Marine Biol. Assoc. U.K.N.S.* 21, 1-27.

25. Carlander, K. D., and Cleary R. E., 1949, "The daily activity patterns of some freshwater fishes," *Am. Midland Naturalist* 41, 447-452.

26. Carlander, K. D., and Ridenhour, R., 1955, "Dispersal of stocked northern pike in Clear Lake, Iowa," *Progressive Fish Culturist* 17(4), 186-189.

27. Childers, W. F., 1956, "Daily activity periods as related to feeding of the black crappie and the white crappie," Master's Thesis, Univ. of Illinois Library, pp. 1-24.

28. Ciampi, E., 1961, "What makes them hit the lure," *Sports Illustrated* 15, 35-48.

29. Cross, J. E., 1964, "Walleye distribution and movements in Berlin Reservoir, Ohio," *Ohio Dept. Nat. Res. Publ.* W-337, 1-9.

30. Crowe, Walter R., 1962, "Homing behavior in walleyes," *Am. Fish. Soc. Trans.* 91(4), 350-354.

31. Delco, E. A., Jr., 1960, "Sound discrimination by males of two Cyprinid fishes," *Texas J. Sci.* 12(1 and 2), 48-54.

32. Durham, L., and Bennett, G. W., 1949, "Bass baits at Ridge Lake," *Illinois Wildlife* 4(2), 10-13.

33. Durham, L., and Bennett, G. W., 1951, "More about bass baits at Ridge Lake," *Illinois Wildlife* 6(2), 5-7.

34. Eschmeyer, P., 1950, "The life history of the walleye in Michigan," *Mich. Inst. Fish. Res. Bull.* 3, 1-99.

35. Eschmeyer, R. W., 1944, "Fish migration into the Clinch River below Norris Dam," *J. Tenn. Acad. Sci.* 19(1), 31-40.

36. Ferguson, R. G., 1958, "The preferred temperature of fish and their midsummer distribution in temperate lakes and streams," *J. Fisheries Res. Board Can.* 15(4), 607-624.

37. Forney, J. L., 1963, "Distribution and movement of marked walleyes in Oneida Lake, New York," *Am. Fish. Soc. Trans.* 92(1), 47-52.

38. Forrester, C. R., 1961, "A note on the practical use of a salmon repellent," *Can. Fish Culturist* 30, 61-62.

39. Frisch, K. von, 1941, "Die Bedeutung des Geruchsinnes im Leben der Fische," *Naturwissenschaften* 29, 321-333.

40. Fry, F. E. J., 1947, "Effects of environment on annual activity," *Univ. Toronto Biol. Ser.* 55, 1-62.

41. Fry, F. E. J., 1957, "The lethal temperature as a tool in taxonomy," *Annee Biol.* [3] 33, (5-6), 205-219.

42. Funk, J. L., 1957, "Movement of stream fishes in Missouri," *Am. Fish. Soc. Trans.* 85, 39-57.

43. Gerking, S. D., 1959, "The restricted movement of fish populations," *Biol. Rev.* 34, 221-237.

44. Graham, J. J., 1956, "Observations of the alewife, *Pomolobus pseudoharengus* (Wilson) in fresh water," *Univ. Toronto Biol. Ser.* 62, 1-43.

45. Greenbank, J., 1956, "Movement of fish under the ice," *Copeia* (3), 158-162.

46. Greenberg, B., 1947, "Some relations between territory, social hierarchy and leadership in the green sunfish *(Lepomis cyanellus),*" *Physiol. Zool.* 20, 269-299.

47. Griffin, D. R., 1953, "Sensory physiology and the orientation of animals," *Am. Scientist* 41, 209-244.

48. Griffin, D. R., 1955, "Hearing and acoustic orientation in marine animals," *Paper in Marine Biol. and Oceanog.,* Deep-Sea Res. 3(Suppl.), 406-417.

49. Gunning, G. E., 1959, "The sensory basis for homing in the longear sunfish, *Lepomis megalotis megalotis* (Rafinesque)," *Invest. Indiana Lakes and Streams* 5(3), 103-130.

50. Hancock, H. M., 1954, "Investigations and experimentation relative to winter aggregations of fishes in Canton Reservoir, Oklahoma," *Oklahoma Agr. Mech. Coll. Res. Found. Pub.* 58, 1-104.

51. Hansen, D. F., 1951, "Biology of the white crappie in Illinois," *Illinois Nat. Hist. Surv. Bull.* 25(4), 211-265.

52. Hasler, A. D., 1954, "Odour perception and orientation in fishes," *J. Fisheries Res. Board Can.* 11(2), 107-129.

53. Hasler, A. D., 1956, "Influence of environmental reference points on learned orientation in fish *(Phoxinus),*" Z. Vergleich, *Physiol.* 38, 303-310.

54. Hasler, A. D., 1960*a*, "Laute und Lauterzeugung beim Susswassertrommler *Aplodinotis grunniens* Rafinesque (Sciaenidae, Pisces)," *Science* 132(3430), 785-792.

55. Hasler, A. D., 1960*b*, "Homing orientation in migrating fishes," *Sonderdruck aus. Ergebnisse der Biologie* 23, 94-115.

56. Hasler, A. D., and Bardach, J. E., 1949, "Daily migrations of perch in Lake Mendota," *J. Wildlife Management* 13(1), 40-51.

57. Hasler, A. D., Horrall, R. M., Wisby, W. J., and Braemer, W. B., 1958, "Sun-orientation and homing in fishes," *Limnol Oceanog.* 3(4), 353-361.

58. Hasler, A. D., and Schwassmann, H. O., 1960, "Sun orientation of fish at different latitudes," *Cold Spring Harbor Symp. on Quant. Biol.* 25, 429-441.

59. Hasler, A. D., and Wisby, W. J., 1950, "Use of fish for the olfactory assay of pollutants (phenols) in water," *Am. Fish. Soc. Trans.* 79, 64-70.

60. Hasler, A. D., and Wisby, W. J., 1951, "Discrimination of stream odors by fishes and its relation to parent stream behavior," *Am. Naturalist* 85, 223-238.

61. Hayne, D. W., 1949, "Calculation of size of home range," *J. Mammal.* 30, 1-18.

62. Hemmings, C. C., 1966, "Olfaction and vision in fish schooling," *J. Exptl. Biol.* 45(3), 449-464.

63. Hergenrader, G. L., and Hasler, A. D., 1967, "Seasonal changes in swimming rates of yellow perch in Lake Mendota as measured by sonar," *Am. Fish. Soc. Trans.* 96(4), 373-382.

64. Hergenrader, G. L., and Hasler, A. D., 1968, "Influence of changing seasons on schooling behavior of yellow perch," *J. Fisheries Res. Board Can.* 25(4), 711-716.

65. Herrick, C. J., 1903, "The organ and sense of taste in fishes," *Bull. U.S. Fish. Comm.* 22, 237-271.

66. Huntsman, A. G., 1942, "Return of a marked salmon from a distant place," *Science* 95, 381-382.

67. Hurst, P. M., Jr., 1953, "Can fish see color?" *Progressive Fish Culturist* 15(2), 95.

68. Huttel, R., 1941, "Die chemische Untersuchung des Schrecstoffes ans Elritzenhaut," *Naturwissenschaften* 29, 333-334.

69. Jaszfalusi, L., and Paskandy, J., 1963, "Die Untersuchung der Biometeorologischen Beziehungen des Karpfenlaichens, *Z. Fisherei* 11(3/4), 189-199.

70. Jones, F. H., 1956, "The behavior of minnows in relation to light intensity," *J. Exptl. Biol.* 33(2), 271-281.

71. Kleerekoper, H., and Chagnon, E. C., 1954, "Hearing in fish, with special reference to *Semotilus atromaculatus atromaculatus* (Mitchell),"*J. Fisheries Res. Board Can.* 11(2), 130-152.

72. Kleerekoper, H., and Roggenkamp, P. A., 1959, "An experimental study on the effect of the swimbladder on hearing sensitivity in *Amelurus nebulosus nebulosus* (LeSueur)," *Can. J. Zool.* 37(1), 1-8.

73. Knight, J. A., 1950, "The solunar theory," in *The Fisherman's Encyclopedia*, Stackpole and Heck, New York and Harrisburg, pp. 244-248.

74. Krumholz, L. A., 1944, "Northward acclimatization of the western mosquito fish," *Gambusia a. affinis, Copeia* 2, 82-85.

75. Lagler, K. F., and DeRoth, G. C., 1953, "Populations and yields to anglers in a fishery for largemouth bass, *Micropterus salmoides* (Lac.), " *Papers Mich. Acad. Sci.* 38, 235-253.

76. Larimore, R. W., 1952, "Home pools and homing behavior of smallmouth black bass in Jordan Creek, Illinois", *Illinois Nat. Hist. Surv. Biol. Notes* 28, 1-12.

77. Larimore, R. W., 1954, "Dispersal, growth and influence of smallmouth bass stocked in a warm-water stream," *J. Wildlife Management* 18(2), 207-216.

78. Larimore, R. W., Childers, W. F., and Heckrotte, C., 1959, "Destruction and re-establishment of stream fish and invertebrates affected by drought," *Am. Fish. Soc. Trans.* 88(1959), 261-285.

79. Larimore, R. W., and Duever, M. J., 1968, "Effects of temperature acclimation on the swimming ability of smallmouth bass fry," *Am. Fish. Soc. Trans.* 97(2), 175-184.

80. Larking, P. A., 1956, "Interspecific competition and population control in freshwater fish," *J. Fisheries Res. Board Can.* 13, 327-342.

81. Loeb, H. A., 1964, "Submergence of brown bullheads in bottom sediments," *N.Y. Fish and Game J.* 11(2), 119-124.

82. Malyukina, G. A., Aleksandryuk, S. P., and Shtefanesku, M., 1962, "On the role of vision in 'schooling' behavior of minnows (*Phoxinus phoxinus* L.) and goldfish (*Carassius carassius* L.)," *Vopr. Ikhtiol.* 2(3), 511-516.

83. Manteifel, B. P., and Protasov, V. R., 1964, "Effect of light intensity on the behavior of fish," in *Techniques for the Investigations of Fish Physiology,* Israel Program for Scientific Translations, Jerusalem, pp. 271-277.

84. Markus, H. C., 1932, "The extent to which temperature changes influence food consumption in largemouth bass *(Huro floridana),*" *Am. Fish. Soc. Trans.* 62, 202-210.

85. Marshall, N. B., 1963, "The biology of sound-producing fishes," in *Symp. on Biol. Acoustics, Symp. Zool. Soc. London* 7(1961), 45-60.

86. McCleary, R. A., and Bernstein, J. J., 1959, "A unique method for control of brightness cues in study of color vision in fish," *Phys. Zool.* 32(3), 284-292.

87. Miles, S. G., 1968, "Laboratory experiments on the orientation of the adult American eel, *Anguilla rostrata,*" *J. Fisheries Res. Board Can.* 25(10), 2143-2155.

88. Miller, H. C., 1963, "The behavior of the pumpkinseed sunfish, *Lepomis gibbosus* Linneaus, with notes on the behavior of other species of *Lepomis* and the pigmy sunfish, *Elassoma evergladei,*" *Behavior* 22(1/2), 88-151.

89. Miller, R. B., 1957, "Permanence and size of home territory in stream-dwelling cutthroat trout," *J. Fisheries Res. Board Can.* 14, 687-691.

90. Mohr, H., 1964, "Netzfarbe und Fangigkeit bei Kiemennetzen," *Arch. Fischereiwissenschaft* 14(3), 153-161.

91. Mottley, C. M., 1938, "Does the full moon affect rainbow trout fishing?" *Am. Fish. Soc. Trans.* 67, 212-214.

92. Mottley, C. M., and Embody, D. R., 1942, "The effect of the full moon on trout fishing," *J. Am. Statistic Assoc.* 37(217), 41-47.

93. Myrberg, A. A., Kramer, E., and Heinecke, P., 1965, "Sound production by cichlid fishes," *Science* 149(3683), 555-558.

94. Olmsted, J. M. D., 1918, "Experiments on the nature of the sense of smell in the common catfish, *Ameiurus,*" *Am. J. Physiol.* 46, 443-458.

95. Olson, D. D., and Scidmore, W. J., 1962, "Homing behavior of spawning walleyes," *Am. Fish. Soc. Trans.* 91(4), 355-361.

96. Parker, R. A., 1956, "A contribution to the population dynamics and homing behavior of Northern Wisconsin lake fishes," *Univ. of Wisconsin Dissertation Abstr.* 16(11), 2248-2249.

97. Parker, R. A., and Hasler, A. D., 1959, "Movements of some displaced centrarchids," *Copeia* 1, 11-18.

98. Pearse, A. S., and Achtenberg, H., 1920, "Habits of yellow perch in Wisconsin lakes," *U. S. Bur. Fish. Bull.* 36, 294-306.

99. Pritchard, A. L., 1943, "Results of the 1942 pink salmon marking at Morrison Creek, Courtenay, B. C." *J. Fisheries Res. Board Can.* 57, 8-11.

100. Privol'nev, T. L., 1956, "The reaction of fish to light," (Reaktsiya ryb na tsvet.), *Vopr. Ikhtiol.* 6, 3-20.

101. Protasov, V. R., 1965, "Sound signals of fishes," in *Bionika* (Bionics), Nauka, Moscow, pp. 251-255.

102. Protasov, V. R., Darkov, A. A., and Malinin, L. K., 1966, "Visual images" in recognition and signalling of fishes," *Izv Akad. Nauk U.S.S.R. Ser. Biol.* 31(1), 59-75.

103. Protasov, V. R., Romaneko, E. B., and Podliaplin, Yu D., 1965, "The biological significance of sounds produced by some fishes," *Vopr. Ikhtiol.* 5(3), 523-539.

104. Roots, B. L., and Prosser, C. L., 1962, "Temperature acclimation and the nervous system in fish," *J. Exptl. Biol.* 39(4), 617-628.

105. Rough, G. E., 1954, "The frequency range of mechanical vibrations perceived by three species of freshwater fish," *Copeia* 3, 191-194.

106. Rubin, M. A., 1935, "Thermal reception in fishes," *J. Gen. Physiol.* 18, 643-647.

107. Schneider, H., and Hasler, A. D., 1960, "Laute and Lauterzeugung beim susswassertrommler *Aplodinotus grunniens* Rafinesque (Sciaenidae, Pisces)," *Z. Vergleich. Physiol.* 43, 499-517.

108. Schwassmann, H. O., 1960, "Environmental cues in the orientation rhythm of fish," *Cold Spring Harbor Symp. on Quant. Biol.* 25, 443-450.

109. Schwassmann, H. O., and Braemer, W., 1961, "The effect of experimentally changed photo-period on the sun orientation rhythm of fish,"*Physiol. Zool.* 34(4), 273-286.

110. Shoemaker, H. H., 1952, "Fish home areas up Lake Myosotis, New York," *Copeia* 2, 83-87.

111. Sieh, J. G., and Parsons, J., 1950, "Activity patterns of some Clear Lake, Iowa, Fishes," *Proc. Iowa Acad. Sci.* 57, 511-518.

112. Smith, D. L., 1960, "The ability of the top minnow, *Gambusia affinis* (B&G) to reproduce and overwinter in an outdoor pond at Winnipeg, Manitoba, Canada," *Mosquito News* 20(1), 55-56.

113. Spoor, Wm. A., and Schloemer, C. L., 1939, "Diurnal activity of the common sucker, *Catostomus commersonnii* (Lac.) and the rock bass, *Ambloplites rupestris* (Raf.) in Muskellunge Lake," *Am. Fish. Soc. Trans.* 68(1938), 211-220.

114. Starrett, W. C., and McNeil, P. L., Jr., 1952, "Sport fishing at Lake Chautauqua, near Havana, Illinois, in 1950 and 1951," *Illinois Nat. Hist. Surv. Biol. Notes* 30, 1-31.

115. Stover, R. E., 1953, "What can fish hear?" *Progressive Fish Culturist* 15(2), 94-95.

116. Stroud, R. H., and Jenkins, R. M., 1959, *Home-Range Finder,* S.F.I. Bull. No. 94, pp. 2-3.

117. Stroud, R. H., and Jenkins, R. M., 1962, *Yellow Perch Habits,* S.F.I. Bull. No. 126, p. 5.

118. Stroud, R. H., and Massmann, W. H., 1965, *Crappie Movements,* S.F.I. Bull. No. 168, p. 4.

119. Sullivan, C. M., 1954, "Temperature reception and responses in fish," *J. Fisheries Res. Board Can.* 11(2), 153-170.

120. Todd, J. H., Atema, J., and Bardack, J. E., 1967, "Chemical communication in social behavior of a fish, the yellow bullhead *(Ictalurus natalis),*" *Science* 158(3801), 672-673.

121. Verheijen, F. J., 1956, "Transmission of a fright reaction amongst a school of fish and the underlying sensory mechanism," *Experientia* 12(5), 202-204.

122. Walls, G. L., 1942, "The vertebrate eye and its adaptive radiation," *Cranbrook Inst. of Sci. Bloomfield Hills, Mich. Bull.* 19, 1-785.

123. Westman, J. R., Smith, R. K., and Harrocks, A. W., 1956, *A report on Some Fishery Research at Farrington Lake, New Jersey,* New Jersey Dept. of Cons., pp. 1-14.

124. Whitmore, C. M., Warren, C. E., and Doudoroff, P., 1960, "Avoidance reactions of salmonoid and centrarchid fishes to low oxygen concentrations," *Am. Fish. Soc. Trans.* 89(1), 17-26.

125. Winn, H. E., 1958, "Comparative reproductive behavior and ecology of fourteen species of darters *(Pisces - Percidae),*" *Ecol. Monographs* 28, 155-192.

126. Winn, H. E., and Stout, J. F., 1960, "Sound production by the satinfin shiner, *Notropis analostanus* and selected fishes," *Science* 132(3421), 222-223.

127. Wisby, W. J., 1952, "Odor perception in salmon fry," Ph. D. Thesis, Univ. of Wisconsin Library.

128. Wisby, W. J., and Hasler, A. D., 1954, "Effect of olfactory acclusion on migrating silver salmon *(O. kisutch),*" *J. Fisheries Res. Board Can.* 11(4), 472-478.

129. Witt, A., Jr., 1948, "Experiments in learning of fishes with shocking and hooking penalties," M.S. Thesis, Univ. of Illinois Library, pp. 1-60.

130. Wood, R., 1951, "The significance of managed water levels in developing the fisheries of large impoundments," *J. Tenn. Acad. Sci.* 26(3), 214-235.
131. Woodhead, P. M. J., 1956, "The behavior of minnows *(Phoxinus phoxinus* L.) in a light gradient," *J. Exptl. Biol.* 33(2), 257-270.
132. Wrede, W. L., 1932, "Versuche uber den Ortduft der Elritzen," *Z. Vergleich. Physiol.* 17, 510-519.
133. Wright, S., 1945, "The effect of moonlight on fishing success in Fish Lake, Utah." *Am. Fish. Soc. Trans.* 73, 52-58.

9

COMMERCIAL ASPECTS OF SPORT FISHING

The various costs of participating in the active sport of fishing range from the expenses of travel and lodging to those of purchasing an annual fishing license and such inexpensive items as earthworms for bait. One is liable not to think of travel and lodging as fishing costs, because the actual fishing operation may be incidental to a larger purpose (that of a vacation trip, for example); but these costs probably should be assigned to fishing because the latter may be responsible for the locale of the trip.

Three National Surveys of Fishing and Hunting have been sponsored by the U.S. Department of the Interior.[2,4,6,28] The latest (in 1965) stated that 28 million people fished and in so doing spent 2.9 billion dollars.[8] We are not particularly interested here with those commercial operations more remotely related to fishing, such as lodging, food, and car services. We are primarily interested in money-making activities directly connected with fishing, such as the propagation and sale of fishes for stocking in private fishing lakes, the propagation and sale of live bait, the operation of a put-and-take fishing pond, or the supplying of lake-management services for lake owners. The extent of these operations may vary on the basis of public demand and on the size of an individual's endeavor. For example, there may be a strong use potential for put-and-take fishing waters around large urban centers of population, but very little around small farm-supported towns (Fig. 9.1). Commercial propagation of golden shiner minnows may encompass individual pond farms of more than 500 acres, or may be limited to a few ponds involving less than 5 acres, depending on the interest and financial backing available to the individual directing the operation.

Fig. 9.1 Anglers participating in a Fishathon at Lakeland, Florida *(Courtesy Art Runnels, Florida Game and Freshwater Fish Commission and Sport Fishing Institute).*

A good deal of research has been done and is being done on the husbandry of fishes and other aquatic animals of economic importance in sport fishing. Also, studies of the ecological life histories of individual fishes composing popular combinations of sport species have brought to light management techniques that may be applied by aquatic biologists to improve production and yields for sport fishermen and lake owners. In the following pages I have considered some of these activities in sufficient detail to introduce them to the reader and expose some of their inherent problems.

THE PROPAGATION OR COLLECTION OF FISHING BAITS

One of the "little businesses" connected with fishing is the live-bait industry, which actually represents thousands of small businesses when one includes all of the "worm farm" operators. Although there are some small minnow farms, there are also some very large ones, each involving several hundred acres of ponds.

Not too many years ago a fisherman who planned to use live bait on a fishing trip had to reserve the time necessary to collect his bait, either the day before if it was not too perishable, or on the way to the lake or stream if it was. Collecting one's own bait was a matter of digging, hand collecting, or seining, and most fishermen were well informed on the location of certain kinds of live bait.

Today fewer people bother to collect their own bait because bait dealers are available in most places where there are fishing waters, and their products can be purchased without loss of time.

Many people engage in the part-time avocation of producing some kind of live bait for fishermen. Some bait producers sell these products locally but many advertise in newspapers and magazines and ship by air mail, express, or truck.

Types of Bait

Earthworms and Other Invertebrates. Baits sold to fishermen for freshwater angling include earthworms, insects and their larval stages, crustaceans, "minnows," and sometimes frogs. The extent of interest in the propagation and sale of earthworms and other baits was evident from the "for sale" ads in a recent issue of a leading hunting and fishing magazine. These ads, which exceeded fifteen percent of the space devoted to all sportsmen's items, offered mostly "red wigglers" or "hybrid red wigglers" or information on raising techniques. Other live baits for sale were crickets, gray crickets, grubs, meal worms, "mousie" grubs (rat-tailed maggots), brownnose worms, wax worms, and Giant African crawlers. Only a few dealers offered night crawlers,* presumably because they cannot be raised without special refrigeration equipment, and are perishable in shipment (some shipments were advertised as available air freight).

The propagation of manure worms** and other annelids for fish bait is sufficiently common to make them available in most cities and towns through local bait dealers who either raise their own or buy from a wholesaler supplying several outlets. In winter these same dealers may handle the larvae of various insects used for ice fishing. The large night crawler worms are usually captured and sold locally, and may bring as much as four to eight cents each because of their desirability and the effort required in catching them. Most state fish and game departments have leaflets on raising various kinds of live baits.

Minnows. The propagation of minnows for both wholesale and retail outlets has become an extensive business. Most of the larger minnow farmers sell their products to truckers that haul on a regular schedule to retail outlets, or they may deliver their minnows directly with their own

Lumbricus terrestris
**Helodrilus* spp.

trucks. The more important kinds of minnows for farming operations are probably fathead,[23] bluntnose,[1] and golden shiners.[7,12,22] Minnow farmers in Missouri alone produce and sell more than 25 million fishes a year. Other fishes raised for bait are goldfish and Israeli carp.[20]

Minnows are raised in shallow ponds or lakes that can be seined or drained and refilled at will. In the operation of a minnow farm, adult fish are stocked in brooder ponds, where they spawn.[22,23] Fatheads and bluntnose minnows deposit their eggs on rocks, boards placed horizontally near the surface, or shingles set at a slant in the pond bottom.[12] Golden shiners spawn on specially constructed spawning mats covered with spanish moss. These mats, to which the eggs adhere, may be lifted out of the brooder ponds and moved to hatching ponds; new mats are then placed in the brooder ponds. In this way the young are separated from the adult fishes, and the latter are prevented from eating them. The young of fatheads and bluntnose minnows are trapped or seined in shallow water and moved to rearing ponds.

Newly hatched minnows are subject to predation by several larval and adult forms of aquatic insects. These are partially controlled by leaving the ponds dry as long as possible before they must be refilled in preparation for the stocking of minnow fry; sometimes the filled ponds are treated with rotenone and calcium hypochlorite a few days before the minnow fry are to be stocked. Kerosene mixed with light fuel oil may be applied at weekly intervals to suffocate submersed air breathing insects.

If ponds are to be fertilized, the program should be started several days before the minnow fry are stocked. Some minnow farmers use both inorganic and organic fertilizers to produce a phytoplankton bloom of sufficient density to blot out a white, 4-in. disc when it is lowered to a depth of about 10 in. Additional fertilizer may stimulate so much algae as to cause oxygen deficiencies at night. Other operators rely on daily or bi-daily feeding of minnows to bring these fishes up to useful sizes in a minimum amount of time. The prepared fish food may be fed in powdered or pelleted form and is made of soybean meal, ground peanut cake, fish meal, and distillers dried solubles.[22,23]

The minnow crop produced in ponds by fertilization and/or feeding may be expected to range between 300 and 600 lb/acre. One of the more common problems in raising minnows is overproduction, which results in too many small fish. It is very important to limit the numbers of fry stocked in rearing ponds to not more than about 40,000 per acre. With limited numbers, small shiners averaging 2 lb per thousand will double their weight in 2−3 mo if fed daily at a rate of 3−5% of their body weight. If almost all of the fish are large enough to sell, the income, less expenses for fertilizer and food, may vary from $500 to $900 per acre.

Minnows may be attacked by diseases and parasites. Although there are treatments for the partial control of these biological problems, prevention is more desirable than a treatment program and it is suggested that a farmer hold over some of his own "clean" stock for breeders rather than bring in fish from outside sources.

In preparing minnows for shipment, farmers often use batteries of concrete troughs supplied with tempered well water and overhead agitator aerators; the troughs are covered by a roof to keep off the sun. Troughs are used for holding and sorting minnows moved in from the ponds. Grading for various sizes of minnows is done by running them through grading boxes with slotted sides (Fig. 9.2). The large minnows are retained in the box while the smaller ones slip through the slots. After grading is completed, minnows are moved directly from the troughs into tank trucks for shipment.

CATFISH FARMING

An extensive catfish-farming operation has developed in the southeastern and south central states wherever a source of water is available and

Fig. 9.2 Minnows are graded by placing them in boxes with slotted sides (shown here). The smaller minnows escape between the openings while the larger ones are retained in the box. Several sizes of minnows may be separated out by the use of boxes with different widths of slots.

the terrain and soils are suitable for the construction of shallow ponds. Roughly this region covers the rice-producing areas and extends somewhat farther northward.

The industry, producing more than 15 million ponds of fish per year,[30] is largely limited to the channel catfish, because of its high market value and the fact that it is considered a high-class sport fish in southern and central parts of the United States. Other food fish such as carp, buffaloes, and sheepshead can be raised successfully in shallow ponds, but the market will take only limited quantities of these fishes and the price is always relatively low compared with channel catfish.

A part of the success of the catfish industry is due to the development of high-quality prepared catfish feeds that may be fed directly to these fishes[34,35] and which make it possible to grow catfish to marketable sizes (1−1.75 lb) in two growing seasons.[21,24] Usually a farmer either hatches catfish eggs and raises the fry to sell at fingerling sizes (yearlings) or buys fingerlings and feeds them to produce marketable-size fishes. Some farmers do both, but the maximum efficiency results from concentrating on one or the other of these operations.

Catfish look for cavities in which to spawn. Milk cans, nail kegs,[19] or any clean metal cans 12−15 in. in diameter and 30−45 in. deep may be used as nests. These are anchored around the edges of the pond in water 2−2.5 ft deep with their open ends toward deep water (Fig. 9.3). These

Fig. 9.3 Catfish spawning pond drained to show the position of spawning cans placed around the pond edges. When the pond is full the cans are 2-2 1/2 ft below the water surface.

cans are located 25 or more feet apart. The spawning ponds are stocked with fewer pairs of catfish than there are cans for them to spawn in. Eggs spawned in the cans are guarded and fanned by the male until the hatch and the small fishes become free swimming. In some catfish hatcheries, egg masses are collected from the cans and placed in troughs supplied with running pond water and turbulence paddles, and hatched in these troughs. Once the young fish are feeding well they are moved to rearing ponds and fed with prepared foods. Growth rate is density dependent and the price received for the fingerlings at the end of the first growing season is related to their size. Therefore, it is essential not to have too many in the rearing ponds.

Farmers raising catfish for market usually buy the largest fingerlings they can afford. These are stocked in growing ponds at the rate of 1000 to 2000 per acre and fed a high protein (32%) pelleted fish food diet prepared especially for this purpose. The feeding program is designed to bring the catfish to useful sizes (1.0−1.5 lb or larger) in three or four months. The fish are then sold alive to sportsmen (Fig. 9.4) or sportsmen's clubs, restaurant owners, hotels, markets, or processing plants. Many are sold to "catch-out" pond owners, or State Conservation Departments for "put-and-take" fishing. Approximately half of the 1966

Fig. 9.4 Many catfish farmers sell fish alive or dressed to customers who drive to their farms from nearby towns.

crop of catfish and food-sized sport fishes for Arkansas were sold alive for recreational fishing.[20]

Since a long growing season (water temperatures above 70°F (21°C) is important in bringing the fingerling catfish to useful sizes in their second growing season, the industry has developed in the southern states rather than in the central and northern states. Catfish farming was an easy step for rice farmers to make because they had the "know-how" and equipment for making pond levees, the water supply, and the pumps for filling shallow ponds. Some rice farmers alternated between rice and catfish.[3]

Recently, the return from catfish farming has been somewhat higher than that for rice and so catfish have often completely replaced rice.[20] This may reverse itself if the catfish market becomes glutted.

Catfish may be raised in pens floating in various kinds of waters, e.g., farm ponds,[36] strip-mine ponds,[10] reservoirs, etc,; in these waters it might be impossible to seine or trap them if they were released. The floating pens may be of any convenient size (Fig. 9.5); they are 2.5−3 ft deep and the sides and bottom are covered with hardware cloth. Catfish are crowded

Fig. 9.5 Floating cages where catfish are confined for feeding on pelleted food. Catfish are held in this floating cage at densities of around 150 per cubic yard of water. At this concentration they apparently are more compatible than when stocked in smaller numbers. Catfish in these cages are always readily available.

in these pens (150 to 170 fish per cubic yard) to the extent that individuals do not form territories and therefore get along with a minimum of fighting. Fish are fed twice each day with floating pelleted fish food which is prevented from drifting out of the pens by a screen wire strip around the upper edge extending above the water line. Waste food that sinks and waste from the catfish may fall through the hardware cloth bottom of the pen and thus does not accumulate near the fishes. The pen method of raising catfish is an extension of a method used in Asia where various food fishes are concentrated and fed in cages in flowing streams.

Because catfish concentratrated in floating cages must depend entirely on food supplied from outside sources, it is essential that they be fed a high-quality food containing all of the necessary proteins, vitamins, and minerals. Hastings and Dupree[36] have demonstrated the value of commercial vitamin premixes along with dried brewer's yeast and wheat for high production of catfish. When catfish are free in a pond they will supplement their diet with some natural food so that a high quality (and more expensive) diet is less essential.

Experiments are in progress in an attempt to raise catfish in a closed system where the catfish are held and fed in water-filled troughs, the water being reused after filtering to remove particulate and dissolved matter originating from waste food and catfish metabolism. If a practical system can be developed for repurifying the water, catfish can be grown indoors the year around in heated buildings in a system analogous to that of raising battery chickens. The long outdoor growing season that is now a deterrent to successful catfish farming in the northern states can then be overcome.

TROUT FARMING

Whereas catfish farming is a rather new venture, the artificial production of trout in the United States has been successfully carried out for many years.[11] Such trout are used for stocking wild waters, for introduction into new waters, and for use in catchout activities; much of the product goes into commercial channels, such as the local grocery store, from which it can be purchased, cleaned, and frozen and ready for the table.

A discussion of this activity is out of place in this treatment of the warmwater fishery and is not dealt with here.

FISHING FOR SALE

When fishing was entirely free it was economically valueless, a time-wasting activity not to be followed by the ambitious, an activity fought with some secrecy, not only because good fishing "holes" were private knowledge, but because overindulgence might brand one as a "loafer." Now that fishing activity is more limited, the opportunity to fish has become quite valuable, and the status of the fisherman creates envy among his friends. When this change of public attitude toward fishing has come the commercialization of certain types of fishing. Some of the more common types are described in the following pages.

"Executives" Fishing and Hunting Clubs

There are a small number of hunting and fishing clubs that cater to the executives of businesses and corporations. Membership is frequently in the name of the corporation; a small group of executives purchases group membership and operates more or less as a unit. These clubs must furnish exceptional hunting and fishing for their members, with nearly an assured take. Pheasants, mallard ducks, wild turkeys, Hungarian partridges, bobwhite quail, and sometimes deer are the hunter's game. Fishing may be done in streams and artificial lakes for brook and rainbow trout, largemouth and smallmouth bass, walleyes, northern pike, and muskellunge. Usually ringneck pheasants and mallard ducks carry the weight of hunting and the trouts and basses that of fishing. Members pay an annual hunting and fishing license fee and are billed for individual items of game and fish that they kill. These are picked (skinned or scaled), drawn, and perhaps quick-frozen by the time the member is ready to leave after a day of field sport. Cost is much less important than services in the operation of this type of club, and members expect an abundance of game and fish that can be taken with a minimum of effort. All of the game birds are hatchery produced and pen reared, but in such a way that they develop strong wings and are able to fly well. Fish are reared in hatcheries and stocked for put-and-take fishing; they are fed artificial food or live minnows and thereby are held in good condition in spite of high concentrations.

The clubs are usually located near large cities or are supplied with air service so that members may reach them without time-consuming travel. These are used extensively for "quick" fishing or hunting trips or for entertaining clients or out-of-town quests, often providing hotel accommodations. A member may leave for the club with a guest in mid-afternoon, shoot or fish until dark, stay overnight, and then, after an early morning fishing or hunting period, return to his office by 10 or 11 a.m.

Fishing-Lake Investments

Occasionally a few individuals who wish to make an investment and are interested in fishing will pool their resources, purchase a site, and build an artificial lake. Sometimes individual owners divide up the lake shore and build permanent homes or summer cottages; other group owners or a company owner may build a community lodge to be used by all families or employees when they are at the lake. If several investors are involved, ownership in the property may be in the form of an investment, to be sold to a new party at any time such a sale is agreeable to the other owners. Group owners are usually incorporated for their own protection against individual law suit.

Sportsmen's clubs are frequently organized in a similar manner. Low-cost membership among a large group usually will not furnish sufficient income for lake construction, but incorporated sportsmen's clubs may solicit donations or engage in money-raising activities to obtain money for a "building fund" to be used for building lakes, club houses, and other facilities. Ownership of these lakes and physical plants resides in the sportsmen's club organization.

Sometimes these sportsmen's groups may purchase an abandoned borrow pit, gravel pit, flooded quarry, or strip mine, instead of building an impoundment. Usually these properties increase in value because of the increasing demand for recreational real estate.

The legal aspects of corporation ownership of lake property make it imperative that legal advice be obtained by any group contemplating the construction or purchase of a pond or lake.

Trespass-Rights Fishing

Owners of ponds or lakes retaining control of their waters and wishing at the same time to receive an income from them may, for a fee, give right of trespass of the surrounding lands to a limited number of individuals on an individual basis for one or more years. When permission is granted, the owner may specify that certain rules and regulations must be followed by the users with the penalty stipulation that should the rules be broken, the lessee loses his right of trespass without the return of his original payment.

Experience has shown that where such "trespass leases" are available within reasonable driving distance of urban centers, owners of waters that are managed to produce angling at an average rate of one or more fish per man-hour often may receive a larger net cash return from an acre of such water than from an acre of productive farm land given over to row crops.[5]

Rules for trespass-fishing lakes usually specify that anyone who fishes must fill out a creel card each time that he terminates a fishing period. At the end of the fishing season a tabulation of the creel cards will furnish the lake owner with the total annual fish yield in kinds, numbers, and pounds, and also the rate of catch in numbers and pounds of fish per man-hour. These records are of interest to those who fish because they indicate whether or not the anglers are receiving a satisfactory return for their money.

This type of operation has another advantage in that the lake owner is able to select only fishermen who are to his knowledge dependable and honest. With selected individuals using his property, he is required to spend a minimum of his time for general supervision.

Facilities other than adequate roads into the area and parking lots are minimal. A creel station where fishermen weigh, measure, and record their catches is, of course, a necessity. Picnic areas are also desirable.

Income from trespass-fishing may vary with size of the water area, the facilities available, the location, and type of fishing.

Fee-Fishing Ponds

Catch-out or fee-fishing ponds are usually small, heavily stocked bodies of water containing a number of kinds of fishes. They may be operated in several ways:

Type I. In this type the fisherman pays a basic fee for the privilege of a day of fishing, and he may also pay a boat rental fee, but he does not pay an additional fee for the fish he catches. The water is usually stocked with fish only once, although the owner may use fertilizer to increase the natural fish production. Fishes available for angling may be trout, large-mouth bass, crappies and other sunfish, channel catfish, or bullheads.

Type II. In a second type of fee-fishing operation the stocked fish are of high quality (usually channel catfish or trout) and are fed daily on prepared fish food. Fishermen are charged a basic fee plus a set price per pound for the fish caught. Operators may also rent boats, sell bait, cold drinks, and snacks, and sometimes rent fishing equipment.

Type III. In a third type of catch-out pond the waters are stocked in great excess, usually with carp, bullheads and sometimes channel catfish (Fig. 9.6). The fish are not fed. The fishermen are required to pay a basic fee for fishing and a small additional fee for each fish caught. In this type of operation the fishes are subjected to virtual starvation, which is supposed to improve their susceptibility to baits.

In 1960 there were an estimated 1500 fee-fishing ponds and lakes in forty-six states;[25,31] in 1968 there were probably more than 2000. Many of the pay lakes, particularly in the western states, have been in operation for more than twenty years, although the greater number were established in the last decade. At least 58% of the catch-out ponds in Colorado (mostly Type II) have exceeded a ten-year operation period.[11] In general,

Fig. 9.6 Fee-fishing pond where anglers pay a daily fee to fish and an additional amount for the total poundage of fish caught. Here fishermen were catching carp and bullheads which have been stocked in numbers and weights exceeding the carrying capacity of the pond.

the business appears quite unstable and in most states there is some turnover from year to year so the absolute number of these lakes in operation fluctuates. Several states have between 200 and 300; in 1960 Pennsylvania had 238.[31] Ohio listed 265 privately owned commercially operated recreational lakes for fishing, this number including some club lakes where the members paid an annual rather than a daily fee.[13]

Most states have passed special legislation to cover the licensing and operation of these pay fish ponds. In some states the operator of the pond must have a license; in others, such as California, no fishing license is required (Dr. Leo Shapovalov, personal communication). Pond owner licenses usually vary in price from $5.00 to $25.00/yr. To be successful, fee-fishing lakes should be close to large centers of population since city dwellers place a greater premium on this type of fishing than do rural dwellers. Ninety percent of the fee-fishing ponds and lakes in Illinois were located within 50 miles of cities of 50,000 or more.[18]

From the biological standpoint there are a number of reasons why the operation of catch-out ponds may be a financial risk. Not only are fishes easily injured in handling and hauling, but when they are stocked in ponds at poundage levels above the natural capacities of these ponds to support fish, and are not fed (Type III), the total weights of the populations move progressively downward until they approach carrying-capacity poundages (see Chapter 4). If all of the fish are of adult sizes, there is little or no chance of their preying upon one another; instead, all will lose weight. Suppose, for example, a one-acre catch-out pond were stocked with 2250 bullheads weighing one third of a pound each or a total of 750 lb. If the normal carrying capacity of this pond for bullheads were 300 lb and fishermen removed only 1000 of the 2250 fish originally released, the average weight of those remaining at the end of the season (provided there was no natural mortality) would be 0.24 lb, a weight reduction of more than 25%. These bullheads would probably be so thin that they would scarcely interest anglers or fish buyers.

The constant threat of disease and parasites in catch-out ponds of Type III is very real because the fish may come from many sources, and because fish are "piled up" above the carrying capacity of these ponds. Parasites brought in with new fish often have an easy time infesting fish already in the pond, and diseases may be transmitted directly and quickly.

Diseases and heavy infestations of parasites may kill the fish outright or cause them to become so emaciated that they either will not bite or else will provide an unacceptable catch. Once the fish in a catch-out pond become sick or heavily parasitized, one would be foolish to introduce additional stock. The best procedure is to kill the fish and take the loss, sterilize the pond, and then restock with "healthy" fish.

In view of the biological problems associated with the mechanics of operating catch-out ponds, it is reasonable to drain the ponds in the fall after the fishing season and dispense with the remaining fish. Ponds should be allowed to remain dry during winter and the pond bottom should be treated with quick lime.

Ponds that cannot be drained should be seined at the end of the season and the fish sold, either alive or dressed. If there is no evidence of disease or parasites, the fish that escape the seining operation may be left in the pond over winter. If fish are diseased or heavily parasitized, the pond should be treated with a fish toxicant to eliminate all remaining fish and then sterilized.

Floating Fishing Docks

Floating fishing docks that are heated in winter have revolutionized winter fishing on many large reservoirs, particularly in the southwest. These docks originated in the 1950s on 46,000-acre Grand Lake O' the Cherokees and on 92,000-acre Lake Texoma in Oklahoma where there are now more than 100 of these enterprises.[15]

A floating fishing dock (Fig. 9.7) usually consists of a rectangular floating barge with a rectangular opening in the center surrounded by a waist

Fig. 9.7 Exterior view of floating fishing dock and fishing lounge (top). Interior view of fishing lounge showing theatre seats arranged around an open well in the center through which
anglers do their fishing (bottom).

high railing. The entire barge is covered by a structure which completely encloses it. Windows along the sides and ends let in light during the day. At night electric lights are turned on, and during cold weather the pier is heated.[29] Some of these floating docks are supplied with television and lunch counters to serve the guests. Fishermen stand or sit in upholstered seats around the open rectangle in the center and fish over the guard railing.

Fish are attracted to these floating barges by brush piles of evergreens suspended below them. Some are baited through the use of cottonseed cake and other types of bait. Dock operators usually sell live bait, fishing tackle, and snacks.

Charges of about $1.00–2.00/day are customary. These fishing docks are very popular with people who would hesitate to go out in small boats, and who would otherwise probably not fish at all in winter.

"An estimated 60,000 fisherman-days were recorded in fishing docks on 19,000-acre Fort Gibson Reservoir, Oklahoma, in the period January through March, 1956."[14] This was probably as much as 90% of all of the winter fishing on the lake. The catch consisted mostly of crappies and continued year-round; these species represented 37% of the fish take on Fort Gibson.

. The effectiveness of these fishing docks is related to their location over natural concentrations of fishes.

ARTIFICIAL FEEDING TO IMPROVE FISH STOCKS FOR ANGLING

Natural food resources of an aquatic environment are variable and at the same time related to the fertility of that environment. Fish production is related in part to the natural food resources of the fishes' habitat, which may or may not rate as superior. Therefore it is sometimes practical, as in the case of catfish farming, to supplement the natural food with feedings of manufactured food if the fish can be induced to take it. Limited experimental work has been done on the artificial feeding of several kinds of warmwater game and panfish other than the catfish.

Bluegills are readily taught to take pelleted fish foods. Such a food in the form of small floating pellets has been used to supplement the natural diet of the bluegills at Ridge Lake (Illinois) each summer, 1965–69 inclusive; in addition, a lake drawdown in early fall of each year prevents overproduction of these fish.[9] This program has increased the bluegill hook-and-line yields by greatly increasing the average length and weight of the bluegills caught, and fishermen have stated that the artificial food improves the bluegill flavor when cooked.

Largemouth bass held at high densities in ponds have been conditioned to accept dead forage and prepared foods.[17,26,27] Those fishes that took this food grew well and remained in good condition. In Lewis' experiments[17] the number of fish that would take prepared food varied from 38 to 70%. Non-feeders showed no interest in the food and became emaciated. The pellets taken by the bass were soft (hard pellets were ejected) and round and about three-fourths of an inch in diameter. These pellets were made up 24 hr in advance of feeding and contained about 50% water. Bass that had been reared on artificial food seemed to have no difficulty in adjusting to natural foods when artificial feeding was discontinued.

Such a program of artificial feeding of bass might be practical if these fish were being grown for use in some aspect of commercialized sport fishing.

The release of large quantities of some type of live natural food for adult piscivorous fishes is probably impractical in most circumstances but is done occasionally. For a number of years the chain of fishing lakes (15.9 acres) on the Fin'n Feather Club near Dundee, Illinois, containing largemouth bass, smallmouth bass, bluegills, and some green sunfish were supplied with emerald shiners seined from Lake Michigan and released alive in the lakes at the rate of about 1000 lb/acre. These shiners were released in February and March and some of these minnows were still present in July and August, although, at that time, they appeared to be badly emaciated.

No draining census was made of the fishes in these lakes, but records of the catch for 1956 and 1957 were analyzed by Dr. D. Homer Buck (unpublished). In these years, the catch was almost entirely of largemouths. In 1956, 46 man-hours of fishing per acre produced a yield of 45.6 lb of largemouth per acre at the rate of 0.99 lb/hr. In 1957, 34.8 man-hours of fishing per acre produced a yield of 60.6 lb of bass per acre, at the rate of 1.74 lb/hr. These statistics indicate that the bass fishing in the lakes was very exceptional; it would be wholly unsafe to estimate the standing crop of bass in the lakes during these years, except to guess that it may have been between 100 and 200 lb/acre. A part of the exceptional fishing must be attributed to the fact that the fishing pressure was so low and intermittent that the bass probably had little opportunity to become "hook-wise." The Supervisor of Fisheries for the Club believed that crayfish ingested by bass imparted a musty flavor to bass flesh; therefore it was thought that the addition of minnows not only increased the poundage of bass in the lakes, but also improved their flavor. He believed that the bass were eating minnows in preference to crayfish (because the former were always readily available). These assumptions could not be verified at the time the catch records were tabulated.

FISH FOR SALE

Private hatcheries selling warmwater fishes can be found in many states. They operate under state fish breeders licenses and sell their products alive to private lake and pond owners, who use the fish for stocking their waters.

In some states these hatchery-reared fish are not subject to state regulations: fishermen using private lakes stocked with commercially raised fish do not need to have a state fishing license. In other states a license is necessary, even if the fish caught were purchased from a fish breeder. However, these fish may not be subject to the same restrictions (length limits, closed seasons, and creel limits) enforced for "wild" fish of the same species in that state.

Most warmwater fishes are raised in ponds. Adults of bass and other centrarchids are allowed to nest in ponds; afterward, the young may be removed to growing ponds, or the adult spawners seined from the spawning ponds. Fishes from which eggs can be removed by stripping may be hatched in jars inside the hatchery building and counted numbers stocked in growing ponds. Most of the hatchery techniques for raising fish are standard, although each operator makes modifications for his specific situation.

Hatcheries selling game fish for stocking may arrange to ship them by air in sealed plastic bags or transport them by truck, since many lake owners have no tank-truck equipment. The fish sold are rarely larger than yearlings, and are, of course, not big enough to catch. These hatcheries are not patronized by catch-out pond owners because the fish are small and too expensive. Fishes sold are largemouth and smallmouth bass, muskellunge, northern pike, walleyes, channel catfish, panfish, and hybrid sunfish. Often live delivery is guaranteed. Much of the business of these hatcheries is with lake and pond owners who know nothing of lake-management techniques and who expect stocking to answer all of their fishing problems. Consequently, their money and the fish are often wasted.

FISH-MANAGEMENT SERVICE

Perhaps the newest commercial operation associated with sport fishing, and one very badly needed in some regions, is fish-and lake-management service. King[16] reports that five years is the average "productive life" of a pond without renovation and restocking.

Since on large country estates artificial ponds and lakes continue to present diverse problems to their owners, this service may involve any and/or all of the management problems described in this book. More common needs, however, are for chemical treatment or biological control of algae and obnoxious rooted aquatic vegetation, or the renovation through chemical treatment of lakes that have become contaminated with undesirable fish, and their restocking with desirable ones.

In some states a limited amount of this type of official extension service has been furnished to private clubs and individuals by state-employed fishery biologists. However, as more state-owned reservoirs are built for public recreation, state biologists will have less time to devote to the problems of private lake owners.

As with most businesses, working capital and training are necessary for a start. The latter may be obtained at universities giving courses in fishery biology and management, as well as basic courses in zoology, botany, physics, and chemistry.

Conceivably, one might set up a lake-management service office in one's own home, but much of the equipment used (boats, trailers, pumps, seines, etc.) is rather bulky and requires a large storage space, usually lacking in the average yard or its accessory buildings. Moreover, ponds are useful for holding a supply of fish while one is engaged in a lake-renovation operation or in stocking a new lake. Thus, a physical situation is required that either furnishes or has the potential to provide office and laboratory space, fish-holding tanks and ponds, and buildings to store bulky equipment.

REFERENCES

1. Altman, R. W., and Irwin, W. H., 1956, "Minnow farming in the Southwest," *Oklahoma Dept. Wildlife Cons.*, pp. 1-35.
2. Anonymous, 1955, "National Survey of fishing and hunting," *U.S. Fish and Wildlife Circ.* 14, 1-50.
3. Anonymous, 1956, "Rice and fish crops in Arkansas," *Progressive Fish Culturist* 18(3), 134.
4. Anonymous, 1961, "National survey of fishing and hunting," *U.S. Fish and Wildl. Circ.* 120, 1-73.
5. Anonymous, 1962, "Rural recreation, a new family-farm business," U.S. Dept. of Agr. Task Force Rept. on Income-Producing Recreation Enterprises on Farm Land, pp. 1-56.
6. Anonymous, 1963, "Shoreline recreation resources of the United States," Outdoor Res. Recreation Rev. Comm. Rept. 4, U.S. Govt. Office, 156 pp.
7. Anonymous, 1965, "Farm reservoir fishes," *U.S. Fish Wildlife Serv. Bur. Sport Fish Wildlife Circ.* 131, 1-13.

8. Anonymous, 1966, "1965 National survey of fishing and hunting," *U.S. Bur. Sport. Fish Wildlife Pub.* 27, 76 pp.

9. Bennett, G. W., and Adkins, H. W., 1968, "The dynamics of a bluegill population fed on a prepared food and subjected to an annual fall drawdown," *Illinois Nat. Hist. Surv. Mimeo.,* 13 pp.

10. Bulow, F. J., 1967, "The suitability of strip-mine ponds for producing marketable channel catfish," *Progressive Fish Culturist* 29(4), 222-228.

11. DeWitt, J. W., Jr., 1954, "A survey of private trout enterprises in the West." *Progressive Fish Culturist* 16 (4), 147-152.

12. Dobie, J. R., Meehean, A. L., and Washburn, G. N., 1948, "Propagation of minnows and other bait species," *U.S. Fish Wildlife Serv. Circ.*12. 1-113.

13. Doherty, W., 1958, "Pay lakes in Ohio," Fish Management Sect., Ohio Dept. Nat. Res., 1-14.

14. Houser, A., and Heard, W. R., 1958, "A one-year creel census on Fort Gibson Reservoir," *Proc. Oklahoma Acad. Sci.* 38, 137-146.

15. Jenkins, R. M., 1961, *Reservoir Fish Management—Progress and Challenge Fish Inst.,* Washington, D. C., pp. 1-22.

16. King, W., 1960, "A survey of fishing in 1959 in 1,000 ponds stocked by the Bureau of Sport Fisheries and Wildlife," *U.S. Fish Wildlife Serv. Circ.* 86, 1-20.

17. Lewis, W. M., Heidinger, R., and Konikoff, M., 1969, "Artificial feeding of yearling and adult largemouth bass," *Progressive Fish Culturist* 31(1), 44-46.

18. Lopinot, A. C., 1966, "Illinois daily fee fishing ponds," *Illinois Dept. Cons. Spec. Fish. Rept.* 14, 1-21.

19. Marzolf, R. C., 1957, "The reproduction of channel catfish in Missouri ponds," *J. Wildlife Management* 21(1), 21-28.

20. Meyer, F. P., Gray, D. L., Mathis, W. P., Martin, J. M., and Wells, B. R., 1967, "Production and returns from the commercial production of fish in Arkansas during 1966," Univ. of Arkansas Agr. Ext. Serv. and U.S. Fish Farming Expt. Sta. Mimeo, 11 pp.

21. Morris, A. G., 1967, "Production of channel catfish to creel size," *Progressive Fish Culturist* 29(2), 84-86.

22. Prather, E. E., 1957, "Experiments on the commercial production of golden shiners," *Proc. 10th Ann. Conf. S. E. Assoc. Game and Fish Comm.* (1956), pp. 150-155.

23. Prather, E. E., 1958, "Further experiments on feeds for fathead minnows," *Proc. 12th Ann. Conf. S. E. Assoc. Game and Fish Comm.,* pp. 176-178.

24. Prather, E. E., 1959, "The use of channel catfish as sport fish," *Proc. 13th Ann. Conf. S. E. Assoc. Game and Fish Comm.* pp. 331-335.

25. Schoumacher, R., 1959, "A survey of catch-out ponds in the United States," Masters' Thesis Univ. of Michigan Library, 35 pp.

26. Snow, J. R., 1965, "Results of further experiments on rearing largemouth bass fingerlings under controlled conditions," *Proc. 17th Ann. Conf. S.E. Assoc. Game and Fish Comm.,* pp. 191-203.

27. Snow, J. R., 1968, "Production of six to eight-inch largemouth bass for special purposes," *Progressive Fish Culturist* 30(3), 144-152.

28. Stroud, R. H., 1956, *U.S. Anglers—Two Billion Dollars,* Sport Fishing Inst. Bull. No. 59, pp. 1-8.

29. Stroud, R. H., 1957, *Cold Weather Fishing Docks,* SFI Bull. No. 62, p. 5.

30. Stroud, R. H., 1968, *Catfish Farming,* SFI Bull. No. 194, p. 8.

31. Stroud, R. H., and Jenkins, R. M., 1960, *Fee Fishing Lakes,* SFI Bull. No. 106, p. 7.

32. Surber, E. W., English, J. McDermott, G., 1962, "The tainting of fish by outboard motor

exhaust wastes as related to gas and oil consumption," USPHS Taft Sanitary Eng. Cent. Mimeo, 2 pp.

33. Tiemeier, O. W., 1962, "Increasing size of fingerling channel catfish by supplemental feeding," *Trans. Kansas Acad. Sci.* 65(2), 114-153.

34. Tiemeier, O. W., Deyoe, C. W., and Wearden, S., 1966, "Experiments with supplemental feeds for channel catfish," *FAO World Symp. on Warmwater Pond Fish Culture. FR, III/E-6,* 15 pp.

35. Schmittou, H. R., 1969, "Developments in culture of channel catfish *Ictalurus punctatus* (Raf.), in cages suspended in ponds," Report given at the Southeast Wildlife Conference, Mobile, Ala., Oct. 19-22, pp. 1-44.

36. Hastings, W., and Dupree, H. K., 1969, "Formula feeds for channel catfish," *Progressive Fish Culturist* 31(4), 187-196.

APPENDIX

Common and Scientific Names of Fishes Referred to in Text

With a few exceptions, the common and scientific names listed below are those accepted by the American Fisheries Society, Committee on Names of Fishes.* One exception is the common name of redear, for *Lepomis microlophus* (G), which is invariably read as "re-dear," presumably because both the prefix "re-" and the word "dear" are more commonly seen in print than are the words "red" and "ear." Other exceptions are the names of a few fishes not native to the United States and Canada.

Common names vary from place to place, and exact identification of any fish must be associated with an accepted scientific name. As most readers will be unfamiliar with the scientific names, and will look first for common names, the Appendix has been arranged with the common *family* names in alphabetical order. Under each family is listed, in alphabetical order, the common names of the species mentioned in the text, and opposite each common name is its corresponding scientific name.

Dr. Philip W. Smith, Head of Faunistics Survey Section, furnished the scientific names not found in Bailey (1960).

*Bailey, R. M., et al., 1960, *"A List of Common and Scientific Names of Fishes from the United States and Canada,"* American Fisheries Society Special Publication 2, pp. 1 - 102.

Anabanted	Anabantidae
Gourami	*Osphronemus goramy* Lae.
Basses (Sea)	Serranidae
Bass, Striped	*Roccus saxatilis* (W)
Bass, White	*Roccus chrysops* (R)
Bass, Yellow	*Roccus mississippiensis* (J&E)
Perch, White	*Roccus americanus* (G)
Bowfins	Amiidae
Bowfin	*Amia calva* L
Catfishes	Ictaluridae
Bullheads	*Ictalurus* spp
Bullhead, Black	*Ictalurus melas* (R)
Bullhead, Brown	*Ictalurus nebulosus* (Le S)
Bullhead, Yellow	*Ictalurus natalis* (Le S)
Catfish, Channel	*Ictalurus punctatus* (R)
Catfish, Flathead	*Pylodictis olivaris* (R)
Madtoms	*Noturus* spp
Stonecats	*Noturus flavus* R
Drums	Sciaenidae
Drum, Freshwater	*Aplodinotus grunniens* R
Gars	Lepisosteidae
Gars, Garfishes	*Lepisosteus* spp
Alligator gar	*Lepisosteus spathula* Lac
Herrings	Clupeidae
Shad	*Dorosoma* spp
Shad, Gizzard	*Dorosoma cepedianum* (Le S)
Shad, Threadfin	*Dorosoma petenense* (G)
Alewife	*Alosa pseudoharengus* (W)
Killifishes	Cyprinodontidae
Killifish	*Fundulus* spp
Lampreys	Petromyzonidae
Lamprey, Sea	*Petromyzon marinus* L
Livebearers	Poeciliidae
Gambusia, Mosquitofish	*Gambusia affinis* (B & G)
Guppy	*Lebistes reticulatus* (P)
Minnows and Carps	Cyprinidae
Carp	*Cyprinus carpio* L
Grass Carp	*Ctenopharyngodon idella* (C & V)
Israeli Carp	*Cyprinus carpio* L
Tawes	*Puntius javanicus - P. gonionotus* (B)
Chub, Creek	*Semotilus atromaculatus* (M)

Dace, Northern Redbelly — *Chrosomus eos* C.
Elritze (European) — *Phoxinus phoxinus* L
Goldfish — *Carassius auratus* (L)
Minnow, Bluntnose — *Pimephales notatus* (R)
Minnow, Fathead — *Pimephales promelas* R
Shiner, Blackchin — *Notropis heterodon* (C)
Shiner, Blacknose — *Notropis heterolepis* E
Shiner, Blacktail — *Notropis venustus* (G)
Shiner, Emerald — *Notropis atherinoides* R
Shiner, Golden — *Notemigonus crysoleucas* (M)
Shiner, Red — *Notropis lutrensis* (B & G)
Shiner, Redside — *Richardsonius balteatus* (R)
Shiner, Sand — *Notropis stramineus* (C)
Shiner, Satinfin — *Notropis analostanus* (G)

Mouthbreeders — Chromides
Tilapia (Asiatic pondfish) — *Tilapia mossambica* P
Tilapia sparmannii S
Tilapia zillii G
Tilapia rendalli (B)
Nile tilapia — *Tilapia nilotica* L

Mudminnows — Umbridae
Mudminnow (Central) — *Umbra limi* (K)

Mullets — Mugilidae
Gray Mullet — *Mugil cephalus* L

Perches — Percidae
Darter, Fantail — *Etheostoma flabellare* R
Darter, Greenside — *Etheostoma blennioides* R
Darter, Iowa — *Etheostoma exile* (G)
Darter, Orangethroat — *Etheostoma spectabile* (A)
Darter, Rainbow — *Etheostoma caeruleum* S
Perch, European — *Perca fluviatilis* L.
Perch, Yellow — *Perca flavescens* (M)
Sauger — *Stizostedion canadense* (S)
Walleye, Yellow Pike-Perch — *Stizostedion vitreum vitreum* (M)

Pikes — Esocidae
Muskellunge — *Esox masquinongy masquinongy* M
Ohio Muskellunge — *E. masquinongy ohioensis* K
Pickerel — *Esox* spp
Pike, Northern — *Esox lucius* L
Chain Pickerel — *Esox niger* L
Grass Pickerel — *Esox americanus vermiculatus* LeS
Redfin Pickerel — *Esox americanus americanus* G

Porgies — Sparidae
Sheepshead — *Arshosargus probatocephalus* (W)

Smelts
  Smelt (American)

Osmeridae
  Osmerus mordax (M)

Sticklebacks
  Stickleback (Brook)

Gasterosteidae
  Eucalia inconstans (K)

Sturgeons
  Sturgeon
  Sturgeon, Lake

Acipenseridae
  Acipenser spp
  Acipenser fulvescens R

Suckers
  Buffalo
  Buffalo, Bigmouth
  Buffalo, Smallmouth
  Chubsucker, Lake
  Quillback
  Redhorse, Golden
  Sucker, Blue
  Sucker, Hog
  Sucker, White or Western
    White

Catostomidae
  Ictiobus spp
  Ictiobus cyprinella (V)
  Ictiobus bubalus (R)
  Erimyzon sucetta (L)
  Carpiodes cyprinus (LeS)
  Moxostoma erythrurum (R)
  Cycleptus elongatus (LeS)
  Hypentelium nigricans (LeS)
  Catostomus commersoni (L)

Chanids
  Milk Fish

Chanidae
  Chanos chanos (F)

Sunfishes
  Bass
  Bass, Largemouth
  Bass, Rock
  Bass, Smallmouth
  Bass, Spotted
  Crappies
  Crappie, White
  Crappie, Black
  Bluegill
  Pumpkinseed
  Sunfish
  Sunfish, Green
  Sunfish, Longear
  Sunfish, Orangespotted
  Sunfish, Red-ear
  Sunfish, Redbellied
  Sunfish, Spotted
  Sunfish, Pigmy
  Warmouth

Centrarchidae
  Micropterus spp
  Micropterus salmoides (L)
  Ambloplites rupestris (R)
  Micropterus dolomieui L
  Micropterus punctulatus (R)
  Pomoxis spp
  Pomoxis annularis R
  Pomoxis nigromaculatus (LeS)
  Lepomis macrochirus R
  Lepomis gibbosus (L)
  Lepomis spp
  Lepomis cyanellus (R)
  Lepomis megalotis (R)
  Lepomis humilis (G)
  Lepomis microlophus (G)
  Lepomis auritus (L)
  Lepomis punctatus (V)
  Elassoma spp
  Chaenobryttus gulosus (C)

Trouts and Whitefishes
  Ciscoes
  Salmon
  Salmon, Coho
  Salmon, Spring (Chinook)

Salmonidae
  Coregonus spp
  Salmo, Oncorhynchus spp
  Oncorhynchus kisutch (W)
  Oncorhynchus tshawytscha (W)

Kokanee	*Oncorhynchus nerka* (W)
Silver	*Oncorhynchus kisutch* (W)
Pink	*Oncorhynchus gorbuscha* (W)
Trout	*Salmo* spp
Trout, Brook	*Salvelinus fontinalis* (M)
Trout, Brown	*Salmo trutta* L
Trout, Cut throat	*Salmo clarki* R
Trout, Lake	*Salvelinus namaycush* (W)
Trout, Rainbow	*Salmo gairdneri* R
Tullibee (Nipigon Cisco)	*Coregonus nipigon* (K)
Whitefish	*Coregonus clupeaformis* (M)
Whitefish, Mountain	*Prosopium williamsoni* (G)

Theraponidae
Zebra Fish   *Therapon jarbua (F)*

Megalopidae
Tarpons   *Tarpon atlanticus* (C & V)

INDEX

INDEX